STAYING IN LOVE FOR A LIFETIME

STAYING IN LOVE FOR A LIFETIME

by
Ed Wheat, M.D.
and
Gloria Okes Perkins

Inspirational Press • *New York*

First Inspirational Press edition published in 1994.
Inspirational Press
A division of Budget Book Service, Inc.
386 Park Avenue South
New York, NY 10016

Inspirational Press is a registered trademark of Budget Book Service,
Inc.

Published by arrangement with Zondervan Publishing House.
Library of Congress Catalog Card Number: 93-80459
ISBN: 0-88486-097-3

Printed in the United States of America.

Scripture Quotation Sources

Contents

LOVE LIFE
FOR
EVERY
MARRIED COUPLE

*My precious wife Gaye and I
dedicate this book to you, the reader.
It is our prayer that you may learn,
not just to hold your marriage together,
but to become united as lovers, experiencing a living,
growing romantic love which becomes more wonderful
every year, making every month a honeymoon
(literally, a month of sweetness).*

Contents

Acknowledgment

I gratefully acknowledge the invaluable work of Gloria Okes Perkins that has gone into the creation and preparation of this book. For three years Gloria has worked with Gaye and me in analyzing hundreds of hours of counseling experience and in formulating these love-life concepts.

As a gifted professional writer, an experienced editor, and women's Bible teacher, Gloria has used her skills to enable us to sensitively and precisely express the deep feelings associated with the pain of loveless marriages and the great joy of love restored. She and her husband Dan enjoy a love-filled Christian marriage that teaches by experience how enriching the emotion of love can be, and it is their desire, as well as ours, to help others find a life of love.

Gloria's commitment to the communication of these truths has made it possible for me to complete *Love-Life* while maintaining my full-time schedule as a family doctor and counselor. Gaye and I are deeply grateful to Gloria and Dan for their part in this ministry.

Introduction

When I began my practice as a family physician in the beautiful little community of Springdale, Arkansas, more than twenty-five years ago, I had no plans of becoming either a certified sex therapist or a marriage counselor. And since I was totally unfamiliar with the Bible, the possibility of becoming a biblical counselor of course never occurred to me.

But I soon discovered that a family doctor has to treat many problems that cannot be resolved medically. Marriage counseling that improved my patients' home life evolved from my desire to meet their needs.

Then about twenty years ago God used a patient who was concerned about my eternal well-being to introduce me to His Son, the Lord Jesus Christ. From the day I became a Christian I poured my life into learning what the Word of God had to say to me as a husband and father, then putting it into practice as best I knew how. This has had unexpected and far-reaching results.

Today I have the privilege of counseling people from all over the world in the area of love, sex, and marriage from the biblical and medical viewpoints. Our published materials, counseling cassette albums, and seminars evoke a constant stream of letters and requests for personal counsel. The issue on the minds of most people is not sex, but the core problem: love, or the lack of it and their longing for it.

In a typical week these burdens are expressed:

A letter from the African continent asks if there is any way a couple can *learn* to love each other.

A husband and wife telephone, bewildered and heavyhearted: "We are married, and as Christians we do not want to resort to divorce. But there is *no love* in our marriage. What can we do?"

"I know I should go back to my wife," a new Christian admits in counseling, "but I don't care for her. Honestly, I never have."

"I'm so torn inside, so disappointed in our marriage," a missionary writes.

A wife confides, "We are both born-again Christians. But my husband doesn't see that it is possible for love to be rekindled in our marriage. I know our God is big enough to handle that!"

The good news I share with all these people and the good news I want to share with you is that you and your marriage partner can have a thrilling love relationship, more wonderful than any romance secular literature has ever written or filmed, *if you will develop it in God's way.*

Many of the principles put forth in this book were tested and proven in a two-year period of marital stress at the beginning of my Christian life when my lovely wife Gaye and our three young daughters were unresponsive both to the gospel and to me. (I am sure they were wondering what had happened to their husband and father as they saw me change so drastically before their eyes.) I have always been grateful for that heartbreaking experience of prolonged rejection, for this drove me to the Word of God to learn exactly what I should do. I learned that it was my responsibility to *love* my wife the way Christ loved me. Many times I did not feel like loving her, for rejection, even quiet, courteous rejection, is hard to handle. But I did it out of obedience to God. I found that as I put the principles of the Bible into practice and as I learned how to really love my wife, this became pleasure as well as responsibility. Obedience took on the bright colors of joy!

As I slowly became the husband God had designed me to be, my wife began to respond with love just as God had planned and promised. When she trusted the Lord Jesus Christ as her personal Savior, it was the real beginning of our own love affair as God had planned it from ages past. We honestly fell in love with each other and found through firsthand experience that God has a genuine *romantic* love rooted in the reality of *agape* love for the husband and wife who will take His counsel seriously.

Our love affair, born out of commitment, encompasses far more than that now. The thrill of romance, the pleasure of friendship, the tranquillity of belonging, the sweetness of intimacy—in fact, all the aspects of love discussed in this book have become an integral part of our marriage. Not because Gaye and I are in some way unique. Certainly, no one would be likely to include a middle-aged doctor and his wife among the world's great lovers. Rather, my point is that the same principles we have used in our marriage will work in yours. They work because they are grounded in biblical truth.

Our prayer is that this book will be used in your life, not just to hold your marriage together, but also to unite you and your mate as lovers in a relationship that becomes more wonderful every day.

Husbands, love your wives, even as Christ also loved the church, and gave himself for it;

That he might sanctify and cleanse it with the washing of water by the word,

That he might present it to himself a glorious church, not having spot, or wrinkle, or any such thing; but that it should be holy and without blemish.

So ought men to love their wives as their own bodies. He that loveth his wife loveth himself.

For no man ever yet hated his own flesh; but nourisheth and cherisheth it, even as the Lord the church:

For we are members of his body, of his flesh, and of his bones.

For this cause shall a man leave his father and mother, and shall be joined unto his wife, and they two shall be one flesh.

This is a great mystery: but I speak concerning Christ and the church.

Nevertheless let every one of you in particular so love his wife even as himself; and the wife see that she reverence her husband.

(Ephesians 5:25-33)

1

A Love Affair:
It Can Happen to You!

THIS BOOK IS about love and marriage: *your* marriage and the love affair that *you* can experience with your own husband or wife.

Most people think of a love affair as a passionate interlude between a man and woman who are not married—at least not to each other. The world for centuries has tried to convince people of the notion that secretive adulterous love is more exciting than love in marriage. But the dictionary defines *love affair* as "an affinity between two persons . . . a particular experience of being in love." The particular experience we are concerned with is the wonderful life-long love affair God designed for husband and wife. He has provided all the pleasures known to man in their normal, healthy, satisfying form, and as the Creator of marriage and the Author of love His provision includes a love affair full of thrills and joy and lasting satisfaction for *every* couple, not just a favored few.

Of course, it is up to each of us to discover this design for our marriage through a careful searching of the Bible and a willingness to follow the principles, instructions, and examples we find there. My purpose in writing this book is to help you, both with the search and the practical application of the truths discovered, so that you can begin to experience all that God has for you in your marriage.

Shining through the scriptural principles and patterns you will find one basic, attitude-transforming truth:

It is God's will in every marriage that the couple love each other with an absorbing spiritual, emotional, and physical attraction that continues to grow throughout their lifetime together.

Another fact follows logically from this great truth: *It is possible for any Christian couple to develop this love relationship in their marriage because it is in harmony with God's express will.*

Because He is the One who made us, who conceived the idea of marriage and ordained it for our blessing, who gave us the potential for love, He is the One who knows best how to build love into marriage. He must be intimately involved in all our efforts to develop the kind of marriage that pleases Him. As we follow His principles and put His concepts into practice, we can begin to experience the marriage that He planned for us from the beginning, filled with "the blaze of newness and the sweet assurance of sameness" all our days.

As a Christian marriage counselor who accepts the Bible as the final authority, I do not offer my patients mere sympathy or set forth pet ideas that may or may not work. The principles I offer are solid biblical principles that will always work when applied properly to individual problems. I have found God's Word, the Bible, to be eternally true and totally dependable. Cultures change; lifestyles fluctuate; modes of thought come and go with the passing of time. But God's principles do not change and human behavior does not really change either. Under the sophisticated exterior of modern man and woman, the same sinful, unworkable patterns of behavior operate with destructive force just as they did in the days of Adam and Eve or Abraham and Sarah. Ancient peoples had the same tendencies to wrongdoing and the same inner desires and needs that you and I have today. Because neither God nor man has essentially changed since the dawn of time, the principles of living spelled out in the Bible are completely relevant to marriage today.

Do you see what this means to you in coping with life in the last two decades of the twentieth century? You have not been left to figure out the solutions on your own or to wonder if your behavior responses are right or wrong. You do not have to indulge in wishful thinking about unsatisfactory relationships. You are told in the Bible what to do about them and you are given every resource you need in order to do those things that will lead to your blessing and happiness. You and I can be affirmative, realistic, and objective about the problems that invade our lives because we are dealing with unshakable truth.

Perhaps this seems idealistic to you in view of the life you are leading with your husband or wife. You may be thinking, "Sounds good. But Dr. Wheat doesn't know what *our* marriage is like!"

Please note that we have titled this book, "Love-Life for *every* married couple." This means you! Because hundreds of couples have discussed their marriages with me, I understand the varied and difficult situations that can arise between two people in marriage. Some are heartbreaking; some are perplexing and unbelievably complicated. But none is beyond solution.

It will be helpful for you at this point to diagnose your own situation and to determine what you would like your relationship to be. Deciding where you are and where you should be is a first step in the direction of constructive change. One or more of the following statements will probably describe your marital situation, so put a mental checkmark where it belongs.

( ) We have a good marriage now, but we want to continue to grow in love for each other.

( ) We have never been in love, not even when first married.

( ) We have lost the love that we once felt for each other.

( ) Frankly, I am no longer in love with my partner.

( ) My partner is indifferent or seems to love someone else.

( ) We do care about each other, but our marriage is dull.

( ) I would like to know what I can do to improve our relationship.

( ) I want to restore our love and save our marriage, but my partner is uncooperative.

( ) My partner wants a divorce.

( ) We have serious problems but are agreed on trying to save our marriage.

( ) Both of us want to learn how to fall in love with each other.

( ) We're newlyweds who want to build a love that will last and become more enjoyable all the time.

Let me encourage you now about the future of your marriage. The relationship you would like to have *can happen,* but not by accident. An intimate relationship seldom improves spontaneously, and a troubled relationship almost never gets better on its own. I have no easy overnight cures to offer you, no happiness pills to transform your marriage automatically. But if you read this book carefully and consistently follow the prescriptions I give you, you are going to learn how to love in such a way that there will be a responding love from your partner. If you have a good relationship now, it will become so much better that you will be thrilled and amazed.

Love can come to you at *any* age in *any* stage of your marriage if you are willing to open the door and invite it into your relationship. No matter how bad your marital situation seems to be, you and your partner can fall in love with each other all over again—or maybe for the first time. If you've been wavering on the edge of a traumatic divorce, you can rekindle your love. You can learn how to handle the most difficult problems in such a way that your marriage will become rooted in love—stabilized and strong enough to withstand the stresses of a lifetime. Even if you are trying to save your marriage all by yourself, without any cooperation from your partner, *it can happen.* When they are properly and consistently applied, there are no exceptions, no unique cases where God's eternal concepts will fail.

I hope that you will approach this book as a counseling manual, rather than just another book to be read lightly at your leisure. These chapters contain the vital, detailed information every married couple needs in order to build love, restore love, and preserve the marriage from forces that would destroy it. A manual is a handy guide or reference book to show you *what* to do and *how* to do it. It implies action. You know that desired results will come from doing, not dreaming. So act upon the practical advice you find here, remembering that it is based on specific biblical instructions as to thought, attitude, and behavior. This is precisely the same counsel that my private patients receive. I hope you will look on it as my personal message to you, just as though I were talking to you in my office. I write with the prayer that you and your partner will learn to love each other in such a way that a world starving for the reality of love can see it manifested through your marriage.

In these pages you will meet people with problems similar to your own. Their stories stand as they told them to me. In all cases I have changed their names and unimportant details in order to protect their privacy.

Allison is just one example. She had been married for thirty years, and although she was a devout Christian, she was struggling with the temptation to divorce her husband because of longstanding problems. He had ignored his financial responsibilities; he had ignored her feelings. One thing above all others troubled her: throughout their long marriage she had never lived in a completed house!

As she described it to me, "There are always building materials in every corner and against the walls. It is a frustration to try to keep house and is so humiliating to me. I no longer will invite people in when they come to the door. I feel like going and hiding. As a younger person I always had hope that some day things would get finished, but when I got to be fifty and it was still the same, I lost hope. I knew that for the rest of my life it would always be the same. At fifty-four a man does not change his whole pattern of living. When you mentioned making our bedroom a love nest, it hurt, because I've always pictured something like that. But how could I with unfinished floors, unfinished walls, and everything makeshift?"

After Allison encountered the love-life concepts that I communicate at every opportunity, she was led by the Lord to make a commitment to learn to love her husband. The process began with a choice of her will and it proceeded through the various stages of restoring love to their relationship. Each step involved another decision to do things in God's way. The result has been what Allison calls "a miracle" in their marriage. Today she says, "I really do *feel* love for my husband now, and my desire for sex is renewed. In the past sex was the last thing I had any interest in. But now that I love my husband I really want to please him in our physical union too."

Allison can be assured that as she continues to love her husband according to biblical principles and patterns, significant changes will occur in him also. Her love already is providing a tremendous motivation for change. At fifty-four—or any other age—a man *can* change his pattern of living with the resources of God at his disposal. This story is not finished yet, but the "miracle" of love has already appeared to bless their marriage.

Allison says, "I know so many miserable, unhappy women who are still fighting their situation. My heart goes out to them. Please encourage them. . . ."

My encouragement is this: I see these miracles happening in marriages all the time. You and your partner can have a wonderful love affair. You can cause it to happen.

2

Discoveries:
The False
and the True

AS A MATHEMATICS major in college I learned that if you do not start with the right premise in problem solving, there is no way you can come up with the right answer. So when I became a Christian, I studied the Bible like a mathematician. That is, I spent more time in the first three chapters of Genesis than any other part of Scripture because I knew that these chapters formed the foundation for everything else in the Bible. I discovered that here in capsule form was the essence of God's truth concerning man and woman and their relationship with God and with each other; here I could begin to understand myself and my wife and to find God's perfect design for our marriage and His purpose for our life together.

So like a mathematician, I plunged into the painstaking study of these seed chapters, knowing that I had to build my life and marriage on the right premises in order to come out right at the end. The outcome has been more wonderful than I expected—a beautiful marriage, a godly home, and a life ministry with the opportunity to show many other couples how to find happiness together by following God's original plan.

Of course, in order to establish an approach to marriage based on Genesis truth, I had to unlearn some concepts I had developed earlier in life. But I could do this because I knew I had accurate information; I could replace wrong ideas with the right ones and then live by them in confidence. I found that I could depend on this truth, that it would never lead me into making bad decisions or giving bad counsel.

How about you? What has shaped your thinking about marriage? Can you depend on it?

I want you to carefully consider the underlying assumptions that govern your attitudes toward marriage and love. Some may be false; some may be true. It is essential for you to determine which premises are correct, which are worth building on, and which concepts should be discarded because they are false and therefore unworkable, even potentially harmful.

A couple I will call Dean and Carol had to come to this place after many years as active Christians in a large evangelical church. Carol regarded her husband as "a wonderful, gentle man" and a good father to their teen-age sons. Their life together was "comfortable." If the thrill seemed to be gone from their relationship, Carol attributed that to twenty years of marriage and their age—a bit past forty.

Then her world was shaken on its foundations when Dean admitted his involvement in an affair with a young woman who worked with him in the church's music ministry. Dean said the affair had ended, but a close Christian friend counseled Carol to divorce him without delay because, as she warned, "Adultery kills a marriage. And it's not right to let yourself be used as a door mat."

While Carol, feeling bewildered and betrayed, withdrew from Dean, the young woman kept on actively pursuing him. Dean had met with the deacons to confess his wrongdoing, but now he became reluctant to attend church with his wife and sons. The church leaders regarded this as proof of Dean's insincerity, and they predicted to Carol that the marriage could not be saved because "Dean is just not right with God."

Dean, deeply depressed, began considering a job transfer to another part of the country for a period of ten months or more. He explained to Carol, "The separation will help us to know if we really love each other, or not." Carol's confidante reacted with angry advice, saying, "Just pack his bags and leave them on the front steps. The sooner he goes, the better!"

When Carol told me her story, I was impressed by the fact that all the people involved in this painful situation claimed to be believers in Jesus Christ who recognized His Word as truth: the wife, the husband, the other woman, the counseling friend, and the church leaders. Yet each of these, in his or her own way, had displayed a lack of knowledge of the biblical principles that could preserve and heal this marriage. So many important biblical principles concerning marriage, love, forgiveness, and restoration were violated or ignored that it is no wonder that Dean and Carol both felt "frozen" into the tragic event and were unable to move on beyond it.

Unfortunately, this is a typical story. I have heard it many times with minor variations on the basic theme. I share it with you because so much can be learned from it.

As I worked with Carol, she began taking a long look at her own thinking and behavior patterns. How valid were her actions and reactions during the crisis and what had prompted them? Were her decisions being shaped by faulty human advice or by the eternal counsels of God? What basic assumptions were guiding her thinking? Were these premises true or false?

Then something very interesting happened to Carol. When she turned to the Word of God, determined to follow His counsel wherever it led, and to leave the results with Him, the unbiblical advice she had received faded out of her thinking, and she began to see clearly the false and the true. She found that there was total disagreement between the Bible and the world's system of thinking on marriage and divorce, and that she had almost been tricked by Satan, the master hypocrite, into believing his lies concerning her marriage. She discovered that Satan can work through even the most well-meaning Christian who takes the human viewpoint on marriage instead of God's clear scriptural teaching. She also learned that when men and women react according to their natural inclinations, they will usually make the wrong decision.

As she described it, both she and Dean had fallen into a pit of muddled thinking, mixed-up feelings, and wrong reactions. Only the truth could set them free. Together they began the relearning process, and they started with Genesis 1-3.

Every married couple needs to know the real truth concerning marriage, but it will never be found in the teachings or examples of the present world system. The best this world can offer is a low-cost, no-fault divorce obtained through the local department store—a new convenience for thousands of people blundering in and out of marriage as though it were a revolving door. It took the words of one social critic to put the situation into clear, hard perspective. He said, "In the 1970s, divorce became the *natural outcome* of marriage!"

If divorce is now accepted, even expected, as the natural result of marriage, this is a chilling heritage for the 80s and 90s. But we certainly do not have to adopt it in our thinking. Bible-believing Christians in every culture, in every age, have found the wisdom and strength to move upstream against the current of prevailing life styles. Note that the scriptural wisdom comes first: then the strength to go against popular opinion, no matter how powerful.

Let me take you on the scriptural tour that Dean and Carol took in their search for foundational truth on which to build their marriage. We'll begin at the beginning with the creation of male and female. Our purpose: to understand marriage as God ordained it in contrast to the opinions of the world around us. We need to look at these verses in Genesis as though we have never seen them before; we will look at them not as cliches but as truth for our individual lives.

1) The idea of male and female was God's idea.

"So God created man in his own image, in the image of God created he him; male and female created he them" (Genesis 1 :27) .

Genesis 1 declares the fact of man's creation while Genesis 2 reveals the process by which this occurred. Here in the first chapter we find the fundamental truth that is so essential to the appreciation of marriage—that God made male and female for His own good purposes. It seems too obvious to mention, but perhaps it should be pointed out that the creation of two kinds of people—men and women—was not a dark conspiracy to thwart the ambitions of the women's liberation movement. It was scarcely a put-down for women. Indeed, it became a testimonial, for creation was incomplete without woman. In a loving, amazing, creative act, the almighty God conceived the wonderful mysteries of male and female, masculinity and femininity, to bring joy into our lives. Think how colorless, how one—dimensional a world would be in which there was only your sex! Who would want to live in an all-male world or an all-female world? Or, for that matter, in a unisex world where all signs of gender were ignored or suppressed? The person who refuses to see and rejoice in the fundamental differences between male and female will never taste the divine goodness God planned for marriage.

2) Marriage was designed by God to meet the first problem of the human race: loneliness.

And the LORD God said, It is not good that the man should be alone; I will make him an help meet for him. And out of the ground the LORD God formed every beast of the field, and every fowl of the air; and brought them unto Adam to see what he would call them: and whatsoever Adam called every living creature, that was the name thereof. And Adam gave names to all cattle, and to the fowl of the air, and to every beast of the field; but for Adam there was not found an help meet for him. And the LORD God caused a deep sleep to fall upon Adam, and he slept: and he took one of his ribs, and closed up the flesh instead thereof; and the rib, which the LORD God had taken from man, made he a woman, and brought her unto the man (Genesis 2:18–22).

Picture this one man in a perfect environment, but alone. He had the fellowship of God and the company of birds and animals. He had an interesting job, for he was given the task of observing, categorizing, and naming all living creatures. But he was alone. God observed that this was "not good." So a wise and loving Creator provided a perfect solution. He made another creature, like the man and yet wondrously unlike him. She was taken from him, but she complemented him. She was totally suitable for him—spiritually, intellectually, emotionally, and physically. According to God, she was designed to be his "helper." This term *helper* refers to a beneficial relationship where one person aids or supports another person as a friend and ally. Perhaps you have thought of a helper as a subordinate, a kind of glorified servant. You will see the woman's calling in a new light when you realize that the same Hebrew word for *help* is used of God Himself in Psalm 46:1 where He is called our *helper,* "a very present help in trouble."

Marriage always begins with a need that has been there from the dawn of time, a need for companionship and completion that God understands. Marriage was designed to relieve the fundamental loneliness that every human experiences. In your own case, to the degree to which your mate does not meet your needs—spiritually, intellectually, emotionally, and physically—and to the degree to which you do not meet your mate's needs, the two of you are still alone. But this is not according to the plan of God and it can be remedied. His plan is *completeness* for the two of you together.

3) Marriage was planned and decreed to bring happiness, not misery.
"And Adam said, This is now bone of my bones, and flesh of my flesh; she shall be called Woman, because she was taken out of Man" (Genesis 2:23).

Here is the world's first love song! Hebrew experts tell us that Adam was expressing a tremendous excitement, a joyous astonishment. *"At last,* I have someone corresponding to me!" His phrase, "bone of my bones, and flesh of my flesh," became a favorite Old Testament saying to describe an intimate, personal relationship. But the fullness of its meaning belongs to Adam and his bride. Dr. Charles Ryrie makes the interesting suggestion that the Hebrew word for woman, *ishshah,* may come from a root word meaning "to be soft"—an expression, perhaps, of the delightful and novel femininity of woman.

So, when the Lord brought the woman to Adam, the man expressed his feelings in words like these: "I have finally found the one who can complete me, who takes away my loneliness, who will be as dear to me as my own flesh. She is so beautiful! She is perfectly suited to me. She is all I will ever need!"

Can you imagine the emotion that must have flamed within both the man and the woman as they realized what they could mean to each other? Can you grasp the purpose with which God created woman for man? All the tired jokes to the contrary, marriage was designed for our joy, our happiness. And God's purpose has never changed.

4) Marriage must begin with a leaving of all other relationships in order to establish a permanent relationship between one man and one woman.
"Therefore shall a man leave his father and his mother, and shall cleave unto his wife: and they shall be one flesh" (Genesis 2:24).

God gave this three-part commandment at the beginning as He ordained the institution of marriage. It remains the most concise and comprehensive counseling session ever presented on marriage. If you will notice, the words are mostly one-syllable words in the English—plain words, easily understood, in spite of their infinite depth of meaning. These twenty-two words sum up the entire teaching of Scripture on marriage. All else that is said emphasizes or amplifies the three fundamental principles originated here, but never changes them in the slightest. They deserve your careful consideration, for any real problem you face in marriage will come from ignoring some aspect of God's Genesis commandment.

We must understand, first of all, that marriage begins with a *leaving:* leaving all other relationships. The closest relationship outside of marriage is specified here, implying that if it is necessary to leave your father and mother, then certainly all lesser ties must be broken, changed, or left behind.

Of course the bonds of love with parents are lasting ones. But these ties must be changed in character so that the man's full commitment is now to his wife. And the wife's full commitment is now to her husband. The Lord gave the man this commandment, although the principle applies to both husband and wife, because it is up to the man to establish a new household that he will be responsible for. He can no longer be dependent on his father and mother; he can no longer be under their authority, for now he assumes headship of his own family.

Scripture makes it clear that the adult must continue to honor his parents and, now that he is independent, he needs to care for them when necessary and to assume responsibility *for* them rather than responsibility *to* them. (See Matthew 15:3–9 and 1 Timothy 5:4–8.) But a leaving must occur, for neither parents nor any other relationships should come between husband and wife.

This means that you and your mate need to refocus your lives on each other, rather than looking to another individual or group of people to meet your emotional needs. This also means giving other things a lesser priority—your business, your career, your house, your hobbies, your talents, your interests, or even your church work. All must be put into proper perspective. Whatever is important to you in this life should be less important than your marriage.

The wife of a successful businessman who has poured all his energies into his business shed some bitter tears in my office, saying, "He keeps giving me *monetary rewards,* and every time he does it, I think how much better it would be to have his time and love. Dr. Wheat, I don't want all those *things.* I just want him to pay some attention to me."

In more than twenty-five years of counseling I have observed that when a man consistently puts his business or career ahead of his wife, nothing he can buy with money will really please her.

There are many different ways of failing to leave something and thus failing to build a real marriage. I have seen women so involved with their jobs or advanced education that they became more like roommates than wives, and other women whose preoccupation with meticulous housekeeping marred what could have been good marriages. I have known men who could not leave the ties with their hunting or golfing buddies long enough to establish love relationships with their wives. Some cannot even tear themselves away from televised sports long enough to communicate with their wives. I have observed situations where either husband or wife became excessively involved in church work to the serious detriment of their marriage. And I have known sad cases where the mother or sometimes the father gave the children top priority. When those children grew up, nothing was left. The marriage was emotionally bankrupt.

The first principle we can learn from Genesis 2:24 is that marriage means leaving. Unless you are willing to leave all else, you will never develop the thrilling oneness of relationship that God intended for every married couple to enjoy.

5) Marriage requires an inseparable joining of husband and wife throughout their lifetime.

"Therefore shall a man leave his father and his mother, *and shall cleave unto his wife:* and they shall be one flesh" (Genesis 2:24).

The next principle to be learned from this ordinance is that it is no use leaving unless you are ready to spend a lifetime *cleaving*. Again, notice that the Lord directs this to the husband especially, although the principle applies to both partners.

What does it mean to cleave? The word sometimes causes confusion because in the English it has two opposite definitions and the most common of these is "to divide, to split, to open." Thus, butchers use a cleaver to cut meat into various pieces. Splitting and dividing is precisely *not* what is meant here, so picture the reverse. "Cleave" (derived from Anglo-Saxon and Germanic speech) also means: "to adhere, to stick, to be attached by some strong tie." This verb suggests determined action in its essential meaning, so there is nothing passive about the act of cleaving. For example, the word "climb" is said to be closely akin to "cleave."

The same feeling of action accompanies the Hebrew word *dabaq* which the King James Bible translates as "cleave." Here are some definitions of *dabaq:* "To cling to or adhere to, abide fast, cleave fast together, follow close and hard after, be joined together, keep fast, overtake, pursue hard, stick to, take, catch by pursuit." Modern Bible translators usually change "cleave" to "cling to" or "hold fast to." When we come to the Greek New Testament, the word means to cement together—to stick like glue—or to be welded together so that the two cannot be separated without damage to both.

From this, it is obvious that God has a powerful message for both marriage partners and a dynamic course of action laid out for the husband in particular. The husband is primarily responsible to do everything possible and to be all he should be in order to form ties with his wife that will make them inseparable. And the wife must respond to her husband in the same manner. These ties are not like the pretty silken ribbons attached to wedding presents. Instead, they must be forged like steel in the heat of daily life and the pressures of crisis in order to form a union that cannot be severed.

The best way to comprehend the force of meaning in the word "cleave" is to consider how the Holy Spirit has used the word *dabaq* in the Book of Deuteronomy. These four prime examples all speak of cleaving to the living God.

"You shall fear the LORD your God; you shall serve Him and *cling to Him,* and you shall swear by His name (Deuteronomy 10:20 NASB).

". . . to love the LORD your God, to walk in all His ways and *hold fast to Him"* (Deuteronomy 11:22 NASB).

"You shall follow the LORD your God and fear Him; and you shall keep His commandments, listen to His voice, serve Him, and *cling to Him"* (Deuteronomy 13:4 NASB).

" . . . by loving the LORD your God, by obeying His voice, and by *holding fast to Him;* for this is your life . . ." (Deuteronomy 30:20 NASB).

This indicates that in the eyes of God cleaving means wholehearted commitment, first of all spiritual, but spilling over into every area of our being, so that the cleaving is also intellectual, emotional, and physical. It means that you will have unceasing opportunity to cleave to your partner even in the smallest details of life. In fact, anything that draws the two of you together and cements your relationship more firmly will be a part of cleaving. Anything that puts distance between you—mentally or physically—should be avoided because it breaks the divine pattern for marriage.

Much of the practical counsel in this book will show you how to cleave to your partner under varying circumstances and in many different ways. However it is expressed, cleaving always involves two characteristics: (1) an unswerving loyalty; (2) an active, pursuing love that will not let go.

If you want to test an action, attitude, word, or decision against the biblical standards of cleaving, ask yourself these questions. Will this draw us closer or drive us apart? Will it build our relationship or tear it down? Will it bring about a positive response or a negative response? Does it express my love and loyalty to my partner or does it reveal my self-centered individualism?

Remember that God's plan for you and your partner is an inseparable union that you bring about as you obey His commandment to cleave to each other.

6) Marriage means oneness in the fullest possible sense, including intimate physical union without shame.

"Therefore shall a man leave his father and his mother, and shall cleave unto his wife: *and they shall be one flesh.* And they were both naked, the man and his wife, and were not ashamed" (Genesis 2:24–25).

We see now that the pattern for marriage that God established at Creation will produce something quite remarkable if it is followed. Two will actually become one. This is more than togetherness! No writer, teacher, or theologian has ever yet explained all that it means for two people to become "one flesh." We only know that it happens!

Several elementary requirements should be noted. For this to take place, the marriage must be *monogamous* (for two people only). At the same time all adultery and promiscuity are ruled out, for, as the Lord Jesus emphasizes in the New Testament, *the two* become one. The Bible graphically portrays the miserable long-term effects of polygamous marriage and the deadly results of adultery. Proverbs 6:32, for instance, says: "The one who commits adultery with a woman is lacking sense; he who would destroy himself does it" (NASB). Certainly none can plead ignorance as an excuse! The marriage must also be *heterosexual.* God made one *woman* for one *man.* The homosexual "marriage" being promoted in some quarters today is a pathetic, squalid distortion of the Creator's plan for holy union between one man and one woman.

Although it goes far deeper than the physical, becoming one flesh involves intimate physical union in sexual intercourse. And this without shame between marriage partners. Shame in marital sex was never imparted by God! Instead, the biblical expression for sexual intercourse between husband and wife is *to know,* an expression of profound dignity. "Adam *knew* Eve his wife; and she conceived . . ." (Genesis 4:1). "Then Joseph . . . took unto him his wife: and *knew* her not until she had brought forth her firstborn son . . ." (Matthew 1:24–25).

This word *know* is the same word used of God's loving, personal knowledge of Abraham in Genesis 18:19: "for I *know* him, that he will command his children and his household after him, and they shall keep the way of the LORD, to do justice and judgment. . . ."

Thus, in the divine pattern of marriage, sexual intercourse between husband and wife includes both intimate physical knowledge and a tender, intimate, personal knowledge. So the leaving, cleaving, and knowing each other results in a new identity in which two individuals merge into one—one in mind, heart, body and spirit. This is why divorce has such a devastating effect. Not two people are left, but two fractions of one.

In the New Testament, the Holy Spirit uses the Genesis mystery of becoming one flesh with its dimension of sexual intercourse to picture an even deeper mystery: that of the relationship between Jesus Christ and His bride, the church. "For this cause shall a man leave his father and mother, and shall be joined unto his wife, and they two shall be one flesh. This is a great mystery: but I speak concerning Christ and the church" (Ephesians 5:3 1–32).

Here is the marriage design as ordained by God at the very beginning—a love relationship so deep, tender, pure, and intimate that it is patterned after that of Christ for His church. This is the foundation for the love-life you can experience in your own marriage, a foundation on which you can safely build.

3
Does the Plan Still Work?

Mᴏʀᴇ ᴛʜᴀɴ ᴏɴᴇ million divorces will split American households this year.

About 75 percent of the family units in this country will need counseling help at some time.

At least 40 percent of all married couples will divorce eventually.

Do these predictions, based on past statistics, mean that the Creator's design for marriage no longer works? We have just been considering the comprehensive marriage ordinance of Genesis 2:24 in all its wonderful wisdom, but we might point out with accuracy that it was given in a world of primeval perfection to innocent people who had not yet tasted the forbidden fruit of sin. Can the Divine pattern for marriage really work outside the Garden of Eden? Or does God take into account how things have changed since then? Has He, in fact, revised His marriage plan to fit prevailing conditions?

This view shows up frequently today as people discuss divorce. Here's how one person expressed it in a letter to the editor of a Christian magazine:

> Just because I married the wrong man for all the wrong reasons, does that mean we should have stayed together to make it "right?" We prayed four years for our feelings to change, for our marriage to change; we saw counselors and went to Marriage Encounter groups. Still we found we disliked each other more and more. Rather than continue to tear each other down, after five years of marriage, we decided to get a divorce. It was the lesser of two evils; either decision we made would have been painful. I feel guilty, thanks especially to the church's attitude, but I also feel that God understands. . . .

A woman made this comment to me at a Christian marriage seminar: "After all, God gave me a brain. If I see that I have made a mistake by marrying the wrong person, then divorce may well be the answer." Apparently she also felt that God would understand her efforts to redeem an unhappy marriage by eliminating it altogether—like correcting a mistake on an exam paper with a very neat erasure.

We must face this issue squarely. Does God still expect people who live in a sin-filled world to carry out the marriage ordinance given in the perfect environment of the Garden?

The Lord Jesus Christ has answered the question. In Mark 10:2–12, which we will quote, and in the parallel passage in Matthew 19:3–12, Jesus communicates the Divine viewpoint of marriage. As you read His words, you will meet the truth in a pure form, untarnished by the hardness of men's hearts.

> And the Pharisees came to him, and asked him, Is it lawful for a man to put away his wife? tempting him.
> And he answered and said unto them, What did Moses command you?
> And they said, Moses suffered a man to write a bill of divorcement, and to put her away.
> And Jesus answered and said unto them, For the hardness of your heart he wrote you this precept.
> But from the beginning of the creation God made them male and female.
> For this cause shall a man leave his father and mother, and cleave to his wife;
> And they twain shall be one flesh; so then they are no more twain, but one flesh.
> What therefore God hath joined together, let not man put asunder.
> And in the house his disciples asked him again of the same matter.
> And he saith unto them, Whosoever shall put away his wife, and marry another, committeth adultery against her.
> And if a woman shall put away her husband, and be married to another, she committeth adultery.
>
> (Mark 10:2–12)

The Pharisees had come to Jesus, hoping to drag him into the stormy controversy surrounding divorce. In that day followers of three different schools of interpretation of Jewish law clashed on the question of acceptable reasons for divorce. Their debate revolved around Deuteronomy 24 where Moses regulated the existing practice of divorce by limiting the cause to uncleanness or indecency of the most serious nature. A careful study of the Old Testament indicates that an act of adultery was not considered legal grounds for divorce. (Numbers 5:11–31 gives specific instructions concerning adultery.) This "uncleanness" or "nakedness" or "indecency" Moses designated as the sole reason for legal divorce usually referred to incest, harlotry, or habitual sexual promiscuity. In the New Testament, Jesus called this uncleanness "fornication." We should note that adultery and fornication are words used distinctively and separately in the New Testament, so that if Jesus had meant to give adultery as the grounds for divorce, He would have said "adultery." Instead, He said, "Whosoever shall put away his wife, *except it be for fornication,* and shall marry another, committeth adultery; and whosoever marrieth her who is put away doth commit adultery" (Matthew 19:9).

Here is how the Jews of Jesus' day variously misinterpreted Moses' statement on divorce. Followers of Shammai claimed that any act of adultery was the uncleanness Moses spoke of. Followers of Hillel defined uncleanness in the widest sense. The wife might burn the soup. That was uncleanness. She might talk too loudly in the home. That was uncleanness. She might appear in public with her head uncovered. Again, uncleanness, if the husband chose to regard it as such. This meant any minor fault could be grounds for divorce. Followers of the most liberal rabbi, Akiba, neatly resolved the matter by asserting that any wife who found no favor in her husband's eyes was unclean and could be put away—a blanket permission to divorce.

Observe that the Pharisees went one step farther and disregarded Moses' exception clause altogether when they questioned Jesus. "Is it lawful for a man to put away his wife *for every cause?*" (Matthew 19:3) they asked. "Is it lawful for a man to put away his wife?" (Mark 10:2).

The way Jesus responded to the Pharisees shows us what our own attitude toward marriage and divorce should be:

(1) He ignored the bickering "religious" authorities of the day and their preoccupation with excuses for divorce.

(2) He focused on the Scriptures as the only real authority.

(3) He went back to the original design of marriage in the Genesis account as the only relevant topic of discussion. Matthew records that Jesus first answered the Pharisees this way: "Haven't you even read Genesis 1:27 and 2:24, you people who are always boasting about your knowledge of the Scriptures?" Or, in other words, "Why don't you go to the original teaching on marriage to find your answers?"

Clearly, Jesus recognized these two Genesis passages as the Divine ordinance for marriage—the first and last word—which remains very much in effect, even in a sin-filled world. Jesus made it clear that the legal concession on divorce given by Moses in Deuteronomy 24:1 simply was not the issue for anyone wanting to understand God's plan and purpose concerning marriage. "He saith unto them, Moses because of the hardness of your hearts suffered you to put away your wives: but from the beginning it was not so" (Matthew 19:8).

From the beginning it was not so! With these words, Jesus directs us back to the beginning where we still find our instruction for marriage and the standards we need to follow. Let us note carefully the one statement that the Son of God adds to the ordinance of Genesis: "What therefore God hath joined together, let not man put asunder" (Matthew 19:6; Mark 10:9).

This adds three important facts to our foundational understanding of marriage:

(1) God Himself has joined husband and wife together. A man and woman marry by their own choice, but when they do so, God yokes them together, changing what has been "two" into "one."

(2) From the Divine viewpoint, marriage is an indissoluble union which all the courts of the land cannot dissolve. How can a piece of paper change what God Himself has done? Only death can part two joined in marriage.

(3) For any individual to *try* to separate what God Himself has joined together is an act of arrogant defiance against the express will of God. Anyone who chooses to do this must live with the results of his action.

To summarize, Jesus told people who were preoccupied with finding excuses for divorce that their emphasis was all wrong. The real issue in the eyes of God then and today is the permanence of marriage and our honoring of this in personal experience.

If any reject these conclusions as hopelessly out of step in today's world, I can only quote the words of the Lord Jesus: "Whosoever therefore shall be ashamed of me and of my words in this adulterous and sinful generation; of him also shall the Son of man be ashamed, when he cometh in the glory of his Father with the holy angels" (Mark 8:38).

Now, how does the issue of divorce relate to your situation? If you are trying to build a love relationship in your marriage, or if you are trying to work out problems in your marriage, even admitting the faintest possibility of divorce will affect your efforts adversely. Retaining the idea of divorce in your emotional vocabulary—even as a last-ditch option—will hinder the total effort you would otherwise pour into your marriage. It will sabotage your attempts to improve your relationship, and an unhappy situation can continue in your home indefinitely. Keeping divorce as an escape clause indicates a flaw in your commitment to each other, even as a tiny crack that can be fatally widened by the many forces working to destroy homes and families.

The gloomy statistics quoted at the beginning of this chapter are due in part to Satan's unceasing attempts to undermine the home, the most valuable institution on earth. They can be attributed to the widely-held idea that if the marriage doesn't work, a divorce should be obtained and another attempt made with a new partner—as we have seen, a totally unbiblical view promoted by the world system under Satan's influence.

Another fundamental cause for marital disharmony exists, and we need to recognize it as we work to develop a real love relationship. I suggest that you thoughtfully read Genesis 3, which describes the failure of man and woman to obey God in an ideal environment; their fall from a state of innocence into sin and death; God's promise of redemption; and the expulsion of the couple from the Garden of Eden to live a life of moral responsibility under new and difficult conditions.

You will find in chapter 3 the origins of sin and shame, of selfishness and self-centeredness and separateness—these all corrupting the magnificent love and unity that Adam and Eve had once enjoyed. Now, in a sense, every couple puts on fig leaves and hides behind trees of their own making! We all have the tendency to withdraw from each other, to be separate, to concentrate on our own needs and wants, to live for ourselves, to blame those closest to us in order to protect or excuse ourselves, and to do that which displeases God.

Sin creates a false hunger, not for communion and fellowship, but for individuality of a destructive nature. Of course, Satan is glad to encourage this tendency. Remember that sin first came on the earthly scene in the first marriage, and in the very first family, division and hatred sprang up. That is where the devil began his deadliest work, and this is why you will never have a strong, happy marriage and a harmonious family life just as a matter of course.

Selfish individuality leading to separateness between husband and wife can be witnessed all around us and is constantly dramatized on television. For example, this dialog between husband and wife appeared on a family television series:

> Young husband comes home exuberantly happy with the news that he has a big opportunity to further his professional baseball career by playing in Puerto Rico for a few months. He is excited about taking his bride with him.
> Young wife answers coldly: "Why should I want to go to Puerto Rico?"
> Husband (just not believing this) stammers: "But . . . but . . . Susan, you're my wife!"
> Susan angrily replies: "Yes, but I'm a PERSON too, and I HAVE MY OWN LIFE TO LIVE!"

The aftershock of Genesis 3 is plainly seen in that interchange. Creeping separateness sometimes affects marriages that the public has taken to its heart. Many were saddened to read the newspaper article concerning an Olympic star who became a household word after his remarkable victory. He and his wife had been admired for their united efforts in working together for years to reach that goal. The Associated Press reported that this young man and his wife were legally separating after seven years of marriage because, to quote their public relations spokesman, "the couple feel their lives have changed in the last year and each wishes to focus on his own life." Hopefully, this marriage may still be saved, but note the reason for their separation: so each can focus on his own life! Again, we see the results of Genesis 3.

In chapter 2, I told you about Dean and Carol, a Christian couple who endured all kinds of onslaughts against their marriage, both from within and without. The pressures on them to separate were enormous. Let's analyze some of these and observe how one mistake led to the next. In each instance there was an absence of understanding or a lack of application of the biblical principles that help and heal such situations.

(1) First of all, they had failed to cleave to each other through the years by neglecting their love relationship. A love affair between husband and wife must be kept in constant repair and always on the growing edge.

(2) This left an emotional vacuum that the other woman happily filled, hoping to separate Dean from his wife so that she could marry him.

(3) Dean's subsequent sin of adultery attacked their one-flesh relationship.

(4) Carol mistakenly opened up her marriage to outside discussion with a friend who constantly criticized Dean, causing Carol to see herself separately from her husband.

(5) This friend also gave unbiblical counsel, urging divorce as a necessity because of adultery.

(6) Carol's physical and emotional withdrawal from her husband during this critical time contributed to the deepening division between them and played into the hands of the other woman who continued to pursue Dean.

(7) The church leaders failed to counsel Dean properly concerning forgiveness and restoration after his open confession of sin to the church board.

(8) As a result, Dean became entrapped by guilt feelings that hindered him from taking the necessary steps toward restoring love and trust in his marriage.

(9) This also affected his ability to go on in Christian growth. Guilt feelings *after confession of sin and repentance* have a satanic origin and are designed to hinder our spiritual growth.

(10) Understandably, Dean felt conspicuous and uncomfortable among the church people who were gossiping about him and criticizing him. He began to stay away from the services.

(11) Some of the church leaders made the mistake of predicting divorce as inevitable for the couple. This brought added confusion to Carol at a time when she needed to hear counsel from God's Word as to how she should meet the situation biblically.

(12) Because Carol failed to forgive her husband and leave the past behind according to biblical principles, they both became almost hopelessly entangled in problems that could have been resolved quickly with proper counseling.

(13) All of these factors, with the emotional pain and confusion involved, prompted Dean to seek escape by moving away, putting physical distance between him and his wife in an effort to determine whether they still loved each other. Separation seldom enhances a troubled marriage, and it is unlikely to prove anything about love. Togetherness in marriage is biblical. Separateness is satanic. This may sound like an oversimplification, but it is in complete accord with the Scriptures on marriage. I hope you will remember it as a rule to be followed in questionable situations.

Both Dean and Carol found that their feelings were leading them astray, that they could not depend on feelings to guide them. Almost everywhere they turned, they heard the word *divorce*. All the pressures on them urged separation rather than unity. But when they discovered the foundational principle of marriage— that in God's eyes husband and wife are one and must remain one—they were able to restore their love relationship and to rebuild their marriage. Today they have great opportunities to minister to other couples who are going through similar difficulties.

You see, it is possible to reasonably recover the Garden situation in marriage, according to the New Testament. We can, to a great extent, return to the ideal in our relationships, and we must if we want love-filled marriages. Although the tendency to selfishness always exists because of the Fall, we can regain the self-giving love, the oneness, the joyous freedom in communication that Adam and Eve once experienced. Through the resources of the Lord Jesus Christ, Christians have not only the pattern for ideal marriage, but also the purpose to fulfill that pattern, and the power to do it.

We earlier posed the question: Has God revised His marriage plan to fit prevailing conditions in a sin-filled world? The answer, we see, is a resounding NO. On the contrary, He expects us to revise our behavior to fit His standards for marriage *for our own good and blessing,* and He knows, because of the new life offered in Christ, that we can do it.

Of course, I am writing to you at the place where you are now. Whatever your past mistakes in the area of marriage and divorce, ask God's forgiveness and accept it, knowing that you have been set free from guilt. He always deals with us in the now, and you have every opportunity to go forward in a new way, "forgetting what lies behind and reaching forward to what lies ahead" (Philippians 3:13 NASB). With your eyes on Jesus and your mind shaped by the Word, you can make a new life for yourself and your partner from this moment forth.

I trust that you will approach your marriage with a new resolve to overcome the outside influences that cause you to see yourself separately from your mate; with a new determination to do all you can to build a love relationship in keeping with God's plan; and with a new confidence that it will be possible for you to improve your marriage and to remold it in the shape of the original design.

A man once said, "Ideals are like stars; we will not succeed in touching them with our hands, but following them, as the seafaring man on the desert of waters, we will reach our destiny."

We will not achieve perfection in our marriage, but as we follow the God-given pattern of Genesis 2:24, we will discover the thrills and wonders He planned for us, and we will fulfill the purpose He has set before us of showing His love to a needy world through the example of our own love.

4
Love:
Solving The Mystery

THE COUPLE SITTING across the desk from me had come from another part of the United States for counsel. Hal, a good-looking young man, who was already a success in his chosen profession, spoke for both of them. "Dr. Wheat, please help us—*if you can.* We're desperate."

As we talked together for a period of hours, I noticed how seldom Hal looked at his wife, Genie. And she, a pretty blonde with a gentle voice and sweet smile, seemed subdued in his presence. At times I detected a sparkle of warmth in her blue eyes, but it was never directed toward her husband. They were like courteous strangers, not even close enough to be hostile, bound by the most intimate of bonds, and yet farther apart than the walls of my office would allow. In spirit they were on opposite sides of the world!

Yet they appeared to have more than their share of good fortune. They were attractive people, financially comfortable, well educated, both with professions, and, most important, they knew and loved the Lord. In fact, they had met through a campus ministry, found that they had the same spiritual goals, and decided to marry after a time of prayerful consideration. To an outsider the marriage might have seemed ideal. But I saw before me two acutely unhappy people, struggling just to get through the next week together.

"We thought it was God's will for us to marry," Hal explained bleakly. "We have studied what the Bible teaches about marriage, and we *know* that divorce is not an option for us as Christians. But what are we going to do? We just don't love each other."

Further discussion clarified that statement. The couple respected, even admired, each other as individuals; they certainly wished each other well. But that was the extent of their real involvement. What was lacking?

"Feelings, Dr. Wheat," they both agreed. "We don't have any of the emotions that go with love. It's no thrill being together. We don't feel drawn to touch each other. We can't seem to talk to each other about our past or make any plans for the future.

"We don't fuss, we don't fight," said Hal. "But we don't enjoy each other either."

Any evening spent alone together resulted in boredom. Hal found Genie's sexual responses uninspiring, although they both regularly experienced sexual release. He admitted that he had no desire to sit close to her or put his arm around her. "I wish that I did," he said.

Genie found Hal to be self-occupied and moody. "But he's good in many ways," she said. "Since we both work, he helps me around the house. He takes me anywhere I want to go. He has told me I'm an excellent wife with a good head on my shoulders. And yet I know I don't please him. For instance, he thinks I look terrible without my make-up first thing in the morning. If he loved me, would that make any difference? I've always believed that real love shaded out imperfections."

"Actually, she's too perfect, too nice a person," Hal said. "Maybe that's why I feel there's no way she could ever understand me and the kind of life I led before I became a Christian."

"We're not on the same wavelength," Genie concluded sadly. "Marriage is nothing like I dreamed it would be. I feel disappointed and let down most of the time."

"Maybe we've cheated ourselves," Hal shrugged. "Our best friends love to be with each other. They light up the room when they're together. But it's different with us. I don't know what we can do about it now. We're married and we're miserable. We just don't love each other!"

I hear this complaint frequently. Often the phrase is, "We don't love each other anymore." Or that devastating admission: "My husband (or wife) doesn't love me anymore." But in a surprising number of cases desolate people tell me that they have never loved each other, not even when first married.

As a counselor, I have to deal with the tragic results of loveless marriages. The dearth of love has caused men who are known for their Christian leadership to become involved in adulterous affairs, or their wives to look elsewhere for the love they feel they are missing. In even more distressing cases, things have been done with legal as well as moral consequences that have virtually destroyed the entire family. Without going into details, I can assure you out of extensive counseling experience that men and women have a desperate longing for the emotion of love in their marriage, and that sometimes Christians shock even themselves by what they will do to find a substitute. Of course, a Christian need never be dominated by his feelings—in marriage or in any other aspect of life. But a marriage without good feelings is terribly incomplete, and the many couples I counsel are almost always concerned about the emotion of love and the lack of it in some phase of their relationship.

This is why, from my perspective, it is not enough to write a book on marriage only. I see the need to focus on love in marriage—the full spectrum of love, including the emotional hungers that God has placed within us to be satisfied. We know that love involves an incredible gamut of feelings ranging from thrills to sweet tranquillity. These can be keenly pleasurable and warmly supportive. They give color and texture to married life. They provide us with happiness and a sense of well-being even in the face of outside problems. But the absence of these feelings forms a painful void that cries out to be filled. We must not ignore the emotions of love and the longings they evoke. It is only when we acknowledge them and handle them in a constructive way that they take their proper place in our life to enrich us without dominating us.

Thus, in the real world of marriage, we have to recognize the importance of love with its accompanying emotions. But we also need to sort out the truth concerning love, just as we did when discussing the foundations of marriage. Dreams and myths must be discarded. I would like for you to carefully distinguish between the false and the true in the realm of love. Please ask yourself, Am I now operating on the basis of truth or fallacy in my love life?

An observer can see that nothing is started with such high hopes and shining expectations, yet fails as regularly as romantic love in marriage. The present divorce rate with almost one out of every two marriages openly admitting failure testifies to this. But why does love so often fail? Surely it is because the "lovers" have no clear understanding of what love is and is not; they do not know how to love; and in many cases they have never made the commitment to love. The behavior and responses of the majority of married couples are influenced not by truth, but by their own private supply of misconceptions about love.

Where does this misinformation come from? Fundamentally, God is Love and communicates the truth about love through His Word, the Bible. Satan is anti-love just as he is anti-Christ, and he disseminates ideas that distort and destroy love through the world system that he controls.

There are three main sources of mistaken ideas about love. As we discuss these, you may find it instructive to analyze your own ideas of love and determine their source, where possible.

Jumbled impressions. Each individual has collected a body of jumbled impressions about love, including odd notions picked up here and there, dating back to earliest childhood. Some of these are absorbed from family practices and philosophies. For example, entertainer Zsa Zsa Gabor, a member of the much married Gabor clan, who herself has been married seven times at this writing, expressed the family philosophy when she told a reporter, "Tiring women are forever asking me why my family and I have had so many husbands. It is not possible for them to understand that you fall in love—but you also fall out of love. When you fall out of love it is better to change partners and remain friends than to stay together and grow to hate each other."

The jumble of misinformation and vaguely defined impressions that most people have collected explains, in part, why so many prefer to look on love as an inexplicable mystery. Apparently, it is because their own view of love is confused and muddled: love *must* be a mystery! Besides, if love is an irrational thing with all its mysterious excitement, then one can be excused for behaving irrationally in the pursuit of it.

This popular view of love as a mystery not to be tampered with was expressed by Senator William Proxmire when the federal government financed a science foundation grant for research into love. He commented that "200 million Americans want to leave some things a mystery, and right at the top of those things we don't want to know is why a man falls in love with a woman and vice versa."

Faulty conclusions based on personal experience. I have found that many people operate on the basis of faulty conclusions drawn from their own experiences with romantic love. Surveys indicate that a good number of people do consider themselves experienced. One sociologist interviewing more than one thousand individuals found that the vast majority had begun with infatuations in their thirteenth year and had one or more "real love affairs" by their twenty-fourth year. But these affairs often bring two different sets of misconceptions about love to a collision course, resulting in emotional fallout. The individuals involved are apt to develop a painful wariness toward love or cynicism rather than real wisdom for the future. Personal experience provides sometimes questionable, always limited, data and leads to faulty conclusions that are of no use in building a lasting love relationship.

Flawed reasoning due to cultural influences. There is no way of measuring how many flawed attitudes toward love emerge from our cultural influences: movies, television, advertising in every form, magazines, novels, prevailing attitudes of friends, the words and example of popular celebrities, etc. These could hardly be classed as reliable sources of truth and wisdom, but their subtle and powerful effect on us cannot be denied.

While people are absorbing these erroneous beliefs about love, the scientific/ intellectual community is, for the most part, staying out of the field. Someone who checked has said that with rare exceptions most psychoanalytic, psychiatric, and psychological books and textbooks do not have the word *love* in their indexes. Not even the *Encyclopaedia Britannica* carries articles on the subject. But one psychiatrist, recognizing that the need for correct information about love is great, has written, "Love is sought by every one, everywhere. It is a constant concern; it is in constant demand. Can it be found? We believe so, if it is sufficiently understood and properly pursued. . . ."[1]

Certainly we all need accurate information and clear thinking about what has been called *the most desired and the most elusive emotion*—so desired that marriages without it range from boring to miserable; so elusive that some people spend their entire lifetime looking for it, leaving a trail of broken relationships in their wake.

My purpose in writing this book is to give you the foundational principles and the information you need in order to experience the fullness of love in your own marriage. The Bible is the primary source of our material; in fact, it is the only authoritative, completely accurate sourcebook on love to be found anywhere.

Now as we consider four basic truths that can reshape your attitudes and re-structure your approach to love, you must realize this: What you believe about love right now—true or false—is presently doing three things for you. It is (1) affecting your marriage; (2) shaping your behavior and responses to your mate; (3) helping determine your future happiness and emotional well-being. What you believe is that important. How much better to believe the truth!

Each of the following principles can help you restore love to your marriage or enrich the love affair you now have with your partner. Each offsets a common misconception of love that may have influenced you in the past. Consider these carefully; then I will show you how they helped the couple introduced at the beginning of this chapter.

1) I can learn what love is from the Word of God. It is rational, not irrational. I can understand love and grow in the understanding of it throughout my lifetime.

Perhaps you have not thought of it in this way, but the entire Bible is a love story that we can learn from—the story of God's unfailing love for an often unlovable human race. It is a pursuing love. Throughout the pages of the Bible we find God wooing, nurturing, caring, doing the best for those He loves, always seeking to draw men, women, boys, and girls to Himself. One verse seems to sum it up: "The LORD hath appeared of old unto me, saying, Yea, I have loved thee with an everlasting love: therefore with loving-kindness have I drawn thee" (Jeremiah 31:3).

The Old Testament tells of the love relationship between the Lord Jehovah and the Israelites, a love often likened to the love of a husband for an erring wife, determined to win her back in spite of her past.

In the New Testament the scope of revelation widens to present a remarkable picture of God's love for all people—a love without limits—as He makes the ultimate sacrifice to bring us into the circle of His eternal caring. We see Him in the form of Jesus, the Man willing to go through death in order to do the best for those He loves. John 3:16 tells us who they are: "For God so loved the *world*, that he gave his only begotten Son, that *whosoever* believeth in him should not perish, but have everlasting life."

If we were to sum up all we can learn about love through a scriptural study of God's dealings with mankind, it might be stated as simply as this: Love is always doing the very best for the object of one's love. This is what love is and what love does, and there is nothing mysterious about that.

But perhaps the motivation for this love is the mystery. What is it that makes us want to do the best for the one we love? The answer, again based on biblical principle, is that love recognizes a unique value in the beloved and chooses to affirm the value of the beloved always. Love is a choice.

Of course there is much more to learn about love from the Scriptures. As we observe the daily life of the Lord Jesus Christ, we can see Him displaying perfect love in every situation. We can learn by example. In Ephesians 5, we find a description of ways in which Jesus Christ shows His love for the church, and these are set before us as the perfect pattern for married love. And 1 Corinthians 13 shows us the nature of love with specific descriptions of how love behaves, especially when tested. We learn that real love is always a choice backed up by action.

So we need not be uninformed concerning love. We can learn from the Word of God, the one accurate source of information about love, what it is and what it does. You and I must understand love in order to build it in our marriage, and this is altogether possible because we have the Scriptures.

2) Love is not easy or simple: it is an art that I must want to learn and pour my life into. I can learn how to love.

This principle corrects a common misconception of love, prevalent particularly among teen-agers who think that love is the simplest thing in the world to understand; that it is easy to love, requiring neither thought nor effort. In other words, no one has to learn about love or even think about it. It's just a matter of doing what comes naturally!

The fact is that love is costly. It requires much from the lover even when the giving is pure joy. If you do what comes naturally you will be wrong almost every time. Love is an art to be learned and a discipline to be maintained. We could compare the art of loving to the art of music or any other disciplined life. In my case, I spent years learning the art of medicine, then learning how to put the theories into practice. Most important, I wanted so much to learn to practice medicine that I was willing to put everything I had into it. Many years later I approached the art of loving my wife in the same manner!

If you want to master the art of loving and want to obtain the rewards of a tremendously happy marriage, you are going to have to learn the principles of building love into your marriage and practice them on a daily basis. Above all, you must want to learn and be willing to pour your very life into it. I can say from experience: it is worth the effort.

How do you learn? Again, the Bible has the information you need. The most concentrated lessons on the art of loving your mate can be found in the Song of Solomon, which we will discuss in chapter 12. But salted throughout the Bible are portions of Scripture that give direct instruction in the art of loving. We will be considering many of these. The real problems of life are not disconnected from the Word of God, and you will find as you go through this counseling manual that the Bible tells you what you need to know to become an expert lover, as a husband or as a wife.

3) Love is an active power that I control by my own will. I am not the helpless slave of love. I can choose to love.

It is important to grasp this principle in light of the propaganda barrage suggesting that love itself is an uncontrollable feeling that comes and goes like a wayward sparrow, landing where it is not wanted and taking off as the mood strikes it. Most of the boy-meets-girl, girl-loses-boy, husband-and-wife-split-up plots of films and television are based on the premise that love is a feeling that just happens. Or else it doesn't happen. Or it happens and then stops happening so that nothing can be done to recapture that feeling, once it goes.

The truth is that love is an active power that you were meant to control by your own will. You are not "just a prisoner of love" as the song goes. If you are a Christian with the love of God shed abroad in your heart, you can intelligently choose to love; you can do what is necessary to restore love to your marriage; and you can refuse to be enslaved by passing emotions.

4) Love is the power that will produce love as I learn to give it rather than strain to attract it.

People today are being taught through the persistence of advertising that they must learn how to be lovable in order to be loved. They are told that they will become more lovable as they choose the proper toothpaste, perfume, shaving cream, shampoo, or deodorant. In fact, the list of products almost guaranteed to bring would-be lovers banging at your door or stopping you on the street is endless. Our media-oriented society measures lovableness by three yardsticks: popularity, sex appeal, and use of the right products.

But God's Word shows the real secret of being lovable and desirable to your marriage partner. It involves learning to give love rather than straining and striving to attract it—a powerful secret that relatively few people know. One word of caution. Many mistakes are made in the name of love. You must learn how to give love in biblical ways that truly will meet your partner's needs and desires. The Bible shows how to love wisely and in reality.

Palm Beach publicist Frank Wright has written hundreds of spontaneous love notes to his wife, some of which have been published in the little book, *Hi Sweetie!* This sample shows how love produces love when it is freely (and wisely) given. The husband writes, "The longer we are married the more I see that happiness in marriage doesn't just happen. Let's always hold hands and tell each other of our love. Let's never take each other for granted. Let's 'give' or 'give in' with a spirit of joy. That's what we have been doing and it works, doesn't it?"

The rest of the note illustrates the fact that the giving of love also produces the romantic emotions of love in full measure. He adds, "I'm just doing some wishful thinking this morning. How about slippin' off after the lunch hour, bags packed, and let's just skip off to some romantic spot for the week-end and keep our destination a secret!"

To summarize:

( ) Real love is not mysterious or irrational.
( ) Real love is not a simple, easy, doing what comes naturally.
( ) Real love is not an uncontrollable feeling.
( ) Real love is not produced by trying to attract it.

( ) I can understand what love is through the Word of God.
( ) I can learn the art of loving.
( ) I can choose to love.
( ) I can produce love by giving it first and giving it wisely.

( ) Love recognizes a unique value in the beloved.
( ) Love chooses to affirm the value of the beloved always.
( ) Love consistently does the best for the beloved.
( ) Love is an active power to be controlled by the will.

( ) Love is always a choice backed up by action.
( ) Love is costly even when the giving is pure joy.

In essence, we have been discussing how *reason* and *feeling* work together in building a love relationship between the husband and wife. While most people consider *feeling* supremely important, I hope you have discovered that what you *think* about love will control your behavior, and that the desired feelings will come as a result of the right thinking and the right actions.

This may sound mechanical and far from romantic, but it is not. Indeed, it points the way to a genuine love affair for you and your mate that should provide enough real thrills and satisfaction to suit even the most romantic individual. When reason is excluded from love's excitements, what results is not love at all but lust, infatuation, or empty sentimentality. And who wants that in his marriage? The Christian, if wise, will build all of his life on the truth. Nowhere is this any more important than in love and marriage.

Hal and Genie, mentioned at the beginning of this chapter, had a sincere desire to build their life on the truth. Yet, as you may have discerned, their chief problem hinged on false ideas about love. In our subsequent talks, Hal admitted that the fault was his, rather than Genie's, although he could not pinpoint the cause. "I suppose it's sin or rebellion or stupidity on my part," Hal said, "because I know I could make Genie fall in love with me if I'd just give her something to respond to. But I feel like Genie is not the right woman, the woman God had for me, and even though I don't believe in divorce, all my fantasies involve another place, another time, another girl."

I asked Hal to take the summary list you have just read concerning biblical principles of love and to measure his own attitudes and actions by the concepts I had explained to him. The results were eye-opening for the young man.

He found that he had some deeply ingrained but faulty ideas about love that dated back to his pre-Christian life and the many romantic affairs he had enjoyed. He still thought of love as a mysterious experience replete with delicious feelings that just came. When he married Genie because she was an outstanding, somewhat sheltered, Christian girl, he expected the thrilling feelings to just come again without any effort on his part. When they did not soon appear, he became resentful and, instead of learning to be a lover, he went from counselor to counselor, trying to find someone who would (magically) get the process started for him. He agreed that although he was an exemplary husband in outward details, he had failed to give his wife what she really needed and desired. He wanted a wife who thrilled him, but he did not want to go through the process that would eventually bring this about. He had never made the choice to love Genie because she was his wife; he had never recognized or affirmed his wife's unique value to him. He had made no attempt to learn the art of loving. Instead, he was waiting for her to inspire the feeling of love in him.

"Even though I didn't realize some of these things before," Hal said, "I did know that I was responsible for Genie just as Christ is for the church. I knew that I was responsible to love her just the way He loves the church. But I was using that 'right woman' bit as an escape clause—really as an excuse for my own self-centeredness. I was kidding myself, because I knew that God's command in Genesis to leave everything else and cleave to and be one flesh applies to the girl I've married, not to some dream girl I've made up in my mind!"

Hal was ready to do whatever I suggested. Learning the art of loving would involve many details that are contained in the rest of this counseling manual. But he could begin by choosing to love his wife and by deliberately giving of himself to her, trusting that the good feelings would come as he changed his behavior.

"God has a triggering action that will stir up romance in you as you do those things that cause a response of love in her," I explained. "If you learn how to love her biblically and *do it,* in six months the two of you will be deeply in love with each other. Try it and see."

Hal and Genie have an exciting time ahead as they begin to put into practice those things that fire up a lasting love affair. In your own case, I suggest that you go over the summary list as Hal did. Make a mental checkmark where you agree with the statement. What about the other concepts? Remember, as you believe them, take them as your own, and act on them, you are preparing yourself to make effective use of the practical instruction in the rest of this book.

5
The Five Ways
of Loving

THE ENGLISH WORD *love* has to be one of the most unusual words in our language! It's supposedly packed with meaning, yet it seems inadequate when we really want to say something. (So much so that Edgar Allan Poe wrote, "We loved with a love that was more than love.") The word is overworked. Some dictionaries list as many as twenty-five meanings for love, and we're apt to use them all in our everyday conversation.

Just having the one word for everything leads to confusion and absurd comparisons. For example, we love our lifelong sweetheart. But we also love fried chicken or quiche Lorraine, thus comparing our marriage partner of thirty years to a French cheese pie! We love our parents and our children. But we also love books or football or skiing vacations, apparently putting Mom and Dad on a par with a weekend at Vail, or little Johnny in competition with the Dallas Cowboys. We love freedom, surely a thing more precious than the shiny machine in the driveway. But we *love* that new car; also we love our pet cat and a certain record album we bought last week. Not only do we love Jesus Christ, King of Kings and Lord of Lords, but we "just love Robert Redford"—or Bob Hope. It all adds up to careless talk and, sometimes, fuzzy thought.

The confusion increases when we read books that have love as their theme. One author speaks of love, and we find that he really means sexual attraction. Another apparently is referring to an abstract ideal. Still another writes of romance. And another of intense family loyalties. The fifth author describes an undying friendship in dramatic terms. Evidently each writer has a different relationship in view. Yet they all use the same word to define the relationship—love.

Fortunately, in writing a book about love in marriage, we can call upon the precise language of the Greek New Testament for help. As one expert pointed out, "Greek is a very subtle language, full of delicately modifying words, capable of the finest distinctions of meaning." The Greeks of the New Testament era had at least five words that we can use to distinguish and describe the various aspects of love in marriage.

As I give you these five Greek words and their meaning in marriage, remember that this is not a language exercise, but a practical explanation of what love-life in marriage should be when love is finding its full expression in the relationship.

By the way, there can be no such thing as window shopping here. You cannot pick and choose the kind of love you prefer and discard the others. Each builds on the other. Each has its own special, significant place, as you will find when you begin putting all these loves into practice in your marriage. But if they are quite distinctive, they are also interrelated so that the physical, emotional, and spiritual processes overlap and reinforce each other in the act of loving.

The first facet of love we will consider is suggested by a Greek word that the Bible never calls love. However, it describes a very important aspect of the love affair between husband and wife. This word is *epithumia*, a strong desire of any kind—sometimes good, sometimes bad. It means to set the heart on; long for, rightfully or otherwise; or it can mean to covet. When used in the Bible in a negative way, it is translated lust. When used in a positive way, it is translated *desire*, and this is the meaning we refer to. In marriage, husband and wife should have a strong physical desire for each other that expresses itself in pleasurable sexual lovemaking.

Sex is not the most important aspect of your relationship, but it is a definite indicator of the health of your marriage. If tension exists in other areas of your life, it will usually show up in your sex life. On the other hand, if you have no sexual closeness, your total relationship may be affected as a result. Sometimes your sexual responses are turned off because of various pressures or problems. This is not uncommon and can, in almost every case, be remedied. Even while you are trying to work out other problem areas of your relationship, you can learn physical communication together and experience mutual pleasure in your sex life, so that restoring and building sexual desire becomes an important part of the whole experience of falling in love with your mate. In the happiest of marriages, couples find they can always improve their sexual relationship through added knowledge, greater understanding, and heightened sensitivity to each other. The facet of love known as physical desire should never be ignored in a marriage.

The next aspect of love to be discussed comes from a familiar Greek word that does not appear in the New Testament, although its Hebrew counterpart is used in the Old Testament. I am speaking of *eros,* the love that, more than any other kind, carries with it the idea of romance. We might think of *eros* as totally fleshly because of our English word "erotic," but this is not the case. *Eros* is not always sensual, but it includes the idea of yearning to unite with and the desire to possess the beloved. *Eros* is romantic, passionate, and sentimental. It is often the starting point for marriage, being the kind of love that lovers fall into and write songs and poetry about. It has been called rapture . . . exquisite pleasure . . . strong, sweet, and terrifying because it is so all-absorbing.

Eros has a problem, however. It needs help because it is changeable and cannot last a lifetime all by itself. *Eros* wants to promise that the relationship will last forever, but *Eros* cannot keep that promise alone.

At this point we need to draw a line between foolish temporary infatuations and the true romantic love to be found in a God-designed marriage. Infatuation has been defined as an emotional and fleshly response to false impressions or mere externals of another that have been overvalued or lusted after. By contrast, genuine falling in love is a spiritual, mental, emotional, and physical response to the actual character and total being of another who embodies attributes long sought and admired.

Eros love, when enjoyed in the lasting context of Christian marriage, offers wonderful emotions and personal rewards that are the gift and creation of God Himself. This kind of love is wholly emotional and cannot be summoned at will, but it appears as a sure response when all the other loves of marriage are set in motion. You will experience *eros* love in a rich, mature, particularly joyous form when you have mastered the art of loving. More than any other kind of love, *eros* transforms a mundane black-and-white existence into glorious living technicolor. It is a delightful part of the love-life designed for marriage.

The third love of marriage, characterized by the Greek word *storge,* could be described as a comfortable old-shoe relationship comprised of natural affection and a sense of belonging to each other. This love, referred to several times in the New Testament, is the kind of love shared by parents and children or brothers and sisters; the kind of love Robert Frost described when he called *home* "the place where, when you go there, they have to take you in . . . something you don't have to deserve." *Storge* love in marriage meets the need we all have to belong, to be part of a close-knit circle where people care and give the utmost loyalty to each other. When the world shows itself as a cold, hard place, *storge* offers emotional refuge. The marriage lacking this quality of love is like a house without a roof, where the rains can pour in. But when present, *storge* provides an atmosphere of security in which the other loves of marriage can safely dwell and flourish.

The fourth love of marriage is described by the Greek verb *phileo,* which often appears in the New Testament. We will be using the verb form as a noun in this discussion because it is the more familiar term to readers. *Phileo* cherishes and has tender affection for the beloved, but always expects a response. It is a love of relationship—comradeship, sharing, communication, friendship. While *eros* makes lovers, *phileo* makes dear friends who enjoy closeness and companionship. They share each other's thoughts, feelings, attitudes, plans, and dreams— the most intimate things they would share with no one else. They also share time and interests. Obviously, it takes two for the full enjoyment of *phileo,* but if you are seeking to restore love to your marriage without much cooperation from your partner, you can aim for *phileo* on your part, looking forward to an eventual response when biblical concepts have been put into practice. A marriage without *phileo* will be unsatisfactory, even if there is plenty of passion in the bedroom. A marriage with *phileo* is sure to be interesting and rewarding.

We are moving from the physical to the spiritual in considering the five ways of loving. I have saved the best for last: *agape,* the totally unselfish love that has the capacity to give and keep on giving without expecting in return. *Agape* values and serves in contrast to *phileo,* which cherishes and enjoys. The New Testament often speaks of *agape,* for it was this love that prompted Christ to come to earth as a man on our behalf. God loves all mankind with an *agape* love. In addition, He has *phileo* love for those who are in relationship with Him through Jesus Christ.

Agape love is of particular significance to those of you who right now are trying to save your marriage and to restore the love you lost. Of all the loves, *agape* is the one you can bring into your marriage immediately, because it is exercised as a choice of your will and has no dependence on feelings. It is a love of action, not emotion. It focuses on what you do and say rather than how you feel.

C. S. Lewis showed the difference between *agape* and the natural loves by using the picture of a garden. He described the natural loves as a garden that would soon run to weeds if left alone. This is inevitable because of self-centeredness, willfulness, and the other sins resulting from the Fall. *Agape* love acts as the rakes, hoes, shears, plant food, and weed killer employed by a skilled gardener to keep the garden thriving, orderly, and beautiful. When God planted the garden of our nature and caused the flowering, fruiting loves to grow there, He set our will to tend them, to watch over them and care for them as a wise gardener should. This operation of the will is *agape* love—a knowledgeable and skillful love always concerned with doing what is best for the beloved.

A marriage possessing *agape* love can survive anything! It is *agape* that keeps a marriage going when the natural loves falter and die. In *Gone With the Wind* we have the classic picture of an intense, longlasting, natural love finally ending. The parting scene of Rhett Butler and Scarlett O'Hara has passed into American folklore . . . Rhett Butler forever at the door saying with complete and final indifference, "Frankly, my dear, I don't give a damn!" We may not care for his language, but we all understand what he is saying: that even the strongest natural love has to end eventually when there is no response.

But *agape* love is different. This is one of the most exciting truths in all of Scripture. *Agape* love is plugged into an eternal power source, and it can go on operating when every other kind of love fails. Not only that! It loves, no matter what. No matter how unlovable the other person is, *agape* can keep on flowing. *Agape* is as unconditional as God's love for us. It is a mental attitude based on a deliberate choice of the will, and so you can choose right now to begin to love your mate with an *agape* love, no matter how much indifference or rejection you must face.

This was the experience of a man who contacted me for help after hearing our counseling cassette album. He wrote,

> I have really appreciated your teaching on Love-Life about agape love, because that is the only thing that is keeping our relationship going. We talk about the kids, other people, the business, etc., but never about anything personal. Kathy will not allow me to put my arms around her, kiss her, or touch her in any way, at any time of the day. If I buy her personal gifts she will not receive them and if I compliment her, she says, "That's not true" or "You don't really mean that" or some other statement that voids what I was trying to say. We have no sexual contact. I want to have a whole, loving relationship with Kathy, but it's like hitting my head against a brick wall. I keep asking God to help me love her and meet her needs, even though there is no response.

What a graphic picture of *agape* in action, preserving a marriage that otherwise would have disintegrated! This is not the end of the story for Zach and Kathy, thanks to *agape* love.

In following chapters I will give you specific suggestions to follow in developing each of these ways of loving in your own marriage.

But first you need to be confident of this fundamental truth: you are commanded by Scripture to have a love affair with your marriage partner! Let's consider this in biblical perspective.

Genesis shows us that woman was created to fill man's loneliness as his lifelong companion and his beloved. Man was instructed to leave all else, cleave inseparably to his wife, and know her intimately over a lifetime—a process designed to establish a powerful love between husband and wife. Other Old Testament writings give us glimpses of love, romance, and sex in the lives of the patriarchs. Then when we come to the Wisdom Literature of Scripture, the private, intensely personal relationship between husband and wife with its romantic love and sexual delight is brought into full view.

In Psalm 45, designated in the King James Bible as *A Song of Loves,* the writer tells of a royal wedding where the queen is exhorted to consider her husband's fairness of appearance, his honor, integrity, and majesty, and to forget her own people and her father's house. In turn, "So shall the king greatly desire thy beauty." The details of the love affair between a king and his bride are exquisitely described in the Song of Solomon as a pattern for all godly lovers to follow.

But the command to engage in a lifetime love affair with one's mate appears in the Book of Proverbs, that book specializing in practical, down-to-earth discussion of life's daily problems and offering counsel out of the Creator's own wisdom. The Proverbs always show cause and effect: if you do *this* in accord with Divine Wisdom, *this good thing will happen.* But if you do *that* contrary to the will of God and all reasonable behavior, *that unpleasant thing will inevitably occur.* The theme of Proverbs 5 could be summed up as: stay away from the adulteress and always be madly in love with your wife. Here is the heart of the message with its clear commandment. "Let thy fountain be blessed: and rejoice with the wife of thy youth. Let her be as the loving hind and pleasant roe, let her breasts satisfy thee at all times; and be thou ravished always with her love" (Proverbs 5:18–19).

The husband has already been warned to avoid the adulteress because she would destroy him *sexually* (v. 9–11), *spiritually* (vv. 12–13), and *socially* (v. 14). The same principle applies to the wife, for she will experience the same injury as the natural outcome of adultery.

But now the reward for marital faithfulness appears, and it is a rich one! The wife is pictured, both here and in Song of Solomon, as a cistern, a well, a spring shut up, a fountain sealed for her husband, whose waters will satisfy to the fullest. Even this may be an inadequate description. To be "ravished" in the Hebrew language means to reel and stagger as if intoxicated, to be enraptured and exhilarated. To be "satisfied" is to have your thirst slaked, to take your fill, to be satiated and abundantly saturated with that which pleases.

That this is a physical love affair seems clear in light of the original language that Hebrew scholars term some of the most graphic lines in Scripture. The verse speaks literally of the wife's nipples and then describes them metaphorically as fountains of wine that will keep the husband intoxicated with her love. Observe that this refers to "the wife of thy youth," indicating the lasting quality of the love affair, and that to "rejoice" together was intended to be an integral part of marriage from beginning to end.

But this is also more than a physical love affair. The word used for love (be thou ravished always with her *love*) is *ahavah,* which includes the element of emotional love in response to attraction, although it is not limited to emotion. *Ahavah* actually is the Hebrew counterpart of New Testament *agape* love, the love of the spirit and the will, committed to doing the best for the beloved at all times. So we see, according to this Scripture, that in marriage we must express *agape* love with its spiritual attributes through the emotional and physical channels of our being to satisfy our marriage partner fully. This is no sacrifice, for in doing so we too will be satisfied.

Here we have the love affair commanded by God for every husband and wife—an absorbing, thrilling interchange of mind, body, spirit, and emotions. Clearly, there are compelling reasons for obeying the Bible in the area of marriage! We remain free to resist love and refuse joy, and nothing can prevent us from following that course if we choose to. But we also are free to love, and if we do so in biblical ways, we will experience the blessings of being essentially and habitually *in love.*

Beyond personal blessing, we should realize that God designed marriage to portray the eternal, wonderful love relationship between Jesus Christ and His bride, the church, and that true romantic love is a necessary component of the marriage relationship in order to complete the picture of Christ's love for His people.

It is an exciting fact that when you enter into the marriage designed by God with your love for each other reflecting Christ's love like a mirror for all to see, you also are entering into a personal ministry that will witness to others, enhance all that you do in the name of Christ, and enable you to serve the Lord in a very special way. Not nearly enough biblical counselors are available to aid all the couples needing help in their marriages today, but a husband and wife who have learned to love each other in the ways we have described can minister to a couple in need with great effectiveness.

I recall the time when I had trusted Christ, but my wife had not yet done so. I really searched for some couple who could by their own example show her how wonderful it was to be *in love* and *in Christ* together! We needed such people as friends. As you seek to develop the kind of love-life the Bible describes, remember that it is not only for your pleasure, but it will also become a ministry as you and your partner are sensitive to other couples who need befriending in this manner.

The example you provide for your own children may be the most rewarding ministry of all. Keep in mind that you are constantly teaching them by example. They will learn about love and marriage (rightly or wrongly) as they observe their father and mother's relationship in the home over a period of time.

A woman, writing a letter to her son and daughter-in-law who were considering divorce, gave them this to think about:

> Your children will feel an insecurity impossible to describe if they cannot count on the love mother has for dad and the love dad has for mother. Children have a right for their parents to love each other. They are their only security. They are the rock or the quicksand under their first steps into adulthood.

As you demonstrate real love for each other and for your children, and as you show them the pattern of biblical marriage working the way God designed it, you will be passing on the gift of love to enrich their marriage and ministry in the years to come.

By now, in light of the biblical concepts we have discussed, I trust that you have the confidence that it is unquestionably God's will for you and your partner to love each other with an absorbing spiritual, emotional, and physical attraction that continues to grow throughout your lifetime together. This means that you can trust Him to work with you and in you as you begin to follow specific counsel on falling in love and staying in love with your mate.

Now I want to show you how you can make each of the five ways of loving a meaningful part of your marriage.

6

How to Love Your Partner Sexually

WHEN I USE the term "love-life," someone usually assumes that I am going to talk about sex. In our culture, sex and love are often confused even though they are not interchangeable terms. The little girl put it into proper perspective when she was being told the facts of life. "Oh," she said, disappointedly. "I thought you were going to explain about love! I already know about sex."

Obviously, love is the ingredient that brings meaning and rich pleasure to sexual activity. Research indicates that out of 168 hours in a week, the average couple seldom spends more than an hour or two in physical lovemaking. It's what you do with the entire week that determines the quality of your love-life.

In order to develop a lifetime love affair, however, you and your partner must maintain a *positive* sexual relationship. The old Johnny Mercer song comes to mind: *You've got to accentuate the positive, eliminate the negative, latch on to the affirmative.* . . . That is what I hope to help you accomplish through the counsel of this chapter. Even if you already have a good relationship, it can be better. A mutually fulfilling sex life will enrich your entire marriage, and it is within your reach!

So let's begin with the affirmative. You have good reason to anticipate increased sexual pleasure year after year. Some people dread the loss of their youthful vigor, or they fear their sex life will become boring and empty through much repetition. But this need not be the case. People growing together in love find that their sexual relationship provides more meaning and enjoyment all the time. In middle age and later years, overabundant sexual energy can be exchanged for mature, sensitive, skilled lovemaking with a beloved partner whose responses are understood intimately. I urge you to read this chapter with a sense of expectancy concerning the positive sexual relationship you and your mate can enjoy throughout your marriage.

But perhaps you are concerned about negatives in your relationship. If you are to eliminate them, you must first understand them. Physical desire with its sexual expression is without doubt the most complicated aspect of love in marriage. So many potential causes of difficulty exist, and problem solving is complicated by silence, suspicion, anger, hurt, misunderstanding, fear, or guilt, which are often hiding in the shadows. The physiological mechanisms of sexual expression are intricately complex and can be shut down at any stage; yet, when hindrances are removed, they work together smoothly, without conscious effort, to transmit an experience of tremendous thrill leading to fulfillment and complete relaxation.

God's physical design for the one-flesh relationship is amazing! I refer you to our book, *Intended for Pleasure* (Revell, 1977), for a thorough explanation. However, you need to understand this about the sexual experience as it relates to negatives: the entire lovemaking episode involves three phases of physical response that are interlocking but separate and easily distinguishable. They are desire, excitement, and orgasm. To use Dr. Helen Kaplan's metaphor, these three phases have a common generator, but they each have their own separate circuitry. Sexual desire comes from a special neural system in the brain; excitement is indicated physically by the reflex vasodilatation of genital blood vessels; and orgasm depends upon the reflex contractions of certain genital muscles. These two genital reflexes are served by separate reflex centers in the lower spinal cord.

Problems arise when an inhibiting "switch" turns off any one of these physical responses in your system. Leading therapists are trying to determine and treat specific causes of inhibition in each phase. As Dr. Kaplan explains, "One set of causes is likely to 'blow the fuses' of the orgasm circuits, another type of conflict may 'disconnect the erection wires,' while a different group of variables is likely to cause interference in the 'libido circuits' of the brain."[1]

For example, fear and hostility are two chief inhibitors of the desire phase. Sexual anxiety for any of various reasons impairs the excitement phase. Excessive self-consciousness will short-circuit the orgasm phase. This is not meant to be a quick diagnosis of sex problems, but a reminder that your sexual relationship will always mirror the larger context of your life, revealing personal fears and tensions, and almost always serving as a barometer of the total relationship between you and your partner—which can fluctuate, depending on how well you are getting along in other areas of your marriage. Negative feelings in a marriage will often show up first in a couple's sex life.

I saw a couple recently who made an appointment for sex counseling because of the wife's inability to enjoy sex. It became apparent that the real problem was a seething hostility on the wife's part that had little to do with sex technique. In a short time, when the real issue was recognized by both partners and dealt with, the couple reported that their sex life was far better than ever before.

Another man told me, "My wife and I have a good, if not excellent, sex life together. But when other problems come up, we use sex in a negative way against each other." He added with a rueful smile, "You need to give a seminar on how *not* to use sex!"

Ironically, negative feelings are easily vented through the very act that God designed to bring two people together as one flesh. Sex can be used to frustrate, disappoint, reject, or "pay back" the mate when the individual does not even realize what he or she is doing, or what has caused the "turn-off." Often, of course, it is done deliberately.

Sexual problems sometimes reflect your feelings about yourself, or negative attitudes toward sex that you will have to unlearn. Many sexual problems stem from ignorance of basic medical facts and can be remedied easily by proper counsel. Any of these negatives we have mentioned can short-circuit some phase of the sexual response so that desire is inhibited, a physical dysfunction occurs, or orgasm seems hopelessly out of reach. That, in turn, can give rise to a whole new set of negatives that will further trouble the couple's love affair.

This is why I stress that you must aim for a *positive* sexual relationship with your mate. To do this you will need three things: (1) correct medical information; (2) a biblical understanding of sex that dispels false fears and inhibitions; (3) the right personal approach to sexual lovemaking in your own marriage.

1) Complete, dependable medical information.

No one should expect to be a natural-born expert! Fortunately, more people today are recognizing the importance of understanding all that God has built into their bodies for sexual delight. My prescription for you is to read our book, *Intended for Pleasure,* or to listen together in the privacy of your own bedroom to our counseling cassette series, *Sex Technique and Sex Problems in Marriage.* These materials contain an enormous amount of medical instruction, explanation, and counsel that cannot be included in this book. For instance, you will learn how to solve the most common sexual problems and precisely how to give your partner sexual release—a necessity. There is a unique advantage in listening to the cassettes together with frequent stops for discussion. It will open your communication lines on this delicate subject, and for most of you this will be better than a session at a sex counselor's office.

You owe it to yourself and your partner to be fully informed. There is no reason why you cannot be a great lover. (I say this to both husband and wife.) Just make sure you know all you need to know. When the aura of mystery is removed from the physical process, you are in a position to understand and resolve the negatives within your sexual relationship.

2) A biblical view of sex.

Most wrong attitudes toward sex are conditioned by early training, but an understanding of God's view of sex that comes directly from the Scriptures can bring freedom to fearful, inhibited individuals. Hebrews 13:4 proclaims the fact that the marriage union is honorable and the *bed* undefiled. The word translated "bed" in the Greek New Testament is actually *coitus,* the word meaning sexual intercourse.

Those Victorians who claimed that sex was something shockingly distasteful that husbands did and wives endured were tragically far from the truth, but they left a legacy of error that is still around. Queen Victoria wrote to her daughter, "The animal side of our nature is to me—too dreadful." There are Victorians of the same mind today who have trained their children (both sons and daughters) to recoil from sex with repugnance or guilt. The result has been acute suffering in marriage for both partners.

One wife in frustration asked me, "How can I help my husband see sex as something *good* . . . that my body is touchable, meant to be seen and enjoyed by him? I know he was brought up to believe that sex was dirty and wrong, something to be ashamed of and done in secret. He's kind and thoughtful. *But I wish he loved me sexually."*

Another wife told me of the "training" that brought her and her husband to the edge of divorce. She said,

I knew nothing about sex except that my mother disapproved of it. So I borrowed a medical book from a doctor just before I got married. I couldn't believe what I read! The idea that married couples would do such a thing was so hard to accept that I almost broke off the engagement. But I loved my fiancé very much, so I went ahead with the wedding. I spent my honeymoon trying to avoid sexual contact. When we got back I tried to talk to my mother about it. She couldn't conceal her disgust that her little girl was involved in something as terrible as sex. Then she assured me that most men did expect it, but it would never be any fun for me. For the first several years I tolerated it and pretended to respond quickly so that we could get it over with as fast as possible. After the birth of our baby, I told my husband I did not ever want to have sex again. I still loved him—but not in that way. I hated the thought of sex. He tried to be kind and understanding with me, but the tension and resentment grew between us. The time came when he said it was all over unless I was willing to change. We had tried a counselor once before, and it was an upsetting experience. This time we went to a Christian counselor

who began by showing me what the Bible teaches about sex in marriage. I understood enough at the first session to see how far my attitudes were from the truth
and to realize that I could trust God to help me change. My husband and I just fell
in each other's arms that night and cried and prayed and asked God to help us love
each other sexually. It was the beginning of something good. I am learning what
sexual fulfillment means, and my husband and I are so much closer.

The Scriptures tell us clearly that the joyous sexual expression of love between husband and wife is God's plan. It is, as the writer of Hebrews emphasizes, *undefiled,* not sinful, not soiled. It is a place of great honor in marriage—
the holy of holies where husband and wife meet privately to celebrate their love
for each other. It is a time meant to be both holy and intensely enjoyable. Uninformed people have actually considered the Victorian view to be biblical
because they think the Bible forbids all earthly pleasures. Certainly not! In fact,
the Bible is far more "liberated" concerning sex than untaught people realize.
In God's view there is a mutuality of experience between husband and wife.
Each has an equal right to the other's body. Each has not only the freedom but
also the responsibility to please the other and to be pleased in return.

These basic principles concerning the enjoyment of sex in marriage are found
in 1 Corinthians 7:3–5. Bible teachers have called them: the principle of need;
the principle of authority; and the principle of habit.

The principle of need. Scripture tells us, not as a suggestion but as a commandment, to meet our mate's sexual needs because we both have these needs.
When husband and wife take hold of this concept and begin to do everything
they can to meet their partner's need, they are sure to develop an exciting relationship.

The principle of authority. Scripture tells us that when we marry, we actually
relinquish the right to our own body, and turn that authority over to our mate.
This amazing principle is certainly an indication of the lifetime scope of marriage as God designed it. It applies equally to husband and wife. Obviously, it
requires the utmost trust. People should understand this principle before they
decide to marry, for on the day they wed, in God's sight, they relinquish the right
of control over their own body. We quickly learn that one of the easiest ways to
hurt our mate is to withhold our physical affection. But we do not have this right!
To put it bluntly, the wife's body now belongs to the husband. The husband's
body now belongs to the wife. This means that we must love our mate's body and
care for it as our own. Thus, unreasonable demands are totally excluded.

The principle of habit. Scripture tells us that we must not cheat our partner
by abstaining from the habit of sex, except by mutual consent for a brief period
of time. Why? Because if we break this commandment and *defraud* our partner

by withholding habitual sexual lovemaking, we will surely open our marriage to satanic temptations. Our Creator knows this; that is why He tells us to participate actively and regularly in sex with our own mate. This is not a debatable issue, biblically. It is an inherent part of the love-life of marriage.

To apply these principles on sex in the most practical terms, I suggest that you make every effort to provide your mate with a good sexual release as an habitual part of your life together. Specific instruction is available to you through biblically-oriented books such as *Intended for Pleasure* and Tim LaHaye's *The Act of Marriage* (Zondervan, 1976).

3) The right approach.

I suggest that you begin by looking on sex in your marriage as an opportunity for genuine lovemaking (the making or building of love) through giving and receiving in ways that arc physically and emotionally satisfying for both of you. Don't worry about fireworks and shooting stars; the thrills will come later when you have learned the highly personalized art of sexual lovemaking. For now, just concentrate on the essentials: physical/emotional closeness and a positive response that may include sexual release.

To develop a real closeness, you will need to view your sex life in the context of your total relationship. A woman at our Love-Life Seminar asked me this question: "What can a Christian wife with a Christian husband do when the husband seems only to want sex and doesn't care about her during the remainder of the day? He forgets her birthday, doesn't care when she has emotional needs, and won't take any spiritual leadership in the family." The lesson is obvious. Sex without signs of love is sure to create resentment, not response, from your partner.

One thing that will always hinder emotional closeness is criticism. You will find it impossible to establish a series of pleasing physical experiences to build on unless you decide to quit criticizing and, instead, begin expressing in the most positive terms your love, your caring, and your desire to please your mate and meet his or her needs. It is not your responsibility to lecture your partner on the biblical commandments we have just discussed, or to insist upon obedience to them. If your mate disappoints you, you must be careful not to say by word or action anything that will make him or her feel like a failure. Even one slip of the tongue can undo weeks of progress, so emphasize your verbal appreciation for your partner. Words are particularly important in this situation. Husband, one sentence of criticism directed at your wife in any area may well drive away the desire she would otherwise feel that day. On the other hand, one sentence of praise and approval (the more specific the better) is going to do wonders for her and for your sense of closeness in the sexual relationship.

Husband, begin showing your wife in other ways that you love her. Give her romantic caresses at times when you are not preparing for sex . . . admiring glances . . . affectionate pats . . . a smile and a wink across the room . . . small attentions that tell her she is a very special person in your sight. Wife, you can do the same for your husband!

All of this sets the stage for the sexual experience. It could be called "before foreplay" technique. Researchers tell us that without affectionate pre-foreplay time together, sexual interest tends to wane. So plan with time as your ally in the development of satisfying closeness in sex. It must be relaxed, enjoyable time. In the busyness of American life, you may find it necessary to plan ahead and to set aside special times for each other. Think of it as a date to take place in the privacy of your own bedroom.

Once you are together, the world should be shut out. Have a lock on your bedroom door and use it. Make sure the children are settled for the night and do all you can to prevent interruptions. You should be able to concentrate on each other completely in a relaxed, pleasant, and *romantic* atmosphere. I receive from wives scores of comments similar to this one: "How do I convey to my husband my need for romance and tenderness before the act of making love? It is seldom there, and without it I just don't enjoy sex!"

A recent survey of women's fantasies revealed that they fantasize romance—not just sex—more than anything else, and most often a romantic interlude with their own husband.

Husband, your wife needs a romantic prelude to sexual intercourse. You may not realize how much your wife desires this or what it means to her. Women must be aroused emotionally as well as physically. They enjoy the closeness and intimacy of sex; they enjoy gentle touching and total body caressing done in a meaningful, not mechanical, way. They want their husband to appreciate their entire body, not just to provide some breast or genital fondling as a means of quick arousal.

The physical side of love rests on the human need for close personal contact, especially the need to be touched in a way that expresses warmth, gentleness, softness, and caring. Men have this need for warmth and affection in addition to sexual satisfaction, but they are much less apt than women to admit it or even to be aware of it. Therapists have found that men often misunderstand this need and seek sex when what they really crave is the physical reassurance of loving closeness.

Husbands who are preoccupied with physical gratification should know that even for their own maximum enjoyment of sexual release, they need to have at least twenty minutes of sexual arousal beforehand. We sometimes call orgasm a *climax* and it should be just that: the highest point of interest and excitement in a series of happenings. How do you reach the high point? By *climbing* to it. Climax is a Greek word meaning "ladder." You move to a climax with a slow, progressive build-up resulting at the highest point in a sudden, thrilling release— something like a roller-coaster ride with its long, slow climb and then its exciting plunge downward from the peak.

So when you come together take time to wind down from the outside pressures of the day. Take time to build desire. Take time to enjoy physical closeness and sensuousness. Take time to love each other with words. You don't have to worry about saying something clever or original. Your partner will not be bored with the same loving phrases over and over when it's obvious you mean them. Treat yourselves to pleasure!

When couples strive to obtain an orgasm without regard to enjoying their time together, sex becomes work rather than pleasure. Remember that orgasm lasts only a few seconds. Emotional satisfaction and gratification occur during the entire episode. Women tell me that they do not *always* need or desire an orgasm during sexual encounter, but their husbands cannot understand this and feel like failures unless an orgasm always occurs.

A recent study was made of the techniques that wives report as hindrances to their enjoyment of sex. Husbands can use this list to see if there are areas where their technique can be improved.

- The husband's stimulation of his wife during foreplay is mechanical rather than spontaneous.
- The husband is more interested in perfecting physical technique than in achieving emotional intimacy.
- The husband seems overly anxious for his wife to have an orgasm because that reflects upon his success as a lover, instead of simply wanting to please her and give her enjoyment whether it results in orgasm or not.
- The husband fails to provide manual stimulation for his wife to have another orgasm after intercourse, even though she desires it.
- The husband is repetitious and boring in his approach.
- The husband is not sensitive to his wife's preferences.
- The husband seems too deadly serious about sex.

So, husband, if you want to build love in your marriage, you will try to avoid these common mistakes in approach and technique. Concentrate on pleasing your wife rather than anxiously pushing her toward a sexual release. If she thinks you are pressuring her, she will begin to dread the possibility of failure rather than relaxing and surrendering to her own physical response. There is no need for you to ask your wife if she has had a good sexual release. Most women will find the question inhibiting. Simply give your wife manual stimulation for additional release after intercourse. If she does not feel a need for it, she can lovingly let you know. Many women who enjoy manual stimulation are afraid their husband will tire of it just as it is becoming pleasurable. Or they are afraid it is boring to their husband. Let your wife know how much you enjoy giving her pleasure and complete satisfaction. If she believes this, she will feel free to show you what pleases her at a particular time.

By all means, be sensitive to your wife's sexual preferences. It may be difficult for her to state her sexual likes and dislikes directly. If she does manage to communicate them and then they go ignored, she is sure to feel resentful and frustrated.

Finally, don't take the sex relationship so seriously. It will be best if you can establish an easy, comfortable camaraderie in the bedroom with laughter as part of your lovemaking. At times, sex should be lighthearted fun—recreation for husband and wife planned by the Creator.

Ask yourself these questions about your lovemaking. Any *no* answers will suggest areas for improvement:

- Is it positive?
- Is it relaxed?
- Is it pleasant?
- Is it romantic?
- Is it physically satisfying?
- Is it emotionally satisfying?

We have discussed what the wife desires from the relationship. The husband greatly desires *response* from his wife. She can give him this beautiful gift and delight his heart. However, judging from my mail and counseling appointments, many women do not understand how important, both physically and psychologically, the sexual relationship is to their husband. They do not seem to realize that their avoidance of sex or their lack of response will affect their entire marriage in the most negative way. To the indifferent wife I must give this caution: When there is no physical intimacy between you and your husband, whatever emotional and spiritual closeness you have had will tend to fade as well.

This is how one husband expressed the painful feelings resulting from his wife's lack of response. He wrote,

My wife and I need help. I feel that all our troubles stem from one cause. My wife does not want to have intercourse with me and I cannot accept this. The situation has existed all of our eighteen years of marriage. We currently have relations about once a month. This occurs normally after many days of my frustrating attempts to have her respond. Then it is not a loving affair, but a surrender or duty attitude on her part. I love my wife. She is an outstanding wife, mother, and friend. Except that she does not physically love me. I'm afraid to face up to the fact that maybe my wife just doesn't love *me* and cannot respond to *me*. I have asked myself many times, What are you still married for? I have no answer. I don't know what to do.

We are not speaking now of a wildly passionate response on the part of the wife, but only of a positive response. When a wife responds, she gives an answer by word and action to her husband's lovemaking. It can be gentle, simple, and loving. It may be enthusiastic; it need not be dramatic. But a wife should meet her husband with open arms and a warm acceptance. A lack of response means that you are ignoring one who in some way is reaching out to you, and there is no worse treatment to give to one who cares for you. Indifference is the enemy of love. So I counsel you to respond to your husband in these simple ways, at least (remembering that your varied spontaneous responses will delight him), and to regard sex with him as an opportunity to build more love into your marriage.

Some interesting studies have been done to determine underlying emotional factors that hinder a partner's response. A primary finding indicates that failure in women to attain orgasm is linked to the feeling that the "love object" is not dependable. All the data gathered seems to suggest that orgasmic capacity in woman is often tied to her feeling concerning the dependability of her relationship with her husband. In other words, the highly orgasmic wife feels she can trust her husband; the low responder fears that her husband will let her down. Since she feels she cannot depend on him and may have to stand on her own, she finds it almost impossible to trust him in the sexual act and to relax and let herself go in his arms. Her deep-rooted apprehension robs her of her ability to respond fully to her husband. Further studies indicate that as her anxieties diminish over a span of time, the potential for sexual response is increased.

What does this mean to the husband who longs for his wife to become sexually responsive? If he wants her to respond passionately with a beautiful relaxation and abandon in lovemaking, he needs to give her the absolute security of his love in the context of permanent commitment. When he convinces her that he will not let her down, he will find her becoming increasingly responsive.

One of these studies also showed that the highly orgasmic women had had fathers who were not passive toward them—fathers who strongly cared about them and their well-being. These fathers had not been permissive; instead, they had set standards and well-defined rules for their daughters' protection in their growing-up years.

Obviously, you cannot change the way your wife's father treated her, but you can give her what she may have needed from her father—a strong, loving concern from a man who is leader, protector, and example to her. If she believes you actively care about every detail of her welfare, and if she can respect you as the spiritual leader of your home, the chances are very good indeed that you will see improvement in her sexual responsiveness over a period of time. (That is, if you also treat her as a lover should in your sexual relationship.)

Those of you who are familiar with Ephesians 5, will realize that these scientific findings bear out the counsel God gives to the husband to provide his wife with a permanent, sacrificial love, a protective love, a nourishing, cherishing love. This is not just something you do in order to gain God's approval. It works! It brings about the kind of marriage God wants every husband and wife to enjoy—a marriage that includes keen sexual desire on the part of the woman as well as the man.

What about the husband whose response to his wife is, for some reason, hindered? The wife whose husband is indifferent should answer the following: Do you respect your husband's leadership as a man, as the head of your home, as the father of your children, and as your lover? If you indicate to him by word, action, or attitude that you do not respect him in some area of his life, you will diminish his desire for you. While this is a biblical principle, it also is a principle emphasized by secular experts in the sex-therapy field. When a husband's self-esteem is reduced because he feels his wife does not respect him, their sex life is sure to suffer.

Also consider this: Have you misused your sexual relationship in the past? Have you used sex as a tool of manipulation or as a weapon against your husband? Have you rejected him on a whim? Have you withheld physical favors to get even with him? Have you been dishonest with him, playing games? Have you battered his sexuality through hostility or criticism or ridicule?

You should realize that your husband is psychologically vulnerable to injury in the area of sex just as he is physically vulnerable to injury. If you have damaged his sense of manhood and participated in producing an attitude of failure within him, you will have to start all over again and build him up by your tenderness, your sensitivity, your respect, and your responsiveness.

Although we have been discussing how your total relationship can affect your sexual adjustment, the opposite is also true. A sexual problem sometimes affects your entire marriage in ways that cannot and should not be ignored. It is most often true of marriages where the wife has never (or almost never) enjoyed an orgasm. This threatens the couple's love relationship when it becomes an issue, and a chain reaction of negative emotions occurs.

Here is what usually happens. The wife begins to feel like a failure because no matter how hard she tries, she cannot work up the right physical response. Of course, the harder she tries, the more the natural reflex action of orgasm eludes her. This lowers her self-esteem and her confidence in herself as a woman. She also senses her husband's disapproval or disappointment, and the sex act becomes increasingly painful for her, emotionally. So she begins to avoid sex. If her husband persists, she feels used, and resentment enters the scene. If he tries to woo her with compliments and caresses, she cannot believe he is sincere because of her low self-image. She thinks he has an ulterior motive in being nice to her.

The husband's confidence in himself as a man is shaken first of all by the sense of failure in being unable to bring his wife to sexual release. It is more deeply shaken as she begins to dislike and avoid sex altogether, and he feels that she is no longer interested in *him*. He wonders if she even loves him. Resentment enters in as he begins to feel that she is not trying to find a solution. The wife's rejection evokes tremendous emotions of depression, as the husband does everything he knows to do to adjust to his wife, believing it is going to work, but rejection still comes. A down draft of anger and discouragement says, Why try anymore?

Actually, both are longing for love and the assurance of love from each other and both are inwardly convinced that they are not loved.

Those of you who are in this situation should realize that this is always a couple problem that has built up over a period of time, so you should not count on an immediate solution. Your belief that the situation is hopeless stands between you and the solution. Once the barriers of persistent discouragement, rejection, and sense of failure are gone, skilled sexual stimulus *will* provide sexual release as a natural result. So both of you need to turn away from concentration on those few seconds of sexual climax and learn to enjoy the whole experience of lovemaking with all its warmth and closeness. Orgasm may be the end of the experience, but your goal should be to please each other, to satisfy the emotional need you both have to know that you are loved and accepted exactly as you are.

Right now you should begin to move toward each other through the uncomplicated avenue of physical touching. As your problem developed, you moved apart. So now come together by warm physical contact, by cuddling and snuggling and holding hands just as you did when you were teen-agers. Sit close to each other every time you have the chance. Sleep close to each other. One couple I counseled held their marriage together by choosing to sleep nude in each other's arms while they were still working out other problems. Take the focus off the sex act altogether for awhile and avoid much discussion of your problem. At the same time begin learning *physical* communication as described in Intended *for Pleasure.*

Husband, take positive steps to meet your partner's emotional needs. Your wife longs to be encouraged, built up, and praised. She wants to feel close to you emotionally. This will come as you love her in the way the Bible describes. A husband can always meet his wife's deepest needs by loving her as Christ loves us, and as a wife begins to respond to that love, she is ready to respond sexually.

The husband's love has been compared to a warm coat he wraps around his wife. As long as she feels encircled and sheltered in his love, she can give herself completely to him. In this safety, she can accept herself as a woman and value her femininity. Then she will be able to entrust herself to her husband in the sexual relationship as the bird gives itself to the air or the fish to the water.

We husbands may not be able to fully appreciate the deep longings that influence our wives, but if we love them with the sheltering love that is described in Ephesians 5:28–29 we will see results! Our wives reflect the love or lack of love we have provided.

As you move toward each other physically and emotionally, you should also move closer in the spiritual dimension of marriage. Sharing in warm personal Bible study and prayer together will help prepare the way for sexual fulfillment as a natural result of the spiritual union that is occurring daily. Then you will find that your sexual union can bring you still closer to God, so that you often want to pray together after making love. Love produces love in all directions!

The principles described in this chapter, when reinforced by a practical knowledge of physical technique, will enable you to build love in your marriage through the avenue of sex by establishing a physical/emotional closeness that is good and satisfying. Remember that this sense of closeness develops best in the atmosphere of security and stability. Within this setting you can give each other the opportunity to be beautiful and varied and unpredictable; open and vulnerable and receptive. Try it. If you are afraid to try it because you are afraid you will be hurt, consider this: the risk of pain is always the price of life.

As we consider how to build the other kinds of love in marriage, we will find that all of them will enhance the sexual relationship. As Dr. Kaplan has observed, "Love is the best aphrodisiac discovered so far!"

7

Romantic Love— The Thrill Factor

AT FIRST GLANCE romantic love seems to be a controversial subject. For instance . . .

Some cynics scoff at romantic love as a myth invented by Hollywood.

Some sincere Christians consider romantic love the whipped cream on the sundae of marriage—decorative, but unnecessary. They see this as a lower form of love that husbands and wives should disregard in their search for higher ground.

Some individuals feel uncertain about the value of romantic love because they confuse the genuine article with that frothy substitute known as temporary infatuation.

Some try to suppress all thought of romantic love because they are not experiencing it. Some rationalize, "I don't have it; it must not exist." Others think, "It's not possible in *my* marriage."

In spite of all this, just about everyone inwardly longs for a thrilling love relationship involving oneness, a deep intimacy with another person, joy and optimism, spice and excitement, and that wonderful, euphoric, almost indescribable sensation known as "being in love." Some people say they are "on cloud nine." They mean that they feel energized, motivated, confident to conquer because they know they are loved by their beloved. There is a sense of awe in feeling *chosen* for this blessed state. With it goes a thrill of anticipation in being together. Most important, a fresh sense of purpose sweetens life because the two have found each other and have, as the expression goes, "fallen in love."

This is not overstating the case. As a physician, I have seen that the emotions of romantic love give people a new outlook on life and a sense of well-being. Romantic love is good medicine for fears and anxieties and a low self-image. Psychologists point out that real romantic love has an organizing and constructive effect on our personalities. It brings out the best in us, giving us the will to improve ourselves and to reach for a greater maturity and responsibility. This love enables us to begin to function at our highest level.

Quite honestly, if you are not in love with your marriage partner in this way, you are missing something wonderful, no matter how sincere your commitment to that person may be. Even contentment can be dull and drab in comparison with the joy God planned for you with your marriage partner.

In this chapter we will suggest ways in which you can revitalize your relationship by adding *eros* love to your marriage and learning how to enhance your present love so that it will become more exciting, not less so, as the years go by.

What if you are having serious problems in your marriage? This chapter is for you too. A film advertisement caught my eye recently. I'm not that interested in what Hollywood is producing, but the headline asked a relevant question: **What Do You Do When Everything Between the Two of You Seems Wrong?** The answer: **Fall in Love!**

This may sound far-fetched, but, in reality, it is good counsel for the couple with a troubled marriage. I have seen couples resolve their problems by falling in love. Other biblical counselors report similar results. Anne Kristin Carroll's book, *From the Brink of Divorce,* includes a number of case histories where marriages hung by a thread. In each of these cases the couple preserved their marriage by falling in love. Nouthetic counselor Jay Adams tells of the many couples who come into his office claiming that their situation is hopeless because they don't love each other anymore. His answer is, "I am sorry to hear that. I guess you will have to learn how to love each other." He says that six or eight weeks later they are likely to go out of his office hand in hand, having the feeling as well as the love if they really mean business.[1]

In all of these cases, the couples have applied specific biblical counsel such as that given in this book. But you may be wondering how it is possible, even under the best of circumstances, to evoke that dramatic happening we call *falling in love*. It seems to be mysteriously compounded of moonbeams and magic. It involves physiological reactions such as quickened breathing and a fast-beating heart. It is one of the most vivid personal experiences a human being will ever have. So how can it be developed— particularly within marriage where two people are caught in the realistic grind of daily life?

The answer is that romantic love can be *learned* emotionally. This brings it into the realm of possibility for all who want to experience it in their marriage.

There are two ways to set up the conditions under which this love can be learned. First, by utilizing your own God-given faculty of imaginative thought; second, by providing the right emotional climate for your mate.

Although you will be using mental, imaginative processes, this does not mean you are to force your emotions. Emotions cannot be commanded to appear, but they will come freely when the conditions are right. Begin by choosing to be willing to fall in love with the person you are married to. Falling in love begins in your mind with the choice to *surrender* to the compelling feelings of love (This is in contrast to *agape,* where the choice must be made to give love consistently.) Surrender means vulnerability and the chance of being hurt; but in marriage it also offers the possibility of great happiness.

Men may find it more difficult to make this deliberate choice to fall in love than women do. Researchers claim that although men have the reputation for being matter-of-fact and practical, they are unlikely to let practical considerations guide their love life. Once their romantic feelings have been strongly awakened, they are more apt to be controlled by the emotions of love than their feminine counterparts and less apt to make decisions based on personal advantage. For instance, the king of England could and did abdicate his throne for the woman he loved. But would the lady have given up her crown, had the situation been reversed? A quarter of a century later, Princess Margaret of England, faced with a similar choice, chose her position and gave up the man.

Researchers have found that women are less compulsive and more sensible when it comes to love. They know how to fall in love instinctively and are more willing to try when they see that it is advantageous for them. As one girl said, "If I wasn't in love with a man, but he had all the qualities I wanted—well, I could talk myself into falling in love!"

In a Christian marriage, the advantages of being in love with each other are so obvious that I hope both husband and wife will make this decision. Begin with the willingness to surrender and to let your emotions take you on together. Roadblocks such as anger and unforgiveness will, of course, get in the way of this surrender and must be removed. (See ch. 14 for instructions.) Then you are ready to set up the conditions for romantic love.

Romantic love is a pleasurable learned response to the way your partner looks and feels, to the things your partner says and does, and to the emotional experiences you share. As you consistently think on these favorable things, your response to them becomes ever more strongly imprinted in your mind. You are learning the emotion of love through your thought processes, and it becomes easier to thrill to the sight, sound, and touch of your partner.

Women's Bible teacher, Shirley Rice, tells her students that she would like to inspire in them the same eager anticipation for growth in their love-life with their husbands that they have toward their growth in Christ. Then she shows them how to use their thought life—the faculties of memory and imagination—to build romantic love in their relationships. She says,

Are you in love with your husband? Not, Do you love him? I know you do. He has been around a long time, and you're used to him. He is the father of your children. But are you in love with him? How long has it been since your heart really squeezed when you looked at him? Look at him through another woman's eyes— he still looks pretty good, doesn't he? Why is it you have forgotten the things that attracted you to him at first? This is an attitude we drift into—we take our men for granted. We complain bitterly about this ourselves because we hate to be taken for granted. But we do this to them. Men are sentimental, more so than women. We weep and express ourselves audibly. Because they don't do it openly does not mean they are not emotional. Your husband needs to be told that you love him, that he is attractive to you. By the grace of God, I want you to start changing your thought pattern. Tomorrow morning, get your eyes off the toaster or the baby bottles long enough to LOOK at him. Don't you see the way his coat fits his shoulders? Look at his hands. Do you remember when just to look at his strong hands made your heart lift? Well, LOOK at him and remember. Then loose your tongue and tell him you love him. Will you ask the Lord to give you a sentimental, romantic, physical, in-love kind of love for your husband? He will do this. His love in us can change the actual physical quality of our love for our husbands.[2]

Husbands need to stop and remember how they felt when they fell in love. One described it this way: "To hold her in my arms against the twilight and be her comrade for ever—this was all I wanted so long as my life should last."[3]

"When a man loves with all his heart he experiences an intensely thrilling sensation," a writer explains. "It has been described as a feeling almost like pain . . . He feels exuberant and light, like walking in clouds. At times he feels fascinated and enchanted with the girl. Along with all of these thrilling and consuming sensations there is a tenderness, a desire to protect and shelter his woman from all harm, danger and difficulty. . . ."[4]

How was it with you when you first fell in love with the girl you married? Or (if you feel that you never were in love) look at her now through another man's eyes. Think about those things that are attractive in her. Love her with a sensitive appreciation and watch her become beautiful as she reflects and radiates the love you have poured out to her.

I am suggesting that both husband and wife must use their imagination to fall in love, renew romantic love, or keep alive the *eros* love they now have. Remember that love must grow or die. Imagination is perhaps the strongest natural power we possess. It furthers the emotions in the same way that illustrations enlarge the impact of a book. It's as if we have movie screens in our minds, and we own the ability to throw pictures on the screen—whatever sort of pictures we choose. We can visualize thrilling, beautiful situations with our mates whenever we want to.

Try it. Select a moment of romantic feeling with your partner from the past, present, or hoped-for future. As you begin to think about that feeling, your imagination goes to work with visual pictures. Your imagination feeds your thoughts, strengthening them immeasurably; then your thoughts intensify your feelings. This is how it works. Imagination is a gift from the Creator to be used for good, to help accomplish His will in a hundred different ways. So build romantic love on your side of the marriage by thinking about your partner, concentrating on positive experiences and pleasures out of the past and then daydreaming, anticipating future pleasure with your mate. The frequency and intensity of these positive, warm, erotic, tender thoughts about your partner, strengthened by the imagination factor, will govern your success in falling in love.

Of course this means that you may have to give up outside attachments and daydreams about someone else if you have substituted another as the object of your affections. Many people who are not in love with their partner begin dreaming about someone else in an attempt to fill the emotional vacuum. Even if it is only in the fantasy stage, you need to forsake it and focus your thoughts on the one you married.

In a book on how to fall *out* of love, a psychologist counsels her patients to practice silent ridicule, microscopically concentrating on the flaws of the other party, even picturing that person in absurd, ridiculous ways, until all respect for that one is gone. This should indicate how important it is, if you want to fall in love, to give up mental criticism of your mate and practice appreciation instead.

To maintain respect for your partner, never allow another person to tear him or her down in your sight. One of Abigail Van Buren's ten commandments for wives says, "Permit no one to tell thee that thou art having a hard time; neither thy mother, thy sister, nor thy neighbor, for the Judge will not hold her guiltless who letteth another disparage her husband." Practice saying good things about your partner to other people. Think about how much your mate means to you and dwell always on the positive side of your partner's character and personality.

While you are doing all that we have just described, you need to provide your mate with the right emotional climate for love to grow in. What do we mean by this? Here's how one man won his bride, as described to me later by her. As you read, remember that these same love-producing practices will work even better in marriage.

> From the night we met somehow we knew God had a special purpose for us. We could hardly keep apart the ten months before we married. He saw to it that we spent a part of every day or evening together. He wrote love letters and sent cards, phoned during the day, and brought special little items to me. He always hugged me when we met. He kissed me passionately and because he spent so much

time just talking and listening to me, I fell head over heels in love with him. He was so proud of me he'd show me off to everyone. I felt like I had been brought back from the dead.

Observe all the ways in which this man established a romantic climate and then ask yourself when you last gave your partner this kind of romantic attention.

In *The Fascinating Girl,* Helen Andelin tells how to create romantic situations. These suggestions can be put to good use by a wife seeking to provide a romantic climate for her husband. The best atmospheres include: dim lights; a cozy winter evening before an open fire; sitting out on a porch or patio in spring or summer moonlight; times spent on or near the water, especially at night; strolls through a beautiful garden; walks on mountain trails or in the woods; drives in the hills; a peaceful, homey setting; romantic, intimate resturants; picnic lunches in a quiet park. Whatever you do, keep it just for the two of you. Men seldom become romantic when other people are around.

Either husband or wife can suggest short trips (even just overnight) that become very special. Shared moments can take on significance. Researchers have found that shared emotional arousal is a catalyst in the development of romantic, passionate love. The emotions do not have to be positive ones, but they must be felt in common. For instance, you may experience an exciting moment together or share the glow of success; but you may also be drawn together as you react to the outside threat of danger. This may explain the noticeable increase in romance during the war years. The key factors are these: there must be a shared emotional experience involving intense feeling, resulting in a physiological response, and the receiving of a label approximating love in the minds of both.

A husband described such an experience to me. He and his wife had been contemplating a separation. He said,

> The other night we had a deep talk about our future. We both felt hopeless and didn't know what to do. She began crying and I cried some. It was strange because we ended up hugging each other. I felt like hugging her and she felt like being hugged. All of a sudden there was an exchange of something important. I felt as if she needed me, and I knew I needed her. It was a rare experience that has given us something to build on.

In providing the right emotional climate, do all that you can to avoid boredom even though your life must of necessity consist of routine. Think of your relationship as a continuing love affair and look at every tender, generous, romantic word or act that you bestow on your partner as an investment in pleasurable memories and emotional experiences that can grow and multiply into romantic love.

There are two additional things you can do to provide the right stimulus for the response of romantic love. The first is physical touching—and lots of it. I am not referring to sexual advances, but to the kind of physical closeness that draws very young people into romantic infatuations. This is how young teens fall in love so quickly and intensely. Married couples with monotonous relationships certainly can learn something from this about building the emotion of love. We all have a need to be held, fondled, caressed, and tenderly touched. As we experience this from our marriage partner and give it in return, love itself is exchanged and the resulting sparks kindle a romantic blaze.

Equally important is eye contact. Psychologists have found by controlled experiments that people who are deeply in love with each other do engage in much more eye contact than other couples. As the old song goes, "I only have eyes for you. . . ." This is true of lovers.

Eye contact shows its significance early in life when an infant's eyes begin focusing at about two to four weeks of age. From then on a baby is always searching for another set of eyes to lock on to, and this becomes a necessity. The child's emotions are fed by eye contact. We never outgrow this need, and when a loved one avoids eye contact with us because of disinterest or anger, it can be devastating.

If you practice warm, affectionate, meaningful eye contact with your partner, you will see how enjoyable this is. When your eyes signal romantic interest and emotional arousal, a spiraling response from your partner is likely.

As everyone knows, *eros* love is visually oriented. This indicates that both husband and wife should be as attractive and well-groomed as possible, whenever possible.

You cannot demand that someone else fall in love with you or expect it as a matter of course, not even from your husband or wife. But you *can* set up the conditions whereby your partner will find it easy to love you. Always be mindful of the kind of emotional response you are establishing in your partner's thought patterns by the way you act, by what you do and say, and how you look at love. Remember to send out signals that are pleasant and pleasurable rather than painful or distasteful, for in a sense you are teaching your partner to respond to you all of the time, either positively or negatively. This is yet another reason why you must never even seem judgmental of your mate—not if you want to spark romantic love and keep it aflame.

One of the greatest hindrances to romantic love is the habit (easily fallen into) of nagging. In a Christian family seminar, J. Allan Petersen analyzed the syndrome of nagging in this manner:

> Nagging is basically a woman's weapon used against the man in her marriage. The recurrent irritation of nagging is designed to get the wife what she wants. When her husband surrenders out of exasperation, he secretly hates himself for doing it and then sets his feet a little more so that the next time around she has to nag more than she did before to accomplish the same purpose. This state of affairs continues until finally the woman has formed a habit of nagging, nagging to get what she wants. She really is achieving her selfish purpose at the expense of her marriage. While she obtains personal and immediate satisfaction of her "want," she sacrifices something very valuable in the relationship. The wife who has to obtain by nagging is a self-confessed failure as a wife. She is admitting, "I don't know how to make my husband so pleased with me, so grateful for me, and so proud of me that he will be happy to do something that pleases me." The nagging wife should ask herself, "How much do I really love? What do I know about real love?" Nagging basically is an expression of a selfish independence.

It should be observed that in some marriages where the wife dominates, a husband may resort to habitual nagging. No matter who does it, it effectively stamps out any spark of romantic love and should be avoided!

At the beginning of this chapter we mentioned some controversies surrounding romantic love. Perhaps we can clarify the facts in these cases. If any reader still thinks of romantic love as a myth invented by the film industry, it can be pointed out that, based on biblical, literary, and historical evidence, romantic love has always existed. Researchers conclude, "Despite the assertions of some anthropologists, the phenomenon is neither of recent origin nor restricted to our culture. Although not always thought of as a necessary prelude to marriage, romantic and passionate love has appeared at all times and places."[5] In a cross-cultural study of seventy-five societies made in 1967, romantic love was found to be surprisingly predominant in other societies.[6]

As Christians we can be sure that romantic love is as old as Time itself, for it came into being in the Garden when the first man and woman gazed on each other. We must recognize that it was our Creator who gifted us with the capacity for the intense and passionate emotions required to fall in love. Clearly, God intended for our emotional potential to be fully developed in marriage and to find its fulfillment in oneness with our beloved.

We spoke earlier of some who feel that romantic love in marriage should be downgraded because it is selfish in origin. They judge it to be selfish because it desires a response. These people have overlooked the fact that romantic love is biblical. One entire book of the Bible, the Song of Solomon, has been devoted to the topic of romantic love in marriage, giving us an ideal pattern to follow in our own marriage. As we consider the five ways of loving within marriage, I hope you will remember that all these loves are God-given and represent different aspects, not degrees, of love. None should be scorned or ignored. Every facet of human love between husband and wife cries out for a response and there is nothing wrong with this. *Agape* may be the most selfless of the loves, but it does not hold exclusive rights to a life of giving. Natural loves also involve giving, even sacrificing, for the loved one. Researchers have observed that a significant component of romantic love is the keen desire to work for the beloved's happiness, no matter how much effort is required.

This brings Jacob of the Old Testament to mind—Jacob, the selfish young man, who, nonetheless, fell so deeply in love with Rachel that he worked seven years for a disagreeable father-in-law, then another seven, in order to marry her. The Book of Genesis says that these years of labor "seemed unto him but a few days, for the love he had for her."

"To be in love," wrote the author of *A Severe Mercy,* "is a kind of adoring that turns the lover away from self."[7] He was describing his own experience in marriage, and lovers will agree with him. In another sense these words can be applied to the compelling emotional love that the believer feels for the Lord Jesus Christ—a love that parallels in many respects the feelings and responses of a husband and wife in love. Theologian Charles Williams wrote that he was "startled to find romantic love an exact correlation and parallel of Christianity."[8] This reminds us that true romantic love, undergirded by *agape,* and enjoyed in the permanent context of Christian marriage, beautifully portrays the love relationship of Jesus Christ and His church. Thus, the goal of building romantic love in marriage can be a matter of confident prayer, for this is pleasing to the Lord.

Some people may be confused about infatuation vs. true romantic love. Infatuation is based on fantasy; true romantic love has a foundation of strong but tender realism. Infatuation is occupied with externals; real love is a response to the whole person. Infatuation fades with time; love keeps on growing like a living thing. Infatuation demands and takes; love delights in giving.

An important guideline for Christians to follow is that of emotions vs. the standard of the Word of God. If you are infatuated, your emotions will clamor to take complete charge and they probably will do so. In real love, your reason, instructed by biblical concepts, guides your emotions and shapes your relationship according to God's wisdom. Deeper channels are carved for the expression of this love than could ever exist in an infatuation. Within the depths of this relationship, thrills and strong emotions can add a sweet savor to the marriage daily.

If you have felt hopeless concerning the possibility of romantic love in your marriage, you can take heart. Romantic love does exist, and not just for others. I challenge you to put these suggestions to the test.

Although infatuation thrives on novelty, insecurity, and risk, true romantic love flowers in an atmosphere of emotional safety. The next chapter explains how to supply this through the gift of belonging.

8

The Gift of Belonging

Do MOST PEOPLE marry for love? Or do the great majority of couples marry for other reasons? It seems unlikely that anyone could arrive at an authoritative answer to those questions, but I have found two secular books that claim to know. Their authors assert that most people only *think* they are in love; that actually they are marrying because of other emotions—sex drive, fear, loneliness, desire to please parents, etc.

The idea of marrying for love, the authors say, is a dangerous myth. Anyway, they insist, a happy marriage does not require love or even the practice of the Golden Rule. In place of romance and love, couples are advised to treat each other with as much courtesy as they would show a distinguished stranger and to try to make the marriage workable.

Interestingly, even these books recognize one of the five loves of marriage. Although they give it no special name, it seems to be the kind the Greeks called *storge*. The authors of one book say that the truly loving union is most apt to be found in elderly couples who have been married for many years, have reared their children, retired, and now face death together. They have a realistic attitude toward each other; need each other's companionship; and care about the other's well-being. The writer of the second book suggests that the couple who married without love may find it ten, twenty, or thirty years down the line. Her description of the relationship again seems to indicate *storge,* the natural affection of marriage.

But does one need to wait thirty years or have a foot in the door of a senior citizens' home in order to qualify for *storge*? Many of you reading this book are young married couples or even newlyweds. I would like to show you the importance of building this love into your marriage now.

Mike and Nan Lawrence have celebrated their twenty-fifth wedding anniversary. But they developed *storge* love early in their marriage. Here's what it meant to their relationship during what they call the "rocky years."

> On the way to our June wedding, we thought we had everything going for us. Our friendship was warm, our romantic feelings even warmer, and, as for the fires of passion, they were just waiting for the match! After we settled into married life, the companionship and sexual desire and romantic thrills were still there. But it was all a little less perfect than we had expected because we were such imperfect people. The pink glow of romance hadn't prepared us for that! We weren't Christians then, so we didn't know that *agape* love could glue us together. Fortunately, something else brought us through those first rocky years when wedded bliss almost got buried under the un-bliss. You might call what developed between us a sense of belonging. We had decided right from the start that it was us against the world— two people forming a majority of one. So whatever happened, or however much we clashed in private, we stuck by each other. We were like a brother and sister on the playground. We might scrap with each other, but let an outsider try to horn in and he had to take us both on! If one of us hurt, the other wiped away the tears. We made a habit of believing in each other while our careers got off the ground. We showed each other all the kindness that two impatient young people could be expected to show—and then some more. It really wasn't long until we discovered something stupendous about our relationship: We found out we belonged. We came first with each other, and always would. Because we belonged to each other, no one could spoil our love and togetherness from the outside. Only we could do that, and we weren't about to! It was too good to lose. A lot of people seem to spend their whole life looking for a feeling of belonging. Maybe they don't know that marriage is the best place to find it.

The New Testament commands *storge* love in Romans 12:10, which tells us to "Be kindly affectioned one to another." Other translations say, "Be devoted to one another" or "Love warmly." An ominous condition of the last days, described in 2 Timothy 3, will be the lack of *storge* love. People shall be "without natural affection."

Applying these biblical insights to your marriage relationship specifically, you can see that to treat your own partner without this warm, kind, devoted affection is unnatural. Why? Because you do belong together. *Storge* is the love within a family—whether it be parents and children, brothers and sisters in Christ, or, most personally, the husband and wife bonded together in a practical oneness that has its roots in Genesis 2:24.

Because this is such an unspectacular, down-to-earth form of love in marriage, its importance may be underestimated. As someone has observed, "Familiarity breeds comfort and comfort is like bread—necessary and nourishing, but taken for granted and unexciting."

I suggest to you that this facet of love we call *belonging* is essential to your happiness in marriage. We all need a place we can call home—not just brick and mortar and four walls, but an atmosphere that is secure, where we feel completely comfortable with each other in the sureness that we belong, and that our happiness and well-being are of the utmost importance to our partner. John Powell has captured the essence of this love in one sentence: "We need the heart of another as a home for our hearts."

Do you already have this love in your marriage? Try the following tests:

Wife, how do you react when your husband comes home wearily and tells you he has been demoted or fired from his job? Or even "chewed out" by the boss?

Husband, how do you react when your wife tells you she's cracked up the new car and says tearfully that the accident was all her fault?

Or picture this scene: An evening of contentment in the living room. Husband watches football on TV while wife crochets and makes an occasional friendly comment (although secretly she has no great interest in the game). Or while he is buried in the technical manuals he brought home from his business, she curls up on the couch with an Agatha Christie mystery. Or they both sit before the fire, unwinding from a hard day, listening to the mellow tones of stereo music, not saying a word, and not needing to. If the husband who has had other things on his mind apologizes for not being good company, the wife answers, "I just enjoy being in the same room with you whether we're talking or not." Could this happen in your home?

Or picture a domestic crisis: Husband stops by the house briefly to discover his wife in a panic. Luncheon guests will be there soon; the dishwasher has leaked soapy water all over the kitchen, and Johnny got sick at school, so she had to go pick him up, and hasn't had time to do the last minute vacuuming. Some husbands might say, "What do you expect me to do about it? I'm in a hurry myself." Or, "Why aren't you better organized?" Or, "Tough luck, Babe," while heading out the door. A husband practiced in *storge* love is going to support his wife by taking a hand in the disaster—mopping the floor or running the vacuum— as well as speaking the words she needs to hear: "Don't worry, Honey; you'll make it." Plus a compliment: "Your table looks great!" And an offer: "Is there anything else I can do for you? I'll check Johnny's temperature again before I leave." Which scene is played out in your home under similar circumstances?

The love of belonging is compounded of many qualities that scarcely can be unraveled from the overall pattern. However, we need to see the qualities separately, if possible, in order to consciously develop this facet of love-life in our marriage. Here are some of the most important elements, but you may think of others to add to the list.

Practical oneness. Husband and wife develop a couple viewpoint. What hurts one hurts the other. What diminishes one harms the other. Personal growth enhances both. Thus, competition is avoided and the petty sniping that sometimes occurs in public as husband and wife try (humorously?) to cut each other down is eliminated.

This oneness developed over a period of time evolves into a couple philosophy in which the personal needs and values of both partners are blended into a common way of life.

Supportive loyalty. One wife told me: "My husband is such a realistic person—he probably sees my faults more clearly than I do. But I know that he is always *for* me, never against me, so he gives me the security and the room I need for personal growth."

Carole Mayhall in *From the Heart of a Woman* shares a lesson she learned concerning loyalty to her husband. She writes,

> Jack was overseas and his letters weren't reaching me regularly. My vivid imagination conjured up all sorts of awful things, not the least of which was, "He just doesn't care that I am here all alone and missing him so. He just doesn't love me the way I love him."
>
> As I was indulging in the world's worst indoor sport—feeling sorry for myself— the Holy Spirit spoke from a freshly memorized verse. "If you love someone you will be loyal to him no matter what the cost. You will always believe in him, always expect the best of him, and always stand your ground in defending him" (1 Corinthians 13:7 LB).

Observe that the combination of practical oneness with supportive loyalty effectively raises the shield against any outside intrusion. A young wife asked me, "What can I do about my mother-in-law's critical attitude toward me? I am so afraid she will persuade her son to agree with her." If this husband loved his wife with the *storge* love we have been describing, she would have no reason to fear her mother-in-law's influence. Or the next door neighbor's subtle interference. Or the predatory woman's activities at the office. A *belonging* love imparts security to the marriage.

Mutual trust. This has been described as "a bond of mutual reliance so deep it is unconscious." The Scriptures say it best: "An excellent wife, who can find? For her worth is far above jewels. The heart of her husband trusts in her, and he will have no lack of gain. She does him good and not evil all the days of her life" (Proverbs 31:10–12 NASB). The same should be said of the excellent husband. Your wife's heart should be able to trust in you as the one who will always be there when needed, helping and not hurting, because you are her husband and because her happiness and security mean as much to you as your own.

The *expression* of confidence in your mate is important. A wife described the difficult period when her husband's work as technical representative and trouble shooter for a corporation required him to travel to inaccessible parts of the world. It was often impossible to get in touch with him even by telephone when a family crisis occurred at home. She said,

> One thing helped me immeasurably. My husband told me often—and meant it—that he left home with complete confidence in my ability to handle whatever came up. He said he knew that I would always do the best under any circumstances, and he backed it up by never criticizing me for actions taken while he was away. His confidence in me has meant so much. And it's made me love him that much more!

A wife can help her husband by listening, understanding, and sympathizing with his problems; then by communicating her confidence in his ability to solve the problems and remove the obstacles. He does not need mothering or a dose of positive thinking or even advice, sensible though that may be. Instead, he needs reassurance from his wife that she has confidence in him, that she sees him as a man capable of conquering his environment. After that is established, he may ask her for advice and benefit from it.

Emotional refuge. If you feel you must hide your hurts from your partner, something is wrong in your relationship. *Storge* (the sense of belonging) was designed to be the soothing, healing love of marriage. Each partner should be to the other a haven of refuge from the harshness of the outside world. We all need our hurts soothed; we all need sympathy and empathy from the one closest to us. Love should mean a shoulder to cry on. If a husband and wife are available to each other at crisis times and if they offer a caring spirit, they will fulfill an important purpose of the God-designed marriage.

As the Scriptures explain,

> Two are better than one; because they have a good reward for their labour. For if they fall, the one will lift up his fellow: but woe to him that is alone when he falleth; for he hath not another to help him up. Again, if two lie together, then they have heat; but how can one be warm alone? And if one prevail against him, two shall withstand him; and a threefold cord is not quickly broken.
>
> (Ecclesiastes 4:9–12)

This describes the benefits of *storge* love, but note that the threefold cord is mentioned for its superior strength. The threefold cord of Christian marriage has these powerful strands: love of husband; love of wife; and the loving presence of God Himself.

Comfortable familiarity. This means you enjoy being together. If you analyze why you feel pleasantly at ease with each other, you will find kindness a key ingredient in your relationship. You are accustomed to spending time together without quarrels and recriminations, so that you feel *safe* with each other. At the same time, familiarity should never breed discourtesy. The courteous kindness we show our partners should be even greater than courtesy shown to anyone else, because ours is based on personal understanding and concern.

Although the warm affection of *storge* love seems as simple and uncomplicated as the comfort of an old shoe, it takes a measure of time and consistent behavior to build this love in your marriage—time spent in proving to each other that you can be depended on to be loyal, supportive, and kind. In short, that you *can* be depended on.

It is possible to begin developing this love now, even if you have failed in the past. It will require forgiving and forgetting past mistakes. It will necessitate the adoption of a viewpoint such as the Lawrences described in their marriage: a practical decision to be *one* against the world. It must include consistent kindness in your daily behavior, for this is fundamental to the continuance of love.

Because this love, like all the others, can begin with a choice to do what needs to be done in order to develop it, you possess the power to give your partner the wonderful gift of belonging.

At this stage, it does not really matter whether you married for love or for some other reason. Let the psychologists debate their theories. Life is meant to be lived this day. If you have a marriage, it *can* become a place of *homecoming* and you can begin moving toward that goal this day, first by making the choice to love, and then by demonstrating your commitment in daily actions, large and small.

"The passions of love are exciting," Nan Lawrence said, "but it's the shared trust that makes every day of marriage so nice."

9

Becoming Best Friends

"WILT THOU HAVE this woman to be thy wife . . . to live with her and *cherish* her?"

"Wilt thou have this man to be thy husband . . . to live with him and *cherish* him?"

These age-old questions put to the two people saying their marriage vows are always answered: "I will!" But what does it mean to *cherish* a marriage partner and how is it to be done?

When we understand the love the Greek New Testament calls (in verb form) *phileo*, we will have the answers, and we will better know how to cherish and become cherished in our own marriage.

Let's consider briefly what the Bible can teach us about *phileo* love. We find that *phileo* is the love one feels for a cherished friend of either sex. Jesus had this love for a disciple: "One of His disciples whom Jesus loved—whom He esteemed and delighted in . . ." (John 13:23 AMPLIFIED).

Peter expressed his *phileo* love for Jesus: "Lord . . . You know that I love You—that I have a deep, instinctive, personal affection for You, as for a close friend . . ." (John 21:17 AMPLIFIED) .

Jonathan and David provide an Old Testament example: ". . . the soul of Jonathan was knit with the soul of David and Jonathan loved him as his own soul"(1 Samuel 18:1). Other translations say that Jonathan loved him "as himself" or "as his own life."

God also loves with a *phileo* love: "The Father dearly loves the Son and discloses (shows) to Him everything that He Himself does" (John 5:20 AMPLIFIED).

The Father loves believers in the same personal way: "For the Father Himself tenderly loves you, because you have loved Me, and have believed that I came out from the Father" (John 16:27 AMPLIFIED).

From biblical evidence we can make these additional observations concerning *phileo:*

(1) It is emotional in nature and cannot be commanded, but can be developed.

(2) It is a selective love, based on qualities in another person that one finds admirable, attractive, and appealing. (One loves *because* . . .)

(3) It is fellowship love requiring enjoyable interaction through comradeship and communication. (Two souls knit together . . .)

(4) It is the manifestation of a living, growing relationship between two friends.

This same *phileo* is the cherishing love of marriage. Biblically, older women are commanded to teach younger women how to develop *phileo* love for their husbands: ". . . the older women . . . are to give good counsel and be teachers of what is right and noble, so that they will wisely train the young women . . . to love their husbands . . ." (Titus 2:3–4 AMPLIFIED).

The fond friendship of *phileo* takes on added intensity and enjoyment as part of the multi-faceted love bond of husband and wife. When two people in marriage share themselves—their lives and all that they are—they develop this love of mutual affection, rapport, and comradeship. They delight in each other's company. They care for each other tenderly. They hold each other dear. This is cherishing!

None of the loves of marriage offers more consistent pleasure than *phileo.* Friendship can reach its zenith in marriage because the other loves of the relationship enhance it. The bond is closer, the setting more secure. The camaraderie of best friends who are also lovers seems twice as exciting and doubly precious.

But *phileo* is by no means a sure thing. It cannot be counted on as a built-in benefit of marriage. It does not automatically appear when the vows are said and the rings exchanged.

In fact, as a counselor, I have observed that *phileo* seems strangely absent from many marriages. Through neglect couples have lost the rapport they once had. Others never bothered to develop it, perhaps because they did not know how. Or, they discounted its importance, leaning more heavily on the romantic and sexual attractions of. their relationship.

This letter to *Dear Abby* describes the dismal (and typical) marriage that has dragged on, even for several decades, without *phileo* love:

> Do all marriages go stale after 25 years? Ours has. My husband and I don't seem
> to have much to talk to each other about anymore. We used to talk about our kids,

but now they're grown and gone, we're out of conversations. I have no major complaints, but the old excitement is gone. We watch a lot of television and read, and we do have friends, but when we're alone together, it's pretty dull. We even sleep in separate bedrooms now. Is there some way to recapture that old magic?

(signed) THE SONG HAS ENDED

The acid-tongued comediennes of the world make a joke of the situation: "My dear, my marriage was so dull that when my husband left me, he was gone two months before I noticed!"

But empty marriages are not so funny, and a lack of *phileo* creates vast spaces of emptiness that couples sometimes take drastic steps to fill. Witness this letter published in the mailbag section of a women's magazine:

> After thirteen years of marriage and two children, my husband and I decided to risk a trial separation. . . . We are allowing each other at least six months separation, dating others and each other, and sharing the bills. If we make it, it will be because we truly want to share each other's lives, not because of habit or established rules.

This couple, while trying to remedy their lack of love, seem to be doing everything wrong in the process. How can a revival of courtship competition inspire the genuine love possible only between two adults committed to each other? How can separation enhance sharing when the two things are mutually exclusive?

There is only one way to learn the joy of sharing yourself with another. That is by doing it! *Sharing is the key that unlocks the emotions of phileo love.* This is the fundamental principle to keep in mind as you seek to develop *phileo* to the fullest in your marriage.

Next, consider that *phileo* consists of emotions. Thus, you must establish the right conditions in your relationship to bring the feelings to life. Once evoked, they need to be maintained, again through providing the right conditions.

Remember that *phileo* is the friendship love. The conditions you set up in your marriage must be conducive to friendship. You will need to be sensitive to the basic dynamics determining how friends are made and kept. Of course, these are known by almost everyone through personal experience. It is a matter of applying what you know. Take a creative look at your marriage as a model of friendship—creative because you are seeing the customary in a new way. How can you put the principles that are tried and true to good use in the setting of your own marriage? Picture your partner (potentially, at least) as your best friend. How can you bring this about in fact, applying your general knowledge of friendship to your specific knowledge of your spouse?

Perhaps the saying comes to mind. "To have a friend, you must be one." That is a good place to begin. We have said that *sharing* on all levels is the key. But *togetherness* turns the key in the lock. Consider these three ingredients of friendship and *phileo* love: comradeship, companionship, and communication. Each begins with *com*, the Latin for "together." Comradeship literally means "together in the same chamber or room"; companionship literally means "taking bread together"; communication literally means "possessing together."

Clearly, then, the two of you are going to have to plan for togetherness—the kind that involves mutual understanding and enjoyment. You will have to find ways to share meaningful time. And that is just the beginning. "Being a friend" demands conscious effort and commitment. But becoming best friends with your marriage partner can turn out to be one of the most rewarding projects of your lifetime.

It will be helpful for you to consider what some psychologists believe to be the three phases of friendship, adapted here specifically to marriage. You will see that these involve sharing on successively deeper levels. They can be expected to evolve as your relationship progresses. However, you will never graduate and leave one behind for the next. The accomplishments of each phase belong in your marriage permanently. If you want to remember the phases by name, just think of the little red schoolhouse with its three R's. Friendship has three R's too: relaxation, rapport, and revelation.

1) Relaxation

This must take place before closeness develops. It is the time to learn to be comfortable with each other while you practice the basics of friendship. Begin with simple, uncomplicated togetherness. Find things you can do together—side by side. It might be refinishing old furniture or playing tennis or taking French lessons or joining a camera club or whatever interests you. You may want to try something new together. Or one of you may have to make some initial sacrifices in order to find common interests. Whatever you do should provide a meaningful togetherness where you can interact and enjoy each other. Christian couples should choose some service that both can become absorbed in—a home Bible study, perhaps, or a church ministry that can be carried out together. In the busyness of our culture, couples need to give their time in areas that bring them together, not fragment their relationship. If you presently are expending your energies on projects that take you in opposite directions, you should change your projects.

Shared time, shared activities, shared interests, and shared experiences lead to shared feelings and shared confidences. "This was the cream of marriage,"

Jan Struther said, "this nightly turning out and sharing of the day's pocketful of memories." Andre Maurois defined a happy marriage as "a long conversation that always seems too short."

As all of this takes place in your relationship, you will find yourselves liking the same things, developing similar enthusiasms, and adopting compatible views. Some couples plan private weekend "retreats" every six months where they can formulate short-range plans and long-range goals for their marriages and their families. Fellowship on a daily basis in Bible reading and prayer will give you one mind in Christ, and you will find shared values and ideals strengthening to your friendship.

During this phase you will learn to trust each other—a critical factor in *phileo*. In a survey of more than forty thousand Americans conducted by *Psychology Today,* these qualities were most valued in a friend: (1) the ability to keep confidences; (2) loyalty (3) warmth and affection. These are the qualities you must communicate to each other, and this will lead to a sense of openness between you that draws you into the next phase. As you move into a deeper level of sharing you take with you the growing joy of being together.

Here is a series of statements describing simple friendship. Use these to evaluate the level you and your partner have reached. You should be practicing all of these as a springboard to the rapport phase. This is just the beginning of *phileo* love.

- We spend time together.
- We have fun together.
- We share activities and interests.
- We know and like each other.
- We talk things over.
- We confide in each other.
- We call on each other for help.
- We count on each other's loyalty.

2) Rapport

The rapport phase has been reached when you are ready to share aspects of yourself that are precious and vulnerable. Not only are you ready, but it becomes real joy to share yourself with your partner. Craig Massey has defined love as "that deliberate act of giving one's self to another so that the other person constantly receives enjoyment. Love's richest reward comes when the object of love responds to the gift." This is what you begin to experience and when it happens, you don't just *like* to be together anymore. You *love* to be with each other. *Phileo* is well under way!

The rapport phase is a time for sharpening communication skills. The complaint I hear most frequently is from the wife who desires to share her inmost thoughts while the husband feels uncomfortable doing so, usually because he has never found it easy to express himself. Difficulties can be overcome with practice in the rapport phase as couples learn to confide in each other and begin to see how rewarding and fulfilling it can be.

I would like to remind wives, in particular, of five basic rules for communication:

(1) Never repeat to anyone else the things your husband shares with you privately.

(2) Give your husband your total enthusiastic attention and listen with interest while he becomes more comfortable in expressing himself. Remember, it may not be as easy for him.

(3) Do not interrupt him or jump to conclusions about what he is saying.

(4) Acknowledge that you understand even if you disagree, and repeat his thoughts and feelings back to him so that he is sure you understand. Do not let your disagreement sound like disapproval.

(5) When you are sharing your thoughts, be careful never to sound as if you are heaping blame on him. When either of you goes on the defensive, your communication goes too, and rapport must be reestablished.

Husbands should realize that silence presents a negative feedback. As a counselor I have seen how a husband's silence, the seeming indifference to his wife's feelings, and his refusal to discuss things with her can destroy a marriage. It is said, "Adultery slays its thousands, and silence its ten thousands!"

Because women usually feel more need to talk than men, husbands should learn that they can love their wives just by listening. I mean real listening: concentration accompanied by eye contact. Dr. Ross Campbell recommends focused attention as a major means of building love in a relationship. Husband, this means giving your wife your full, undivided attention so that she feels without question that she is completely loved; that she is valuable enough in her own right to warrant your appreciation and regard. Here are some ways to implement focused attention in your marriage:

(1) Spend time together alone—really listening to your wife because you want to understand her better. Of course, this means the television will be turned off!

(2) Look at your wife and move close to her while you are talking.

(3) Plan for times when you will be uninterrupted and then give her the gift of your interested attention.

(4) Arrange longer periods for this so that both of you can warm up, let defenses down that may have been temporarily erected, and feel free to share your inmost selves.

(5) Pay attention to your wife when other people are around. This will mean more to her than you can ever know!

Husbands need this same quality of focused attention from their wives with the personal reassurance that it brings. Through the operation of *phileo*, two separate selves begin to merge and mesh together as you develop a rapport—a harmonious oneness. At the same time this friendship love gives the assurance that you both are unique and valuable individuals. According to the laws of human behavior, this will cause you to become more lovable and even more free to love in return.

Feeling accepted is a necessity in the rapport phase as you learn to share parts of yourself. As someone has observed, "There is great power in being loved by one who does not walk out on you when you are at your worst, or even hold it against you." Love may be blind, the proverb says, but friendship closes its eyes!

As you become practiced in rapport love, its joy will sweep you into the most mature phase of friendship where a willingness to learn more about your partner becomes an eagerness to know the beloved completely and to be as close as possible. The movement of *phileo* through these phases could be likened to a wheel rolling along, picking up speed. As the momentum builds, the pleasures of togetherness increase, closeness becomes a way of life, and cherishing your partner is now a reality, not just a wedding promise.

3) Revelation

This is the phase of mature and steadfast understanding. "I think a man and a woman should choose each other for life," J. B. Yeats said, "for the simple reason that a long life is barely enough for a man and woman to understand each other; and to understand is to love."

Married partners will agree that understanding each other is a lifelong process. It requires sensitivity, a quality developed as a part of total loving. To be sensitive is to be aware of your lover as a whole person; to recognize your beloved's uniqueness; and to discern what will best meet your mate's needs.

In the revelation phase both partners are freely open to one another. Both have gladly exchanged the original state of independence for an emotional interdependence that is unafraid to lean, to trust, and to seek fulfillment of personal needs and desires. On this level, both the needs and longings of the two personalities are understood and met in a process that becomes almost as natural as breathing.

But a warning must accompany this description of *phileo* love as it consistently matures and deepens in marriage when the conditions are right. A wheel can turn in two directions. If it can roll forward swiftly, it can also roll backward under given conditions, and a backward momentum can occur so unexpectedly that you will be caught by surprise. When a seeming betrayal of trust occurs or personality needs begin to be ignored, a reversal of *phileo* will naturally occur. Remember that *phileo* feeds on response and cannot survive too long without it.

Picture the friendship of your marriage as a fire capable of dying out through indifference. But the fire can be rekindled and its intensity increased until the enjoyment of rapport between you becomes a live thing—like sparks igniting the space you share.

Or picture your friendship as a valuable house. If neglected, it will soon show it. Friendship will fade when neglected. Your relationship may need some repairs, but, like a valuable house, restoration can take place if you care to invest the time and attention.

Always remember that friendship requires attention. It must have something to feed on and respond to. Ask yourself and your partner: What are we overlooking that could make our relationship better? If we are a bit bored, what are we doing to add zest to our friendship?

Any marriage can benefit from more *phileo*. Since this friendship is a living entity, it must constantly grow or it will begin to wither. So think of tangible things you can do to help it grow.

I find it interesting to hear from couples actively engaged in building *phileo* together because they go about it in so many different ways. For Paul and Olivia it meant blueberries and a baby!

This couple had found real unity in their marriage, particularly in the joy of Christian ministry and spiritual growth. But they were still aware of emotional distance. Paul was not affectionate by nature. Olivia was reticent about expressing her needs. They became conscious of living in two separate worlds: Paul in his schoolroom and Olivia in her home. He coped with young people all day, while she developed her skills as a full-time homemaker and mother. At night there seemed to be little meaningful conversation. After eight hours of interaction with students, Paul said that he felt too tired to talk. Finally he told his wife, "You couldn't understand my day, and I don't feel up to explaining what goes on by the time I get home." When they faced this problem, they found a solution: Olivia came to school for visits and observed Paul's world. A deeper understanding developed.

Then they decided to begin a project together—a blueberry patch with money-making potential. The real bonus, however, was the long hours spent together over the bushes—row by row—providing plenty of opportunity for leisurely conversation while they learned the pleasure of working together. Paul says now that weeding time just means more time he gets to spend talking with Olivia!

The most exciting project for this couple, however, has been the coming of their third baby—an arrival planned with delight from the beginning. Paul and Olivia decided that this time they would totally share in the delivery through prepared childbirth training. "Before, with the other children, it had been an anxious time for me," Olivia explained. "But this became an adventure. Paul was enthused about doing the whole thing with me. He even studied what foods would be best for me to eat. He put so much time and effort into learning with me—attending classes, spending time on the exercises with me—it meant a lot to me emotionally. Especially because childbirth is such an emotional happening, and we were in this together."

"It brought us together in every way," Paul said. "My job was to massage her when the contractions came, keep her relaxed, talk to her, and become sensitive to what she was feeling. We practiced this long before the time of delivery. It taught me the importance of physical touching in a non-sexual way. As I learned to touch her with a gentle, caring touch, I saw a real response, and I *knew* that my touch comforted her."

"We had been married eleven years," Olivia said, "but we had never been as close. I think for the first time Paul realized just how much l needed him. I had never felt free to show him before. Now I am sure that I am cherished and I can express my needs because of the way he demonstrated his loving care for me all during those nine months—and ever since!"

"As I worked with her, I did become much more sensitive to her," Paul said. "As Olivia realized this, she began to trust me more and this has continued since the birth of our baby. It's part of us now."

"We developed a new admiration for each other through this experience," Olivia added. "And a new confidence in the other's ability to cope with the situations of life. I was so impressed with Paul's care and concern, and his wisdom and sensitivity. And he was impressed with my ability to deliver our baby in a natural, wonderful way. The three of us were able to come home from the hospital the same day. When we got home we couldn't believe we had done it so easily! We accomplished it *together*. What a beautiful feeling!"

Paul summed it up: "We're much more *one person* now."

One of the most interesting examples of the development of *phileo* love can be found in the marriage of Anne and Charles Lindbergh. It is well worth considering because of what it illustrates about friendship in marriage.

The world called it a storybook romance—the ambassador's daughter and the famed "Lone Eagle." But the shy, introspective girl who would marry aviation hero Charles Lindbergh saw it another way: she, "the youngest, most self-conscious adolescent that ever lived" and he, like "a bomb dropped into our college-bred, forever book-reading family."[1]

The sheltered young poet and the man of whirlwind action. He was always in the public eye, his mind fastened on the scientific rather than the poetic—could such radical differences between them be overcome in marriage? Anne Morrow, admittedly "very much in love," recognized their differences in background, training, personality, interests, and way of life, and she tried to draw back.

To one sister she wrote, "I . . . think dazedly, Who *is* this man anyway? I can't *really* like him. It is a dream and a mistake. We are utterly opposed."

To her other sister she wrote, "I am completely turned upside down, completely overwhelmed, completely upset. He is the biggest, most absorbing person I've ever met, and he doesn't seem to touch my life anywhere, really."[2]

When the decision to marry was made, she wrote a friend with painful honesty:

> Apparently I am going to marry Charles Lindbergh. It must seem hysterically funny to you as it did to me, when I consider my opinions on marriage. "A safe marriage," "things in common," "liking the same things," "a quiet life," etc. All those things which I am apparently going against. . . . It must be fatal to decide on the kind of man you *don't* want to marry and the kind of life you *don't* want to lead. You determinedly turn your back on it, set out in the opposite direction—and come bang up against it, in true *Alice in the Looking Glass* fashion. And there he is—darn it all—the great Western strongman-open-spaces type and a life of relentless action. But . . . what am I going to do about it? After all, there he is and I've got to go.

She added, "Don't wish me happiness—I don't expect to be happy, but it's gotten beyond that, somehow. Wish me courage and strength and a sense of humor—I will need them all."[3]

And so the writer and the aviator set out to develop the comradeship, communication, and togetherness that would make them best friends and loyal lovers through almost fifty years of living—years full of ordinary happiness as well as triumph, tragedy, controversy, and accomplishment.

The published diaries and letters of Anne Morrow Lindbergh reveal the intense effort given to melding two such individualists into a deep, close union. The greater effort seemingly was made by her, even as the Bible counsels throughout the New Testament: Wives, adapt yourselves to your husbands.

Anne's adaptation involved learning navigation, radio, and aerial photography—even becoming a skilled pilot herself; hiding her fear on their hazardous pioneer missions; traveling without a settled home for the first years; and coping with endless crowds in the constant glare of publicity. Charles' contributions to the process of developing their close relationship, if less obvious, were substantial and abiding.

Most significant for us, this couple proved that *phileo* love can be developed between two dissimilar people even under extreme conditions when the two care enough to pour their lives into it.

Cherishing! It never happens quickly. As the middle-aged couple with six children said, "Love is what you've been through with somebody." But two of you cooperating can bring this cherishing about, slowly, beautifully, like the unfolding of a flower.

10
The Agape Way

"BUT, DR. WHEAT, what do you do about a marriage that isn't *emotionally real*?" The wife posing that question had good reason to ask. Barbara, who at age thirty is as lovely as any model, spends her days at home with two young children while her husband, a high-living executive, crisscrosses the continent on business (and pleasure), often accompanied by his mistress.

I think of many others committed to emotionally barren marriages that are devoid of the wonderful feelings of love we have been describing. Not much friendship or affectionate belonging or physical, romantic love in these marriages! Not presently.

I am reminded of Eric, whose wife, caught up in the sophisticated trappings of a new job, thinks she no longer wants what he can offer her and demands a divorce....

Of Fran, whose husband pours all his affection and attention on his thoroughbred horses and tells her to "go find a hobby"....

Of Quentin, whose wife has exhibited a sudden personality change and after an episode leading to her arrest refuses to come home....

Of Iris, who has to stand alone in rearing the children, maintaining the home, and coping with finances, "all without a word of approval, encouragement, or even a love pat" from her husband, a brilliant but self-centered scientist.

Of John, whose wife coldly rejects him as friend and lover....

And of Una, whose husband has been spending most of his free time at home in an alcoholic stupor....

What is the answer for these people and for others who have no reason to *feel* love for their marriage partners?

God has provided a remarkable solution: a love directed and fueled, not by the emotions, but by the will. Out of His own mighty nature, God supplies the resources for this love, and they are available to any life connected with His by faith in Jesus Christ: ". . . God's love has been poured out in our hearts through the Holy Spirit Who has been given to us" (Romans 5:5 AMPLIFIED). This is the *agape* love of the New Testament—unconditional, unchanging, inexhaustible, generous beyond measure, and most wonderfully kind!

No book on the love-life of husband and wife can be complete without a consideration of *agape*. Even in the best of marriages, unlovable traits show up in both partners. And in every marriage, sooner or later, a need arises that can be met only by unconditional love. *Agape is* the answer for all the woundings of marriage. This love has the capacity to persist in the face of rejection and continue on when there is no response at all. It can leap over walls that would stop any human love cold. It is never deflected by unlovable behavior and gives gladly to the undeserving without totalling the cost. It heals and blesses in unpretentious, practical ways, for it is always realistically involved in the details of ordinary life. To the relationship of husband and wife, which would otherwise lie at the mercy of fluctuating emotions and human upheavals, *agape* imparts stability and a permanence that is rooted in the Eternal. Agape is the Divine solution for marriages populated by imperfect human beings!

Two verses among hundreds in the New Testament will suffice to illustrate the nature of *agape* love:

"For God so loved the world, that he gave his only begotten Son, that whosoever believeth in him should not perish, but have everlasting life" (John 3:16).

"But God commendeth his love toward us, in that, while we were yet sinners, Christ died for us" (Romans 5:8).

We can make these observations concerning *agape:*

(1) *Agape* love means action, not just a benign attitude.

(2) *Agape* love means involvement, not a comfortable detachment from the needs of others.

(3) *Agape* love means unconditionally loving the unlovable, the undeserving, and the unresponsive.

(4) *Agape* love means permanent commitment to the object of one's love.

(5) *Agape* love means constructive, purposeful giving based not on blind sentimentality but on knowledge: the knowledge of what is best for the beloved.

(6) *Agape* love means consistency of behavior showing an ever-present concern for the beloved's highest good.

(7) *Agape* love is the chief means and the best way of blessing your partner and your marriage.

Let me illustrate with a case history—the most beautiful example of *agape* love that I have observed personally:

In this case a man loved his wife tenderly and steadfastly for a total of fifteen years without any responding love on her part. There could be no response, for she had developed cerebral arteriosclerosis, the chronic brain syndrome.

At the onset of the disease she was a pretty, vivacious lady of sixty who looked at least ten years younger. In the beginning she experienced intermittent times of confusion. For instance, she would drive to Little Rock, then find herself at an intersection without knowing where she was, or why, or how to get back home. A former schoolteacher, she had enjoyed driving her own car for many years. But finally her husband had to take away her car keys for her safety.

As the disease progressed, she gradually lost all her mental faculties and did not even recognize her husband. He took care of her at home by himself for the first five years. During that time he often took her for visits, she looking her prettiest although she had no idea of where she was, and he proudly displaying her as his wife, introducing her to everyone, even though her remarks were apt to be inappropriate to the conversation. He never made an apology for her; he never indicated that there was anything wrong with what she had just said. He always treated her with the utmost courtesy. He showered her with love and attention, no matter what she said or did.

The time came when the doctors said she had to go into a nursing home for intensive care. She lived there for ten years (part of that time bedfast with arthritis) and he was with her daily. As long as she was able to sit up, he took her for a drive each afternoon—out to their farm, or downtown, or to visit the family—never in any way embarrassed that she was so far out of touch. He never made a negative comment about her. He did not begrudge the large amount of money required to keep her in the home all those years, never even hinted that it might be a problem. In fact, he never complained about any detail of her care throughout the long illness. He always obtained the best for her and did the best for her.

This man was loyal, always true to his wife, even though his love had no response for fifteen years. This is *agape,* not in theory, but in practice!

I can speak of this case with intimate knowledge, for these people were my own wonderful parents. What my father taught me about *agape* love through his example I can never forget.

Now I would like for you to apply the principles of *agape* love to your own marital situation. Remember that *agape* gives the very best to the one you love. In your own marriage, your partner needs one thing from you above all else: *unconditional love*! Christian therapists speak of "the almost unbelievable need for *agape.*" Psychiatrist Ross Campbell points out that there is no substitute for the incomparable emotional well-being that comes from feeling loved and accepted, completely and unconditionally.

You will both experience tremendous benefits when unconditional love becomes a part of your marriage. First, your partner's self-image will be greatly enhanced. The better a person feels about himself, the better he is able to function in a marriage relationship. One who feels loved all of the time, knowing it is not based on his performance but on his unique value as a person, is going to be able to relax and love generously in return. The person who *feels* lovable can express all the loves of marriage. The person who feels he has something to give will gladly give it. Your partner will feel at ease with himself and, as a result, will become a more enjoyable companion.

Second, this habit of unconditional love can carry your partner safely through periods of severe stress. At times when our mates are most vulnerable to hurt because of stress, they are apt to behave in unattractive ways. That is the signal that we need to give more love than ever. Unconditional love will meet your mate's needs during the troubled periods that come to almost everyone at some time. Designed by the wisdom of God, *agape* is the best medicine for mental health.

Third, in an atmosphere of unchanging love, the two of you can find the security and stability that will help you to grow and become the individuals you want to be. The writer of Psalm 52 illustrates this when he begins by affirming that "The goodness of God endures continually" and concludes by describing himself as a green olive tree in the house of God, trusting in the mercy of God forever—planted, rooted, living, and growing. Unconditional love does this for us.

Fourth, unconditional love makes every day a smoother experience, even the most trying of days. Because you have established the habit of expressing *agape,* you do not behave disagreeably just because you are feeling depressed, worried, ill, or fatigued. You continue to treat your mate with courtesy and kindness, and you avoid those uncontrolled outbursts that can be devastating to the love-life of marriage. Because you are practiced, you know how to draw on the Divine supply of patience. Therefore your partner does not become your emotional football because you consistently behave with love, no matter how you feel.

Fifth, unconditional love removes the spirit of defensiveness on both sides. Thus, you do not feel the need to defend yourself from attack or to cut the other down by criticism. The syndrome of incessant complaining and explaining is happily absent from your home.

Unconditional love means that we can love our mates even in the face of extremely unlovable behavior. It means, for instance, that a husband can go out looking for his wife when she has run away from him to become a prostitute. He can find her in the gutter (literally) and take her home to love her back to health and restore her to a place of honor. Does that sound too drastic? Too improbable? A husband named Hosea loved his wife with unconditional love, and their story had a happy ending. You can read it in the Old Testament and in chapter 15 of this book, where it appears in a dramatic narrative form. But this still happens today. In my counseling I have encountered several Hoseas—both men and women—who exhibited this pursuing, unconditional love for their mates.

It is important for you to stop and evaluate your own approach to love. Do you presently love with conditional love? Or unconditional love? Try to answer these questions honestly:

- Is my treatment of other people usually based on their behavior?
- Does my partner's performance determine the degree of love I give him or her?
- Do I think that love should be shown only as a reward for good behavior?
- Do I feel that my partner has to change before I can love him or her *more?*
- Do I think I can improve my partner's behavior by withholding love?
- Am I reacting to other people most of the time?

As you may be aware, people who constantly react are never really free. Someone else is always in control, determining how they will feel and behave.

Your attitude toward unconditional love may well determine the ultimate happiness of your marriage. Remember, *agape* can begin with just one person. It can start with you, no matter what your partner is doing. That is the genius of this love.

By giving your mate acceptance through *agape*, you will find it immeasurably easier to work out whatever problems you have. But acceptance must be given in the framework of permanent commitment. To feel that you are accepted today but just might be rejected tomorrow is of little value. The total commitment of *agape* becomes the bedrock foundation of your marriage. As you express *agape* habitually, you will have a new serenity of heart because now you are not reacting like a rubber ball to everything that happens. You are behaving consistently with a giving love that flows right from the heart of God into your heart and on to bless the life of your marriage partner.

Here is how to make *agape* the central force of your marriage:

1) Choose with your will to love your mate unconditionally and permanently through attitude, word, and action.

When God created us, He gave us a wonderful faculty in addition to minds that think and emotions that feel. He gave us a free will. With our will we want and choose, and our will becomes the most influential part of our personality. When our will exercises its power of choice, it acts for our total person and the rest of our being falls into line with what we have chosen.

Thus, we choose to apply God's scriptural principles concerning love, and we choose to give this love to our mate without limits or conditions.

2) Develop the knowledge you need in order to do the very best for the object of your love.

Knowledge is indispensable in the exercise of *agape* love. If the loving actions of *agape* are not guided by precise knowledge of your partner, they will miss the mark.

Two kinds of knowledge are involved. The first is biblical. When I became a Christian and discovered that I could and must love my wife with *agape*, I had to study the Scriptures to learn how a husband is to love his wife and what a wife needs from her husband. As our Creator, God knows how we can best relate to each other, and He has not hidden these facts from us.

Through simple Bible study a man finds that the best thing he can do for his wife is to become the kind of husband described in Ephesians 5. A woman learns that the best thing she can do for her husband is to become the kind of wife described in 1 Peter 3. A number of good books have been written on the husband/wife roles in Scripture, and you will want to read some of them as you make your own study. In brief, the husband will find as he studies the New Testament and the Song of Solomon that God has designed him to be a protective, competent leader who will take care of his wife, and a tender, kind, and courteous lover who initiates love for her. This is what his wife needs from him. The wife who studies these Scriptures will find that God has designed her to be a responder to her husband's love; one prepared to help, who can gracefully adapt to her husband's calling in life; who possesses the beauty of a gentle, quiet spirit as she respects and affirms her husband; and who continues to delight him all through his life. This is what he needs from her.

This basic design, established by God in His loving wisdom, reflects the inmost natures of husband and wife and cannot be altered by those who would try. It lies deep within the plan of God, dating from the dawn of Creation, and no matter what cultural changes people attempt to bring about in the name of unisex, the fact remains that God created us male and female with distinctive privileges and responsibilities. Men and women are *different,* thank God, and so we can enrich each other and bring the full measure of joy into our marriage.

To love your mate meaningfully, you must add personal knowledge to biblical knowledge. This must be an intelligent, intimate, perceptive knowledge of the unique individual you are married to. If you do not understand your mate's highly specialized needs and desires, you will be unable to meet them with *agape* love.

Husband, you are told in 1 Peter 3 to dwell with your wife according to knowledge. You are to be totally relaxed and at home with her because you understand her so well. Because you understand her, you will know what she desires and needs; how to meet her needs; what will make her *feel* loved; and how to do the very best for her on a consistent basis.

The wife should study her husband in the same way to discover what makes him feel loved and to find out what he desires and needs and how she can best meet those needs. This is the creative project of a lifetime for both partners. Remember that *agape* is always an appropriate love, not given to suit your own hangups, but to ensure and enhance your partner's well-being. One of the thrills of marriage is knowing that you are providing what your beloved desires!

Strangely enough, one can be loved and accepted unconditionally and still not *feel* genuinely loved. What feels like love will vary with the individual— this is why you must know your mate so well. One person may measure love by the way his material needs are met, or by tangible items such as expensive gifts. Another may feel loved when her husband helps her with the dishes. One will measure love by the amount of time spent together, or by the quality of openness and sharing of thoughts between the two. Another desperately needs to hear often the words: *I love you.* Still another measures love by physical affection— hugs and kisses. One person puts a heavy emphasis on the loyalty shown by the mate, especially in public. Another values sensitivity shown to feelings. Some will measure love by the support given to their personal growth and development. There are so many languages of love! While all I have mentioned are important, some of them will have special, even critical, significance for your mate on an emotional level. Learn what speaks love to your own partner; then express your love in ways that cannot be doubted.

If the two of you are reading this book together, set aside some time to talk about each other's feelings. Share with your mate exactly what it is that makes you *feel* loved. Always keep the discussion on a positive basis without hint of reproach for past mistakes your partner may have made. Remember, you can never enhance or rekindle the emotions of love by heaping a sense of failure on your partner. I cannot overemphasize this. *Never* in the slightest way put a feeling of guilt upon your mate.

If you are more concerned about building love in your marriage than your partner is, and you are unable to discuss your feelings together, then begin to concentrate on a deeper understanding of your mate so that you, to begin with, can learn his or her special language of love by observation and discernment.

3) Apply everything that you know in giving agape love. Pour your life into it.

Never forget that *agape* is action, not just attitude. Make a specific effort to *do* loving things for your partner daily in addition to what you *are*. The wise husband or wife listens with the heart to consider and understand what the partner needs and desires, then acts to meet those longings.

Here is how one wife met her husband's deepest needs through the knowledgeable expression of *agape:*

"This began as a bleak time for us," Sue explained. "Because of my husband's change of job we left our pleasant life in a small town and moved to the big city where nothing seemed right. The house we rented was like a prison to me. I felt as if I had lost contact with the outside world! The neighborhood was unsafe, and I had no women friends, not even one good neighbor. Our church was so far away—clear across the city. Rob worked the evening shift so I was all alone with plenty of time to feel sorry for myself. I turned to the Bible during those long, lonely evenings.

"Rob and I had been Christians for years, but we had never enjoyed the oneness in the Lord that I had hoped for. Now, as I turned to Bible study and prayer— struggling with my fears and unmet needs—the Lord directed my attention to Rob and *his* unhappiness and *his* needs. I love my husband, and I could not bear to have him living such a joyless, sterile life.

"I began asking the Lord to teach me the right way to love my husband. I searched the Scriptures to find out how to meet Rob's needs. Do you know, the Lord took me to I Peter 3 and kept me there for months! I used to think of verse I as speaking of the lost husband: 'In the same way, you wives, be submissive to your own husbands so that even if any of them are disobedient to the Word, they may be won without a word by the behavior of their wives.' Now I realized that saved husbands are not always obedient to the Word either. Many of them don't know what it says. My husband was in that category, and he needed to be 'won without a word.' *Without a word* was something new for me! I had always tried to push my husband along in the Christian life. Now I made the *choice* to love Rob by obeying 1 Peter 3:1–6 in daily behavior and attitudes. Those were conditions that had to be met if I was to obtain this promise.

"I also determined to turn all my thoughts and my heart to God and to my husband. Every day I claimed Philippians 1:6, for I knew that a good work was begun in Rob long ago. I was confident that the Lord would complete it—now that I wasn't standing in His way. I also read Psalm 112 daily as an affirmation of God's purpose for Rob, putting his name in there. What a beautiful portrait of the righteous man. This is what Rob is becoming.

"It's been six months now, and I can tell you there is a transformation going on here that Rob and I can hardly believe. God's Word is absolutely true if we just do what it says in faith! We are developing such a beautiful relationship with each other, with God at the center of our marriage. Rob and I have a wonderful time together now. It is as grand as I always believed it could be. Fifty years old, and I am so in love with my husband! Such a beautiful life! Rob now wants to do things for me and with me. He seems to really enjoy talking with me, reading Scripture to me, and sharing insights about spiritual matters. Now the Lord has miraculously answered Rob's prayer that he would be able to work days and be home with me in the evenings.

"Rob told me recently that for a long time he had had one great desire—that the joy of his salvation would be restored. And now, Rob says, that desire has been fulfilled! The Lord allowed me to have a part in giving my husband what he wanted most when I chose to love him with *agape* love."

This wife has given us a concrete example of the way *agape* can transform the love-life of marriage when even one partner chooses to do the very best for her beloved—the best, scripturally, and the best, personally. (The two always seem to go together.) *Agape* love often clashes head-on with our old learned habits of conditional loving, so when you choose the *agape* way as Sue did, you have an adventure before you.

I must caution you on one important point. Please don't start loving with *agape* just because you want to reform your mate. This is not *agape* at all, but another form of conditional love. Change comes only from inner motivation. So accept your partner exactly the way he or she is now and seek to change your own behavior in accord with biblical standards to lovingly meet your mate's needs. The rest is accomplished by the Holy Spirit working through the Word of God.

You may be interested to know that almost all of the individuals mentioned at the beginning of this chapter did set their feet on the *agape* way. Faced with "no response" in their marriage, they had only two options: give up or learn to love a new way. Quentin quickly became discouraged and gave up. Tragic disintegration of home and family resulted. Una, on the other hand, has already seen her marriage totally transformed. The others are faithfully continuing to love their mates with *agape,* some with dramatic personal results. Barbara, for instance, has become a radiant Christian in the process, and the change in Eric has been remarkable. He is a new man in Christ.

As a counselor for many years I can promise this: no one who has ever really tried the *agape* way has regretted it. After all, it is commanded by God, and He always has surprises of love for those who obey Him!

11

The Secret of Staying in Love
(*Especially for Newlyweds*)

I<small>T</small> IS A remarkable fact that while millions of men and women have no difficulty in falling in love, at least half of that number seem unable to *stay* in love. This chapter offers the secret of staying in love for any couple interested in a lifelong love affair. The secret in one potent word is: *intimacy.*

Although couples of all ages and at all stages of marriage can use this information to improve their relationships, we want to speak directly to couples just beginning their married life. Ideally, this is where the intimacy building process should begin.

As a family physician and premarriage counselor, I have had some part in preparing hundreds of couples for the adventure of marriage. It is interesting to observe the varying attitudes of these couples as they approach the most significant event of their lives.

Some come into my office wrapped in a romantic haze that can scarcely be penetrated. They are walking on clouds, feeding on dreams, and feeling no need for counsel or advice. "Happily ever after" seems guaranteed from their point of view. It is impossible for them to believe that their emotional euphoria could ever be eroded by daily routine, growing irritations, competing attractions, or financial and family pressures. After all, they are in love, and isn't that all that matters?

Some come in rather anxiously, afraid of admitting any inadequacy within themselves or any need for information. They think that whatever happiness they feel now is going to be so much better after marriage. It is as if they are counting on the *fact* of marriage to provide them with something it can never deliver. In reality, marriage will magnify whatever problems they are trying to overlook in their present relationship or in themselves. (To paraphrase John F.

Kennedy, we should not ask what our marriage can do for us, but what we can do for our marriage.)

Others are in a hurry to take care of the premarriage business as one more in a long list of errands, carelessly confident that their marriage can succeed without any instruction in love. A few tips on sex and a blood test to meet state requirements will suffice! Their high expectations invariably are based on their partner's ability to meet all of their wants, needs, wishes, and desires for the next fifty years. Thus their happiness is going to depend on how well their partner performs for them—always a shaky business.

Sadly, I see many of these couples later under very different circumstances. Now, buried under a load of problems, they welcome every word that can help them work their way out of marital conflict and grief.

Then there are the couples I consider fortunate—those with realistic goals; eager to learn everything they can about developing a positive, loving relationship that will endure; and ready to put conscious, intelligent effort and careful planning into the development of the intimacy that can keep them in love for a lifetime.

Van and Terri, for instance, drove eight hundred miles for premarriage counseling. They came well prepared, having already listened to our counseling tapes and having studied our book, *Intended for Pleasure,* as well as other Christian materials on marriage. They had written their questions out in advance, anticipating problems that could arise and planning how to prevent them. It was obvious that they expected a wonderful life and did not want to miss out on any good thing that would enhance their marriage. Van and Terri believed their relationship was worth all the planning and effort they could possibly put into it. They were totally committed to the challenge of staying in love for a lifetime and enjoying every minute of it!

So together we discussed the principles of building intimacy in marriage— the principles that every newlywed couple should be putting into practice. The urgency of this can be understood by noting that the median duration of marriage before divorce is only seven years and, according to researchers, a mere three to five years for people drawn together by sexual attraction. *Now is the time for intimacy*! should be engraved in every newlywed's home—or heart.

What is intimacy? It is a fashionable word these days that describes the kind of relationship people have always longed for. Intimacy (derived from the Latin *intimus,* meaning inmost) refers to the state of being most private, most personal in relationship. It depicts a special quality of emotional closeness between two people in which both are constantly alert and responsive to fluctuations of feeling and to the well-being of the other. It can mean to understand and to be fully understood by one who cares for us deeply.

Of course, to become so finely tuned to each other demands time and conscious effort from both partners, but the resulting closeness lifts the relationship out of the commonplace and into the unique and irreplaceable.

Dr. Helen Kaplan terms intimacy "an important ingredient in the quality of love and of life. A high degree of intimacy between two lovers or spouses contributes to the happiness and emotional stability of both. All activities are more enjoyable and life is richer and more colorful when shared with an intimate partner.

"An intimate relationship acts as a buffer, providing shelter from the pressures and tensions of daily life," Dr. Kaplan observes, warning that "without intimate relationships we tend to get lonely and become depressed. The availability of intimate relationships is an important determinant of how well we master life's crises."[1]

There is no intimacy as precious or rewarding as that which can be experienced in marriage. When it is absent the effects range from dull to dismal to devastating. As Dr. William S. Appleton has pointed out, "It is essential to remember that marital dullness is *not* confined to middle and later years; indeed it can and does occur in the first year of marriage."

He calls boredom the warning signal with "preventive maintenance. . . the answer." And he emphasizes that "people are now less willing to tolerate boredom. . . . Magazines and television have raised expectations. Americans expect the good life materially and interpersonally. They want fulfilling marriages, high-quality leisure time, exciting sex, warm intimacy, stimulating conversation, good-looking bright spouses 24 hours a day! Unfortunately, their knowledge of and patience with necessary marital maintenance is often so minimal that their chances of achieving their high relationship goals are almost zero."[2]

Certainly, an emotionally flat, chronically dull marriage signals the need for positive steps toward building intimacy, injecting new life into the relationship. Recently a young husband said to me with a note of despair, "My wife and I have already lost touch with each other." It was a graphic description of their lack of intimacy, for to experience intimacy is to *touch*—emotionally, physically, mentally, and spiritually.

Here are some of the strands that make up the bond of intimacy between a husband and wife. They are given in no particular order, and you may have others of your own to add.

- Physical touching of an affectionate, non-sexual nature
- Shared feelings
- Closeness without inhibitions

- Absence of psychological defenses
- Open communication and honesty
- Intellectual agreement on major issues
- Spiritual harmony
- Sensitive appreciation of the mate's physical and emotional responses
- Similar values held
- Imparted secrets
- Genuine understanding
- Mutual confidence
- A sense of warmth, safety, and relaxation when together
- Sensuous nearness
- Sexual pleasures lovingly shared
- Signs of love freely given and received
- Mutual responsibility and caring
- Abiding trust

Couples who enjoy intimacy have their own special tokens of it. One wife, speaking of the ease of long intimacy, defined it as "understanding without words . . . family jokes that don't have to be explained . . . and a warm back in a wide bed."

In general, intimacy consists of a blending of the five facets of love that have been described in previous chapters. It does not happen easily in a marriage for there are too many hindrances that would impede its growth. And it will never happen automatically. To use W. H. Auden's description, an intimate longterm marriage "is not the involuntary result of fleeting emotion but *the creation of time and will.*" *Time* and *will* are primary factors in developing the intimacy that will cause you to stay in love! Auden concludes that this makes a marriage "infinitely more interesting and significant than any romance." As newlyweds set out, determined to build intimacy because it is worth doing and because it offers them lifetime rewards, they will find Auden's conclusion to be true. Their marriage will become the most interesting, significant relationship on this earth in their view. Romantic fiction will pale in comparison with the realities they enjoy every day.

But *time* and *will* must be joined by the *knowledge* and *patience* Dr. Appleton referred to—"knowledge of and patience with necessary marital maintenance." If marriages are made in heaven, their maintenance occurs in an earthly setting, which requires not only knowledge but also patience in the process.

Biblically, the Lord allotted one year of concentrated togetherness for newlyweds in order to establish the patterns of intimacy that would last a lifetime.

"When a man hath taken a new wife, he shall not go out to war, neither shall he be charged with any business: but he shall be free at home one year, and shall cheer up his wife which he hath taken" (Deuteronomy 24:5).

The Hebrew word translated "to cheer up" meant: to delight his wife, to know her, and to discover what would be pleasing to her.

In today's economy very few men can afford to take off for a year of honeymooning, but important scriptural principles are here for every newly married couple to consider:

(1) Nothing is as important as the health of your marriage and your growth in oneness.

(2) To concentrate on knowing each other and building an intimate relationship is pleasing to the Lord.

(3) It takes time spent *together* to properly lay the foundations of marriage.

(4) It is essential that the husband learn how to meet his wife's needs.

(5) Knowledge of one's mate is necessary in order to live according to biblical patterns. You must know your partner in depth if you are to love, understand, help, and encourage.

(6) Marriage mates are meant to be teammates yoked together to serve God effectively. Becoming teammates takes time and cooperation in an atmosphere as free from distraction as possible.

(7) According to the Creator's wisdom, the first year is crucial in any marriage and should be lived with care and forethought.

Another principle may be observed. It is that strong marriages are in a nation's best interests. So much of the health of society depends on the marriage unit, that in Israel the forming of a strong marriage took priority over business or military duties. Evidently the nation's *internal* strength was considered of primary importance.

Here are specific ways to build intimacy in your marriage along with some hindrances to avoid. Because we experience intimacy by touching in the different areas of our relationship, these principles will come under four headings: Touching—Physically; Touching—Emotionally; Touching—Mentally; and Touching—Spiritually.

1) Touching—Physically

I am referring to non-sexual physical caresses between husband and wife—of cuddling, snuggling, hugging, holding hands, sitting and sleeping close to each other, not as an occasional happening, but as an integral part of your daily life.

Touching is the most natural act in the world, and our need for it is more basic than our need for sex. Sex falls into the category of *desire,* for unmarried people can live happy, fulfilled lives without it. But the caring touch of another human being is a *need* that should not be ignored. At birth, touch was our first line of communication. The cuddling and loving we received was necessary for our emotional development, even for our physical well-being. Now that we are adults, very little has changed. We still have a deep need for the warmth, reassurance, and intimacy of nonsexual touching whether we are conscious of it or not. Often we turn to sex when what we really want is the comfort of loving closeness. As one husband observed, "Sex is a lot of extra effort when all you need is a real warm hug!" Psychologists believe that American preoccupation with sex these days is really a longing for the emotionally supportive physical affection that every human craves, but which has been in short supply in our culture.

If you are in doubt about how to begin developing intimacy physically, consider Webster's definition of *caress:* "An act of endearment; a tender or loving embrace, touch. To touch, stroke, pat; tenderly, lovingly, or softly." Begin doing these things, weaving simple physical touch into the fabric of your daily life. For instance, hold hands at the table when you pray. Take some time for closeness early in the morning and snuggle together at night. Sit on the couch so that you are touching in some way, rather than choosing chairs across the room. Hug and kiss when you go your separate ways for the day and do the same when you come together in the evening.

As you do this habitually you will share the same good sensations of warmth, security, and psychological satisfaction that you felt in childhood when you were held close by your mother. This is the tangible base of your intimate relationship. It is real because you can touch it.

Betty Ford in *The Times of My Life* says, "What stands out most in my memory about Mamie and Ike (Eisenhower) is their affection for each other. . . . I document my observation with photographs. So many pictures of them look unposed, as if they'd been caught in the act of touching." She recalls what Mamie, then widowed and eighty years old, said about her husband's "wonderful hands." "Every knuckle," she said, "was broken from football or whatever, but I always felt in all the years we were married that I could grab onto them when I felt sick or worried, and nothing was ever going to happen to me."

A young wife expressed her need for tangible expressions of caring in this poem to her husband:

Please—
Come take my hand
    Let's walk!!

Give me you—
    Eyes saying—Hi!
    Glances saying—I care!
    Handholds that let me know you were only teasing;
    Hugs saying—Thank you for being you!
    Kisses that—gently want me;
Then Love—
    That says, I'll be here tomorrow and everyday hereafter.[3]

Physical contact is absolutely essential in building the thrill of intimacy and kindling the flame of romantic love between husband and wife. I have observed that the people who come to my office saying, "I love my partner but I'm just not *in love* with him (or her)," are the ones who are having little affectionate touching in their marriage—no hugs or love pats, few kisses, no snuggling at night.

While physical touching is the easiest and most effective way to begin to build intimacy in your marriage, several hindrances sometimes exist and can become problems if allowed to continue.

First, many young couples who built an intense love relationship by caressing while dating often quit affectionate touching after marriage. The reason? Now they are using touch only as a sexual signal to communicate a readiness to make love. At other times they carefully stay apart lest an affectionate gesture be misinterpreted.

Couples must break the habit of using touch exclusively as a signal for sex. This will deprive you of the warmth and physical tenderness that every marriage should have. It may be interesting to know that building true intimacy in marriage will decrease your need for sexual signals. A greater openness will exist between you, a more comfortable relationship even in the sensitive area of sex. Many times the wife feels more free to initiate sex. Husband and wife are relaxed with each other and yet beautifully sensitive to the feelings and desires of the other. So I encourage you to keep up the physical closeness that helped you to fall in love in the first place. And rid yourself of the myth that touching itself must always lead to sex. Lovingly talk it over so that you both agree that touching casually and often will signal your growing intimacy. You must be able to touch each other in a relaxed way without fear of rebuff or misunderstanding.

The second hindrance is caused by the individual who goes into marriage convinced that he or she is just not naturally affectionate. Some are quick to tell me that they are different from other people. . . that they do not like to be touched . . . that it is not their nature. In most cases this can be traced to their early upbringing. But whatever the reason, anyone can *learn* to express his love through physical closeness. Anyone can *become* affectionate, even in a few months, with the right motivation and encouragement. Remember that the Christian does not have to see himself in a certain mold: "This is just the way I am, so I can't change." It is a fact of the Christian life that we do not have to remain as we are, because God will change us as we are obedient to Him. We have the spiritual resources to make any changes that are needed.

Couples who have experienced this change say that their new patterns of affectionate touching are bringing them feelings of comfort, support, and optimism that are wonderful. They have found out that giving and receiving physical affection adds a new dimension of pleasure to their life together.

But what if you have developed some negative attitudes toward each other? Does that mean you have to stay apart until you are over your anger? The answer is no! Therapists have found that actions do change attitudes and that physical closeness should be resumed immediately. Even when couples have experienced years of hostility and bickering, they are helped by learning to touch warmly and intimately.

One husband told me that his wife was not an affectionate person. When he began to practice the principles of building intimacy, it took months of patient, consistent, gentle, loving advances before she began to respond. But recently she said to him (as they cuddled in bed on a Saturday morning), "This is so much fun. I wonder why we waited so long to do it!"

2) Touching—Emotionally

A university professor who has taught a class on love for twelve years says that the most common problem discussed in his class is the basic difficulty people have in forming a deep, meaningful relationship with another person. Obviously, touching emotionally is far more complicated than touching physically! When we consider the complexities of emotional intimacy we can understand why the Lord set aside the first year for newlyweds to concentrate solely on each other. Creating emotional intimacy involves the meeting and merging of two different sets of emotions. The challenges are compounded because the two personalities learning to harmonize are masculine and feminine.

"A man who can understand his own wife can understand just about anything," a homespun philosopher mused, and, indeed, Scripture seems to indicate that women are more delicate and far more emotionally complicated than men. The godly wife also is incredibly valuable, according to Proverbs 31. Her value goes beyond the most priceless jewel. But she must be intimately known and understood to be appreciated. Thus, Peter, in his first epistle, counsels husbands to give top priority to understanding their wives: "Ye husbands, dwell with them according to knowledge, giving honor unto the wife. . . . Be ye all of one mind. . . ." Husbands should study their wives so that they can feel at home with them, totally at ease together, with full knowledge of each other. Craig Massey suggests that a man must learn to understand his wife's responses to herself, to him, and to the world's influence on her.

But if the greater responsibility has been put on the man, it still takes the wholehearted cooperation of both partners to develop the emotional intimacy that will keep them in love.

Emotional intimacy begins when two people deliberately share the same world—sharing time, interests, feelings, thoughts, goals, and ideals. It is possible for "in love" newlyweds to quickly develop two different worlds like separate continents without bridges *unless* they make a concerted and consistent effort to spend their free time together, developing absorbing interests in common, and doing the tasks of life in partnership, side by side. That most prized relationship of understanding and being fully understood by one who deeply cares comes into being as both are willing to communicate with each other—sharing experiences, dreams, fears, and secrets they would tell to no one else. Talking in private about private matters builds emotional intimacy as nothing else can! Many students of love believe that sharing is the key, that it is growing separateness in the minds of marriage partners that kills love. Couples, then, must knit their individual lives together in that important first year to form one pattern of intimacy, consisting of many threads of togetherness.

Intimacy can grow only in a place of safety. When husband and wife are afraid of hurt, rebuff, criticism, and misunderstanding, they will find it difficult to touch and share freely. So if you want real intimacy in your marriage, you will have to establish trust in your relationship.

God's Word shows how to do this in two concise statements: "Love covers over a multitude of sins" (1 Peter 4:8 NIV); and "Love builds up" (1 Corinthians 8:1 NIV). In other words you must: (1) overlook mistakes and never criticize; and (2) always encourage and give your partner the gift of sympathetic understanding.

As a counselor I observe many people attempting to improve their marriage partners by criticizing them, pointing out their faults and mistakes. But this never changes anyone for the better. It only puts miles of emotional distance between a husband and wife who may be secretly longing for closeness.

The truth about criticism is almost startling when fully grasped: criticism can actually be the death blow to love, intimacy, and all the good things you want to build in your marriage. So think before you speak! Remember the potent power of praise and form the habit of consistently building up rather than tearing down. I do not recall when my wife and I last criticized each other. After years of edifying, we are not even conscious of personal flaws in the other because we are so caught up in the pleasure of living every day together. Gaye and I can enthusiastically recommend this pattern of interaction to couples just beginning their marriage because we know that it works so well.

There is another element that will contribute to your mutual trust. In plain words, the rule should be: never let your partner down in something that really matters to him or her. The application of this rule will be determined by your partner—not you. You might feel that you are behaving correctly, yet this may clash violently with your partner's emotional perceptions of what he or she needs from you. A marriage often begins with fantasies and unreasonable expectations of a partner who will be all things, perfectly meeting every desire. But wise newlyweds will learn to replace these dreams (which could never be fulfilled by an imperfect human being) with realistic expectations. This requires a dialogue of loving honesty. What can you realistically expect from each other? What really matters to you down in the fibers of your unique emotional makeup?

One couple, the Xaviers, gave me examples from their own marriage. *She* said, "My husband thought I was being too demanding when I asked him to give up his plans so he could go with me to the dentist—an emergency trip. Until he understood that I was simply terrified of the prospect and I *needed* his support. If he had refused I would have felt he had failed me badly. But because we discussed it, he understood my need and met it in a loving way." *He* said, "I will never forget the sight of my wife dropping everything else to type my research paper—and staying up half the night to do it. She really bailed me out without a word of complaint because I explained how important it was to me."

The kind of dialogue that leads to genuine understanding is far more than conversation. It involves *listening to each other from the very beginning of the conversation* with an attentive ear to what the other person really is saying and feeling. Communication has been defined as the ability to send and receive messages accurately—not only factual messages, but signals of an emotional nature. To learn to listen and to communicate is an essential part of perfecting the art of loving.

John Powell calls dialogue "an act of purest love." He explains, "The listening and speaking of dialogue are each directed to the other. Dialogue is essentially other-centered. . . .

"There are no winners and losers in dialogue," he points out, "only winners. Neither partner is ever required to give up or give in but only to give, to give of himself. In a dialogue we can never end up with less than we were but only more. To live in dialogue with another is to live twice. Joys are doubled by exchange and burdens are cut in half by sharing."[4]

These three guidelines should be followed as you practice communication in the early days of your marriage:

(1) Talk more freely about your feelings, but not in such a way that your partner feels rebuked or criticized.

(2) Be willing to show your vulnerable side to your mate. A cardinal rule of developing intimacy is: Dare to be needy; do not be afraid to *say,* "I need you."

(3) Remember that silence is almost always a negative feedback unless it is accompanied by nonverbal signals that your partner shares your feelings, such as by a squeeze of the hand or a smile.

Obviously, to build intimacy and establish trust, any emotional conflict must be settled quickly. In fact, I give this guideline in premarriage counseling: *Never go to bed with unresolved conflict.* The biblical principles are: "Let not the sun go down upon your wrath" (Ephesians 4:26) and "Forgive . . . as Christ forgave" (Colossians 3:13). Conflicts are inevitable in any marriage, but they become problems only when they are not quickly and lovingly resolved. Real love acts as the inhabitant to anger. When you love someone and have developed a satisfying level of intimacy, anger disappears rapidly. It is a relief to forgive and forget and to feel close to each other again. You will both need to recognize times when your behavior is less loving than it should be, and readily admit this to your partner with a sincere "I'm sorry." An apology is recognition of the fact that your relationship is so important to you that you want to keep it in good repair. When you "keep up" with each other through emotional intimacy, the relationship can be easily restored. Keeping up is far easier than "catching up" after years of emotional distance.

Some of the hindrances that can pose serious threats to your emotional intimacy show up like warning lights in this letter from Walt, a heartbroken husband:

> My wife's divorce proceedings are just days away. By way of my attorney, I postponed answering the papers, but have run out of time.
> There is no doubt, Dr. Wheat, that I am guilty of most everything you warned against. Neither Yvonne nor I were fully aware of our obligation to God and each other when we made our vows. As time went on we managed to draw away from each other by not sharing in each other's world. Yvonne placed manipulative conditions on our sex life. I had to do certain things such as wash dishes, etc., to win a few intimate moments. I realize that I failed to follow most of the guidelines you give for love. It was not a matter of not loving her in my heart, but my blindness to her needs, as well as my own selfishness. My job requires quite a bit of time, which was bad enough, but I also didn't open the rest of my life to her as I should.

Her parents never let us be, constantly interfering with our lives. Her mother constantly wanted her to "come by" and go places with her. So I did not really feel necessary in her life. I began to come home to supper on the stove and a quickly scribbled note about "gone so and so with Mama."

In my failure I didn't set about to improve our situation. Instead, I found ways to amuse myself, and in time our lives became two different paths, and our home a pit stop for sleep. Our separate paths began to bring about sexual hunger in me, and once again I failed. I had an affair to try to counter this frustration. I knew this was sin and my conscience ate at me. I see now that I was substituting selfishness for the patience I should have had and thinking only how to fulfill myself.

When I finally came to the point of suggesting that we seek help for our marriage, it was too late for Yvonne. I have tried fervently to seek forgiveness and to reconcile, but her response has been hatred. . . . Our four-year-old prays each time I am with her for God to help Mommy and Daddy get back together. . . .

As Walt's letter illustrates, in-laws can be a most serious hindrance to establishing intimacy. The Lord recognized this in His commands to Adam (before sin had entered into the human race). He gave Adam two commands and one of them was to keep in-laws out of marriage. Looking down the corridors of time at future causes of marital disharmony, God said that in-laws should not be involved in your marriage—that an entirely new social unit is to be established. This means that separation from both sets of parents is a necessity:

Physically. Do not live with your parents after marriage. Do not even spend a great deal of time together. I occasionally hear of couples who take their in-laws with them on the honeymoon trip. No matter how well-intentioned this is, it sets up an undesirable pattern. Intimacy in marriage is a private thing. It is something you just do not share with others. You might have a good time with a group of people on a trip, but that is not intimacy. Real intimacy can flower only when you are alone together. By the way, never discuss intimate marital problems with your parents.

Emotionally. Do not marry if you cannot be emotionally independent of your own family. Recent research indicates that "going home to mama" when conflicts appear is as prevalent in marriage today as ever in spite of the new thirst for independence. Do not allow a parent to fill an emotional role that should be reserved for your mate alone. No genuinely loving parent will expect this or seek it.

Financially. Do not marry if you cannot maintain a household. Help in financing education should be accepted only if you can be completely free from domination by those providing the funds.

Another hindrance to intimacy expressed so vividly in Walt's letter was that of living in separate worlds until coming home for both meant only taking a pit stop for sleep!

This lonely state of affairs begins when a young couple does not make any effort to build a new life together. Instead they each pursue their separate interests and sometimes keep their separate friends. In a *Moody Monthly* article, "Satan's Doctrines of Marriage," Craig Massey points out that Satan's lie says: *"You can spend time away from one another without hurting the marriage relationship."* No wonder this is a favorite satanic lie! Intimacy—physical, emotional, mental, and spiritual—simply cannot be accomplished by separation, and it is this intimacy that fulfills and satisfies, which causes two to become one according to God's design.

The third serious hindrance to emotional intimacy is that ubiquitous annoyance we call the television set. Some TV shows are informative and enjoyable, of course. But few people seem to have the discipline required to choose only the best programs and keep the set turned off otherwise. In premarriage counseling I encourage every couple to refrain from getting a TV set for the first year. I tell them that television robs them of wonderful hours that could be spent together, sharing and learning to relate to each other. There can be no giving, no receiving, when you have your eyes and mind glued to the set.

Dennis Guernsey in *Thoroughly Married* says:

> It's folly to try to communicate with the television blaring in the background, in between football timeouts. . . . Quality time requires a focus of attention that is impossible to achieve if the slightest distraction persists. Most of us would be shocked if we totaled up the amount of face-to-face time we spent with each other during the last week, the last month, or the last year. Weeks can go by without a meaningful time for the sharing of our lives.

He calls attention to the special value in deliberately and regularly setting aside time to be with each other:

> Many couples successfully manage the "hurt" in their relationship because they know for sure there will be a time and an opportunity to work their problems through. In contrast, the smallest annoyance in a marriage can become unbearable if it appears it will be there forever. . . . We end up trying to go in all directions at once and then wonder why we've lost touch with each other.

No husband or wife should take the matter of emotional intimacy lightly. Intimacy will cause you to stay in love. But without intimacy one or both of you may be strongly tempted to seek it elsewhere. Dr. Mary Ann Bartusis in a study of marital triangles found that all too often an affair occurs with the spouse's best friend. Why? Because human beings have an "insatiable quest" for a meaningful one-to-one relationship that is not being satisfied within the marriage; and because so many opportunities for intimacy exist with the marriage partner's "best friend." Intimate talks are often a key factor in developing the feeling of being in love. Dr. Bartusis suggests that familiarity, availability, and acceptance are the keys—conditions easily fulfilled with a close friend of the family.[5]

So, invest in emotional intimacy with your own partner and find a happiness that carries with it no regrets or bitter aftereffects.

3) Touching—Mentally

This level of intimacy involves coming to an agreement about all the important issues that determine the direction of your life. It requires practice in making intelligent plans for your lifestyle and the well-being of your family. Couples who learn to develop this kind of intimacy find real pleasure in setting goals together and then accomplishing them together.

One example will suffice. The area of financial habits is crucial to the future of the marriage. Experts believe that 50 percent of all divorces are now caused by financial disagreements, and with the growing instability of our economy, this number is sure to rise. Just the frustrations of keeping a home and family solvent these days are enough to create conflicts unless the financial difficulties become challenges that draw husband and wife together. A beautiful intimacy can develop as husband and wife face and overcome the budget shortages together. It is not just a matter of eliminating causes for conflict, but the positive value of working together to build a God-honoring life of financial freedom that makes this such an important aspect of intimacy-building.

George and Marjean Fooshee in *You Can Beat the Money Squeeze* warn of "the debt trap." They define a trap as attractive, easy to get into, and almost impossible to escape from—an accurate description of the credit card lifestyle. The easy credit available for so long in our culture has taught people to overspend consistently, hoping to make enough in the future to pay for what they are using up today. Probably the majority of married couples today find themselves more or less financially entrapped.

Newlyweds who want to establish a pattern of financial freedom should be very sensitive to these warning signs:

- You are preoccupied with thoughts about money, at the expense of thoughts about God.
- You don't give what you feel God wants you to give.
- You are not at peace to live on what God has provided.
- You argue within your family about money matters.
- You can't or don't pay credit cards debts in full each month.
- You need or have considered a consolidation loan.

- You receive notices of past-due accounts.
- You charge items because you can't pay cash.
- You use spending as emotional therapy.
- You spend impulsively.
- You invade savings to meet current expenses.
- Your net worth does not increase annually.
- You "just can't save."
- You are underinsured.
- You wish you had a plan for spending and saving and are frustrated because you don't.

The goal to be financially free requires two basic decisions, the Fooshees say: (1) Decide at the outset that you will not spend what you do not have. (2) Trust God instead of trusting a loan.

Christian Financial Concepts, a non-profit organization headed by Larry Burkett, can give you knowledgeable and practical help in carrying out these decisions by handling your finances according to biblical principles and wise economic policies. I highly recommend their books, counseling cassette albums, and their seminars that are held in churches across the country. Write to the organization at 209-A Norcross-Tucker Road, Norcross, GA 30071 for further details.

Finances always prove to be divisive in marriage no matter what your economic level unless the two of you develop the right attitudes together—another important step in intimacy growth.

4) Touching—Spiritually

Another of my premarriage recommendations is: *Have some Bible study together every day.* This is the basic way to develop spiritual intimacy. As the Word of God courses through your minds, you are shaped and transformed together into new people with united attitudes and goals and with a common outlook that comes from taking in God's viewpoint of every aspect of life. It is really the responsibility of the husband to initiate daily Bible study. If you don't know how, one way is to listen together to Bible teaching on cassette. Bible Believers Cassettes, Inc., a *free-loan* library, offers the best in Bible teaching by the finest teachers in the English-speaking world today. There are more than ten thousand different messages available with many on the subject of marriage and the Christian home. You may wish to begin with these. Send one dollar for your catalog to Bible Believers Cassettes, Inc., 130 N. Spring St., Springdale, AR 72764.

I also recommend that every newly married couple become actively involved in a local church where they can learn and grow and serve the Lord in company with other people who will get to know them well and to care for their well-being.

Nothing can draw a couple closer than genuine, heart searching prayer together. I appreciate the testimony my wife Gaye shared in *Intended for Pleasure* concerning the rewards of spiritual intimacy. She wrote,

> Now that we are Christians, I know that the love Ed has for me is the same kind of love that Christ has for me. I am safe and secure in that love. I know that I can always talk to my husband and that I can trust his wisdom as the spiritual leader of our family. As we have become so used to pouring our hearts out together in prayer, we now are free to communicate about anything to each other. We are not afraid to expose ourselves and our faults, because we know that we accept each other just as we are, with all our frailties and faults and good points. How wonderful it is to know that I am not on a performance basis: No matter how poorly I perform, I am still going to be loved. And that has to make me perform better.

At the beginning of this chapter I referred to Van and Terri, a couple who came eight hundred miles for premarriage counseling. It has been a pleasure to hear of their progress in building a close, intimate, and wonderfully happy marriage. They started off wisely with a private honeymoon in the mountainous beauty but inexpensive facilities of a state park. Their goal was not to go somewhere to be entertained, but to focus on each other, and they report that they had a meaningful time together that will never be forgotten.

Now they have agreed on a specific goal for their life. When Van receives his graduate degree, they will be going to Africa where he plans to teach. While he completes his education, Terri is working, but their lives are carefully integrated. He helps her with the housework, and she works with him on the preparation of his papers. In fact, she is also auditing a course he teaches, and they are experiencing a real intellectual intimacy.

Terri comes from a warm, united home, while Van's parents are individualists who lead virtually separate lives. They have already agreed to model their home after the example of Terri's parents, and to fulfill this plan, they give their relationship and their "face to face" time top priority. Because their financial resources are slim, they have a carefully planned budget and enjoy inexpensive activities—exploring every resource of their area of the country in the process. She makes most of her clothes, and he is tremendously supportive of her efforts, even going with her to choose materials. He is quick to show appreciation and lets her know how thankful he is for her willingness to prepare the dinner meal after a hard day at work.

With accurate information concerning sexual adjustment at the beginning of their marriage and with a loving openness of communication, they already have developed a satisfying sex life.

Personality clashes have been avoided through forethought and understanding. Terri had found Van's strength and forcefulness appealing, but she thought there might be difficulties because of her own stubborn and independent nature. However, Van values her ability to make decisions and to cope with challenging situations. While abdicating none of his leadership role, he is encouraging her to use her strong characteristics in the most positive way.

Terri and Van often share spiritual insights. While they are cleaning up the kitchen together, they memorize and discuss Bible verses. As committed Christians, they have an active involvement in a local church and are growing together spiritually.

A close friend says their relationship is characterized by togetherness, and by their constant concern for each other. "They are always looking for ways to help each other," the friend observes.

In this day of disintegrating marriages, I would judge their chances for a good, enduring marriage and an evergrowing love to be almost 100 percent. Their secret: intimacy!

12

A Pattern for Lovers

E<small>VERY</small> M<small>ARRIED</small> C<small>OUPLE</small> with a Bible in their home should become experts on the one book of the Bible devoted exclusively to love and marriage. I refer to "The Song of Songs, which is Solomon's." The Song of Solomon gives us the pattern of married love as God intended it to be, revealed in such striking detail that it can serve as a practical model for our own marriages almost three thousand years after it was written.

Through the inspiration of the Holy Spirit, we are told of a marriage between the king of Israel and a beautiful, unsophisticated country girl whom he met in the northern vineyards of his kingdom. At this point it may sound like one of those storybook tales that end, "And they lived happily ever after." But this is no pretty fantasy spun by some story teller. It is the Word of God relating truthfully, as always, the events experienced by one couple and the words and emotions they expressed that portray for all time the love-life in marriage that honors and pleases God.

It is hardly surprising that Scripture speaks so clearly on the subject of love and sexual fulfillment in marriage. After all, the Bible deals with every other area of human behavior. And we need more than admonitions as we enter into the complicated relationship of marriage; we need examples to follow! What *is* remarkable is the range and degree of practical insights to be gleaned from the Song, applicable to any marriage in any civilization. Only the guiding hand of the Creator could have made this small book of exquisite love poetry about a king and queen in 945 B.C. (or thereabouts) so amazingly relevant to the average couple today. Again we see proof that God's principles concerning marriage transcend time and cultural differences and will always work when applied. In just eight short chapters constituting the world's greatest romantic literature, the Song of Solomon not only shows today's husband and wife *how* to love each other, but realistically presents problems of marriage and the principles for solving them.

As you and your partner study this wonderful little book, you will discover how to obey God in your marriage by being very much in love and very expressive of that love while working out your natural differences.

Of course, it is impossible to make a thorough study of the Song of Solomon in one chapter, and we will not try. Instead, we want to help you enhance your love-life by emphasizing principles and conclusions drawn by the finest Bible scholars of recent times. I trust this will whet your appetite for more study on your own.

"Which way do you interpret the Song of Solomon?" a young Christian (a student) asked me recently. "I've heard that some people say it's talking about marriage and some say it's talking about spiritual things—Jesus Christ and His love for us. Which interpretation is right?"

"Both views are correct," I explained, "in the sense that you could not have one without the other. The New Testament makes it clear that marriage is intended to be a reflection on earth of the love relationship between Christ and His church. So, whenever the Bible speaks of marriage as God designed it, we are going to find applications to the spiritual relationship we enjoy with our Lord. On the other hand, as we learn more about Jesus Christ and His love for us, we will know more about the way we should behave in marriage. The principle is, 'Husbands, love your wives, even as Christ also loved the church, and gave himself for it' (Ephesians 5:25)."

"You mean all that is in the Song of Solomon?" the young man asked.

"Yes," I said. "Look at the way the bridegroom in the Song loves his wife. You'll find innumerable parallels to the way the Savior loves His people—the way He loves you personally. If you study how the bride responds to the bridegroom, you can learn a lot about how you are to respond to the Savior on a spiritual level. Just remember that the primary teaching of the book concerns love and marriage. These truths should never be spiritualized away."

"Okay," he nodded. "You're saying that the Bible communicates truth on different levels at the same time. So we can learn about marriage from the Song of Solomon and also see the spiritual dimensions of the book without any contradiction."

Later, with a grin, he showed me his literature textbook which analyzed a brief poem at length, explaining its "three tiers of meaning." "The man in this poem was literally writing about sundown," he said, "but also about the decay of civilizations, and about his own death, all at the same time. If poets can do that, I guess people shouldn't be surprised that God's Word contains different applications of truth in one book."

This young Christian's questions are understandable in light of the confusion that has reigned in the past concerning the Song of Solomon. In fact, no book of the Bible has been as attacked or misunderstood through the ages as this one. It may sound strange to contemporary ears, but for centuries theologians did not want to admit the plain truth: that the Song of Solomon was speaking of godly marriage between a husband and wife who loved each other!

We need to understand that from the beginning some of Satan's strongest attacks on the biblical viewpoint have been mounted against Christian marriage. To undermine biblical truth in this area, Satan effectively used the philosophies of the pagan world to permeate the church. The attitude of the Gentile pagan in the ancient world toward love, marriage, and sex clashed head-on with the biblical view as given in Genesis 1 and 2; Proverbs 5; Jesus' teachings in the Gospels and His attendance at the wedding feast; 1 Corinthians 7:1–5; 1 Timothy 4:1–5; Hebrews 13:4; Ephesians 5:22–33; *and* the Song of Solomon.

What *did* the pagan believe about sexual love in marriage? While the Bible taught that marriage was good, that human sexuality was created and commanded by God for marriage, and that marriage with its one-flesh relationship provided a sacred picture of Jesus Christ and the church, the pagan thought of sex in marriage as unholy, impure, and certainly as *not good.* The pagan indulged in sex, all right, often in perversions of sex. The temples of the pagan gods were, in effect, sordid houses of prostitution and debauchery of every kind in the name of "worship." But to the pagan mind, holiness and purity belonged to the people who had renounced sex forever—never to a married couple still engaging in the act of marriage.

Virginity became the symbol of spirituality, just as the Roman Vestal Virgins had represented ideal Virtue. At least three streams of philosophy totally foreign to the Word of God crept into the thinking of Christians and distorted the perspective of the church on the sacredness of married love for centuries to come.

First, the Greek Stoics, scorning human emotions, began the custom of allegorizing human passions in literature until human feelings became only pale symbols of "spiritual" concepts. This approach the church applied to the Song of Solomon. Second, the Greek philosopher, Plato, had taught that you could not have *both* earthly love and spiritual love; therefore, it was better to renounce the earthly and physical in hope of acquiring the spiritual. This view strongly influenced Christian teachers. Third, the Gnostic cults taught married couples to renounce all human sexuality in marriage in favor of a mystical "marriage" with the Spirit.

Obviously, the Song of Solomon contradicted these views and could not be tolerated by churchmen who held them unless its teachings were "spiritualized" so that the marriage described in the Song became only a symbol of mystical marriage with God.

Not surprisingly then, the church throughout the Middle Ages regarded celibacy as the greatest of virtues, and its teachers continued the attempt to turn the Song of Solomon with its joyous celebration of sacred married love into something else—a spiritualized allegory free from the "carnal taint" of human love in marriage. Only a few brave monks and an occasional bishop taught the Song in its plain sense as a work praising marriage and the dignity and purity of human love springing from God's love.

The holy beauty of wedded love was rediscovered by Christians in the sixteenth century when the Puritans and other reformers looked to the Bible as the final authority for doctrine and conduct. The Puritans unanimously declared that the sex drive was created by God and therefore was good in principle. And some of them pointed to the Song of Solomon as providing instruction in perfect married love.

Today the uninformed tend to tag Puritans as prudes—perhaps because they always insisted on the sacredness and privacy of sex in marriage and were appalled by sexual perversions just as the Bible is. But their attitudes toward sexual love between husband and wife were expressive, not repressive; positive, not negative; and both joyous and reverent. In *Paradise Lost,* the great Puritan poet, John Milton, hailed wedded love as a

> Perpetual fountain of domestic sweets,
> Whose bed is undefiled and chaste pronounced.

Unfortunately, the Victorian embarrassment with sex in the nineteenth century kept allegorical interpretations of the Song of Solomon in vogue. Those who saw the Song as plainly teaching the stages of true and chaste love in marriage were shouted down, sometimes by absurd arguments. For example, in a debate on the Song of Solomon, when Dr. J. Pye Smith showed the allegorical method to be "contrary to all the laws of language and reason and detrimental to real religion," Dr. James Bennett answered that there *had* to be an allegorical interpretation because "the language of the Song in its literal sense is contrary to the nature and modesty of women!"

We can better understand the basis for that remarkable statement by hearing what the medical expert on Victorian sexuality believed about women. In a book called *The Functions and Disorders of the Re-productive Organs,* Dr. William Acton asserted:

> The majority of women (happily for them) are not very much troubled with sexual feelings of any kind. . . . The best mothers, wives, and managers of households know little or nothing of sexual indulgences. Love of home, children, and domestic duties are the only passions they feel. . . . A modest women seldom desires any sexual gratification for herself.

For the past few decades the air has been clearing. Bible scholars have returned to the literal interpretation of the Song of Solomon as the foremost biblical teaching on love in marriage by example. It is now recognized as a carefully constructed unit with a clear message rather than (as some had said) an odd assortment of writings carelessly put together like sheet music stuck in a music rack. New scholarship is being directed to the understanding of the metaphors that make up the poetic imagery of the Song of Solomon. Nowhere can the fruits of this study be enjoyed more than in *A Song for Lovers* by S. Craig Glickman—an excellent book for you to use in your further study of the Song of Solomon.

Long ago the "mysteries" of Solomon's Song were likened to a lock for which the key had been lost. But, as Marvin H. Pope, Professor of Northwest Semitic Languages at Yale University, observes,

> The door to the understanding of the Song was not locked, nor even shut, but has been wide open to any who dared to see and enter. The barrier has been a psychological aversion to the obvious, somewhat like the Emperor's New Clothes. The trouble has been that interpreters who dared acknowledge the plain sense of the Song were assailed as enemies of truth and decency. . . . In recent decades there has been a general and growing tendency to reject allegory and freely admit the application of the Song to human physical love.[1]

As we consider the Song, we need to keep in mind the inspired view of the Hebrews who wrote the Old Testament. To them there was no real division between the love of God, the love of neighbor, and the sensuous love of husband and wife. In each case the same root word—*ahavah*—is used:

"You shall love (*ahavah*) the LORD your God" (Deuteronomy 6:5 NASB).

"You shall love (*ahavah*) your neighbor as yourself" (Leviticus 19:18 NASB).

"How fair and how pleasant art thou, O love (*ahavah*), for delights!" (Song of Solomon 7:6).

Love between husband and wife is seen as a Divine imperative, as the fulfillment of the will of God. The Song of Solomon teaches the searcher of its truths that romantic, sensual love is His gift and creation for marriage—that He honors and blesses true romantic love between husband and wife: therefore, love can be developed in one's marriage to the glory of God.

The very thing that offended and perplexed the Victorians such as Dr. Bennett is the characteristic that sets the Song apart from other poetry of its day. This is the total absence of male chauvinism and the equal role of the wife in the love affair. In the wisdom of the Holy Spirit, the book was written from the woman's viewpoint. This dramatically differs from other ancient oriental writings, according to Professor Chaim Rabin of the Hebrew University in Jerusalem. The bride (we will call her *Shulamith,* the feminine counterpart of Solomon, i.e., *Mrs. Solomon*) frankly expresses her longing for her husband in a way that reflects the reality of Genesis 3:16: "Unto the woman he said, I will greatly multiply thy sorrow and thy conception; in sorrow thou shalt bring forth children; and *thy desire shall be to thy husband,* and he shall rule over thee" (italics mine). But, as we will see, this desire is met with equal intensity by the husband. It is as if in a marriage rightly corresponding to God's design that part of the curse on mankind is reversed in the free interchange of love between husband and wife.

If Shulamith is the central figure of the narrative, the husband (Solomon in the early years of his reign) is sensed and seen through her eyes as the strong, vital, attractive man who finds her working in the vineyards, woos her, wins her love, makes her his queen, and causes her love for him to deepen and intensify with the passing of time.

Briefly, let us consider how this man loved his wife. What were his "secrets"? The husband trying to follow New Testament admonitions in carrying out his role can find no better guidelines and examples of Ephesians 5 in action than those provided by Solomon in the Song of Solomon.

Shulamith, we are told, was a country girl, chastely brought up, but required by her stepbrothers to work in the vineyards so that her skin became deeply tanned in contrast to the elegant, pampered, white-skinned ladies of the court. She felt inferior, unworthy to be Solomon's queen, but her husband skillfully and lovingly built up her self-image. He did this first of all by praise. He sensitively praised her in the areas where she felt most insecure. He voiced appreciation of her physical appearance and her lovely character in specifics, not in vague generalities. He compared her with all other women so favorably that she could rest in the sureness that she pleased him as no other woman could. He told her, in fact, that she was flawless . . . perfect in his eyes . . . *altogether lovely.* He did not say this just when they were courting or on their wedding night. He continued to praise her in the maturity of their marriage.

Husband, your wife needs to hear these same things from your lips. Every wife needs to be praised for her beauty by her husband. It is this that will make her beautiful!

But more is to be learned from this husband. He not only praised Shulamith; he also totally refrained from criticizing her. Never was there a word of criticism, not even when, perhaps, she deserved it. His words to her were always positive, and they bore fruit in the kind of loving, responsive wife she became.

His love and approval was not just a private matter. The king showed publicly his adoration and respect for his wife. In the royal banqueting house, his banner over her was love. In other words, it became obvious to everyone that Shulamith was the most important person in his kingdom—to be honored, respected, and protected in every way. He treated her like a queen, and that is what she became in truth. At the same time he privately loved her in such a way that she could finally give herself completely to him, withholding nothing of her trust, her thoughts, and her love.

Husband, how do you treat your wife publicly? Do you open doors for her . . . seat her at the table . . . hold her coat for her? These small courtesies give honor to the wife as the more delicate vessel. After all, your wife cannot *see* your mental attitude toward her. You must show it by simple actions that display your love for her and your care and protective concern for her wellbeing. Is your love a banner over her when other people are present? Do you often look at her? Respond to her glances? Listen to her? Make her feel she is the most important person in *your* kingdom? If you want a queen for a wife, publicly treat her as one.

Of course, the marriage in the Song of Solomon had problems of adjustment as all marriages do. It is no sin and is not unusual to have natural differences with your mate. The test of emotional and spiritual maturity is how you work these problems out.

Let's take one example from the Song. Shulamith had difficulty in adjusting to Solomon's demanding schedule as chief of state. One night, perhaps when he had promised to come home early, he did not arrive until very late. By this time she may have been offended; at the least she was more concerned about her own comfort and schedule than about loving her husband. So she said she was not ready to see him, and she would not open her bedroom door to him.

Now observe how he handled the situation. Instead of making an issue of it, he quietly withdrew for a few hours to let her think it over. He left her alone, and gave her time to deal with her negative feelings. Please note that he did not rebuke her. Instead, he left a sign of his love for her at the door—a gift of rare perfume.

Because he had not reacted as an irate husband, but had behaved as a lover, his wife quickly realized that she was in the wrong and should correct her mistake. As soon as he withdrew she began to long for him and went out to look for him. When the two were together again, the husband reassured his wife with tender love words repeated from their wedding night. In other words, "I love you just as much as ever." And wrapped up in his love, unspoken, was instant forgiveness for her rejection of him.

Certainly it was necessary for Shulamith to learn to adjust to her husband's occupation. The same is true for all wives. The New Testament Scriptures tell the wife to adapt herself to her husband. Even though your husband is not a king, his calling should be as important to you as if he were a monarch. You should show a vital interest in his work, not just in his paycheck. You should respect what your husband does for a living and should be able to admire the way in which he does it.

I want you to consider how this wife loved her husband. It was by her response. Brought up as a chaste young woman, she now was free to delight in her husband's caresses, and she wholeheartedly, exquisitely responded to his lovemaking. Obviously, she thought much about her husband. Her thoughts were occupied with him even when they could not be together because of his duties. She respected his manly character and often expressed her admiration of him to others. When he complimented her, she responded with her own apt expressions of praise and left him in no doubt as to her feelings for him. She was thrilled by his touch at all times, eager for his embraces, and she let him know it. She enjoyed his company and planned delightful times for the two of them. She stored up delights for him—both new and old ways to please him.

To see how she blossomed in the security of his love, we can compare three statements she made. When she first fell in love with him, she said, "My beloved is mine and I am his" (2:16). Her possession of him was uppermost in her mind. But later in their relationship she said, "I am my beloved's and my beloved is mine" (6:3). Note that she reversed the order! Now his possession of her was more important. Finally, in the fullness of their love, she said, "I am my beloved's and his desire is toward me" (7:10). By this time she was so focused on him that she had forgotten about possessing him. She had lost herself in the greatness of his love, and she gloried only in his desire for her. It is here that we see the seeming reversal of the situation pronounced in Genesis 3:16, for the word in the original language translated *desire* in "his desire is for me" is the same word used in Genesis 3:16 to describe the woman's strong, often unreturned desire for her husband—a word used only three times in all of Scripture. Now, this desire has become mutual!

Husbands, I want you to especially consider this request that Solomon made of Shulamith. He said, "Let me see thy countenance, let me hear thy voice; for sweet is thy voice, and thy countenance is lovely" (2:14).

This speaks of a man who loved to look into his wife's eyes, who loved to talk with her and to hear what she had to say to him. No wonder she became completely secure in his love! As a result of this openness and communication between them, their relationship could grow and mature until it became many-faceted, expressing all the aspects of love that we have discussed in this book. He was her brother, lover, teacher, friend, companion, husband; she was equally everything to him. Their conversation, their lovemaking, their enjoyment in being together became even deeper and richer in quality.

It is interesting that at the end of the Song, the husband's last words were, "Let me hear your voice" (see 8:13). These were like the words he had first whispered to her when they were courting. Then he had compared her to a gentle dove hidden from him whose voice he wanted to hear so that he could come to know the inmost person of her heart. Now he still longed with the same intensity to grow in the knowledge of his fascinating wife. And his wife repeated her longing to make love to him. The romance of their marriage had only increased with the years! At the same time, their physical love-life had become better and better, nourishing their entire relationship.

No doubt their experience enabled Solomon to write so feelingly in Proverbs 5:18–19: "Rejoice in the wife of your youth. As a loving hind and a graceful doe, let her breasts satisfy you at all times; be exhilarated always with her love" (NASB).

At the conclusion of this chapter you can read Glickman's "Interpretive Paraphrase of the Song of Solomon" to see for yourself the ways this couple built their love for each other. You will note that physical caressing was an important aspect of their relationship, but that all the facets of love sparkled in this marriage like the many-sided reflections of a perfectly cut diamond.

Then I encourage you to study the Song of Solomon in several modern translations of the Bible, using A Song for Lovers as a guide, always noticing the delicacy of this couple's language of love and remembering that they chose certain metaphors to express their deepest feelings in a most vivid and memorable way.

It is important for you to share the Song with your marriage partner so that you both can be aware of the truth that the love relationship you experience is a part of your worship of God.

A high point of the Song comes in chapter 4 with the wedding night of the bride and groom after the wedding procession of chapter 3. The first verse of chapter 5 contains the joyous words of the husband after their lovemaking: "I have come into my garden, my sister, my bride; I have gathered my myrrh along with my balsam. I have eaten my honeycomb with my honey; I have drunk my wine with my milk" (NASB). The young husband is describing their love as a beautiful garden and as a wonderful feast he has celebrated.

Then another voice speaks—a mysterious voice. Who can it be? Wedding guests? On the wedding night? Hardly! Only One could be with the couple at this most intimate time and that must be God Himself, the Creator who had prepared this couple for their night of His design. It is God who is approving and affirming the love physically shared this night. As Glickman explains, "He takes pleasure in what has taken place. He is glad they have drunk deeply of the fountain of love. Two of his own have expenenced love in all the beauty and fervor and purity that he intended for them."

God's words are: "Eat, O loved ones; drink and be drunk, O Lovers" (Song of Solomon 5:1b). In other words, Continue to enjoy the feast of love I have prepared for you!

When we study the Song of Solomon we begin to realize just how fortunate we are to have this inspired pattern for our own love-life. Now let it bless your marriage from this time forth. A good way to begin is by reading the following paraphrase aloud *together* preferably while sitting close to each other.

THE MOST BEAUTIFUL LOVE SONG EVER WRITTEN

Shulamith's First Days in the Palace (1:2–11)

The King's fiancée, Shulamith, in soliloquy

How I wish he would shower me with kisses for his exquisite kisses are more desirable than the finest wine. The gentle fragrance of your cologne brings the enchantment of springtime. Yes, it is the rich fragrance of your heart that awakens my love and respect. Yes, it is your character that brings you admiration from every girl of the court. How I long for you to come take me with you to run and laugh through the countryside of this kingdom. (You see, the King had brought me to the kingdom's palace.)

Women of the court to the King

We will always be very thankful and happy because of you, O King. For we love to speak of the inspiring beauty of your love.

Shulamith in soliloquy

They rightly love a person like you, my King.

Shulamith to women of the court

I realize that I do not display the fair and delicate skin of one raised in the comfort of a palace. I am darkened from the sun—indeed, as dark as the tents of the humble desert nomads I used to work beside. But now I might say that I am also as dark as the luxurious drapery of the King's palace. Nevertheless, what loveliness I do have is not so weak that the gaze of the sun should make it bow its head in shame. And if the glare of the sun could not shame me, please know that neither will the glare of your contempt. I could not help it that my stepbrothers were angry with me and demanded that I work in the vineyard they had leased from the King. It was impossible for me to care for it and for the vineyard of my own appearance.

Shulamith to King

Please tell me, you whom I love so deeply, where you take your royal flock for its afternoon rest. I don't want to search randomly for you, wandering about like a woman of the streets.

Women of the court to Shulamith

If you do not know, O fairest among women, why not simply go ahead and follow the trail of the flocks, and then pasture your flock beside the shepherds' huts?

King to Shulamith

Your presence captivates attention as thoroughly as a single mare among a hundred stallions. And how perfectly your lovely jewelry and necklace adorn your lovely face.

Women of the court to Shulamith

We shall make even more elegant necklaces of gold and silver to adorn her face.

In a Palace Room (1:12–14)

Shulamith in soliloquy

While my King was dining at his table, my perfume refreshed me with its soothing fragrance. For my King is the fragrance and my thoughts of him are like a sachet of perfume hung around my neck, over my heart, continually refreshing me. How dear he is to me, as dear as the delicate henna blossoms in the oasis of En-Gedi. What joy I have found in that oasis!

In the Countryside (1:15–2:7)

King to Shulamith

You are so beautiful, my love. You are so beautiful. Your soft eyes are as gentle as doves.

Shulamith to King

And you are handsome, my love, and so enjoyable. It's so wonderful to walk through our home of nature together. Here the cool grass is a soft couch to lie upon, to catch our breath and to gaze at the beams and rafters of our house—the towering cedars and cypresses all around. Lying here I feel like a rose from the valley of Sharon, the loveliest flower in the valley.

King to Shulamith

Only the loveliest flower in the valley? No, my love. To me you are like a flower among thorns compared with any other woman in the world.

Shulamith to King

And you, my precious King, are like a fruitful apple tree among the barren trees of the forest compared with all the men in the world.

Shulamith in soliloquy

No longer do I labor in the heat of the sun. I find cool rest in the shade of this apple tree. Nourishment from its magical fruit brings me the radiant health only love brings. And he loves me so much. Even when he brings me to the great royal banquets attended by the most influential people in this kingdom and beyond, he is never so concerned for them that his love and his care for me is not as plain as a royal banner lifted high above my head.

How dear he is to me! My delightful peace in his love makes me so weak from joy that I must rest in his arms for strength. Yet such loving comfort makes me more joyful and weaker still. How I wish he could lay me down beside him and embrace me! But how important it is I promise, with the gentle gazelles and deer of the countryside as my witnesses, not to attempt to awaken love until love is pleased to awaken itself.

On the Way to the Countryside (2:8–17)

Shulamith in soliloquy

I hear my beloved. Look! He is coming to visit. And he is as dashing as a young stag leaping upon the mountains, springing upon the hills. There he is, standing at the door, trying to peer through the window and peep through the lattice. At last he speaks.

King to Shulamith

Come, my darling, my fair one, come with me. For look, the winter has passed. The rain is over and gone. The blossoms have appeared in the land. The time of singing has come, and the voice of the turtledove has been heard in the land. The fig tree has ripened its figs, and the vines in blossom have given forth fragrance. Let us go, my darling, my lovely one; come along with me. O my precious, gentle dove. You have been like a dove in the clefts of the mountain rocks, in the hidden places along the mountain trails. Now come out from the hidden place and let me see you. Let me hear the coo of your voice. For your voice is sweet and you are as gracefully beautiful as a dove in flight silhouetted against a soft blue sky. My love, what we have together is a valuable treasure; it is like a garden of the loveliest flowers in the world. Let us promise each other to catch any foxes that could spoil our garden when now at long last it blossoms for us.

Shulamith in soliloquy

My beloved belongs to me and I belong to him—this tender King who grazes his flock among the lilies.

Shulamith to the King

How I long for the time when all through the night, until the day takes its first breath and the morning shadows flee from the sun, that you, my beloved King, might be a gazelle upon the hills of my breasts.

Shulamith Waits for Her Fiancé (3:1–5)

Shulamith in soliloquy

How I miss the one I love so deeply. I could not wait to see him. I thought to myself, "I must get up and find him. I will get up now and look around the streets and squares of the city for him. Surely I'll be able

to find this one I love so much." But I could not find him. When the
night watchmen of the city found me, I immediately asked them if they
had seen this one I loved so deeply. But they had not. Yet no sooner did
I pass from them than I found my beloved. I held on and on and would
not let him go until I could bring him to my home. I still held on until my
fearful anxieties left me and I felt peaceful once again. How hard it is to
be patient! You women of the court, we must promise ourselves, by the
gazelles and deer of the field, not to awaken love until love is pleased to
awaken itself.

The Wedding Day (3:6–11)

Poet

What can this be coming from the outskirts of the city like columns of
smoke, perfumed clouds of myrrh and frankincense, clouds of the scented
powders of the merchant? Look! It is the royal procession with Solomon
carried upon his lavish couch by his strongest servants. And take a look
at all those soldiers around it! That is the imperial guard, the sixty
mightiest warriors in the entire kingdom. Each one is an expert with his
weapon and valiant in battle. Yet now each one has a sword at his side
only for the protection of the King and his bride. Look at the luxurious
couch Solomon is carried on. He has had it made especially for this day.
He made its frame from the best timber of Lebanon. Its posts are made
of silver, its back of gold, and its seat of royal purple cloth. And do you
see its delicate craftsmanship! It reflects the skill of the women of the
court who gave their best work out of love for the King and his bride.
Let us all go out and look upon King Solomon wearing his elegant wedding crown. Let us go out and see him on the most joyful day of his life.

The Wedding Night (4:1–5:1)

King to Shulamith

You are so beautiful, my love, you are so beautiful. Your soft eyes are as
gentle as doves from behind your wedding veil. Your hair is as captivating as the flowing movement of a flock descending a mountain at sunset.
Your full and lovely smile is as cheerful and sparkling as pairs of young
lambs scurrying up from a washing. And only a thread of scarlet could
have outlined your lips so perfectly. Your cheeks flush with the redness
of the pomegranate's hue. Yet you walk with dignity and stand with the

strength of a fortress. Your necklace sparkles like the shields upon the fortress tower. But your breasts are as soft and gentle as fawns grazing among lilies. And now at last, all through the night—until the day takes its first breath and the morning shadows flee from the sun—I will be a gazelle upon the hills of your perfumed breasts. You are completely and perfectly beautiful, my love, and flawless in every way. Now bring your thoughts completely to me, my love. Leave your fears in the far away mountains and rest in the security of my arms.

You excite me, my darling bride; you excite me with but a glance of your eyes, with but a strand of your necklace. How wonderful are your caresses, my beloved bride. Your love is more sweetly intoxicating than the finest wine. And the fragrance of your perfume is better than the finest spices. The richness of honey and milk is under your tongue, my love. And the fragrance of your garments is like the fragrance of the forests of Lebanon.

You are a beautiful garden fashioned only for me, my darling bride. Yes, like a garden kept only for me. Or like a fresh fountain sealed just for me. Your garden is overflowing with beautiful and delicate flowers of every scent and color. It is a paradise of pomegranates with luscious fruit, with henna blossoms and nard, nard and saffron, calamus and cinnamon with trees of frankincense, myrrh and aloes with all the choicest of spices. And you are pure as fresh water, yet more than a mere fountain. You are a spring for many gardens—a well of life-giving water. No, even more, you are like the fresh streams flowing from Lebanon which give life to the entire countryside.

Shulamith to King

Awake, O north wind, and come, wind of the south. Let your breezes blow upon my garden and carry its fragrant spices to my beloved. May he follow the enchanting spices to my garden and come in to enjoy its luscious fruit.

King to Shulamith

I have rejoiced in the richness of your garden, my darling bride. I have been intoxicated by the fragrance of your myrrh and perfume. I have tasted the sweetness of your love like honey. I have enjoyed the sweetness of your love like an exquisite wine and the refreshment of your love like the coolness of milk.

Poet to couple

Rejoice in your lovemaking as you would rejoice at a great feast, O

lovers. Eat and drink from this feast to the fullest. Drink, drink and be
drunk with one another's love.

A Problem Arises (5:2–6:3)

Shulamith in soliloquy

I was half asleep when I heard the sound of my beloved husband knock-
ing gently upon the door of our palace chamber. He whispered softly,
"I'm back from the countryside, my love, my darling, my perfect wife."
My only answer was a mumbled, "I've already gone to sleep, my dear."
After all, I had already prepared for bed. I had washed my face and put on
my old nightgown.

But then my beloved gently opened the door and I realized I really
wanted to see him. I had hesitated too long though. By the time I arose to
open the door, he had already walked away, leaving only a gift of my favorite perfume as a reminder of his love for me. Deep within my heart I
was reawakened to my love for him. It was just that the fatigue and distractions of the day had brought my hesitating response. I decided to try
to find him. I threw on my clothes, went outside the palace and began to
call out to him.

But things went from bad to worse. The night watchmen of the city
mistook me for a secretive criminal sneaking about in the night. They ar-
rested me in their customarily rough style, then jerking my shawl from
my head they saw the face of their newly found suspect—a "great" police
force we have!

O, you women of the court, if you see my beloved King, please tell
him that I deeply love him, that I am lovesick for him.

Women of the court to Shulamith

What makes your husband better than any other, O fairest of women?
What makes him so great that you request this so fervently of us?

Shulamith to women of the court

My beloved husband is strikingly handsome, the first to be noticed among
ten thousand men. When I look at him, I see a face with a tan more richly
golden than gold itself. His hair is as black as a raven's feathers and as
lovely as palm leaves atop the stately palm tree. When I look into his
eyes, they are as gentle as doves peacefully resting by streams of water.

They are as pure and clear as health can make them.

When he places his cheek next to mine, it is as fragrant as a garden of perfumed flowers. His soft lips are as sweet and scented as lilies dripping with nectar. And how tender are his fingers like golden velvet when he touches me! He is a picture of strength and vitality. His stomach is as firm as a plate of ivory rippling with sapphires. And his legs are as strong and elegant as alabaster pillars set upon pedestals of fine gold. His appearance is like majestic Mt. Lebanon, prominent with its towering cedars.

But beyond all this, the words of his heart are full of charm and delight. He is completely wonderful in every way. This is the one I love so deeply, and this is the one who is my closest friend, O women of the palace court.

Women of the court to Shulamith
Where has your beloved gone, then, O fairest among women? Where has he gone? We will help you find him.

Shulamith to women of the court
Oh, I know him well enough to know where he has gone. He likes to contemplate as he walks through the garden and cares for his special little flock among the lilies. I know him, for I belong to him and he belongs to me—this gentle shepherd who pastures his flock among the lilies.

The Problem Resolved (6:4–13)

King to Shulamith
My darling, did you know that you are as lovely as the city of Tirzah glittering on the horizon of night? No, more than that you are as lovely as the fair city of Jerusalem. Your beauty is as breathtaking as scores of marching warriors. (No, do not look at me like that now, my love; I have more to tell you.)

Do you remember what I said on our wedding night? It is still just as true. Your hair is as captivating as the flowing movement of a flock descending a mountain at sunset. Your lovely smile is as cheerful and sparkling as pairs of young lambs scurrying up from a washing. And your cheeks still flush with the redness of the pomegranate's hue.

King in soliloquy
The palace is full of its aristocratic ladies and dazzling mistresses belonging to the noblemen of the court. But my lovely wife, my dove, my flaw-

less one, is unique among them all. And these ladies and mistresses realize it too. They too must praise her. As we approached them in my chariot, they eventually perceived that we were together again.

Women of the court to one another
Who is that on the horizon like the dawn, now fair as the moon but now plain and bright as the sun and as majestic as scores of marching warriors?

Shulamith in the chariot in soliloquy
I went down to the garden where I knew my King would be. I wanted to see if the fresh flowers and fruits of spring had come. I wanted to see if our reunion might bring a new season of spring love for my husband and me. Before I knew what happened, we were together again and riding past the palace court in his chariot. I can still hear them calling out, "Return, return O Shulamith; return that we may gaze at the beloved wife of the King."

King to Shulamith
How they love to look upon the incomparable grace and beauty of a queen.

In the Royal Bedroom (7:1–10)

King to Shulamith
How delicate are your feet in sandals, my royal prince's daughter! The curves of your hips are as smooth and graceful as the curves of elegant jewelry, perfectly fashioned by the skillful hands of a master artist. As delectable as a feast of wine and bread is your stomach—your navel is like the goblet of wine, and your stomach is the soft warm bread. Your breasts are as soft and gentle as fawns grazing among lilies, twins of a gazelle, and your neck is smooth as ivory to the touch. Your eyes are as peaceful as the pools of water in the valley of Heshbon, near the gate of the populous city.

Yet how strong you walk in wisdom and discretion. You are, indeed, as majestically beautiful as Mt. Carmel. Your long flowing hair is as cool and soft as silken threads draped round my neck, yet strong enough to bind me as your captive forever. How lovely and delightful you are, my dear, and how especially delightful is your love! You are as graceful and

splendrous as a palm tree silhouetted against the sky. Yes, a palm tree—
and your breasts are its luscious fruit.

I think I shall climb my precious palm tree and take its tender fruit gently into my hand. O my precious one, let your breasts be like the tender fruit to my taste, and now let me kiss you and breathe your fragrant breath. Let me kiss you and taste a sweetness better than wine.

Shulamith to King

And savor every drop, my lover, and let its sweetness linger long upon your lips, and let every drop of this wine bring a peaceful sleep.

Shulamith in soliloquy

I belong to my beloved husband and he loves me from the depths of his soul.

In the Countryside (7:11–8:14)

Shulamith to King

Spring's magic flowers have perfumed the pastel countryside and enchanted the hearts of all lovers. Come, my precious lover; every delicious fruit of spring is ours for the taking. Let us return to our springtime cottage of towering cedars and cypresses where the plush green grass is its endless carpet and the orchards are its shelves for every luscious fruit. I have prepared a basketful for you, my love, to give you in a sumptuous banquet of love beneath the sky.

I wish we could pretend you were my brother, my real little brother. I could take you outside to play, and playfully kiss you whenever I wished. But then I could also take your hand and bring you inside and you could teach me and share with me your deep understanding of life. Then how I wish you would lay me down beside you and love me.

Shulamith to women of the court

I encourage you not to try to awaken love until love is pleased to awaken itself. How wonderful it is when it blossoms in the proper season.

Shulamith to King

Do you remember where our love began? Under the legendary sweetheart tree, of course, where every love begins and grows and then brings forth a newborn child, yet not without the pain of birth. Neither did our love begin without the pain, the fruitful pain of birth. O, my darling lover, make me your most precious possession held securely in your arms, held close to your heart. True love is as strong and irreversible as the onward march of death. True love never ceases to care, and it would no more give up the beloved than the grave would give up the dead.

The fires of true love can never be quenched because the source of its flame is God himself. Even were a river of rushing water to pass over it, the flame would yet shine forth. Of all the gifts in the world, this priceless love is the most precious and possessed only by those to whom it is freely given. For no man could purchase it with money, even the richest man in the world.

King to Shulamith
Do you remember how it was given to us?

Shulamith to King
My love, I truly believe I was being prepared for it long before I even dreamed of romance. I remember hearing my brothers talking one evening. It was shortly after my father died, and they were concerned to raise me properly, to prepare me for the distant day of marriage. They were like a roomful of fathers debating about what to do with their only daughter. They finally resolved simply to punish and restrict me if I were promiscuous but to reward and encourage me if I were chaste. How thankful I am that I made it easy for them. I could see even when I was very young that I wanted to keep myself for the one dearest man in my life.

And then you came. And everything I ever wanted I found in you. There I was, working daily in the vineyard my brothers had leased from you. And you "happened" to pass by and see me. That's how our love began.

I remember when I worked in that vineyard that a thousand dollars went to you and two hundred dollars for the ones taking care of its fruit for you. Now I am your vineyard, my lover, and I gladly give the entire thousand dollars of my worth to you; I give myself completely, withholding nothing of my trust, my thoughts, my care, my love. But my dear King, let us not forget that two hundred dollars belongs to the ones who took care of the fruit of my vineyard for you. How thankful we must be to my family who helped prepare me for you.

King to Shulamith
My darling, whose home is the fragrant garden, everyone listens for the sound of your voice, but let me alone hear it now.

Shulamith to King

Hurry, then, my beloved. And again be like a gazelle or young stag on the hills of my perfumed breasts.*

*Taken from A Song for *Louers* by S. Craig Glickman. © 1976 by Inter-Varsity Chrlstian Fellowship of the USA and used *by* permission of InterVarsity Press.

13

Prescription for a Superb Marriage

IF YOU HAVE read and absorbed the love-life principles we have discussed up to this point, you are ready for my prescription for a superb marriage.

The prescription involves a practical course of action for husband and wife that is both uncomplicated and effective. You will be able to remember it readily because it is called the B-E-S-T, an acronym representing the four positive elements that will transform any marriage. These are not steps to be tried one at a time, but four measures to be taken simultaneously and maintained consistently. If necessary, they can be implemented by either partner alone. In many cases, one of you will have to make the first move without any promise of cooperation from the other. So, if you want the best marriage possible with the mate you have chosen, then give your partner the *best:*

> *B lessing*
> *E difying*
> *S haring*
> *T ouching*

1) Blessing

Perhaps you have never thought of blessing as a practical element to be introduced into marriage. The principle of blessing is a biblical one, and the Christian is commanded to practice it, most particularly in response to annoyance or provocation. Learning this important technique of response will carry you through the difficult moments that occur in any marriage and will bring peace to the troubled waters of your relationship. The practice of blessing puts an end to the volley of sharp words that mars so many love affairs, and that is only the beginning of its benefits for you

The word *"blessing"* in the New Testament (*eulogia*) is based on two Greek words: *eu,* meaning "well," and *logos,* meaning "word." The first way of blessing your marriage partner is to speak well of him or her, and to respond with good words even when your partner's speech becomes harsh, critical, or insulting. The Lord Jesus gave us an example we are advised to follow: when He was reviled, He did not revile in return, and when He suffered, He uttered no threats, but kept entrusting Himself to His Father in heaven. *In the same way,* Scripture says, we are to live as husbands and wives. The wife described in Proverbs 31 receives praise because she opens her mouth in wisdom and the law of kindness is on her tongue. James warns us about the inconsistency of sending forth both blessing and cursing from our mouth as if we were a fountain pouring out a mixture of fresh and bitter water. And Peter tells us that if we love life and want to see "good days," we will keep our tongue from speaking evil in any form.

To put this in the most practical terms, you have the power to bless your marriage by the words you speak to your partner. You can also bless by learning when to be silent.

Three other aspects of blessing are found in Scripture. You bless by bestowing practical benefits upon; simply by doing kind things for another person. When is the last time you did something kind for your mate just to please, not as a duty, but as a gift of blessing? This should be a daily part of your marriage.

You also bless by showing thankfulness and appreciation. Whatever you can find to appreciate in your partner, make it known verbally. Thank your partner and thank God too.

Finally, you bless by calling God's favor down in prayer. How much are you praying for your partner? And on what basis? So things will be easier for you? Or is it prayer for your partner's good and blessing?

To sum up, you bless your partner and your marriage in these four ways: (1) through your good and loving words spoken to him and about him; (2) through your practical behavior, which shows loving kindness toward him in actions large and small; (3) through conveying your attitude of thankfulness and appreciation for him; (4) through your prayer to God on his behalf. Good words . . . kind actions . . . thankful appreciation . . . and intercessory prayer for your partner.

Blessing in its fullness will work wonders when applied to your marriage. No matter how your partner treats you, blessing should be your response. Scripture tells us that the Lord protects and honors the husband or wife who applies biblical principles all the time. You have been promised good days as a result of giving blessing. The Lord has promised to protect you and hear your prayers. And, when blessing your partner, you take yourself out of the way so that the Lord is free to work in the life of the partner who may be rendering evil.

If all of this helps a troubled marriage, think of how a good marriage can be enhanced when two people begin to bless each other!

2) Edifying

Edifying, a biblical term often used in the New Testament, refers to the building up of individuals. Although Christians can be edified spiritually by preaching, I do not recommend this means of edifying your marriage partner. When I suggested to one wife that she begin to edify her husband, she said, startled, "Do you mean I am supposed to *preach* to him?"

I quickly assured her that preaching was not what I had in mind; that by edifying, I meant building her husband up in every aspect of his personality, cheering him on in every area of life, and increasing his sense of self-worth with the result that his capacity to love and give of himself would be increased as well.

Elizabeth Barrett Browning expressed the principle of edifying in a few succinct words when she wrote to the man she would marry, "Make thy love larger to enlarge my worth." When we speak of edifying, we are referring to an expanded love expressed in positive ways that enlarges the self-worth of the beloved. You see, this is a great gift that you can give to your partner.

We can appreciate the psychological connotations of edifying by considering the root meaning of the word. The English word *edify* goes back to an old Latin word *aedes,* which originally meant a hearth or fireplace. A fireplace has emotional associations for most of us, representing cozy warmth, loving togetherness, and, perhaps, a special tranquillity. The hearth was the center of activity in ancient times, the only place of warmth and light in the home, and the place where the daily bread was prepared. Certainly it was the place where people were drawn together, comforted, and sustained in the midst of the harsh realities of life.

In today's marriage, the process of edifying holds a similar place of importance in the emotional sense. We find as we study the New Testament passages that speak of edifying that three golden strands are interwoven: personal encouragement, inner strengthening, and the establishment of peace and harmony between individuals. For example:

"So let us then definitely aim for and eagerly pursue what makes for harmony and for mutual upbuilding (edification and development) of one another" (Romans 14:19 AMPLIFIED).

"Let each one of us make it a practice to please (make happy) his neighbor for his good and for his true welfare, to edify him—that is, to strengthen him and build him up spiritually" (Romans 15:2 AMPLIFIED).

"Therefore encourage one another and build each other up, just as in fact you are doing" (I Thessalonians 5:11 NIV).

1 Corinthians 8:1 sums up the matter of edifying: "Love builds up (NIV).

But how do you build up your mate? A careful study of New Testament principles and the example of the Song of Solomon indicates that husbands and wives each have their own ways of edifying. In brief, the husband edifies his wife by praising her. The wife edifies her husband by her loving response to him.

Husbands are commanded in Ephesians 5 to nourish and cherish their wives. This is at least partially accomplished through the giving of verbal praise and encouragement. A wife's sense of her own beauty depends greatly on what her husband thinks of her. She needs to be nourished emotionally with praise and never diminished by criticism, especially in the areas where she feels most insecure and vulnerable. She needs to be cherished in public, and the test of this is how her husband treats her socially. You can be sure that a genuinely beautiful wife has been protected and cherished by a husband who has shown a sensitive response to her special needs.

Remember, edification builds up, never tears down. So love gives your partner freedom to grow and develop as a person without fear of failure and fear of hurtful criticism.

Some husbands who manage to refrain from criticism still have not learned the art of praise for their wives. It is said, "The best way to compliment your wife is *frequently.*" On the other hand, relationships die because of what you *don't* say. They simply dry up!

Edifying begins in the thought life where Philippians 4:8 is applied: "If there is any excellence and if anything worthy of praise, let your mind dwell on these things" (NASB). Practice thinking about things you find attractive in your mate— every positive quality your partner possesses. Let the words of your lips be governed by this principle: Will these words build up or tear down? Then ask yourself: What can I say to my partner right now that will edify and build up, encourage, strengthen, and bring peace?

Biblically, the wife best edifies her husband by her response to him. In the full meaning of the language of the Greek New Testament, the wife is told to respect, admire, be in awe of, defer to, revere, adore, esteem, praise, and deeply love her husband. This is presented as her full-time job, and the original language of the Bible indicates that she will be personally benefited as she does it.

God has designed marriage so that a husband is dependent on the affirmations of his wife, the appreciation she shows him for all that he gives her, and her demonstration of respect for his manhood. It is wounding when a husband criticizes his wife. It is equally wounding when the wife criticizes what her husband provides for her.

Both husband and wife have a tremendous need for encouragement by word, by focused attention, by eye contact, and by loving touch to keep them alive as growing, confident individuals. Psychologists call this *healing attention*. We call it *edifying*.

The New Testament Greek word for "edify" reminds us of an important fact. It is *oikodomeo,* a combination of two words: *oikos,* meaning a family, home, or house, and *demo,* meaning to build. While you are edifying and building each other up, you also are building a home together. Your home can never be what it should be until you have developed the practice of edifying. Let it begin with you!

3) Sharing

We have already discussed this third element in building a superb marriage. You may wish to refer again to chapters 9 and 11. I would like to reemphasize several points. The more ways you can find to be in relationship with each other, the stronger your love will become. Sharing should touch all areas of life— your time, activities, interests and concerns, ideas and innermost thoughts, spiritual walk, family objectives and goals, etc.

Sharing demands giving of yourself, listening to your partner, and, as you live life together, developing a sensitive awareness of moments that offer possibilities for deepening the love between you.

Picture it as taking an adventurous voyage of discovery together, for you will be discovering interesting new territory in each other through the experience of sharing on successively deeper levels.

Yes, this too is a biblical principle. Husband and wife are to become *one* flesh. The Book of Acts tells us that all the believers were *one* in heart and soul and, at that time, even had their possessions in common. If this sharing could happen within a group of people, how much more possible it is to de-

velop oneness of heart and soul between two people who want to build love in
their marriage!

4) Touching

If you have read this book carefully up to this point, you already know how
essential physical touching is to every human being. God created us with hundreds of thousands of microscopic nerve endings in our skin designed to sense
and benefit from a loving touch. A tender touch tells us that we are cared for. It
can calm our fears, soothe pain, bring us comfort, or give us the blessed satisfaction of emotional security. As adults, touching continues to be a primary
means of communicating with those we love, whether we are conscious of it or
not. Our need for a caring touch is normal and healthy and we will never outgrow it.

But if touching is so valuable and pleasurable, why is it necessary to advise
couples to do more of it? The answer lies in our culture. While our western civilization is highly sexual, it frowns on or ignores touching apart from sex. This
is particularly true for men, for there are only three acceptable kinds of touching in today's world: the superficial handshake, aggressive contact sports, and
the sexual encounter. Men have been conditioned to turn to sex whenever they
feel any need for loving closeness. No wonder experts believe that our extreme
preoccupation with sex in this society is actually an expression of our deep,
unsatisfied need for the warmth, reassurance, and intimacy of nonsexual touching.

Those of you who begin to practice physical touching in your marriage in all
of its pleasant nonsexual forms will find that you may be having sex a little less
often, but enjoying it much more. Snuggling and cuddling, sleeping close to
each other, sharing affection through simple touch, will meet many of the emotional needs that you hoped sex would provide. At the same time, this pattern
of affectionate closeness provides a delightful prelude to the entire sex relationship, preparing the way emotionally for wonderful times together.

I must emphasize that even though you apply every other principle I have
given you in this book, it will be of little avail unless you learn to touch each
other often and joyfully in nonsexual ways. Physical contact is absolutely essential in building the emotion of love. You may take it as a sobering warning
that most of the time marital infidelity is not so much a search for sex as it is for
emotional intimacy. The Scriptures indicate that touching a woman kindles a
flame that should be natural within marriage. If you would like to kindle a flame
in your own marriage, then begin to show your love through physical touching.

Blessing . . . Edifying . . . Sharing . . . Touching . . . a four-point prescription for a superb marriage! But prescriptions are useful only when taken as directed. As a family doctor, I find that some of my patients do not take their prescriptions or do not follow the directions on them. At their next visit, when there has been no improvement, the truth comes out.

In your own case, if you add these four elements to your marriage according to directions, you will soon see a dramatic improvement. I often hear these words from a happy husband or wife: "It works! The B-E-S-T really works!"

To be sure you are applying these principles correctly, I want to give you some additional helps in each area. This time we will begin with the simplest of the four elements—touching—and conclude with the more challenging part of the prescription—blessing.

TWENTY-FIVE SUGGESTIONS FOR TOUCHING

1. When dating, young people can scarcely be kept apart. Most married couples have forgotten how much fun physical closeness can be! So set aside practice times at night (at least once a week) to learn the delights of nonsexual body caressing. Make a date ahead of time. Anticipate pleasure and relaxation together.

2. Show each other where you like to be touched and the kind of touch that pleases you. Usually, a light touch is the most thrilling. Be imaginative in the way you caress.

3. Remember the purpose: to establish a good emotional climate of warmth, love, and affection; *not* to initiate sex. If sex results later because you both want it, that's all right. But you need to learn to enjoy *nonsexual* touching during these exercise times.

4. Demonstrate to each other how you prefer to be held. Kiss your partner the way you would like to be kissed—not to criticize past performances, but to communicate something your partner has not sensed before.

5. Use lotion or baby oil in body caressing; use K-Y Jelly when touching the more sensitive areas of the body. Physical caressing should be totally pleasant.

6. Try caressing (not tickling!) each other's feet. For almost everyone this is a pleasurable and nonthreatening form of touch communication. Some people bathe, dry, and oil each other's feet gently and leisurely.

7. Cleanliness is essential for enjoyment of these sessions.

8. Some evenings take your shower or bath together. Make this a lighthearted, sensuous experience.

9. Americans habitually do everything in a rush, including lovemaking. But to learn the art of expressing warm, sensual feelings, you will have to slow down. If what you are doing feels good, take the time to enjoy it. This may become the best part of your day.

10. Caress each other's back. Pay special attention to the back of the neck at the hairline and the area just above the small of the back.

11. Maintain a positive attitude (the attitude of yes, rather than no). If some manner of caressing or the area chosen does not feel particularly enjoyable, gently lead your partner on to something you do like. Never say, "Stop doing that!" or similar words. The atmosphere should be delightfully permissive.

12. Practice communicating warmth. Learn to be emotionally aware of your own feelings and those of your partner. Focus on expressing your love through the medium of touch. Caress each other's face in the dark, becoming more aware of your partner and spelling out love through sensitive fingertips.

13. Make sure that both of you are having equal opportunity to give and to receive. Take turns giving pleasure to each other.

14. When you caress, use a slow, tender, appreciative touch, indicating how much you enjoy your partner's body—each part of it. When people feel negative about some part of their body, it is more difficult for them to relate freely to their partner. Help your mate realize that every part of his or her body is pleasing, attractive, and desirable to you.

15. Develop positive feelings toward your own body given to you by God. This is biblical! Meditate on Psalm 139. "I praise you because I am fearfully and wonderfully made; your works are wonderful, I know that full well" (Psalm 139:14 NIV).

16. Communicate verbally during your exercises, telling each other what you especially enjoy and how it makes you feel.

17. Sleep in as few clothes as possible at night. Clothes are only a hindrance during these touching sessions.

18. Practice breathing together in rhythm, both of you lying on your side, the other pressed up against your back, hand on your abdomen to gauge your breathing and adjust his rhythm to yours. Then reverse places and do it again.

19. Try to go to bed when your partner does *every* night.

20. Have a period of fifteen to thirty minutes every night to lie in each other's arms in the dark before you drift off to sleep. Whisper together, sharing private thoughts and pleasant little experiences of the day. Avoid controversial or negative topics. This is the time to build intimacy and wind down

for sleep. You will become used to sharing things with each other that you would not otherwise mention. In each other's arms the hurts and frustrations of the day are healed. You may want to pray together at this time, or just relax in the comfort of physically-felt love.

21. Establish the cozy habit of staying in some sort of physical contact while you are going to sleep—a hand or a leg touching your partner's, for instance.

22. Begin every day with a few minutes of cuddling and snuggling before you get out of bed. A husband can tell his wife how nice she feels and how glad he is to be close to her. A wife can nestle in her husband's arms and tell him she wishes they didn't have to leave each other that morning. Just be close and savor gentle physical contact for awhile. It will make the morning bout with the alarm clock far more pleasant, so allow a few minutes in your schedule for this, even though one or both of you must soon be up and off to work.

23. Hold hands often. Think of all the different ways you can enjoy just touching with your hands, and all the different feelings that can be conveyed.

24. Become aware of the many ways you can have physical contact in the course of a week. Touch when you are talking and maintain eye contact. Sit close to each other in church. Kiss each other when there is no occasion for it. Add variety to your kisses, your touches, and your love pats.

25. While you watch television, make sure you sit close together and use the time for some physical communication. A wise wife will cuddle close to her husband when he chooses to watch his football games, even if she is not interested in the program. Since so many people spend so much time before the TV set, it need not be wasted if they are at least together physically.

My final word on touching: even if you practice everything else in this book, but do not touch each other frequently and lovingly, the thrill of romantic love will be absent from your marriage. It's up to you to add the spark.

A CREATIVE VIEW OF SHARING

1. Take another look at sharing through the eyes of two lovers whose love endured:

We talked deeply. . . about justice between lovers and about how to make love endure. What emerged from our talk was nothing less, we believed, than the central "secret" of enduring love: sharing.

"Look," we said, "what is it that draws two people into closeness and love? Of course there's the mystery of physical attraction, but beyond that it's the things they share. We both love strawberries and ships and collies and poems and all beauty, and all those things bind us together. Those sharings just happened to be; but what we must do now is share *everything*. Everything! If one of us likes *anything,* there must be something to like in it—and the other one must find it. Every single thing that either of us likes. That way we shall create a thousand strands, great and small, that will link us together. Then we shall be so close that it would be impossible—unthinkable—for either of us to suppose that we could ever recreate such closeness with anyone else. And our trust in each other will not only be based on love and loyalty but on the *fact* of a thousand sharings—a thousand strands twisted into something unbreakable."

Our enthusiasm grew as we talked. Total sharing, we felt, was the ultimate secret of a love that would last forever. And of course we *could* learn to like anything if we wanted to. Through sharing we would not only make a bond of incredible friendship, but through sharing we would keep the magic of inloveness. And with every year, more and more depth. We would become as close as two human beings *could* become—closer perhaps than any two people have ever been. Whatever storms might come, whatever changes the years might bring, there would be the bedrock closeness of all our sharing.[1]

2. Now, creatively evaluate where you can develop sharing in your own marriage. Look at your life together in these four areas:

    *   *Common Ground.* Think of all the things you actually share right now. How can you enjoy it more?
    *   *Separate Ground.* Parts of your life, particularly in the area of work and responsibility, may be separate. You may also have special interests that your partner will never become directly involved in. How can you bridge these gaps in order to share your separate worlds? Through communication? Through mutual understanding and encouragement?
    *   *New Ground for One.* What interests can you begin to enjoy because your partner enjoys them? If you each develop new enthusiasms to match your partner's, life will become more interesting than ever.
    *   *New Ground for Both.* What new, absorbing interests can you develop together?

The above should jog your own thinking as you plan creatively for more meaningful sharing in your marriage. Here's how Rich and Celia, a couple married four years, revised their approach to sharing:

"We had to start by admitting there were some segments of our personalities that would never quite mesh," Rich said. "I enjoy running a mile or two a day—

the hotter the sun, the better. Cele likes to curl up in the shade with a book of poetry. I do a lot of heavy reading, while she's into crafts of all sorts. I'm a research scientist, and she's a second-grade school teacher. But we can share even our differences through conversation. We're beginning to communicate a lot more about the work and interests that we each have. And we're becoming more consciously proud of each other. Cele makes some beautiful art objects, and I insist that we use them in our home. I know she respects the work I do in meteorology and I tell her about it because she always seems interested. On the other hand, she brings her problems home from the classroom, and we discuss the best way to handle them. We often pray together for the children she's concerned about. It's amazing how close two people can become through sharing their separate worlds.''

"I've become excited about photography," Cele said, "because it's one of Rich's favorite hobbies. He's taught me so much, and it satisfies my need to be creative. In the process, I've done a lot of strenuous hiking with him because we like to photograph the beauty of the mountain trails. Now we're learning something new together—cross-country skiing! Another world we're exploring together is classical music."

"This winter Cele suggested that we read *The Lord of the Rings* trilogy by J. R. R. Tolkien together—a chapter a night," Rich said. "It was a great idea sharing the pleasure of those books with each other."

"Rich never cared much for table games," Cele smiled, "but he's learned to play them because I enjoy them."

"And Cele has returned the favor by cooperating with me in organizing our financial affairs into a definite system that takes a lot of record-keeping," Rich added. "Now we do the housework and yardwork together instead of separately and talk while we're working. Sharing gets to be a habit—a nice habit. The more you do it, the more you want to."

Every couple's plan for sharing will be different. Just make sure you have a plan. The natural tendency is to go your separate ways. Sharing helps to create an *enduring* love.

NINE WAYS TO EDIFY

1. Make the irrevocable decision to never again be critical of your partner in word, thought, or deed. This may sound like an impossibility, but it is not. It is simply a decision backed up by action until it becomes a habit you would not change if you could.

2. Study your partner. Become sensitive to the areas where your partner feels a lack and think of ways to build up your partner in those areas particularly.

3. Think every day of positive qualities and behavior patterns you admire and appreciate in your mate.
4. Consistently verbalize praise and appreciation for your partner. Be genuine, be specific, be generous. You edify with the *spoken* word.
5. Recognize your partner's talents, abilities, and accomplishments. Communicate your respect for the work he or she does.
6. Husband, show your wife publicly and privately how precious she is to you. And do not express admiration for another woman. This is never edifying to your wife. Keep your attention focused on her!
7. Wife, show your husband that he is the most important person in your life—always. Seek his opinions and value his judgment.
8. Respond to each other physically and facially. The face is the most distinctive and expressive part of a person. Your mate wants to see you smile, eyes sparkling in response to him or her.
9. Always exhibit the greatest courtesy to each other. You should be VIPs in your own home!

SCRIPTURAL COUNSEL ON BLESSING

Do not repay evil with evil or insult with insult, but with blessing, because to this you were called so that you may inherit a blessing. For,

> "Whoever would love life
>   and see good days
> must keep his tongue from evil
>   and his lips from deceitful speech.
> He must turn from evil and do good;
>   he must seek peace and pursue it.
> For the eyes of the Lord are on the righteous,
>   and his ears are attentive to their prayer,
> but the face of the Lord is against those
>   who do evil."   (1 Peter 3:9–12 NIV)

This New Testament Scripture with the passage quoted by Peter from Psalm 34:13–17 is very plain. God has called every Christian into a lifestyle of consistent blessing of others through (1) *words;* (2) *behavior.* This means consistently blessing those in our own household—our marriage partner first of all. Blessing in word and action is most especially required of us in response to any manner of evil behavior or insulting speech. As you apply this to your own marriage, understand that you never have any justification for speaking to your partner scornfully, angrily, or deceitfully. Your partner's bad behavior can never excuse your own in God's eyes. If you fail to bless, God says that your mouth will bring more trouble on you; you will miss out on the blessing that He had planned for you; and, instead, His face will be against you (i.e., nothing you try to do in your marriage will prosper).

The rewards of blessing are also plainly spelled out: God will see to it that we are blessed by Him (no matter what our partner does); that we will "love life" and experience good days; that He will watch over us with special protective care; and that He will hear and answer our prayers.

Few choices of life have been given to us more clearly. Often we hesitate between this path and that, wondering what the outcome will be. In this case, we know. If we choose the disciplined path of blessing in our marriage (the road surely less traveled by!), it will make all the difference in our life. We know it because God has said it.

The way is simple, if challenging, and can be followed by anyone who uses the spiritual resources the Lord Jesus Christ provides. Here are the directions.

Negatives:
(1) Keep your tongue from evil and your lips from speaking deceitful words.
(2) Turn away from evil.

Positives:
(1) Do good.
(2) Seek peace and pursue it.
More detailed counsel can be found in Romans 12:

"Bless those who persecute you; bless and do not curse. Rejoice with those who rejoice; mourn with those who mourn. Live in harmony with one another. Do not be proud, but be willing to associate with people of low position. Do not be conceited.

Do not repay anyone evil for evil. Be careful to do what is right in the eyes of everybody. If it is possible, as far as it depends on you, live at peace with everyone. Do not take revenge, my friends, but leave room for God's wrath, for it is written: "It is mine to avenge; I will repay," says the Lord. On the contrary:
"If your enemy is hungry, feed him;
   If he is thirsty, give him something to drink.
In doing this, you will heap burning coals on his head."
Do not be overcome by evil, but overcome evil with good.

(Romans 12:14–21 NIV)

In short:
- Bless and do not curse the one who is giving you a hard time.
- Be empathic and understanding with your partner.
- Live in harmony with your mate.

- Do not think you are better than your partner.
- Do not act proud; do not act conceited.
- Do not repay evil with evil (even in the most petty detail).
- Be careful to do what your partner considers to be right.
- As far as it depends on you, live at peace in your marriage.
- Never take revenge.
- Consistently do kind things for your partner, no matter what treatment you receive.
- Do not let yourself be overcome by evil. Instead, overcome evil with good!

14
Removing
the Barriers

ONE OF OUR American generals made a profound observation about war. He said, "The only way to *win* a war is to prevent it."

As a marriage counselor, I recall these words when I work with couples who are at open war. No one is winning. No one *can* win. But the hostilities go on— husband and wife treating each other like bitter enemies!

In other marriages, hostilities exist under the surface, just as real even if semi-concealed. In the long run they will be equally deadly unless they are recognized and checked in time.

Let me ask you a personal question. Are there hostilities in your marriage, standing between you and the happiness you long for? Occasionally I counsel couples where either husband or wife will not admit to any bad feelings. They claim they feel nothing but indifference. Only after deeper consideration do they realize that their indifference is the direct result of buried anger that has led to depression, numbing all of their emotions, both happy and unhappy ones. It is important to understand that a negative attitude represents psychic energy that cannot be ignored or hidden away. This psychic energy is a force that must be reckoned with. When one tries either to maintain it or conceal it, so much emotional strength is required that the individual ends up drained and therefore very depressed.

We have been describing the incomparable joy experienced by husband and wife who learn to love each other with the fullness of love—*agape*, romance, belonging, cherished friendship, and physical fulfillment blended into a wonderful, enduring intimacy.

Now we must warn that this love cannot grow in the same heart with negative attitudes and bad feelings—anger, bitterness, resentment, pride, disillusionment, despair, or hostility (veiled or otherwise). Facing these and dealing with them in your own life will not only prevent a disastrous war, but can open up the way to a host of blessings. Not the least of these may be a love affair you no longer thought possible in your marriage.

We are going to concentrate only on *your* attitudes, not those of your partner. As you change for the better, this will inevitably have its effect on your mate.

I would like for you to visualize your negative attitudes as barriers obstructing the passage that leads to a genuine love relationship. Barriers separate and keep apart; they hinder and impede progress. But they are not *necessarily impassable.* So, if negative attitudes have taken root in your heart, I want to help you face them and remove them so that the way will be clear for the interchange of love. These attitudes go by different names because people react differently. One wife confessed to me that she was so angry with her husband that she had a desire to smother him as he slept, while another retreated into an icy resentment that caused her to say that now she could not respond to her husband even if he were perfect!

Whatever name you give to *your* negative attitudes, the common denominator will always be the same—an unforgiving spirit that can rob you of all that makes life good if you let it continue.

"But, Dr. Wheat, I am justified in my feelings," a husband or wife sometimes protests. "You don't know how I've been treated!"

My answer is that this is not the issue. You personally are faced with a choice. Let me spell it out so that you can make a conscious, rational decision. Otherwise you will slide into a choice almost unconsciously, a decision based on emotion with neither logic nor the Word of God to back it up.

If you want a marriage full of love, you cannot afford the luxury of resentment or self-pity or anger. Unforgiveness toward your mate in any form (including the self-protective shield of distrust) will be the death blow to love. If you choose to cling to your bad feelings, they will cripple your marriage relationship and at the same time they will take their toll of your physical health and emotional well-being.

Of course, all normal people want health and happiness and love in their marriage. But they often do not know how to handle the past; how to deal with their negative attitudes; how to cope with their resentments; or how to recognize their own anger buried under a layer of depression. Many do not know how to forgive, and they think it must be very complicated or even impossible. But it is not. God never asks His children to do anything that He does not provide both the instructions for and the strength to accomplish.

Let me share two basic principles that will help you at this point. First, *you do not have to be controlled by your feelings.* Second, *you are not the helpless prisoner of your past.*

These are the chief objections people offer when told they need to forgive. Their answer goes like this . . . "Maybe so, but I can never *feel* any forgiveness toward my husband after what he *did.*" Or, "I'd like to forgive my wife, but I can't change the way *I feel. I can't change the past.*" These people are confessing a state of slavery. They are picturing themselves as enslaved by their own feelings, as prisoners of events that happened in the past. And yet Christians have already been set free! Jesus said, "You will know the truth, and the truth will set you free. . . . If the Son sets you free, you will be free indeed" (John 8:32, 36 NIV). If you are a Christian, trusting in Jesus Christ alone for your salvation, right now you are more free than you know!

Even in the secular world counselors are dramatically changing their approach in a way that is much more in accord with biblical principles. Counselors no longer give exclusive attention to the patient's *feelings;* many of them now concentrate on the importance of the individual's *behavior.* The most effective counselors no longer attempt prolonged treatment of the patient's past; instead, they emphasize the present—the here and now—with marked success.

So begin by realizing that you are in control of your behavior. This is what counts because it is a proven fact that feelings change as behavior changes. Then you must understand that God is not even asking you to change your feelings. He never does that. Throughout Scripture He tells us the way He wants us to behave and to think. Because He created us, He knows full well that as we think rightly and behave rightly, right feelings will appear in us as a matter of course. You need to realize that God is not asking you to work up a *feeling* of forgiveness toward your mate, but He is asking you to make a choice (no matter how you feel) to forgive him or her.

Is God making selfish demands on us? Hardly! He asks us to forgive because He knows we will benefit from it. As a God who loves you and me with a fatherly heart, He desires the best for us. That *best* includes the spiritual and emotional wholeness and the physical health that spring out of a spirit of forgiveness.

Is God making an unreasonable request? Never let us forget that God forgave *first* in a way that we can neither discount nor overlook. When Jesus Christ was rejected, falsely accused, taunted, abused, tortured, then nailed to the cross to experience the most agonizing death hatred could devise, He prayed, "Father, forgive them. . . ." God asks no more, indeed, far less, of you and me. If any man ever had the right to be bitter, it was Jesus Christ. But He wasn't. He forgave instead, and established the pattern of forgiveness for all His followers from that time forth. Remember that every command of God carries a promise in its heart. Because He commands, "Forgive as Christ forgave" (Colossians 3;13), the ability to forgive accompanies the choice to do so.

Forgiveness involves three steps: (1) Using your free will to make the choice to forgive; (2) Deliberately behaving in the manner that the Lord has shown in the Bible to be right; (3) Trusting Him to do His part by renewing your mind and giving you new, transformed attitudes.

STEP ONE: CHOOSING TO FORGIVE

To help us make the choice to forgive, the Lord provides an urgent warning in the letter to the Hebrews: "Make straight paths for your feet, lest that which is lame be turned out of the way; but let it rather be healed. Follow peace with all men, and holiness, without which no man shall see the Lord: looking diligently, lest any man fail of the grace of God; *lest any root of bitterness springing up trouble you, and thereby many be defiled"* (Hebrews 12:13–15).

The one who clings to the misery of an unforgiving spirit will be crippled in the living of life, God warns. And not only will that person be troubled by the root of bitterness crowding out good things in his life, but many others will be injured by it as well.

The word *bitterness* in the Greek New Testament is *pikrias,* giving the idea of a cutting, pricking, puncturing that is at the same time pungent and penetrating. It vividly communicates the sensations of torture, and this is just what you are doing to yourself and your loved ones when you refuse to forgive your mate. Radio Bible teacher Charles Swindoll has suggested that it is like locking yourself in a concentration camp of your own making. Corrie Ten Boom describes it as sitting in a very dark room in the daytime with heavy draperies closing off the sunlight and fresh air.

You will indeed suffer by your own choice until you decide to fully and completely forgive any wrongs done to you. It may be one big thing or years of small hurts adding up to one large resentment. Certainly it will cost you something; it cost God more than we can ever know to forgive us. But once you have made the choice with your will, you will discover that you have taken a big step into freedom and emotional health and spiritual growth. You have come into what the psalmist called "a more spacious place." When you choose to forgive your husband or wife totally and wholeheartedly for any and all wrongs, you will find yourself entering the "kingdom of love." I have never known anyone who later regretted that step.

As soon as you choose to forgive with your mind and your will and commit this matter to God, you free both yourself and the one who offended you from the power of the past. Then, whatever happened is historical fact, and no longer emotional fact. In a real way you have opened up the wound to the Great Physician, and you will find that His love poured on it will so heal that you will no longer feel the sting.

Recall the words the Lord Jesus used to describe His ministry. He said, "The Spirit of the Lord is upon me, because he hath anointed me to . . . set at liberty them that are bruised" (Luke 4:18). There He offers us both the deliverance and the healing. There is no bruise, no emotional wound in your marriage that the Lord cannot heal when you choose to forgive and commit this matter and your subsequent behavior to Him. No hatred can hold you prisoner when you choose freedom. No negative attitude can dominate you when you choose to let it go as an act of obedience to the Lord Jesus Christ. His love simply overpowers old resentments. It is like raising the shade and opening the window in that dark room. The sunshine floods in and dispels every corner of darkness. The air is fresh and sweet and exhilarating.

STEP TWO: CHANGING YOUR BEHAVIOR

We find the second step in forgiveness expressed in capsule form in Ephesians 4:31–32: "Let all bitterness, and wrath, and anger, and clamour, and evil speaking, be put away from you, with all malice: And be ye kind one to another, tenderhearted, forgiving one another, even as God for Christ's sake hath forgiven you." It is time to look into the Bible to see what mode of behavior the Lord counsels and then begin to carry it out. In this Scripture passage, God shows the process of first choosing to put away the negative attitudes, then of assuming positive attitudes and behaving in positive ways, summed up in the instruction, "Be kind. Be tenderhearted. Be forgiving."

The essence of kind treatment of your partner is to treat him or her precisely as you want to be treated. Kindness, as expressed in connection with your partner's wrongdoing, will certainly include these proofs of forgiveness. You will never use the past against him. You will never talk about it again either to him or to anyone else. You will never dwell on it in your thoughts. If you think of it in passing, you will immediately remember that it has been forgiven, just as God has forgiven you for many things far worse.

I want to emphasize this point so that there will be no misunderstanding. When authentic forgiveness takes place, your behavior will change. It must change. I am reminded of a husband whose wife was unfaithful to him a number of years ago. He says that he has forgiven her. Yet even today his behavior toward her clearly shows that he does not trust her. Obviously, this husband has never really forgiven his wife, and she is only too aware of it. You can imagine how difficult it is for love to grow in that environment.

To forgive is to say good-by forever to the pain of the past and to be rid of its effects in the present. This brings us to the third phase of forgiveness.

STEP THREE: RENEWING YOUR MIND

Now is the time to forget the past and move into the future. This is possible as you allow God to do His part by renewing your mind through the Word of God, thus replacing the negatives with good attitudes that will bless your marriage relationship.

As we have already observed, this ability to leave the past behind belongs to God's people. The Christian life is all present and future. God has so designed it that the Christian can always begin where he is right now to live life in a new way—God's way. How comforting to know it is impossible for us to tangle up things so badly that God cannot work them together for our good. It is hard to understand how God can (seemingly) start over with a new set of plans dating from this moment, but He can and He will. He always responds completely in love to our efforts to follow His counsel. The biblical principle is that the steadfast love of the Lord never ceases. His mercies never come to an end. They are new every morning. Great is His faithfulness! (See Lamentations 3:22–23.)

So it is altogether possible for us to say with Paul "This one thing I do, *forgetting* those things which are behind, and *reaching forth* unto those things which are before . . ." (Philippians 3:13). Forgetting . . . reaching forth. This is the way to continue beyond that moment of forgiveness into the kingdom of love to live there for the rest of your life.

Now, you may be wondering what you can do about the negative attitudes your partner holds—the barriers he or she has erected against the free movement of love. You need to take the initiative and seek his or her forgiveness. First of all, stop doing the thing that caused the feeling of estrangement between you. Show by your speech and actions and attitudes that you are aware of your wrongdoing and would like to right it. Never use the word *if* when you are speaking to your partner about the matter. Simply admit your wrong and ask for forgiveness. This means much more than saying, "*If* I have hurt you in some way, I'm sorry." Be careful not to project any blame for the problem onto your partner. Making your mate feel guilty is one of the worst things you can do if you want to restore love to your marriage.

If after all this, your mate does not immediately respond, continue to show by your consistent loving behavior that you have forgiven on your side and that you are committed to loving your partner for the rest of your life. Remember, forgiveness can begin as a unilateral action. So let it begin with you!

Now, in spite of all we have said, you may still have some mental limitations tacked on to your scope of forgiveness. In other words, "I can forgive everything else . . . but I could never forgive my partner for being unfaithful. . . ." Or, " I could never forgive my husband for *this* or my wife for *that*. . . ." Insert any unpleasant, unthinkable situation in the blanks. You name it, I have seen it, and counseled a person with the problem—usually a Christian. Sin is sin, and every person is fully capable of committing sin. It all needs to be dealt with and forgiven whatever the category. If you are feeling bitterly disappointed in your mate, that attitude also is a signal that you need to choose to forgive. Remember that God's grace covers *every* category. The love of God can cover every kind of problem. I have seen in many years of counseling that no situation is so difficult or so shocking that God cannot restore the marriage and bring glory to His name in the process.

Many people think that of all sins, adultery automatically destroys the marriage. No, it is only marriage to someone else that destroys the marriage bond. Biblically speaking, adultery need be no more destructive to your marriage than any other sin. I have seen a surprising number of Christian marriages attacked by unfaithfulness. I have also seen many of these restored in such a way that the relationship has become much better than before.

Recently a pastor said to me in reference to some very troubled marriages: "Only God could heal *those* relationships!" This is true, but God is able to heal as people are willing to apply the Word of God to their situation. When you are ready to forgive and let go of your negative attitudes, God will be more than ready to heal you and renew your love for each other. He's been waiting for that all this time!

15
How to Save Your Marriage Alone

THIS CHAPTER IS directed to a special group of readers: those individuals who want to save their marriage at all costs, even though they have to do it alone without any help from their partner. In fact, their partner may be actively pursuing a divorce.

If you are in this group, I do indeed consider you *special*. First, by your stand you indicate a commitment to the sacredness and permanence of marriage that is God-honoring; second, you have the courage to face your own problems instead of running from them or hiding behind false pride; and, third, you exhibit the maturity which, even when there is no response, can choose to love with a steadfast love that is tough and real, intelligent and purposeful, wholly committed to your partner's well-being.

Christian psychiatrist Paul D. Meier says that there are "only three choices for any person involved in an unhappy marriage: (1) get a divorce—the greatest cop-out and by far the most immature choice; (2) tough out the marriage without working to improve it—another immature decision but not quite as irresponsible as divorce; and (3) maturely face up to personal hangups and choose to build an intimate marriage out of the existing one—the only really mature choice to make."[1]

In your case, the moment of truth has come, for your partner probably has already ruled out the second option and chosen the first without even considering the third. The question is, What will *you* do? Surrender to the pressures of the world's way of thinking and the emotions of the moment? Or make a choice based on confidence in the eternal truths of Scripture?

The stakes are higher than one may realize at the time. One choice clearly leads to the bitterness and defeat of divorce as well as lost opportunities for blessing. "Divorce is more painful than death," a woman told me the other day, her voice husky with pent-up emotion, *"because it's never really over."* Dr. Meier says that when couples run away from their problems by divorcing and remarrying, "then there are four miserable people instead of just two. . . . Why spread misery?" he asks. "Bad marriages are contagious! Numerous psychiatric research studies have shown that when couples with neurotic marriage relationships get divorced—no matter how good their intentions may be—they nearly always remarry into the very same type of neurotic relationship they had before."[2]

When you choose the pathway of irrevocable commitment to your mate and your marriage—regardless of how troubled your relationship may seem—you will find that choice leading you into a place of *agape* love and peace and personal growth. These are just some of the rewards, for the chances are very good that you will also be able to enjoy the blessings that God has wanted to bestow on your marriage from the beginning.

I am not suggesting that the healing of a marriage is an easy process when one partner resists it. But are any easy choices open to you, after all? Torn relationships involve pain, whatever you do about them. As Peter points out in his first letter, it is far better to suffer (if suffer you must) for doing *right,* than for doing wrong. He makes it clear that God's favor and blessing shine on the one who patiently suffers, if necessary, in order to do His will. Meeting your marriage problems in a biblical manner is productive rather than pointless, and whatever hurts you encounter will be less damaging than the long-term effects of divorce would be.

"The very word *divorce* should be cut out of the vocabulary of a couple when they marry," a woman with a restored marriage said, "because God's way is so much better for anyone who is willing to give it a try."

Another woman, considering the turbulent events of the past year that had driven her to grow emotionally and spiritually while she "loved her husband back" to their marriage, said, "You know, it's been all gain for me. I'm a different person now. The process was humbling, but it was worth it!"

A man said, "During the time when I was trying to win my wife's love and hold our family together, sometimes I got so tired of rejection that I didn't feel anything except a determination to do what the Bible said and leave the results with God. The only thing I was sure of was that somehow God would work it out for my good because He promised that in His Word. I never imagined the love affair He has actually given us. He really does do more than we can ask or think!"

While these comments from the far side of the problem are encouraging, I understand that the feelings you may be experiencing right now within the problem are less than pleasant. Many others have been where you are now and can empathize with what you are going through: shock, hurt, rejection, emotional confusion, temptation to bitterness, and, of course, pressures from all sides that sometimes make you want to give up.

My heartfelt goal in this chapter is to help you clarify your thoughts, stabilize your emotions, and learn to behave in a consistent, purposeful way that will save your marriage and bring a new dimension of love into your relationship.

So, if you are willing to make a commitment to your marriage based on the eternal principles and promises of the Word of God, you can take heart and let hope grow in proportion to your commitment. Contrary to what the world believes, one person *can* save a marriage. In fact, most of the people I counsel belong in this category. Even when both come to see me, one is usually dragging the other along, in a manner of speaking, and only one really cares about the outcome in most cases.

Marriage counselor Anne Kristin Carroll says, "If you think there's no hope because you are the only one in your relationship who wants or cares enough to try to save your marriage, you are wrong!" She adds, "In my experience most torn marriages are brought to new life, new vitality, by the interest, basically, of only one party."[3] This has been my experience as well. I have seen numerous marriages saved when only one partner applied biblical principles in a wholehearted commitment to the mate and the marriage.

Some have not been saved. Usually this is because the individual is convinced that nothing will change the partner—that the longstanding problem of alcoholism or financial irresponsibility or whatever cannot be solved, and he or she simply gives up. Occasionally, the partner desiring a divorce has developed such a strong emotional attachment to another person that it is not broken off *in time* to save the marriage. Often, however, this infatuation ends while the divorce is being delayed, and the unfaithful partner thanks the committed mate for standing fast and preserving the marriage. In a relatively few cases, one partner pressured by family and "loyal" friends, develops a deep bitterness toward the other and is actually encouraged in this hostility by parents and even, sometimes, church members so that efforts at reconciliation may be unavailing.

But in the great majority of cases, the outcome depends squarely on the committed partner's ability to behave consistently in accord with biblical principles designed by the Author of marriage. So, in a very literal sense, it is *all* up to you. You need not expect your partner to do anything constructive about the marriage if he or she wants out.

CLARIFYING YOUR THOUGHTS

When the Bible says, "Gird up the loins of your mind" (1 Peter 1:13), it means to get your mental powers in a state of alertness for proper action. You must do this without delay. Often the Lord will provide the opportunity for some quiet, uninterrupted Bible study and prayerful consideration of God's plan for your situation. You may also learn some important things about yourself during this time. When one husband moved out, his parents lovingly helped the wife by keeping the children for several weeks while she prepared mentally and spiritually for the challenges ahead.

One young wife was ready to dissolve her marriage until a friend in her garden club led her to the Lord. "I only knew two Scriptures at the beginning," the wife said, "but they were exactly what I needed: 'God is not a man, that he should lie' (Numbers 23:19) and 'With God nothing shall be impossible' (Luke 1:37).

"With those truths as a foundation I began to study the Bible, desperately trying to dig out God's purpose for marriage and all that He had to say about it. I found out for myself that if I were to obey Him, then I would have to become committed to my marriage and my husband, even though he was involved with another woman and we were on the verge of divorce.

"Coming to this decision didn't make things any easier emotionally at first, but it did show me a clear path of action, and the situation actually became less complicated because there was no more confusion about *what* to do! I refused to sign the divorce papers. I had gathered evidence identifying the other woman and proving my husband's unfaithfulness. I destroyed it all. I didn't need it anymore."

A University of Chicago professor described this generation's dilemma with the now familiar quotation: "We lack the *language* to teach what is right and wrong." But the Bible-believing Christian caught in an emotionally fraught situation does not have that problem. The language of God concerning divorce is plain enough for any reader. For example:

For the Lord, the God of Israel, says: I hate divorce and marital separation, and him who covers his garment [his wife] with violence. Therefore keep a watch upon your spirit [that it may be controlled by My Spirit], that you deal not treacherously and faithlessly [with your marriage mate] (Malachi 2:16 AMPLIFIED).

He replied, Have you never read that He Who made them from the beginning made them male and female. And said, For this reason a man shall leave his father and mother and shall be united firmly (joined inseparably) to his wife, and the two shall become one flesh? So they are no longer two but one flesh. What therefore God has joined together, let not man put asunder (separate) (Matthew 19:4–6 AMPLIFIED).

As you try to gain clarity of thought concerning your marital situation viewed in light of the teaching of Scripture, I suggest that you re-read the first five chapters of this book and *search the Scriptures* that have to do with marriage. Let me remind you once more of the eternal principle that undergirds the biblical counsel we offer: *It is God's will in every marriage for the couple to love each other with an absorbing spiritual, emotional, and physical attraction that continues to grow throughout their lifetime together.* It should be crystal clear that God intends for you and your mate to picture the love-bond of Christ and His church and that you must beware of substitutes who sometimes find their way into the vacuum of a troubled relationship. Obviously, infidelity and divorce are paths that move away from God's plan and blessing. But when you pour yourself into restoring love to your marriage, you can be sure that the force of His will is at work with you in the process.

It is important to fill your mind with positive biblical input: biblical counseling, preaching, and teaching; good books and Bible-study tapes; and friends who will affirm you in your commitment to your marriage. You need to take in truth from those who are as committed to the permanence of marriage as the Bible is. And don't listen to anyone else! Develop tunnel vision in this area as Proverbs 4:25–27 commands:

> Let your eyes look directly ahead, and let your gaze be fixed straight in front of you. Watch the path of your feet, and all your ways will be established. Do not turn to the right nor to the left; turn your foot from evil (NASB).

You need to maintain this total mental commitment to the truth or you will be swamped by waves of human opinion and bad advice, sometimes from seemingly religious people.

One young man came to me, confused because he had been told to do nothing to win back his wife. He had been told to concentrate on his vertical relationship with God. I said to him, "This is true, but you can please God only when you are doing what the Bible says you are to do. You must be right in line with God's Word. We have no other direction for this life. When we are in total accord with the Word, then we can relax and God has the freedom to work with us. He always works with us on the basis of the information that we have from His Word. So the more you know of the Word of God concerning marriage and love and His abhorrence of divorce, the more equipped you will be to let God do His full work and have His full way in your life."

"I had to take a stand on this matter of outside influence," a wife told me. "Everyone has been anxious to give me advice about my marriage. I refuse to discuss it with people who hold an unbiblical viewpoint, or people who try to turn me against my husband, or people who make me feel sorry for myself and encourage weakness in me. I can't afford to be around worldly friends anymore. They tear me down; they tear my husband down. They may mean well, but they are so misguided. I want to be with people who will stand with me and support me when I might falter."

When your mind is settled, your thoughts clarified, and your commitment made, you will find that you no longer lie at the mercy of outside events, reacting to every new circumstance with fresh pain and bewilderment. Instead, your viewpoint becomes, "This is what I am going to do, *no matter what,* because it is God's way to do it. I can count on His wisdom, and I can trust Him with the results of a course of action based on His Word."

"I'm not standing by my marriage anymore on the basis of what the outcome will be," one woman told me. "People urge me to dump my husband, give up on him because he's made my life miserable; they tell me I deserve someone better, that I wouldn't have any trouble finding someone else to love me. My answer is that marriage is sacred; marriage is permanent; I am committed by my marriage vows; I am one flesh with my husband; and then I really shock them! I tell them that even if there is no happy ending for our marriage, I will not regret the stand I have taken. I will know that I made the right decision and followed the only course possible for me. I will have done all that I could.

"But my trust is not in what I am doing," she added. "It is in God and His Word. He has a perfect, loving plan for my life, and He's wise enough and powerful enough to carry it out, if I cooperate by following His counsel. So I'm going to keep on obeying Him in my marriage and I'll leave the results with Him. I am at peace with that."

STABILIZING YOUR EMOTIONS

As a medical doctor I often know when a marriage is in trouble because my patients come to me for something to alleviate their highly nervous state. One wife whose husband was intensely infatuated with someone else came to me convinced that she was on the verge of "losing her mind." She feared that she might not survive and had pleaded with her in-laws to keep her children away from contact with the other woman if something happened to her. Her mental anguish was indeed acute.

Months later I was impressed by the transformation in this woman—alert, poised, attractive, well-balanced in thought and speech, she now seemed to possess a central core of peace. Although her marital problems were not completely resolved, her husband had returned home and they were working together to build a real love relationship.

"Before he could tell me he loved me, even before he came back home, he was impressed with how I had changed," she explained. "He was in such a turmoil, and the peace and stability that I had found really attracted him to me." She opened her Bible. "Did you know that Proverbs 5:6 says an adulteress's ways are *unstable?* My husband found that out! The contrast with the spiritual maturity that I had gained the hard way inspired his respect and made him want to be with me."

"How do you account for this change in you?" I asked, although I was sure I already knew the answer.

"The Lord changed me through the Word of God," she said. "It was as if I were drowning, and the Word was the lifeline. I spent hours every day in the Bible. To begin with, the Lord showed me how wrong I had been as a wife. I couldn't feel betrayed and mistreated anymore; I couldn't even blame my husband for looking for someone else to make him happy when I had failed so badly. I saw that I had to change, and the Word showed me how.

"Then the Lord showed me that I couldn't be bitter toward the other woman. Bitterness was out. Love was in. And all the time the promises of the Word of God were stabilizing me, giving me a steadiness to face each new day. When something occurred that seemed like a severe setback, I could calmly go to the Word and study and begin to understand the new lesson He was teaching me.

"As *you* know," she said, "when this all started, I just had to have someone I could call day or night to talk to because I was so scared, so hurt, so desperate. But the time came when I learned to go straight to the Lord. It took a while to reach that, but it's the greatest blessing for me out of this whole experience. I've learned that all I really need is the Lord!"

This wife's testimony points the way to emotional stability for any individual who needs it—and most people faced with the disintegration of their marriage desperately need it.

In a magazine article, "Fly by the Instruments," Gloria Okes Perkins compares times of trial and emotional instability in the believer's life with the clouds, fog, and air turbulence an airplane pilot experiences. The answer in both cases is to fly entirely by the instruments.

"When there is no visual contact with the earth . . . when no horizon is in view, stability can be achieved only by depending on what those vital gyros have to say," she writes. "What is true for pilots in the skies is just as true in another sense for believers in the difficulties of life when normal conditions of stability seem to vanish in clouds of sorrow and confusion. Sooner or later every believer will have to 'fly by instruments' spiritually and emotionally through bad times. . . .

"While piloting a plane in a thick fog, a pilot cannot be sure of his direction unless he gives full attention to his instruments. When flying through a thunderstorm, the turbulence will throw him about, and the darkness within the clouds will threaten to disorient him. Sometimes he will feel as though he is going up or down or turning around. But he cannot depend on his feelings. Only the gyros can be trusted, so the pilot must hang on to the controls in the turbulence and discipline his mind to concentrate on the instruments while he flies through the storm.

"The parallel truth for the Christian in troubled times is clear. Undisciplined feelings . . . can cause a crash unless one keeps himself stabilized by the facts of the Word of God. . . . Every promise in the Word of God is like a gyro giving information to stabilize him in a specific situation. . . . With daily practice one learns not to panic but to believe a specific truth from the Bible fitted for his own unique circumstances. By experience one learns not to fight his feelings, but to look away from them to the 'instrument panel' of the Word of God which is utterly dependable.

"One discovers that if he will just hang on in the worst of the turbulence, no matter how disrupting, his mind and heart steadied by the great truths of the Word and his eyes intently fixed on God Himself, he will eventually break through rain-black clouds to soar once more in the clear, tranquil atmosphere."[4]

This is the way *you* can gain emotional stability at this time, no matter what your situation.

LEARNING TO LOVE

We come now to the practical behavior that can save your marriage. Your challenge is to learn how to love your partner day in and day out in such a way that there will be a responding love. Remember, you become lovable by loving, not by straining to attract love. So be careful how you love. Loving your mate in God's way does not mean clinging, complaining, or making demands. Moodiness, anger, and temperamental displays will only hinder your efforts. Loving your mate in God's way does not mean playing games—trying to inspire jealousy or insecurity, playing hard to get, taking petty revenge, or any of the other approaches you may have used in your early teens that are wholly inappropriate for marriage.

I recommend that you read 1 Corinthians 13, in as many different modern English translations as you can find. Read it again and again to learn the behavior patterns that characterize the genuine loving that God can use in healing a marriage. Fill your mind and spirit with these basic behavior responses so that they can reshape your attitudes and change your actions.

One wife asked her husband, "What can I do to show you that I love you?" This was his answer: "You could be nice to me all of the time, not just when you're in the mood. You could treat me as if I were really special. You could show me that you love me by respecting me and not trying to take over."

A wife expressed her desire in this way: "I just want my husband to keep telling me that he loves me and approves of me. Not only with words but also with kisses and thoughtfulness and understanding and protectiveness. I suppose what I'm really saying is that I want him to love me the way the Bible says—to love me the way Jesus Christ loves the church!"

We all hunger to be loved. And we want tangible proof that we *are* loved. But someone in the marriage has to take the initiative and begin the loving process. When misunderstandings piled upon misunderstandings erect walls between husband and wife, this can be difficult. Robert Louis Stevenson spoke the truth when he said, "Here we are, most of us, sitting at the window of our heart, crying for someone to come in and love us. But then we cover up the window with the stained glass of pride or anger or self-pity so that no one can glimpse the lonely self inside."

Is it possible in your own marriage that two lonely people are crying out for love on the inside, yet confused about what the other really wants and feels? There is only one constructive answer. You must choose to love your partner, unilaterally at first, and show it by meeting not only his or her needs, but desires as well.

In short, you will need to apply all the principles we have discussed in previous chapters concerning the five ways of loving and how to love. The easiest way to establish an effective habit of loving behavior is to follow the B-E-S-T prescription of chapter 13 of our book.

At one of our Christian marriage seminars in the South, a middle-aged couple came up to Gaye and me, smiling broadly and obviously happy. The wife's first words were, "We just wanted to meet the people responsible for the *Love-Life* cassette album that saved our marriage!" Taking turns, their faces radiant, they explained how they had given up on their marriage with their relationship problems seemingly insurmountable. But then a Christian counselor gave them our *Love-Life* cassette album, and they found hope for the first time. They had carefully followed our suggestions step by step and discovered that they worked. The wife reached in her purse, pulled out her billfold, and took a card out to show us. On it she had outlined the B-E-S-T prescription with a few lines under each point. She said, "I used to look at this many times in the course of a day, and I still use it daily to remind me how to love. Our marriage is so good now—I do not want to slip back into the old patterns of behavior that almost destroyed it!"

Loving your partner by blessing, edifying, sharing, and touching should become a lifetime habit. Not only does it inspire a responding love, but it will bring to life your own feelings of love and keep them alive. This occurs because feelings are determined by actions—not the other way around. If you behave as if you love someone, the *feelings* will inevitably follow in a short time. And by behaving in a positive way through the B-E-S-T plan, you can avoid the emotional numbness you would otherwise develop as a result of your mate's continued rejection.

Even while applying all the rest of the counsel in this book, if you alone are trying to save your marriage you are in a special situation that demands special measures and additional counsel. For, how can you show love when your partner is occupied with someone else? Or has moved out of the home? Or meets your love with hostility? Or totally ignores you?

The special advice I have for you will run counter to everything the worldly mind teaches, and it will go against your own nature to do it. But if you want to save your marriage, you cannot afford to indulge your pride or exalt yourself. You will not even be able to carry out this counsel on your own because only the individual with spiritual resources through a knowledge of the written Word of God and the abiding presence of the Lord Jesus Christ can consistently and effectively do what needs to be done.

The spiritual principle you must comprehend and lay hold of is this: "He (the Lord) has said to me, 'My grace is sufficient for you, for power is perfected in weakness.' Most gladly, therefore, I will rather boast about my weaknesses, that the power of Christ may dwell in me . . . for when I am weak, then I am strong" (2 Corinthians 12:9–10b NASB).

In the light of that principle, which operates in the Christian's life whenever applied, here is preparation you need to make in your purposeful effort to save your marriage.

1) Prepare for the worst, knowing you have a sufficiency of grace.

Usually when a troubled relationship exists, the mate who wants to leave either is involved with another person or anticipates involvement with someone else. So, when a person comes to me with a marriage problem, one of the first things I ask is this:

"Is your partner involved with someone else?"

Often the answer is a reluctant, "Yes, somewhat. . . ."

"All right," I say, "what would you do if your mate were involved in adultery with that person?"

"Well," the individual may say, "it hasn't gone that far yet!"

Then I explain that he or she must be prepared to face the possibility. One wife clung to the belief that her husband (an active Christian) could not possibly have gone as far as the act of adultery with the other woman (a Christian "friend"). When the truth came out, it was doubly devastating because she was totally unprepared to handle it.

Another wife began to prepare emotionally and spiritually for the possibility of her husband's unfaithfulness as a result of Gaye's counsel to her at a seminar. The wife called later to tell us that her husband had come to her soon after the seminar with a confession: he had had a lengthy affair with his secretary. "I'm so glad I was prepared," the wife told us. "He wanted to stay with me, but he thought it would be hopeless once I knew the truth about his past. I had been listening to the *Love-Life* cassettes over and over again, and I was able to handle the situation with calmness and love and forgiveness. I already had my mind focused on the important thing—saving our marriage. We're going to do it."

Adultery probably is the worst sin that most mates can think of their partners committing. It is wise to be prepared practically, emotionally, and spiritually for the worst. Then other problems will become easier to handle if they are "all" you have to contend with. Prepare for the possibility of infidelity by realizing that adultery is sin—the same as any other sin, because God can forgive that individual and so can you! You must forgive if you are to be free to love and live and grow as a person.

Karen Mains, in *The Key to a Loving Heart,* vividly describes the connection between forgiveness and love:

> The key that opens the door to the locked rooms of our hearts is forgiveness. It is only when we have experienced forgiveness (. . . I mean being overwhelmed by the reality of forgiveness, being able to touch, taste, and smell its results) that we find the locks are sprung, the doors flung open, the windows tossed high, the rooms inhabited, the fires lighted on the hearths. It is then we discover that our hearts are finally free to love. They have become what the Creator intended them to be, places with immense capacity to embrace.

After you have forgiven, you must prepare yourself to cope with a continuation of the affair and decide exactly how you will handle it, even rehearsing in your mind how you will respond to certain situations that might arise. You must be prepared to respond in a loving way, even to a continuing infidelity. It's not that you are condoning it; it's not that you are ignoring it. But early on in the process of resolving your marriage problems you have to come to the powerful realization that you cannot reform your mate, no matter how hard you try. Your only option is to become the husband or wife God has commanded you to be in Scripture, and to apply every principle of behavior from the Word of God to the day-by-day challenges of your situation. You may well save your marriage. Without question, you will enjoy God's blessing and favor.

What will change your mate? Sometimes the change comes through a personal knowledge of the Scriptures. One Christian husband forsook his adulterous affair and came home because through personal Bible reading he realized how deeply he had fallen into sin and how terrible the results of that could be. His wife told me, "I thought he had come home because he loved me. But he admitted that he came back in obedience to God's Word. That really did something to my pride at first! My husband said, 'God promises me that He will teach me how to love you as you should be loved.' Then I realized how dumb I had been with my hurt pride. I should be thanking the Lord because this is the best way for us to begin building a real love relationship. If he had come back just because I looked more attractive to him at the moment, it wouldn't have lasted. Now, with *both* of us, our strength and hope to rebuild our marriage rests with the Lord."

But what about the mate who will not go to the Word of God for counsel? In that case, he or she must see in you a living, walking example of God's truth being applied faithfully in every situation. Never leave the impression that you are behaving this way just to change your mate. You do it because God said that you must, whether it seems to work or not.

In severely troubled marriages, it is usually the husband who comes and goes from the family home, perhaps spending part of the time with another woman. While this is obviously distasteful, I sometimes counsel wives to accept this situation on a temporary basis as it is preferable to total separation leading to dissolution of the marriage.

For this reason, your husband is given the freedom to be in both worlds for a time while he tries to live out his fantasy. If you are doing your part at home, a clear contrast will become evident to him. "The lips of an adulteress drip honey, and smoother than oil is her speech; But in the end she is bitter as wormwood, sharp as a two-edged sword. Her feet go down to death. . . . She does not ponder the path of life; her ways are unstable, she does not know it" (Proverbs 5:3–6 NASB). Sooner or later, this will become apparent to your husband. You have the opportunity, if he is still coming home at least part of the time, to show him genuine sweetness with no bitter aftertaste and the gracious, stable serenity that only Christ can give. Your behavior can remind him of the continuing joy and dignity of remaining as the head of his family in contrast to the social, spiritual degradation that biblically is promised to the man who casts his lot with an adulteress. You will not accomplish this by trying, but by *being:* being the loving, gracious wife God would have you to be as defined in the Scriptures.

This is why I urge all men and women under my counseling to avoid separation no matter how serious their problems are. (The only exception is in the case of actual physical injury that could require a legal separation.) As long as the two of you live in the same household, you have the daily opportunity to put powerful biblical principles into action. Don't underestimate your advantage. You are in a position to love so unchangingly that the impact on your partner will intensify with the passing of time. As you consistently apply eternal concepts to your daily relationship, time and togetherness become your helpers in restoring love to your marriage. If you are living apart, then you must take advantage of every common bond you have, such as children or business, to display love through your behavior and attitudes.

The rule is to show him the difference when he is home; make him glad to be there! One wife described how she behaved toward her husband who was beset by financial problems and wavering between home and the other woman's apartment. "I was willing to let my husband have what we had accumulated (mostly debts)," she smiled. "But the other woman was pressuring him to leave home and telling him what she would allow him to give to his children. I thought, He's got one woman pressuring him. He doesn't need two. So I left him alone, coped without demanding money from him, and refused to charge to his accounts. Originally, in his own thinking, he had placed me in the middle of his financial problems while the other woman represented freedom to him—the fantasy of starting over unhindered. But that soon changed. He saw I was on his side—concerned about him, and trusting the Lord to provide for the children and me financially. In contrast, she was demanding expensive furniture and clothes from the best shops. Yes, it hurt to go without a new coat and see her sport a $250 model. But I had to laugh. I knew it wouldn't last long. And it didn't. He's home now—permanently. Our marriage is on a new, solid footing."

In preparing to face the worst that could assault your marriage, you must remember that people ensnared by infatuation and involved in an extramarital affair are suffering from a kind of temporary insanity. They are not thinking clearly: they may behave in totally irresponsible ways; they seem beyond the reach of normal judgment. You will have to realize that this does occur. Even this has to be accepted and dealt with in your own emotional preparation. As one wife said, "While my husband was 'out of it' I didn't try to reason with him. I didn't condemn or judge or scorn or rebuke. I just accepted him the way he was. During that period, I used the waiting time to grow in the Lord myself. Happily, my husband is back to normal now and a lot wiser than before."

When the wife in the marriage becomes infatuated with someone else she will usually move out of the home permanently or demand that her husband leave the home. I counsel the husband not to move away. There is no way he can be forced out of his home if his behavior is moderate and reasonable.

Husbands must be prepared to actively pursue their wives and win them back. But the wife should never be allowed to feel that he is doing this out of duty. Only love will have the force to prevail over the warring emotions that have brought an unfaithful wife to this point.

For instance, a church-going wife's one-time indiscretion became public knowledge. Deeply ashamed and emotionally confused, she left her husband and moved into an apartment where, in a combination of guilt, defiance, and loneliness, she continued to see the other man. Her husband had all the sympathy from their family and church friends. But was he blameless in the matter? Or had he failed to love her as he should before the act of infidelity occurred? In almost every case, the injured party has to bear some responsibility for the breakdown of the marriage. In this situation, the wife's out-of-character behavior had developed after the tragic loss of their child. The husband recognized that he perhaps had failed to exhibit the sensitive understanding he should have shown her at that time. Clearly, he had failed to meet her needs and desires.

Now he had a choice. He could let her go or he could win her back (as did Hosea in the Old Testament), restoring her to her former place of honor. I reminded him of two scriptural principles from Ephesians 5. First, he and that girl were intimately united whether they were living apart or together. As the church is Christ's body, so the wife is, in a sense, the husband's body. Public opinion and her temporary indiscretions and foolish behavior could not change that eternal fact. Second, "He who loves his own wife loves himself; for no one ever hated his own flesh, but nourishes and cherishes it" (Ephesians 5:28–29 NASB).

I counseled this husband to love his wife back to their marriage by nourishing her emotionally and cherishing her in every possible way during this upheaval in her life. "If you approach her as though you are being noble and doing her a favor, you will get nowhere," I warned. "You have to convince her that you love her, that she is valuable and precious beyond any other woman in your sight, that you need her and do not want to live without her."

Another husband had been told by Christian friends to pray and ask God to bring his wife back, then to do nothing, trusting God to work in some supernatural way.

"But your marriage relationship is to picture the relationship between Christ and the Church," I pointed out. "Jesus Christ did not stay with the Father. He came to earth out of love for us and gave everything that He had to establish the relationship with us. Look, the Bible says you are to love your wife the way Christ loves the church. That means an active, pursuing love on your part."

I say to any husband who is trying to restore his marriage that he needs to understand that the only thing that will reach his estranged wife is a convincing, consistent demonstration that he really wants *her*. He is not trying to win her back because it is the right thing to do, or because it is best for the children, or because God is directing him this way. He needs to convince her that he wants her for himself. He has realized that the qualities she has are the ones he needs the most; he feels now that he is able to become the husband he ought to be; and he is eager for every opportunity to show her that he *can* and he *will* love her.

Notice that a husband must win his wife back by initiating love and pursuing, when necessary. A wife must win her husband back by responding with love at every opportunity. This is in keeping with the biblical roles and distinctive natures of husband and wife since the Creation.

The husband who has reason to believe his wife has been unfaithful should beware of asking her for information about the affair. It is enough to accept the fact that she has been indiscreet. The more you know, the more difficult it will be to handle it emotionally.

As Dr. Carlfred Broderick has noted, "In response to an informed spouse's assertion of the right to know 'everything,' repentant mates all too often supply details so vivid and concrete that they can scarcely be set aside."[5]

At the present time I am counseling two husbands, each of whom was determined to build a new love relationship with his wife after an episode of unfaithfulness on her part. But each made the crucial mistake of discussing the affair, probing for details, and they have since been tormented by the information they obtained.

As a general rule, there should be honesty between mates, and in answer to a direct question the affair must be admitted, but details should not be revealed. Tell your partner the subject is too painful to discuss and that you are much more interested in the love affair the two of you can have in your marriage. Unless you are asked, never confess an affair from the past that would come as a shock to your partner. Confession in this case is not virtuous honesty; it is a cruel act that puts the burden and pain on your mate. Keep the knowledge to yourself, confess your wrong to God and rest in His forgiveness.

In this extensive discussion of coping with adultery in marriage, I am in no way minimizing the sin of adultery or discounting the intense suffering it causes. But Christians should be the most realistic people in the world, enabled by the resources of Christ to confront and heal the deepest problems of human relationships. Some researchers say that more than 50 percent of Americans have committed adultery at some time in their marriage. From my vantage point as a family physician for twenty-five years, this estimate sounds quite conservative! But I want to emphasize that a one-time experience of adultery or even an affair of some duration need not destroy your marriage relationship. I can second Dr. Meier's observation that while the wounds from adultery run very deep, mature human beings have a tremendous capacity to forgive one another. Dr. Meier says, "Patients have told me that they never thought they would be able to forgive their mate if he or she ever committed adultery—until it actually happened. Then they were amazed at their own ability to forgive. They realized how much they wanted to restore intimate fellowship with their mate."[6]

So, when you must face the possibility of unfaithfulness on the part of your partner, remember that the Lord has grace enough for you, not only to endure or accept the situation, but also to redeem it.

2) Prepare to be "perfect," knowing you have a sufficiency of grace.

This may come as shocking information, but if you want to save your marriage, you cannot be just a "good" husband or wife. You have to be perfect in your behavior toward your partner. You must *do* and *be* everything the Bible prescribes for your role in marriage, and you must be very sensitive to avoid anything that will set your partner off. The least slip in word or action will give your mate the excuse he or she is looking for to give up on the marriage. Since resentment and rationalization are two of the key issues in the thinking of an unfaithful partner, even one remark spoken out of turn can fan the flames of old resentments and give weight to rationalizations that the partner is manufacturing to excuse his or her behavior.

One wife said, "I had to prove over a period of time that I had changed before my husband could believe it. He kept expecting to face my anger or a miserable silence when he walked in the door. For years, I was so moody, he never knew how he would find me. But now he is beginning to realize a new pattern has formed and things are not the way they used to be."

In talking about "perfect" behavior, we must always recognize the fact that it is the Lord who makes this possible, providing the pattern, the purpose, and the power for fundamental change in our behavior and attitudes. One wife married to an alcoholic said, "I had tried for years to manipulate the situation and change my husband by my own efforts. By nature I am strong-willed and ready to fight for what I want. But I just gave up one day. I remember beginning to cry in the bathtub and praying, 'Lord, you know that I can't handle my own life. Just take over for me, because I have learned that I can't control *anything.*

"And that," she went on, "was the turning point for our marriage. For both of us! Change came slowly. But I had the opportunity to pour out my heart to my husband and tell him how much I needed to be loved and to be put first in his life. He really took me seriously. He had a new motivation to quit drinking. A friend took him to Alcoholics Anonymous, and he has not had a drink in the last seven years. He's again become the wonderful man that I married. I thank God every day for my husband's sobriety and dignity and the love and respect we have for one another now. But the Lord had to change *me* before it could happen."

Three rules should be followed as you learn to love your partner with a love that can save your marriage:

First, *consistently do everything you can to please your mate and meet his or her needs and desires.* Love your partner in such a way that it will be interpreted as love. Study what your partner needs. One wife said, "I used to work in my husband's business, and I thought I was really helping him—really impressing him with my wisdom and efficiency. After our marriage ran into deep trouble, I discovered that wasn't what he needed at all. Now I am staying at home and becoming what he needs—not a whirlwind worker, but a woman who quietly loves him and believes in his ability to handle things well."

Pleasing your partner involves action—sometimes drastic action. A striking example of this is the wife who had had endless fights with her husband over flying in their plane. He was an enthusiastic private pilot; she was terrified of flying. But when it came down to saving her marriage, she went alone to the airport and took flying lessons, trusting the Lord to remove her fears. Today she is a pilot too, and they have a better marriage than ever before. She says, "I have found that spiritual growth gives me the courage I need to change."

Second, *consistently show your mate the respect and honor commanded in Scripture whether your mate personally merits it or not.* I cannot overemphasize this. All of the scriptural admonitions concerning marriage are rooted in this one principle. Study the New Testament passages on this subject, particularly Ephesians 5, Colossians 3, and 1 Peter 3 as translated in the Amplified Bible and other modern English versions. The husband, whatever his behavior, is by position the head of the wife and is to be treated with respect at all times. The wife, whatever her behavior, as an equal heir of the grace of life, is to be given the place of highest honor and special privilege by her husband. As someone has said, she is to be treated like a Ming vase instead of an old garbage can!

Third, *totally avoid criticism of your mate.* Accept whatever your partner is or is not doing without comment or histrionics. Do not even suggest a secret disapproval. Again, the New Testament provides an abundance of instruction.

In Colossians 3, for example, we read:

> Clothe yourselves therefore . . . [by putting on behavior marked by] tenderhearted pity and mercy, kind feeling, a lowly opinion of yourselves, gentle ways, [and] patience—which is tireless, long-suffering and has the power to endure whatever comes, with good temper. Be gentle and forbearing with one another and, if one has a difference (a grievance or complaint) against another, readily pardoning each other; even as the Lord has freely forgiven you, so must you also [forgive]. And above all these [put on] love and enfold yourselves with the bond of perfectness—which binds everything together completely in ideal harmony. And let the peace (soul harmony which comes) from the Christ rule (act as umpire continually) in your hearts. . . . And be thankful—appreciative, giving praise to God always (Colossians 3:12–15 AMPLIFIED).

3) Prepare to be rejected, knowing you have a sufficiency of grace.

What about rejection while you are trying to carry out these principles of love? I can only say that Jesus Christ was perfect and He was rejected! We should not be surprised when it happens to us. But do not give up your efforts because of rejection. One husband told me how he had sent a Valentine's Day flower arrangement to his estranged wife with a card from himself and their little girl. When he came home from work that night, the flowers were on the front step waiting for him—returned in scorn. Later, when she called him at his business, he told her, "I just want you to know that I love you. The hatred you are throwing at me right now cannot change that. I've discovered since we separated that my love for you has much higher limits than I ever realized."

She was quite taken aback by the loving way he had responded to her rejection of his gift. She said, "But you wouldn't want to live with a woman who doesn't love you?"

He answered, "Honey, love is something that doesn't grow overnight, especially when it has been treated the way both of us have treated our relationship in the past. You can't buy love. You aren't born with it. It's something you work at and build together. We haven't even tried that yet."

A happy wife wrote me a note of thanks for my counsel which gave her the courage to stick with her marriage. She said, "One little thing you said to me meant so much. You said, 'So what if your husband doesn't tell you he loves you right now!' I knew you were right. It really wasn't that important." This wife found that putting up with a little rejection was worth it in the long run in order to have a revitalized marriage.

I have talked with many women who tell me that when they do not feel their husband's love, the Lord has a way of loving them that is almost tangible. "Like being in the sunshine, just feeling the warmth of His love," several wives agreed.

A lovely young wife carried that a step further in her own trying situation. She said that it was often difficult dressing to go out for the evening with her husband because she knew in advance that he would not treat her the way she longed to be treated. So she developed the habit of thinking of the Lord Jesus as her friend and escort for the evening. "It helped me tremendously," she said. "I looked my best for Him, I behaved my best for Him, and I was constantly aware of His steadying presence with me!"

In summary, you need to give love to your mate biblically, emotionally, and physically whether you receive a response or not. This is altogether possible through *agape* love. One wife, whose husband was involved with another woman, said, "I tried to show him that my love for him did not depend on how he treated me. I still showed him physical affection. I said to him sometimes, 'I love you, no matter what you are doing right now, and I believe the Lord means for us to be together.' I sent him little cards with appropriate messages that expressed my caring while we were apart. And, do you know, when we reconciled, I found that he had saved every one of them!"

I asked some wives who had been through the experience to give me their list of do's and don'ts for any woman trying to save her marriage. Here are the excellent suggestions they compiled:

- There can be no growth in your relationship as long as there is doubt as to your commitment to your marriage. Make your commitment!
- When your husband withholds his love, trust the Lord to meet your emotional needs. He won't let you down!
- Give your husband honor, love, and biblical respect even though his actions do not deserve it. Give him warm acceptance no matter what. The more hopeless your situation is, the more your loving behavior is apt to be accepted as genuine.
- Don't try to reform your husband. Just love him.
- Live one day at a time.
- Don't try to do it on your own. The Lord is with you!
- Don't be bitter against anyone in the situation. Never turn your children against their father. Forgive!
- Don't ask family or friends to take sides against your husband.
- Don't discuss your intimate marriage problems. Don't give fuel to gossip. Confide in the Lord, your counselor, and perhaps a close Christian friend whom you can trust to keep silence.
- Choose your biblical counselor wisely. *Never* discuss your problems with a friend of the opposite sex.

- Spend as much time in the Word of God as possible.
- Concentrate on yourself, redeeming the mistakes you have made, and asking God to show you how to change, rather than concentrating on your partner's failures.
- Do not separate. Encourage your husband to stay in the home, no matter what.
- Do not give your husband a divorce. Do all in your power to delay or prevent it. If you must consult a lawyer, make it clear to the lawyer that it is only for your financial protection and that of your children. Find a Christian lawyer who will help you preserve your marriage.
- Spend your time with people who will encourage you in spiritual growth.
- Do not overcompensate with your children. They need your love and stability while their father is gone, but they still need discipline. It will be hard to build a new love relationship with your husband when he does come home if the children are out of control.
- Do not try to defend yourself from gossip or criticism. Keep your mouth shut. The Lord will fight for you and you will hold your peace.
- Remember that the most innocent thing you say will get twisted. Avoid loose talk and do not listen to tale-bearing.
- When you do anything (large or small) to pull the marriage apart, you are going against God's will. Let that be your guideline for all decisions.
- Don't expect your husband to change overnight when he does come back home.
- The hardest time may be when you are reconciled and you have a tendency to fall back into old habit patterns. Don't do it!
- Hope all things, believe all things, endure all things.

The Book of Hosea in the Old Testament gives us the ultimate pattern for a love without limits which eventually reunites husband and wife in spite of great obstacles. This holds particular meaning for the husband whose wife has left him for someone else. Read the following narrative account of the love story of Hosea and ask God to strengthen your own resolve through this retelling of His Word.

THE LOVE STORY OF HOSEA

(A first person narrative expository dramatic sermon by Dr. John W. Reed, Associate Professor of Practical Theology, Dallas Theological Seminary. Used by Permission)

I have been called the prophet of the broken heart, but I would rather be remembered as the prophet of love and hope. I am Hosea, prophet of God to Israel, my homeland.

Come with me to my home on the outskirts of Samaria. There beneath the oak tree is Gomer, my wife; I love her as I love my own life. You will learn to love her too. Sitting beside her is our son, Jezreel. He is eighteen now, handsome and strong—a young man with a heart for God. At Gomer's feet and looking up at her is Ruhamah, our daughter. Do you see how her raven hair glistens? She is the image of her mother. She was sixteen just half a year ago. And then Ammi, her brother—fifteen and as warm and bubbling as the flowing brook that you hear in the background.

We are happy and at peace. It has not always been so.

I began my ministry as a prophet almost thirty years ago during the reign of Jeroboam II. Those were years of prosperity. The caravans that passed between Assyria and Egypt paid taxes into Jeroboam's treasury and sold their goods in our midst. But they also left their sons and daughters and their gods. These gods and the gods of the ancient Canaanites and of Jezebel have wooed the hearts of my people. Altars built for sin offerings have become places for sinning.

If you were to walk through my land today, you would see images and altars in all the green groves. My people have many sheep and cattle. Some think that Baal, the so-called fertility god, is the giver of lambs, of calves, and the fruit of the field. Every city has its high place where Baal is worshiped. There is a high place not far from here—you are never far from a high place in Israel in these days! Sometimes at night we hear the beat of the priest's music and the laughter of the sacred prostitutes. Last week a man and woman who live three houses from us sacrificed their infant son to Baal.

You may wonder how Jehovah's people could sink to such unholy ways. It is because the priests of God have departed from Him. They delight in the sins of the people; they lap it up and lick their lips for more. And thus it is "Like priests, like people." Because the priests are wicked, the people are too. Surely God will judge. My beautiful land is just a few short years from being crushed under the iron heel of the Assyrian military might.

Yes, thirty years ago God appointed me a prophet in Israel. My father, Beeri, and my honored mother had taught me early to fear Jehovah, the One true God of Israel. They taught me to hate the calf deity of the first Jeroboam. Daily we prayed. Daily we longed to return to the Temple in Jerusalem. Daily we sang the songs of David and hungered for the coming of Messiah.

My ministry has always been hard. The first ten years were the hot-blooded days of my twenties. My sermons were sermons of fire. My heart bled for my people. I was little heeded and generally scorned. When I was thirty-two, God stirred me and I spent many days in prayer and meditation. I felt lonely and in need of a companion.

The first frosts of fall had tinted the leaves when I went with my parents to visit the home of Diblaim. In the busy activity of my ministry I had not seen the family for several years. We were engaged in lively conversation when through the door swept a young woman, Gomer, the daughter of Diblaim. I remembered her as a pretty and somewhat spoiled child. But now she was a hauntingly beautiful woman. Her ivory face was framed in a wealth of raven black hair. I found myself fascinated by her striking beauty and had great difficulty in turning my eyes from her.

As we returned to our home that day, my father and I talked of many things. Yet, in my mind hung the image of a raven-haired Israelite. My father's friendship with Diblaim flourished and often I journeyed with him to visit. I was strangely drawn to Gomer. Diblaim and my father talked incessantly. Then one day my father astounded me with the proposal, "Hosea, it is my desire that you should marry Gomer." I did not question that I loved Gomer. But something about her troubled me. As most young women of her time she had a love for expensive clothing, jewelry and cosmetics. That I accepted as part of her womanhood. But she seemed somehow to be experienced beyond her years in the ways of the world.

Yet, I loved her. It was my father's will that I should marry her. I knew that my burning love for Jehovah would win her from any wanton ways. God confirmed to me that indeed Gomer was His choice as well.

I wooed her with the passion of a prophet. God had given me the gift of poetry and I flooded Gomer with words of love.

She responded to my love. We stood together beneath the flower-strewn canopy of the Hebrew marriage altar and pledged eternal love to God and to each other. We listened together to the reading of God's laws of marriage. We heard the reminder that our marriage was a symbol of the marriage between Jehovah and Israel, His wife.

I took Gomer to my home. We read together the Song of Songs which is Solomon's. We ate the sweet fruit of its garden of love. She was as refreshing to me as the first fig of the season. Gomer seemed content in the love of God and of Hosea. I looked forward to the future with hope.

Shortly after the anniversary of our first year of marriage Gomer presented me with a son. I sought God's face and learned that his name was to be Jezreel—a name that would constantly remind Israel that God's judgment was surely coming. It was a stark reminder to me of the times in which we lived.

With the birth of Jezreel, Gomer seemed to change.

She became distant and a sensual look flashed in her eye. I thought it a reaction to the responsibility of caring for our son. Those were busy days. The message of God inflamed me and I cried out throughout the land.

Gomer was soon with child again. This time a daughter was born. I learned from God that she was to be named Lo-Ruhamah. It was a strange name and troubled me deeply for it meant, "Not loved." For God said, "I will no longer show my love to the nation of Israel, that I should forgive her."

Gomer began to drift from me after that. Often she would leave after putting the children to bed and not return until dawn. She grew worn, haggard, and rebellious. I sought every way possible to restore her to me, but to no avail. About eighteen months later a third child was born, a boy. God told me to call him, Lo-Ammi—meaning, "Not my people." God said to Israel, "You are not my people, and I am not your God." In my heart a thorn was driven. I knew that he was not my son and that his sister was not the fruit of my love. Those were days of deep despair. I could not sing the songs of David. My heart broke within me.

After Lo-Ammi was weaned, Gomer drifted beyond my reach—and did not return. I became both father and mother to the three children.

I felt a blight upon my soul. My ministry seemed paralyzed by the waywardness of my wife. My prayers seemed to sink downward. But then Jehovah stirred me. I came to know that God was going to use my experience as an illustration of His love for Israel.

Love flamed again for Gomer and I knew that I could not give her up. I sought her throughout Samaria. I found her in the ramshackle house of a lustful, dissolute Israelite who lacked the means to support her. I begged her to return. She spurned all my pleadings. Heavy-hearted, I returned to the children and mourned and prayed. My mind warmed with a plan. I went to the market, bought food and clothes for Gomer. I bought the jewelry and the cosmetics she loved so dearly. Then I sought out her lover in private. He was suspicious, thinking that I had come to do him harm. When I told him my plan, a sly smile crept over his face. If I could not take Gomer home, my love would not let me see her wanting. I would provide all her needs and she could think that they came from him. We struck hands on the bargain. He struggled home under his load of provisions. I followed in the shadows.

She met him with joy and showered him with love. She told him to wait outside the house while she replaced her dirty, worn apparel with the new.

After what seemed hours, she reappeared dressed in radiant splendor, like the Gomer I saw that first day at the home of her father. Her lover approached to embrace her, but she held him off. I heard her say, "No, surely the clothes and food and cosmetics are not from your hand but from the hand of Baal who gives all such things. I am resolved to express my gratitude to Baal by serving as a priestess at the high place."

It was as if I were suddenly encased in stone. I could not move. I saw her walk away. She seemed like the rebellious heifer I had seen as a youth in my father's herd. She could not be helped but would go astray. The more I tried to restore her the further she went from me. Feeble with inner pain, I stumbled home to sleepless nights and days of confusion and grief.

Gomer gave herself with reckless abandonment to the requirements of her role of priestess of Baal. She eagerly prostituted her body to the wanton will of the worshipers of the sordid deity.

My ministry became a pilgrimage of pain. I became an object of derision. It seemed that the penalty for the sin of Gomer—and of all my people— had settled upon me.

I fell back upon Jehovah. My father and mother helped me in the care and instruction of the three children. They responded in love and obedience. They became the Balm of Gilead for my wounded heart. The years passed as I sounded the burden of God throughout the land. Daily I prayed for Gomer and as I prayed love sang in my soul.

She was my nightly dream and so real that upon waking I often felt as if she had just left me again.

The years flowed on but the priests of Baal held her in their deadly clutch.

It was just over a year ago that it happened. The blush of spring was beginning to touch our land. In the midst of my morning hour of meditation, God seemed to move me to go among the people of Samaria. I was stirred with a sense of deep anticipation. I wandered through the streets.

Soon I was standing in the slave market. It was a place I loathed. Then I saw a priest of Baal lead a woman to the slave block. My heart stood still. It was Gomer. A terrible sight she was to be sure, but it was Gomer. Stark naked she stood on the block. But no man stared in lust. She was broken, haggard; and thin as a wisp of smoke. Her ribs stood out beneath the skin. Her hair was matted and touched with streaks of gray and in her eye was the flash of madness. I wept.

Then softly the voice of God's love whispered to my heart. I paused, confused. The bidding reached thirteen shekels of silver before I fully understood God's purposes. I bid fifteen shekels of silver. There was a pause. A voice on the edge of the crowd said, "Fifteen shekels and an homer of barley."

"Fifteen shekels, an homer and half of barley," I cried. The bidding was done.

As I mounted the slave block, a murmur of disbelief surged through the crowd. They knew me and they knew Gomer. They leaned forward in anticipation. Surely I would strike her dead on the spot for her waywardness. But my heart flowed with love.

I stood in front of Gomer and cried out to the people. "God says to you, 'Unless Israel remove her adulteries from her, I will strip her as naked as the day that she was born. I will make her like a desert and leave her like a parched land to die of thirst.'"

I cried to a merchant at a nearby booth, "Bring that white robe on the end of the rack."

I paid him the price he asked. Then I tenderly drew the robe around Gomer's emaciated body and said to her, "Gomer, you are mine by the natural right of a husband. Now you are also mine because I have bought you for a price. You will no longer wander from me or play the harlot. You must be confined for a time and then I will restore you to the full joys of womanhood."

She sighed and fainting fell into my arms. I held her and spoke to my people, "Israel will remain many days without king or prince, without sacrifice or ephod. Afterward Israel will return and seek the Lord her God and David her king. She will come trembling to the Lord and to his benefits in the last days. And where it was said of Israel, 'Lo-Ru-hamah—you are not loved, it will be said Ruhamah—you are loved.' For the love of God will not give you up, but pursue you down your days. And where Israel was called, 'Lo-Ammi, you are not my people,' it will be said, 'Ammi, you are the people of the living God,' for I will forgive you and restore you."

I returned home with my frail burden. I nursed Gomer back to health. Daily I read to her the writings of God. I taught her to sing the penitential song of David and then together we sang the songs of David's joyful praise to God. In the midst of song I restored her to God, to our home, to our children.

Do you not see how beautiful she is? I have loved her always, even in the depth of her waywardness because my God loved her. Gomer responded to God's love and to mine. She does not call me "my master" but "my husband." And the name of Baal has never again been on her lips.

Now my people listen to my message with new responsiveness for I am a prophet that has been thrilled with a great truth. I have come to know in the depth of my being how desperately God loves sinners. How deliberately He seeks them! How devotedly He woos them to Himself!

16
Resources for Change

LOVERS NEVER SEEM to tire of sharing tender reminiscences about their love affair: the intrigue of first meeting . . . the sweet moment when they confessed their caring . . . the thrill of their surrender to each other.

Intimate conversations of this nature are recorded in Scripture in the Song of Solomon. For example, when Shulamith and her beloved husband are vacationing in the countryside, Shulamith says, "Do you remember where our love began? Under the legendary sweetheart tree, of course, where every love begins and grows . . . Neither did our love begin without the pain, the fruitful pain of birth. . . ."

Of course, such reminiscences lead to a quickened desire for physical expression of their love: "O, my darling lover, make me your most precious possession held securely in your arms, held close to your heart," Shulamith whispers.

But the lovers are irresistibly drawn to speak of the quality of the love they share: its strength and its ultimate source. "True love is as strong and irreversible as the onward march of death," Shulamith says. "True love never ceases to care, and it would no more give up the beloved than the grave would give up the dead. *The fires of true love can never be quenched because the source of its flame is God himself.*"

These are the fires that I pray will be set ablaze in your own marriage!

My personal message to you in these pages has been that you and your mate do not have to live together in boredom or separate in misery. The alternative: to become *lovers* through the resources of what I will call *ultimate* love. This is what I would have you to focus on in this final chapter of *Love-life.*

In marriage, the delights of all the human loves are mingled and made fragrant as a garden when ultimate love permeates the relationship. Even more important, the human loves are stabilized by the abiding presence of ultimate love. Feelings are momentary; ultimate love is lasting. The emotions of love are like those of other natural energies, always ebbing and flowing, even as the metabolic rate of the body incessantly changes, or the wind rises and falls. No passion endures on a consistent level. But your experience of love can be so reinforced by the tensiled strength of ultimate love that you will keep on loving and continue growing in love, no matter what your marriage must face in the course of a lifetime.

The Bible teaches (and in honesty we must agree) that we cannot save ourselves by any method: the Son of God had to become the Man Jesus, to live a perfect life, die for our sins, and live again in order to save us. Equally so, we cannot truly love by our own efforts. Again, God who is Love intervenes by giving us the priceless gift of ultimate love to be poured out to others.

Your own marriage partner should be the first, last, and in between recipient of ultimate love. It is this that will save, restore, transform, and bless your marriage beyond your highest hopes.

How is this love expressed in human relationships—this love beyond which there is no other? We have described its qualities in other chapters, but let us take one more look from a different perspective. We can search out love's characteristic behavior by reading the letters the apostles wrote to believers of the early church. For example, if we read 2 Corinthians 12 we will find these qualities of love shining through the pages, and these are the very attitudes and actions that should be pervading our own marriage:

- Ultimate love pursues the beloved. It is a love of action that perseveres against great odds and never gives up. "I come to you," Paul writes.
- Ultimate love is unselfish—undemanding and compassionate. "I will not be a burden to you," Paul says.
- Ultimate love values the beloved. "I do not seek what is yours, but *you*," Paul reassures.
- Ultimate love freely assumes responsibility for the welfare of the beloved. "I am responsible for you," Paul states.
- Ultimate love gives to the limit without totaling the cost. "I will gladly spend and be expended for you," Paul affirms.
- Ultimate love grows in expression and does not diminish, regardless of the nature of the response. "I will love you the more," says Paul.
- Ultimate love is pure in motive and action, unadulterated by self-centered considerations. "I will not take advantage of you," Paul promises. "I will not exploit you. Everything I do is for your strengthening and building up."

Surely this love is fitted for the hard realities of life! When two people love this way, their marriage is touched by heaven despite the earthly problems from which no people are exempt.

Do you want to love and be loved like this? God is the only source of ultimate love; His is the power supply that feeds the fires of true love between husband and wife. It will not be enough to learn *about* God and this love. You must learn *from* Him and become linked to Him in an eternal relationship through new life in Jesus Christ.

Let me explain how this occurs. Romans 10:9–10 says, "If thou shalt confess with thy mouth the Lord Jesus, and shalt believe in thine heart that God hath raised him from the dead, thou shalt be saved. For with the heart man believeth unto righteousness; and with the mouth confession is made unto salvation."

The Bible teaches that the Lord Jesus Christ is the Son of God who came to earth through the miracle of the virgin birth. He lived a perfect life as a man and, at a specific moment in history, He died on a cross to bear the sins of the whole world—the sins of every individual who will ever live. He died for you personally! Through that mighty act He paid the death penalty for sin and opened the way whereby your sins and mine can be forgiven and remembered no more.

After three days in the grave, Jesus demonstrated to all people for all time that He is God by rising from the dead—a legally authenticated fact of history. After more than a month spent on this earth in His resurrection body, He ascended to heaven with all power and authority in His possession. It is written in John 1:12: "But as many as received him, to them gave he power to become the sons of God, even to them that believe on his name."

Colossians 1:13–14 explains that the Father "hath delivered us from the power of darkness, and hath translated us into the kingdom of his dear Son: in whom we have redemption through his blood, even the forgiveness of sins."

Second Corinthians 5:17–18 promises that "Therefore if any man be in Christ, he is a new creature: old things are passed away; behold, all things are become new. And all things are of God, who hath reconciled us to himself by Jesus Christ. . . ."

Salvation and new life come through believing in Jesus Christ, the Son of God, as your Savior and receiving Him by faith. You must believe these things in your heart, then confess them with your mouth—both to God and to men.

Here is a prayer that you may wish to follow in expressing your faith in Jesus Christ as your Savior:

Heavenly Father, I realize I am a sinner and cannot do one thing to save myself. Right now I believe Jesus Christ died on the cross, shedding His blood as full payment for my sins—past, present, and future—and by rising from the dead He demonstrated that He is God. As best I know how, I am believing in Him, putting all my trust in Jesus Christ as my personal Savior, as my only hope for salvation and eternal life. Right now I am receiving Christ into my life, and I thank You for saving me as You promised, and I ask that You will give me increasing faith and wisdom and joy as I study and believe Your Word. For I ask this in Jesus' name. Amen.

When we put our trust in Jesus Christ and our lives link up with His, we become new people. Our problems may seem the same, but our ability to cope with them is all new. We have suspected that we needed to change. Now we can face it and draw on new resources to effect that change.

We as Christians have a source of love beyond ourselves. We have a sufficiency of grace for every situation. We have a new kind of strength—the power of the Lord Jesus Christ--that manifests itself through our own weakness. We now have the ability to behave in the ways that will bring order and blessing into our lives. It is now possible for us to apply every biblical principle concerning marriage and to resolve relationship problems with those closest to us.

As Christian psychiatrist Frank B. Minirth has observed, "Christian counseling is unique because it depends not only on man's willpower to be responsible, but also on God's enabling, indwelling power of the Holy Spirit to conquer man's problems. I do not wish to imply that man has no responsibility for his actions, for he does; and many Christians choose to act irresponsibly. However, our willingness and attempts to be responsible must be coupled with God's power. Through God's power, man need no longer be a slave to a weak will, his past environment, or social situations. Problems do not disappear when one accepts Christ, but there is a new power to deal with them."[1]

The chances are good that you have read this book through to the end because you are hungering for a change in your marriage. You have, no doubt, seen many areas of your life that cry out for improvement. And, by now, you have realized that change must occur within yourself before you can hope for your partner to change. You know for a certainty that running away from your problems will not cause change within. You can go a thousand miles away, start a new life, get a divorce, remarry, and you will still find yourself on the old emotional treadmill, facing compounded problems and an even greater need to change.

But if you have trusted Jesus Christ as your Savior, the answers are within your grasp. You do not have to run away from yourself or your problems any longer. The question now is not: *Can* I change? but *Will* I change?

No writer has made this point more clearly than Charles (Chuck) Swindoll, radio Bible teacher, in a column entitled "CAN'T OR WON'T?" He writes:

No offense, but some of you don't have any business reading this today. Normally, I do not restrict my column to any special group of people. But now I must. This time it is *for Christians only*. Everything I write from now to the end is strictly for the believer in Christ. If you're not there yet, you can toss this aside because you lack a major ingredient: the power of God. Non Christians are simply unable to choose righteous paths consistently. That divine response upon which the Christian can (and *must*) draw is not at the unbeliever's disposal. That is, not until personal faith in Jesus Christ is expressed.

But if you know the Lord, you are the recipient of limitless ability . . . incredible strength. Just read a few familiar lines out of the Book, *slowly* for a change:

> I can do all things through Him who strengthens me (Philippians 4:13).

> . . . "My grace is sufficient for you, for power is perfected in weakness." Most gladly, therefore, I will rather boast about my weaknesses, that the power of Christ may dwell in me (2 Corinthians 12:9).

> For this reason I bow my knees before the Father. . . that He would grant you, according to the riches of His glory, to be strengthened with power through His Spirit in the inner man (Ephesians 4:14, 16).

> . . . He has granted to us His precious and magnificent promises, in order that by them you might become partakers of the divine nature . . . (2 Peter 1:4).

And one more:

> No temptation has overtaken you but such as is common to man; and God is faithful, who will not allow you to be tempted beyond what you are able, but with the temptation will provide the way of escape also, that you may be able to endure it (1 Corinthians 10:13).

Wait a minute now. Did you read every word—or did you skip a line or two? If so, please go back and *slowly* graze over those five statements written to you, a Christian. It's really important.

Okay, what thought stands out the most? Well, if someone asked me that question, I'd say, "special strength or an unusual ability from God." In these verses it's called several things: strength, power, divine nature, ability. God has somehow placed into the Christian's insides a special something, that extra inner reservoir of power that is more than a match for the stuff life throws at us. When in operation, phenomenal accomplishments are achieved, sometimes even *miraculous*.

Let's get specific.

It boils down to the choice of two common words in our vocabulary. Little words, but, oh, so different! "Can't" and "won't."

We prefer to use "can't."

"I just *can't* get along with my wife."
"My husband and I *can't* communicate."
"I *can't* discipline the kids like I should."
"I just *can't* give up the affair I'm having."
"I *can't* stop overeating."
"I *can't* find the time to pray."
"I *can't* quit gossiping."

No, any Christian who really takes those five passages we just looked at (there are dozens more) will have to confess the word really should be "won't." Why? Because we have been given the power, the ability to overcome. Literally! And therein lies hope in hoisting anchors that would otherwise hold us in the muck and mire of blame and self-pity.

One of the best books you can read this year on overcoming depression is a splendid work by two physicians, Minirth and Meier, appropriately entitled *Happiness Is a Choice*. These men agree:

As psychiatrists we cringe whenever (Christian) patients use the word *can't*. . . . Any good psychiatrist knows that "I can't" and "I've tried" are merely lame excuses. We insist that our patients be honest with themselves and use language that expresses the reality of the situation. So we have our patients change their *can'ts* to *won'ts*. . . . If an individual changes all his *can'ts* to *won'ts*, he stops avoiding the truth, quits deceiving himself, and starts living in reality. . . .

What a difference one word makes!

"I just *won't* get along with my wife."
"My husband and I *won't* communicate."
"I *won't* discipline the kids like I should."
"I just *won't* give up the affair I'm having."
"I *won't* stop overeating."

"I *won't* find the time to pray."

"I *won't* quit gossiping."

Non-Christians have every right and reason to use "can't," because they really can't! They are victims, trapped and bound like slaves in a fierce and endless struggle. Without Christ and His power, they lack what it takes to change permanently. They don't because they can't!

But people like us? Hey, let's face it, we don't because we won't . . . we disobey because we want to, not because we have to . . . because we choose to, not because we're forced to. The sooner we are willing to own up realistically to our responsibility and stop playing the blame game at pity parties for ourselves, the more we'll learn and change and the less we'll burn and blame.

Wish I could find a less offensive way to communicate all this, but I just can't.

Oops!

Chuck Swindoll
(used by permission)

Poet and hymn-writer Annie Johnson Flint expressed the same truth in words that countless Christians have sung with grateful hearts:

His love has no limits; His grace has no measure;
His power has no boundary known unto men.
For out of His infinite riches in Jesus,
He giveth, and giveth, and giveth again!

And so some crucial choices lie before us. We must choose first of all whether to become Christians and to be linked eternally with the God of love and the Lord of life. Then we must choose whether to use the great resources He makes available to every believer.

We also determine by action or inaction the quality of love-life we will have in our marriage. It is vain to hope that a troubled relationship will get better on its own, or that somehow time will bring about more love, or that we will (accidentally?) draw closer to each other. It is up to each of us to build our house of love.

The Bible makes the choice clear in the Book of Proverbs. We are told, "The wise woman builds her house, but the foolish tears it down with her own hands" (Proverbs 14:1 NASB). "He that troubleth his own house shall inherit the wind . . ." (Proverbs 11:29) and will live to regret it.

But this need not be so! For, "By wisdom a house is built, and by understanding it is established; and by knowledge the rooms are filled with all precious and pleasant riches" (Proverbs 24:3–4 NASB). Our wisdom comes from a daily study of the Word of God, applying its counsel to the details of life and letting it shape our attitudes and behavior in every situation.

As you continue gathering biblical information on your role as husband or wife and learning how to love, and as learning is followed by doing, and principle by practice, you will find your obedience transformed into the passionate and joyous pleasure of loving your mate.

Isobel Kuhn in *Stones of Fire* quotes a phrase from Dr. G. Campbell Morgan that perfectly describes the uniqueness of the love-life that is available to every Christian couple:

> Principle shot through with passion,
> Passion held by principle.

This is the pattern we aim for. And as we aim we find 2 Chronicles 25:9 wonderfully true: Whatever plateau you have reached in your love-life, *"The LORD is able to give thee much more than this!"*

Notes

Chapter 4

[1]Silvarlo and James Arieti, *Love Can Be Found* (New York: Harcourt Brace Jovanovich, 1977), Preface, IX.

Chapter 6

[1]Helen Singer Kaplan, *Disorders of Sexual Desire* (New York: Simon and Schuster, 1979), p. 6.

Chapter 7

[1]Jay E. Adams, *Christian Living in the Home* (Phillipsburg, New Jersey: Presbyterian and Reformed, 1972), p. 100.

[2]Shirley Rice, *Physical Unity in Marriage* (Norfolk, Virginia: The Tabernacle Church of Norfolk, 1973), pp. 3-4.

[3]Sheldon Vanauken, *A Severe Mercy* (New York: Harper & Row, 1977 Bantam Books), p. 20.

[4]Helen B. Andelin, *The Fascinating Girl* (Santa Barbara: Pacific Press Santa Barbara, 1969), pp. 15-16.

[5]Glenn Wilson and David Nias, *The Mystery of Love* (New York: Quadrangle/The New York Times Book Co., Inc., 1976), p. 48.

[6]Mary Ellen Curtin, ed., *Symposium on Love* (New York: Behavioral Publications, 1973), p. 120.

[7]Vanauken, *A Severe Mercy*, p. 36.

[8]Mary McDermott Shideler, *The Theology of Romantic Love: A Study in the Writings of Charles Williams* (Grand Rapids: Eerdmans, 1962), p. 1.

Chapter 9

[1]Anne Morrow Lindbergh, *Bring Me a Unicorn* (New York: Harcourt Brace Jovanovich, Inc., 1971), Introduction, p. XXV.

[2]Ibid., pp. 239, 245.

[3]Ibid., pp. 248–249.

Chapter 11

[1]Kaplan, *Disorders of Sexual Desire, p.* 183.

[2]William S. Appleton, "Why Marriages Become Dull," *Medical Aspects of Human Sexuality* (March 1980): 73, 81.

[3]Jan Ensley Troutt, *Sensitivity Plus* (Rogers, Arkansas: Waggoner-Shumate Printing Co., 1979).

[4]John Powell, *The Secret of Staying in Love* (Niles, Illinois: Argus Communications, 1974), p. 188.

[5]Mary Ann Bartusis, "Falling in Love with a Best Friend's Spouse," *Medical Aspects of Human Sexuality* (February 1980): 32–43.

Chapter 12

[1]*The Anchor Bible, Song of Songs,* Introduction by Marvin H. Pope (Garden City, New York: Doubleday, 1977), p. 17.

Chapter 13

[1]Vanauken, *A Severe Mercy,* pp. 27–28.

Chapter 15

[1]Paul D. Meier, You *Can Avoid Divorce* (Grand Rapids: Baker Book House, 1978), p. 4.

[2]Ibid., pp. 5–6.

[3]Anne Kristin Carroll, *From the Brink of Divorce* (Garden City, New York: A Doubleday-Galilee Original, 1978), p. 19.

[4]Gloria Okes Perkins, "Fly by the Instruments," *Good News Broadcaster* (October 1978): 26–27.

[5]Carlfred B. Broderick, "Guidelines for Preserving Fidelity," *Medical Aspects of Human Sexuality* (May 1980): 21.

[6]Meier, *You Can Avoid Divorce,* p. 8.

Chapter 16

[1]Frank B. Minirth, *Christian Psychiatry* (Old Tappan, New Jersey: Revell, 1977), pp. 31–32.

Suggested Reading

Adams, Jay E. *Christian Living in the Home* (Phillipsburg, New Jersey: Presbyterian and Reformed Publishing Company, 1972). A precise and powerful application of scriptural principles to the problems of today's home and family.

Augsburger, David W. *Seventy Times Seven: The Freedom of Forgiveness* (Chicago: Moody Press, 1970). A classic on the subject of forgiveness and resolving of hostility.

Brandt, Henry, with Landrum, Phil. *I Want My Marriage to Be Better* (Grand Rapids, Michigan: Zondervan Publishing House, 1976). A Christian psychologist explains how walls arise in marriage and shows how they can be removed.

Burkett, Larry. *Your Finances in Changing Times* (Campus Crusade for Christ, Inc., 1975). God's principles for managing money described by a Christian financial counselor. Recommended for every marriage.

Campbell, Ross, M.D. *How to Really Love Your Child* (Wheaton, Illinois: Victor Books, SP Publications Inc., 1977). Valuable instruction in how to love those closest to you with many applications to the husband-wife relationship.

Carroll, Anne Kristin. *Together Forever* (Grand Rapids, Michigan: Zondervan 1982). Wise, sympathetic advice for the individual caught in a problem marriage. A must for those who want to save their marriage.

Cooper, Darien B. *You Can Be the Wife of a Happy Husband* (Wheaton, Illinois: Victor Books, SP Publications Inc., 1974). A helpful explanation of the wife's God-given role.

Dillow, Linda. *Creative Counterpart* (Nashville, Tennessee: Thomas Nelson, Inc., 1978). Good ideas for the Christian wife to implement.

Dobson, James. *What Wives Wish Their Husbands Knew About Women* (Wheaton, Illinois: Tyndale House Publishers, Inc., 1975). This popular book includes an important section on hormonal problems during menopause.

Fooshee, George and Marjean. *You Can Beat the Money Squeeze* (Old Tappan, New Jersey: Power Books, Fleming H. Revell Company, 1980). Practical principles of finance for the marriage of the '80s.

Glickman, S. Craig. *A Song for Lovers* (Downers Grove, Illinois: InterVarsity Press, 1976). Perceptive discussion of love in marriage based on the Song of Solomon.

LaHaye, Tim and Beverly. *The Act of Marriage* (Grand Rapids, Michigan: Zondervan Publishing House, 1976). Excellent suggestions for improving the sex relationship in any marriage.

Landorf, Joyce. *Tough and Tender* (Old Tappan, New Jersey: Fleming H. Revell Company, 1975). A sensitive consideration of husband and wife roles in marriage.

Lewis, C. S. *The Four Loves* (New York: Harcourt Brace Jovanovich, Inc., 1960). A refreshing view of the basic kinds of human love.

Mayhall, Jack and Carole. *Marriage Takes More Than Love* (Colorado Springs: NAV press, 1978). Down-to-earth solutions for marital conflicts.

Meredith, Don. *Becoming One* (Nashville, Tennessee: Thomas Nelson Publishers, 1979). Realistic suggestions for a successful marriage.

Merrill, Dean. *How to Really Love Your Wife* (Grand Rapids: Zondervan Publishing House, 1980). A thought-provoking job description for the married man.

Miles, Herbert J. *Sexual Happiness in Marriage* (Grand Rapids, Michigan: Zondervan Publishing House, 1967). Written by a pioneer in the field of sex in marriage from the biblical viewpoint.

Minirth, Frank B., M.D. *Christian Psychiatry* (Old Tappan, New Jersey: Fleming H. Revell Company, 1977). A balanced, biblical approach to personal problems.

Minirth, Frank B., M.D., and Meier, Paul D., M.D. *Happiness Is a Choice.* Two Christian psychiatrists explain how to conquer depression and establish a sense of well-being.

Powell, John. *Why Am I Afraid to Love?* (Niles, Illinois: Argus Communications Co., Revised, 1972). A sensitive discussion of the barriers that hinder loving and how to overcome them.

Rice, Shirley. *Physical Unity in Marriage* (Norfolk, Virginia: The Tabernacle Church of Norfolk, 1973). An excellent treatment of the subject from the wife's view.

Short, Ray E. *Sex, Love, or Infatuation* (Minneapolis: Augsburg Publishing House, 1978). A good overview of genuine love as it should be experienced in marriage.

Strauss, Richard L. *Marriage Is for Love* (Wheaton, Illinois: Tyndale House Publishers, 1973). How to make your marriage work by applying God's principles.

Swindoll, Charles R. *Killing Giants, Pulling Thorns* (Portland, Oregon: Multnomah Press, 1978). Strong encouragement, biblical teaching in exciting language. Tells how to deal with the giants and thorns in your own life.

Timmons, Tim. *One Plus One* (Washington, D.C.: Canon Press, 1974). A detailed look at the scriptural plan for oneness in marriage.

Trobisch, Ingrid. *The Joy of Being a Woman* (New York: Harper & Row Publishers, 1975). A guidebook to the Christian woman's own body and spirit.

Trobisch, Walter. *I Married You* (New York: Harper & Row Publishers, 1971). A creative, compassionate approach to the meaning of marriage based upon the author's insight as a counselor and as a husband.

Wessel, Helen. *The Joy of Natural Childbirth* (San Francisco: Harper & Row Publishers, 1973). A useful book for those considering natural childbirth, written from a Christian perspective.

Wheat, Ed, M.D., and Gaye. *Intended for Pleasure* (Old Tappan, New Jersey: Fleming H. Revell Company, 1977). Sexual fulfillment in Christian marriage clearly and sensitively explained from the medical, emotional, and spiritual perspectives. Indexed and illustrated.

Wright, H. Norman. *Communication: Key to Your Marriage* (Glendale, California: G/L Publications, 1974). Good ideas for the husband and wife who want to enrich their marriage through better communication.

THE FIRST YEARS
OF FOREVER

With thanksgiving for
our wonderful marriage partners,
Gaye and Dan,
whose love and encouragement
shine through every page of this book.

Contents

Preface

Readers who are familiar with the byline Ed Wheat, M.D. and Gaye Wheat will note another name on this volume, which rightly belongs on all our books. For the past ten years we have had the privilege of working closely with Gloria Okes Perkins, a gifted professional writer and biblical counselor. The result has been *Intended for Pleasure*, which has found its place as the standard reference book for Christians concerned with sex in marriage from the medical and biblical perspectives; *LOVE LIFE*, the Zondervan book that has been read by more than half a million couples seeking to rekindle love in their marriage; and *How To Save Your Marriage Alone*, the little book in large demand by individuals facing the personal threat of divorce. Together, Gloria and I have also produced a videocassette series of premarriage counseling albums and three counseling cassettes, including "Before the Wedding Night," which is the forerunner of *The First Years of Forever*.

Since the Lord brought Gloria and her husband, Dan, to northwest Arkansas, Gaye and I have had the joy of observing their beautiful relationship and the way they share their love and their home with others. By consistent example and friendship, by teaching and counsel, they have had a positive effect upon many marriages. Singles of all ages are drawn to them, too. I know of no one more qualified to develop and communicate these concepts for newlyweds and engaged couples. Dan and Gloria, and Gaye and I have a wholehearted commitment to helping others find the wonderful, lasting happiness that God has designed for man and woman in marriage. Our prayer is that this book will come to you in God's timing just as you are making the decision of a lifetime, and that you will find in the clear light of reality the happiness that every couple dreams of.

Your friend in Christ,
Ed Wheat, M.D.

Acknowledgements

Whenever I open a new book, I read the Acknowledgements with keen interest because it helps me to understand the writer in a more personal way.

My "thank you's" are very personal: first, to my beloved family and closest friends, who lived through this time with me, protected me with their prayers, and inspired me with their love.

Also, to my editor, Nia Jones, who knew how to encourage me when I needed it most.

Always, my gratitude to Dr. Wheat. His vision for transformed marriages, his steadfast faith in the Lord Jesus Christ, his love of the Scriptures, his unquenchable hope, and his wisdom and kindness are a continuing inspiration to me. We share one special prayer at every meeting in my office or his: "Lord, please allow us to produce this book to help many couples experience how wonderful a lasting, love-filled marriage can be!"

Gloria Okes Perkins,
Springdale, Arkansas

Introduction

This book has been written for you who are just starting out in marriage because we care about your future. In fact, without knowing you by name, we've been praying for you and picturing you as we have developed this new-marriage handbook.

We asked that our book would find its way into the hands of couples who love each other so much that, in spite of all the statistics, they are determined to build a quality marriage that will last and are seeking to learn how to do it because, realistically, they know it won't be easy. We have the information that you will need to accomplish your goal, along with the solid assurance that, *if you want it badly enough,* a wonderful marriage is within your reach.

We hear from so many people who, not long ago, stood in your place as newlyweds with high expectations of happiness. Now they are wondering what to do about the problems, which have sprung up like fast-growing weeds in what they believed would be their own little Garden of Eden. Most of them acknowledge that they were overconfident: they just assumed their love would carry them through any difficulties. They also say that they were poorly prepared for the realities of marriage. They ask with bewilderment, "Why didn't someone tell us how hard it is to make it work, that it doesn't just happen?" And most of them admit to unrealistic expectations of what marriage would do for them.

Said one young woman, "I thought marriage to my guy would bring automatic happiness with it; I expected it to settle him down and take away all my insecurities. I guess I assumed marriage was some kind of a miracle drug."

Another agreed, "Even though our friends were already getting divorces, we just knew we would be different. We counted on being in love. We thought that would keep us together and make all our dreams come true. But it wasn't enough."

An ex-husband said bitterly, "I wish I'd known some of this sooner. I can look back now and see that our divorce was unnecessary. But we didn't even know enough to know what we didn't know. By the time we tried to get help, it was too late."

Unfortunately, these stories are all too common. Among the disturbing marriage/divorce statistics, here are two that you need to think about. Researchers report that nearly half of all serious marital problems develop in the first two years of marriage. Yet, on the average, couples who seek counseling for the first time have already been married seven years.[1]

Many divorces can be attributed to this five-year counseling gap—a time when the relationship deteriorates, but warning signals are ignored. Usually the couple doesn't seek help until one partner resorts to a drastic move, such as leaving home or having an affair. In our continuing survey over the past five years, it's no wonder that three-fourths of the respondents urge new-marriage counsel as a preventive measure.

We have designed *The First Years of Forever* to stand in this gap by offering you much-needed, but hard-to-obtain, counsel at the time when you need it most, with major chapters devoted to counsel in the critical areas of sex and communication.

You have exciting times ahead! As Paul Tournier has said,

Marriage becomes a great adventure, a continuous discovery both of oneself and of one's mate. It becomes a daily broadening of one's horizon, an opportunity of learning something new about life, about human existence, about God.[2]

If you have not yet married, we encourage you to request a premarriage counseling session with your pastor. In some cases he will use *The First Years of Forever* as a counseling resource; you may even have received your copy as a gift from your church. Remember, as you plan your new life together, that a Bible-believing pastor, and Christian friends can offer tremendous support and encouragement for your marriage.

And now we trust that *The First Years of Forever* will become a well-thumbed "help book" in your home and a good friend during this time of exciting beginnings.

1

The Feelings of Love:
Guarding Your Treasure

As NEWLYWEDS OR an engaged couple, you undoubtedly qualify as experts on the feelings of love. Since few parents today are in the business of arranging marriages, most couples marry because the feelings of love draw them together in an almost irresistible fashion. You know for yourself the euphoric wonder of new love—the magic, the mystery, the miraculous sense of well-being (often described as walking on air) when just being together makes you supremely happy. To love and be loved in this way within the security of marriage is probably one of the greatest pleasures in life.

But can you maintain these wonderful feelings for the next fifty years or more? In our new-marriage handbook, we want to show you how to relate to one another so that you never lose this most precious treasure: your feelings of love.

A dynamic truth that you need to recognize now, at the beginning of your marriage, comes not from a counselor, but a poet. Robert Frost observed that love (like a good poem) *begins in delight and ends in wisdom.*[1] He wasn't saying that delight comes to a dead end because the lovers have learned better. He meant that ecstasy cannot stand still because it has a life of its own. It must move on—hopefully, in the direction of wisdom.

What does this say to you? That if you expect your love affair to remain the same or count on it to get better and better without effort on your part, you will be disappointed. Your love relationship must change because it is a living entity. And you will determine the nature of that change by the direction you set now and the course you follow over the years. Your love will either grow or diminish, progress or fall back. It will be more wonderful than you could have imagined, or, for some unhappy couples, it will be dreadful. Some may have to search very hard to find even the faintest trace of love left over from years of neglect.

The feelings of love will always require your attention. Think of it as an investment that yields high returns. Five or seven years down the road your love relationship will reveal just how much both of you have put into it.

LIVING WITH YOUR FEELINGS

To preserve your feelings of love, you need a clear understanding of them— what they are, essentially; what they can and cannot do; and how to nurture and intensify all the good feelings while you confront the negative ones that can threaten your love relationship when you least expect it. Here, in seed form, is the information you need to begin building the love affair of a lifetime. It will happen through treasuring, guarding, and nurturing the feelings of love you now share.

One husband offered this definition of feelings: "Feelings are thoughts of the heart rather than thoughts of the mind." In other words, your feelings give you an inner awareness of your emotional condition from moment to moment.

Your feelings are more immediate than thoughts, of course. They are more like vibrations or signals you must interpret—signs of your humanness. The Lord says in Psalm 33:15 that He fashions all hearts alike. But some people are more *in touch* with their feelings than others. Individuals differ greatly in their ability to recognize their feelings quickly and interpret them accurately.

Feelings are a gift from God to provide both protection and pleasure. They are indicators that can suggest and offer input, but they have neither authority over you nor power to control you. As children most of us learned we could not always do what we felt like doing. As adults we know that our feelings (our emotions) are not capable of conducting our daily affairs, so we do not give them control. This principle should also apply in our love relationships. Certainly, feelings have helped to bring you together as a newly-married or engaged couple, but they were never designed to *drive* you anywhere.

Your feelings are neither all-powerful nor all-wise. You can appreciate them as indicators—the things that let you know what's happening to you—but never as infallible guides. Only God's Word, the Bible, can guide us surely. If someone tells you, "Do whatever feels good!" BEWARE! Never let your feelings become the deciding factor in anything without checking all the available data first. Respect your feelings, listen to their warnings, but do not let them control you. God has given you a free will and the power to choose. You are in charge.

You must recognize, however, that feelings will always have persuasive force because of their ability to occupy and dominate the moment. George MacDonald describes the deceptive nature of feelings in this way:

They had a feeling, or a feeling had them, till another feeling came and took its place. When a feeling was there, they felt as if it would never go; when it was gone they felt as if it had never been; when it returned, they felt as if it had never gone.[2]

Feelings are so fragile and explosive that they must be handled with special care. How you consider your partner's feelings will tell a great deal about you as a lover. As we have already suggested, the feelings of love are the treasure within the earthen vessel of marriage, but they can change unexpectedly, so never look to them as the last word. Always remember, you are *more* than your feelings!

Throughout the Bible God reveals a whole tapestry of feelings. The Song of Solomon offers a vivid display of the feelings of love experienced by a bride and her husband. But nowhere in the New Testament does God ever command us to *feel* anything. Rather, He would have us to behave in certain ways or to adopt certain attitudes, which will produce certain feelings. It is a principle worth learning that if we obey God with right actions, the right feelings will soon follow.

TOUCHING THE MAGIC

Feelings are the music of life and the magic that makes marriage exciting, pleasurable, and satisfying. Let's "touch the magic" by analyzing what happens when a man and woman fall in love. It's important to understand the dynamics of falling in love because they are the very dynamics you will want to keep alive in your marriage relationship. Don't take them for granted because the weight of everyday living can smother the magic of love before you realize it.

Two people falling in love is a powerful emotional event. That it happens to both lovers at the same time intensifies the sense of delight. There is the thrill of newness and a sense of wonder as if the two lovers have entered into a new reality—almost like time-space travel—in which they see themselves and their old world in a different light. C. S. Lewis said, in describing his relationship with his wife Joy, that even his body "had such a different importance" because it was the body his wife loved![3]

The term *falling* accurately depicts the suddenness and drama of the situation. The phrase *in love* correctly implies that the lovers are no longer where they were. They have left themselves as individuals to dwell in a new place together—"a safe and intimate world."

Falling in love has to do with summoning up . . . rapturous feelings of engulfment in a safe and intimate world—one in which two are as one, perfect company, and in which perfect nurturance exists. It has to do with the visions of Eden, buried within, before human aloneness had been perceived.[4]

Four significant things usually occur when love is genuine.

1. The lovers long to be together.

In fact, they may even feel shock-waves of emotion when they must be apart, incomplete when they are separated—a foreshadowing of the time when two will become one in marriage. This powerful sense of need for the other may express itself in a sensation of "homesickness." This happens because they have become bonded emotionally and now crave that feeling of security and *at-homeness,* which they find only in the other's presence.

As a newlywed told us, "We fell in love one weekend when he came to see me at school. It was incredible! On Thursday I was my own person. On Sunday when I took him to the airport, I was someone new. When he left to board the plane, I thought I would die. . . . I felt so alone, as though half of me had gone with him."

Another bride said, "I used to hate having to say good-bye to him. It had nothing to do with wanting to be with him for sexual reasons. I just wanted to be with him! For me, marriage means not having to part at the end of the evening, but being together, whatever we're doing and wherever we happen to be."

2. The lovers see each other in a unique way.

Lovers begin to see each other almost as if through the eyes of God. One husband said, "My wife sees a side of me that no one else sees. I feel as though she knows the true me, and her love filters out all the faults that other people might notice. Maybe this is the way God sees us when our sins have been covered by Jesus Christ. I know that her admiration and acceptance make me want to be my very best."

True romantic love seems to open a lover's eyes to see the loved one the way God sees that person—as extraordinary, priceless, like no one else ever created, as unique with an eternal identity.

The lovers place such high value on each other that they are willing to give up their selfish independence so as to belong to one another. As one young man said, "When I fell in love with her, I knew it meant changing direction for my life. I had planned on a life of travel . . . alone. I valued fast cars and my airplane. But that was worth nothing compared to the value of knowing her and building our life together. Sure, I had a brief, passing regret. But I realized that genuine happiness for me meant loving this girl and being loved by her for the rest of my life. And I haven't been sorry!"

3. The lovers desire to commit themselves to one another.

Real love always wants to commit itself. Judith Adams Perry, M.D., in answering a question about love in a medical magazine, points out that we commit ourselves to whatever we love most:

The *Psychiatric Dictionary* defines love as pleasure. Love usually also involves commitment, regardless of which type of love is expressed—self-love, family, work, spiritual, erotic, or love for life itself. The combination of pleasure and commitment leads to a dynamic process of movement toward the person or ideal.[5]

The Lord Jesus Christ said it first in words we cannot easily forget: "For where your treasure is, there will your heart be also" (Matt. 6:21).

4. The lovers want to marry, to be together "forever."

Falling in love usually leads to the couple's mutual desire to make a new world for themselves, to seal their commitment in marriage. Commitment not only demonstrates the quality of their love but attempts to preserve it . . . forever.

> It seems there is an intrinsic connection between "forever" and some commitments. The most convincing way that people have hit upon to state the fact that they are not placing conditions on the giving of themselves to another is to confess that they are not setting a predetermined time span within which the relationship is to work. In other words, the most congenial way we humans have of showing that our commitments are unconditional is to say "forever." Granted this is a resort to quantity terms in order to prove quality, but who has found a better way to express total commitment to another person than to say that we include him or her in our entire future? . . . Commitment is the most natural way of . . . expressing the love one has for another . . . and of proving as well as preserving that same love. All other things being equal, permanence will be a property of every commitment that flows from love and continues in love.[6]

If all these exciting events have occurred, can we then conclude that they will "live happily ever after"? No. We don't know if they will apply wisdom in their relationship as they shape their lives together. But this is the place where most couples begin—this period of falling in love. And the principles involved in falling in love can help any couple stay in love and grow in love. Here they are in capsule form:

STAYING IN LOVE

1. Concentrate on building an intimate relationship. Nurture each other emotionally. Touch lovingly, share thoughts and feelings. Spend private time together so that you can continue to feel secure and at home in each other's presence
2. Avoid the negatives that could change the way you see each other. Live in an atmosphere of approval, and forgive quickly and generously.

3. Live out your commitment to one another in such a way that strong links of trust are established and maintained.

4. Build your marriage on a solid biblical base. Always think and talk in "forever" terms.

Now let us share with you one of the fascinating surprises of marriage. If— and this is an important *if*—you both move from the falling-in-love stage to the in-love stage and, even more importantly, into the practice of *loving* your partner (which involves giving and always doing the very best for him or her), you will have the delightful experience of falling in love all over again many times during the course of a full and happy marriage. All the enjoyable emotions will be there, even the sense of fresh wonder, of seeing each other and life itself through love washed eyes.

BEWARE OF THE MYTH

We have analyzed the experience of falling in love; now let's examine the widely held myth that falling in love is an uncontrollable event.

As an illustration imagine being married, but things are not going well in your relationship. You feel distant from your mate, maybe offended. You begin having intimate talks at work with someone who is lonely and sympathetic. Your eyes meet across the room; you begin sharing secrets; your hands touch, and presto! the magic strikes and you think you're in love. Your emotions have you convinced that, obviously, you don't love your mate anymore. "It's no one's fault," you say. "It just happened."

Wrong!!! Your feelings, which can get out of "sync" temporarily, are playing tricks on you, and you are experiencing the impulses of an infatuation that you incorrectly label "love," although it has very little in common with what genuine love is or how it behaves.

This, of course has been an exercise in imagination. But one young man who came in for counseling—we'll call him Jim—had just such an experience. His wife Beth was working the night shift as a nurse to make extra money to furnish their new home. Jim didn't see much of her, and when he did, they were usually both tired and frustrated. Then Jim became acquainted with a co-worker who was going through the trauma of divorce. Sympathy drew him to her at first, but soon he was infatuated and thrilled by this woman's dependence on him. Jim was also bewildered. How could he love two women at once? Should he move out of his home? Should he seek a divorce? He suddenly felt obligated to both women, and sought counsel.

Jim's feelings were playing tricks on him. He had only one commitment—the one he had made four years ago when he married Beth. What he was experiencing had no real control over him, regardless of how powerful his emotions were toward this woman. To save his marriage, Jim needed to stop spending time with this woman, to ignore the feelings, and rearrange his life so he and his wife could have time together to fall in love all over again.

Beth was able to change her work schedule, and she and Jim began pouring their lives into loving each other. Jim recognized his deceptive feelings for what they were, and the co-worker turned her sights elsewhere. The episode ended happily for Jim and Beth.

The message of this true story—which is played out in ten thousand cities around the country—is that the feelings of love cannot survive alone. They must be accompanied by the facts of love. Then "walking on air" becomes moving ahead together on solid ground, and delight is transformed by wisdom into something even better.

2

The ABCs of Forever: Living by the Facts of Love

THE TITLE OF our book, *The First Years of Forever*, carries with it a promise—that we will show you how to form a forever relationship with the one you love. But what is a forever relationship? You will find the "ABCs" of it in this chapter.

Let's start by thinking of a forever relationship as the kind that begins with the best intentions. A man says to his fiancee, "Sweetheart, I want to be with you *forever.*" And she whispers, "I'm yours for the rest of our lives—and *forever!*" Five years later he's lost his job, they've quit communicating, and their sex life is almost nonexistent. What happened to "forever?" As one young man said, sadly, "It's like a dream we lost along the way."

The forever relationship does not have to be a dream that vanishes in the light of cold, hard day. In fact, it will actually thrive on adversity and become more precious when the rest of life has temporarily lost its joy. How does one acquire anything so valuable? Well, it cannot he found or fallen into, but *formed*—by a man and a woman who want it enough to pour their lives into the building process.

First, it must be understood. So let's consider the fundamentals—the ABCs of forever.

Most couples begin with love. But who can say how love really begins? Each of you has a different story to tell, for romantic love takes surprising turns in its development. For one person, love warms slowly out of a good friendship; for another, love sparks a blaze fueled by sexual desire. Love may begin with admiration in the classroom, or find its root in good conversation on a blind date. Perhaps you discovered someone who really understands you, and life seems magically transformed because you are no longer alone! It matters little whether your love found its beginning when you first locked eyes with someone across a crowded room, or whether you've been in love since you met in junior high. If it leads to your passionate desire to belong to each other exclusively, you are embarking on the adventure of a lifetime.

BELONGING LOVE

We can call this kind of love that first sparks a relationship *belonging* love and let it represent all that is delightful and exciting and comforting about loving and being loved.

As Malachi Martin has described it,

> The surest effect of love in an individual is an increase of what we all recognize as happiness. It is unmistakable. When we love, and are loved, that happiness is irrepressible in us. Like fresh spring water, it bathes everything within us and spills out into our lives. It seeks to splash and sparkle and wash the world about us until everything in and around us reflects a new light.[1]

As wonderful as belonging love is, it cannot be counted on to produce the forever relationship lovers long for. *Belonging love,* though it seems perfect for the moment, is not guaranteed to last, even within the context of a marriage. The Bible compares this kind of love, which can change so quickly, to the dew of early morning and the misty clouds that disappear before the day is half begun (Hos. 6:4). And our country's rising divorce rate suggests that the institution of marriage has seemingly lost its power to bond a couple together in a lasting relationship.

THE MISSING ELEMENTS

What is missing if the best love two people can have for each other in marriage cannot be depended upon? The story of a couple we'll call Joe and Evie best illustrates the problem of missing elements in a relationship.

When they married in their late teens, Joe and Evie displayed all the signs of two people in love. "She was the most beautiful girl I had ever seen," Joe said. "We're in our forties now, and she's still a very lovely woman. We've gone through tough times together financially and survived. We've gone through grief and trouble. We lost our oldest son in an automobile accident when he was sixteen, and our youngest daughter has had a bad marriage and emotional problems. But she's doing okay. Evie and I could really begin to enjoy life now if only . . ."

Joe's "if only" meant, if only Evie had not filed for divorce. Her reason for wanting to end the marriage went back many years to their newlywed experiences. Their sexual relationship had been less than fulfilling for Evie, but the couple had never sought help for their problem. Instead, she became increasingly resentful and avoided sex. This continued until Joe's mother died unexpectedly.

"Then I was desperate for comfort and love," Joe said. "I turned to my wife, but when she was so cold and kept rejecting me, I found someone else. I ran around for close to two years, although Evie and I had a son during this time. It was seeing myself as a father that caused me to straighten up and get my act together. I asked Evie to forgive me, and I promised to be a good husband and father. I've never been unfaithful to her since. I've tried to make it up to her."

Unfortunately, things continued to go badly for this couple. As Joe tells it, "She never forgave me, I guess. Held a grudge against me all this time. She even told me recently that she blamed me for our son's death. Said it wouldn't have happened if we hadn't moved to this part of the country. She's just been waiting, evidently, until the financial conditions were right for us to divorce.

" But," he went on, "I thought we had a good life together. I still love her although she says she has no love for me, that I killed it when I went out with other women so many years ago. So we're dividing our property, our kids are divided over the situation, and we're both facing middle age alone with nothing to look forward to. I can't believe it turned out like this. We were so much in love when we married!"

So much in love when they were married . . . Such is the refrain of many failed marriages. But Joe and Evie, like others, lacked the love that never fails, the love that could have given them a compassionate tenderness for one another and a longing to meet one another's needs; the love that heals all bitterness and makes forgiveness possible. Married, yes. But they lacked the essential ingredient of *commitment* to their marriage covenant and to each other.

A *LOVE-CENTERED* MARRIAGE

To form a forever relationship, you will need a *Love centered* marriage. The love you have at the beginning with its intensely personal quality of belonging and possessing fluctuates because it is fed by feelings, and feelings change, especially if needs and desires are not being met. But the God of Love has made His own love available to each of us. That love, which the Bible calls *agape,* never changes. It is unconditional and does not depend on a person's behavior. It goes right on showing kindness to the beloved, no matter what, because it is controlled not by our emotions, but by our will. The ability to love this way is a gift from God through His Son Jesus Christ; His love channeled through us blesses our mate and our marriage. The nature of agape love is described in our book, *LOVE LIFE for Every Married Couple:*

> Out of His own mighty nature, God supplies the resources for this love, and they are available to any life connected with His by faith in Jesus Christ: "God's love has been poured out in our hearts through the Holy Spirit Who has been given to us" (Rom. 5:5 THE AMPLIFIED BIBLE). This is the agape love of the New Testament— unconditional, unchanging, inexhaustible, generous beyond measure, and most wonderfully kind![2]

ABSOLUTE LOVE

It is important for you to understand that the love you feel for each other needs to be grounded in agape love. This love is *Absolute* love and comes directly from God; there is no substitute for it, and you could never crank it out on your own. Consider some of the synonyms for the word "absolute" to help you better understand the nature of this love: actual, authentic, bona fide, genuine, indisputable, real, sure, true, undeniable, complete, consummate (which means perfect), and godlike.

We have, then, two loves that merge into one to bless our life together: *absolute* love and *belonging* love. Both need to be at the heart of a relationship. These loves can only be fully enjoyed within the protective structure God has designed. We might think of the structure of marriage as our House of Love. We enter this house by our free choice. Our decision is both legal and public, and, most importantly, spiritual. When we marry we cannot escape the fact (even if we wanted to) that we are entering into a sacred covenant, established and ordained by God from the beginning of human history. As Jay Adams has said in his book *Marriage, Divorce and Remarriage:*

> God designed marriage as the foundational element of all human society. Before there was . . . a church, a school, a business instituted, God formally instituted marriage, declaring, "A man shall leave his father and mother and shall cleave to his wife, and the two shall become one flesh.''

Dr. Adams also points out that

> if marriage were of human origin, then human beings would have a right to set it aside. But since God instituted marriage, only He has the right to do so. . . . Nor can marriage be regulated according to human whims. [It] is subject to the rules

and regulations set down by God. If He had said nothing more about marriage after establishing it, we might have proceeded to draw up such rules on our own. But He did not leave us in the dark; God has revealed His will about marriage in the pages of the Bible.[3]

COMMITMENT TO MARRIAGE

But one of our problems is that marriage today is taken so lightly. It is no longer a place of safety. Only through *commitment* to the absolute permanence of marriage, a commitment made by both partners, based on deep beliefs and the choice of the will, can marriage become the sure guardian of love. If we have made this once-and-for-all-time commitment, the structure of marriage will preserve our love. And the couple who has undergirded their marriage by their commitment will be prepared for those inevitable times when their marriage will be tested.

Those who have given up on a love-filled, enduring marriage do not understand the ABCs of forever: *Absolute* love strengthens and turns to pure gold our *Belonging* love, and *Commitment* to the permanence of marriage guards and preserves our love relationship for the rest of our lives.

A FOREVER RELATIONSHIP

To answer the question posed earlier in this chapter: A forever relationship consists of a Love-centered life built and shared by a man and a woman who maintain total commitment to one another and to their marriage as the permanent structure of their lives on this earth, and as the safeguard of their love—a love which has its origin and continuance in the eternal love of God and thus never ends.

The biblical equation for a forever relationship is this:

Absolute Love +
Belonging Love +
Commitment to Marriage =
a Forever Relationship

HEAVEN'S RESOURCES

During premarriage counseling sessions we ask the engaged couple, "How do you plan to celebrate your twenty-fifth wedding anniversary?" While this may seem to be the least of their concerns, the question is more relevant than they know. The marriage that lasts and lasts happily begins with the confident assurance that there will be a twenty-fifth wedding anniversary, or a fiftieth or more if God permits.

We'd like to give you some good reasons for this assurance, even in a day when divorce *seems* to be a natural consequence of marriage. We call these Heaven's Resources. They are truths you can count upon concerning God's readiness to help you build the kind of marriage you dream of now.

1. It is God's will in every marriage that the couple love each other with an absorbing spiritual, emotional, and physical attraction that continues to grow throughout their lifetime together.

God intends for you and your mate to experience this love-bond together, not with substitutes, and will show you how to bring this about.

2. Because God is the one who made you, who thought up the idea of marriage and ordained it for your blessing and gives you the capacity to love, He is the one who knows best how to build love into your particular relationship. You can trust Him to be intimately involved in your efforts to develop a love-filled marriage.

A third principle follows logically from these great truths:

3. It is possible for any Christian couple to develop this love relationship in their marriage because it is in harmony with God's express will.

If the time should come when you are feeling discouraged about your relationship, remember that Heaven's Resources are at your disposal. Any couple who want and choose to build a love-filled marriage *can* do so.

To sum up the counsel of these first two chapters, here is a sure formula for a lasting, love-filled marriage: Enjoy the *feelings* of love and guard them well, but live by the *facts* of love.

> *Keep the delights of your love*
> *ever-green and growing*
> *by planting their roots deep into truth*
> *and watering them with wisdom.*

3
Faithfulness: The First Essential

HOW WOULD YOU answer this question: What one quality do you believe will contribute most to the continuing development of love and growth in your marriage relationship?

Think about it! Finding the most satisfactory answer to this question will give you insight into what will be most important in building your forever relationship.

This question was recently put to a husband and wife who have loved each other for more than a quarter century. Their responses were completely honest since each gave a response without knowing how the other responded. Consider their answers. What essentials have been at work to make their marriage last?

The wife took her time before giving an answer, obviously considering the many good aspects of their relationship. "It has to be *faithfulness*," she finally said. "Steve's faithfulness to me all these years is so unmistakable that I don't have to live with fear and uncertainty. I never doubt that he will *be there*, loving me as long as he has strength left in his body."

She also added, "The two qualities that mean almost as much as Faithfulness are Steve's tremendous *kindness*—I can always count on him to be kind!—and his *responsiveness* to me. I never go to him for comfort that his arms do not open to receive me. And if I reach out, his hand is always there, warm and strong and waiting for me.

"But as I thought about it," she went on, "I realized that his kindness and responsiveness are just other ways of showing his faithfulness to me!"

Steve answered the same question with a prompt assurance. "Whatever you want to call it," he said, "the most important quality is being able to trust my wife. I trust her to be true to me, and I trust her to keep on loving me, looking out after my best interests, and being loyal to me. That's the bottom line."

What is particularly interesting about this couple's answers is that in designing this new-marriage handbook, we reached similar conclusions about those qualities that make for a lasting marriage.

How then can you make faithfulness, this first essential quality, a cornerstone of your relationship?

Faithfulness in marriage means firmly adhering to the commitment you have made. In both attitude and action you are loyal, true, and constant to your marriage partner. Although *faithfulness* implies *duty,* with an allegiance, vows, and promises to live up to, the husband and wife who are truly faithful live out their loyalty to one another not out of duty, but joy.

This loving loyalty has two requirements. First, a faithful couple must never allow a third person to intrude into their love relationship. When you are faithful to your mate, you not only avoid adultery, you don't even give the appearance of interest in another person. Your partner should never feel the need to compete with someone else for your attention or admiration.

The second requirement for faithfulness involves loving your partner in ways that meet his or her needs and deepest desires. We can never plead ignorance as to how to do this; in the Scriptures God has shown us how to faithfully love one another. (See chapters 8 and 9.)

Faithfulness begins as a choice. It is, in fact, always a choice. As one Christian therapist has explained:

> Central to marriage is this "choosing" process wherein a unique relationship with one person is established. What keeps it vital is a faithfulness which continues to choose the same person even in the midst of pain, frustration and disillusionment. Apart from this, the institution of marriage cannot sustain the blush of its initial days or the vows of its partners.[1]

The ongoing choice to be faithful to the one you have chosen makes all the difference between an empty relationship (in which one or both eventually look for other ways to meet their emotional needs) and a warm, vital, intimate relationship, which continues to grow in the security of steadfast love.

Faithfulness is not only an ongoing choice. It is a continuing call to action. If you don't express it, if you don't demonstrate it in your daily life, it can't be faithfulness.

To illustrate faithfulness at work, consider this true story told in *What Will Make My Marriage Work?* A couple was married only a year when the wife became ill with multiple sclerosis. Unable to bear the thought of being a burden to her husband, this young woman decided she would "set him free." But her husband refused to leave her. Instead he showered tender care and love on her as long as she lived. Why did he do it? "Because," he said, "when I vowed before God 'for better or for worse' and 'in sickness and in health,' I meant it." Did he ever regret it? No! This faithful husband emphatically remarked, "God made both of us unbelievably happy."[2]

By contrast, consider another true story of a husband whose wife of many years came to the last months of her terminal illness. He decided that he could not give her all the attention she needed, because it was necessary for his survival to live his own life, which must come first.

Both men had made their vows, but only one continued to choose faithfulness under difficult circumstances. One man lived his faithfulness; the other, his own life. Their actions reflected their choices.

While few of you will be forced to make such difficult choices early in your marriage, later in life one mate may need tender, protective care because of serious health problems. There is great comfort when you can count on each other to be faithful, whatever comes. This sense of security cannot depend on blind faith. You may have gone into marriage with blind faith, but now you must build trust and faithfulness. The ways you demonstrate your faithfulness today will build bridges of trust for a lifetime. Here are seven ways to demonstrate faithfulness.

1. Behave in faithful ways consistently. As the Bible says, "Ever follow that which is good" (1 Thess. 5:15).

In other words, do everything you can to express your faithfulness in action. Support and encourage your partner by helping out whenever and wherever it is possible. When you see a job that needs to be done, do it without being asked. Be consistently honest in all your dealings, showing yourself trustworthy in even the smallest detail. As a troubled wife once said, "It takes a lot of energy to love someone you can't trust!" Being trustworthy means keeping your word. If you say you will meet your mate at a certain place and time, make sure you are there. Most of all, show kindness in your actions, not just your words. You've heard the old expression, "Pretty is as pretty does." Well, love *is* as love *does*.

2. Avoid doing things to offend or disappoint your mate, and don't do anything to create suspicion in your partner's mind. As the Bible says, "Abstain from all appearance of evil" (1 Thess. 5:22).

Consider these two cases of couples who received counseling because of problems in their marriage. The husband had a habit of casually putting his arm around other women in social situations. It meant nothing to him, but it disturbed his wife, and consequently affected their relationship. In another case, the wife sometimes praised other men she admired and respected. Her husband felt threatened, believing his wife found him inadequate compared to other men. If you are unsure whether some action may offend your mate, ask yourself this: "Will this seem like faithfulness or unfaithfulness to my mate?''

3. Let your partner know that being faithful brings you joy; you are not faithful just out of a sense of duty. Be happy and show it! As the Bible says, "Rejoice evermore" (1 Thess. 5:16).

Your happiness is the greatest compliment you can give your loved one, and the expression of joy gives marriage vitality. But sometimes one partner will go through times of sadness, brooding, worry, or depression. And the other will also experience some anguish, wondering: "Have I done something wrong? Doesn't my mate love me anymore? If my partner's not happy, it must be my fault." Be open with each other during these times, reassure each other, and pray together about all your concerns.

4. Consistently show appreciation for all the ways your partner blesses your life. Thank him or her for even the smallest things. Speak positively about your partner to other people, and give thanks to God, too. As the Bible says, "In everything give thanks . . ." (1 Thess. 5:18).

Showing appreciation not only demonstrates faithfulness to your partner, it builds more loving faithfulness in your own heart. It is amazing how we tend to believe our own spoken words. So be careful what you say and always speak positively.

5. Learn to be sensitive to your partner in even the smallest detail. A faithful lover goes to a great deal of trouble to understand the beloved. Quench not the spirit of your mate through misunderstandings!

Take the case of Karen and Gary. Karen's family had always made much of birthdays, while Gary could forget his own birthday if not reminded. When Gary casually postponed his wife's birthday celebration to the weekend when it would be a more convenient time, Karen felt devastated and unloved. Gary had made some special plans for her he thought would delight her, so he was astonished when Karen was hostile and tearful that day. "But why didn't you give me my birthday card on my birthday anyway?" she exclaimed. "That would have made it all right." Gary could only answer, "Because I didn't think. Because I didn't know the timing was so important to you." It's up to you to *know* what's important to your mate.

Keep in mind how different you and your partner are—not just your backgrounds, but your emotional make-up. You cannot demonstrate faithfulness if you do not "dwell together according to knowledge" (1 Peter 3:7). Learn what really matters to your partner, learn his or her emotional language of love, and then act accordingly.

6. Pray that you will be faithful. It's not always easy to be what your partner needs, and we can use all the help we can get. The Bible says, "Pray without ceasing" (1 Thess. 5:17). Keep the goal of faithfulness ever uppermost in your mind, and maintain a heart attitude of prayer.

Praying will keep you alert and watchful of anything that might draw you away from the oneness of the marriage relationship. If a passing fantasy about some other attractive person has you distracted, a prayerful attitude will redirect your focus. Pray for faithfulness in every season of life.

7. Look to God who is the faithful One. What you can't do in your own strength, He can empower you to do. The Scripture says, "Faithful is he that calleth you who also will do it" (1 Thess. 5:24).

4
Forgiveness: The Second Essential

Marriage becomes a series of surprises for most of us, and one of them is how frequently we need to forgive and be forgiven. Faithfulness may be the first essential of a love filled marriage, but even the best relationship cannot remain intact for long without forgiveness: the second essential of marriage.

EVERY MARRIAGE NEEDS THE HEALING TOUCH

Every husband-and-wife combination needs the healing touch of forgiveness. Where else could there be more opportunity to annoy, insult, offend, or ruffle another person than in the intimacy of married life when we're constantly under foot, get in each other's way, and have to share all things in common (whether we like it or not)? That's just ordinary living, without taking into account the astonishingly hurtful things husbands and wives do, which demand more forgiveness than any of us could work up on our own.

To learn how to forgive, and how to draw on spiritual resources to accomplish the task, is one of the most important "skills" newlyweds can acquire. *Skill* seems an inadequate word for something as glorious as forgiveness, but it's a beginning point.

FORGIVENESS AS A WAY OF LIFE

Think, for a moment, of forgiveness as a way of life. Picture your relationship growing year by year with forgiveness as an essential nutrient in the soil of your marriage, keeping your love alive and thriving. Or think of forgiveness as an element of the emotional air you breathe, as important as oxygen in the physical world; a natural ingredient in the wholesome environment of your marriage. In other words, forgiveness needs to become habitual in your relationship— something both of you do lovingly, consistently, and *forgetfully* because you don't keep score!

What is forgiveness? There's some confusion about that. When most people think of forgiveness, they think of changing their feeling toward someone who has wronged them, of teary-eyed sweetness replacing anger and a thirst for revenge.

But forgiveness is not a feeling at all. It is a choice you make, which may go against every self-centered fiber of your being. So forget the easy, mushy sentiment that the world inserts into the idea. True, you may feel some emotions when you forgive, perhaps gladness at being reconciled and close again. But if you are acting only on sentimental impulse, there's no assurance that your forgiveness will last beyond that impulsive moment. True forgiveness is a strong, rational decision based on spiritual values, fueled by spiritual resources, and modeled after the spiritual principle of God's forgiveness.

HOW GOD'S FORGIVENESS WORKS

To understand how forgiveness can work in your marriage relationship, it's necessary to go to the Bible to understand the quality of God's forgiveness. Although the entire New Testament resonates with the wonder of God's forgiveness through Jesus Christ, one verse will suffice for our purpose "And be kind to one another, tender-hearted, forgiving each other, just as God in Christ also has forgiven you" (Ephes. 4:32 NASV).

1. **Be kind,** *chrestoi* **(what is fitting to a need).**
2. **Be compassionate,** *eusplanchnoi* **(tender-hearted).**
3. **Be forgiving,** *charizomenoi* **(giving freely and graciously as a favor).**
4. **Just as God in Christ has forgiven (another form of the same verb,** *charizomai*) **you.**

The same wonderful word is used here for forgiveness whether it be divine or human. *Charizomai* means to bestow a favor graciously, unconditionally, and freely. It represents a gracious, beautiful act of showing favor—the favor, grace, and goodness of God to man—of the worthy to the unworthy.

Obviously, we can't forgive like this on our own, but if we have experienced this favor ourselves—God's personal forgiveness through Jesus Christ—then we can draw upon this resource in our marriage. When husband and wife are both in Christ—both pouring out this gracious, beautiful favor upon one another—what a love-filled marriage they can have!

This much is clear then. We can forgive because we have been forgiven first. We can learn how to forgive from God's example. And we can draw upon His resources to show this gracious favor to one another.

FORGIVENESS IS A PROMISE

The next question is, how do we show this gracious favor? Jay Adams explains in *More Than Redemption,*

> Forgiveness is a *promise.* When God forgives a sinner, He does not simply become emotional over his repentance. No, instead, He goes on record that He has forgiven by making (and keeping) a promise to that effect: "Your sins and iniquities will I remember against you no more. . . ." (Jer. 31:34).

> Our forgiveness is modeled after God's forgiveness (Ephes. 4:32). That means that for us forgiveness is also a promise that offers assurance for the future. So when a counselee says, "I forgive you," to another, then he also makes a promise. This . . . is an essential element of forgiveness.[1]

Dr. Adams defines forgiveness as

a formal declaration to lift the burden of one's guilt and a promise to remember another's wrong against him no more.

HOW FORGIVENESS WORKS IN A CRISIS

Let's test this definition by writing a scenario to use as an example. A husband (we'll call him Mark) has deeply wounded his wife (we'll call her Lucinda) by paying too much attention to her former college roommate (Shirley) at a party. They have a stormy discussion after they get home. (She's sending forth the thunder bolts; he's trying to come in out of the rain.) He finally manages to communicate that he feels bad about it, that it meant nothing, and he wishes she could forgive him.

Lucinda would prefer to stay angry; after all, he deserves it! But she remembers three things: how much she loves him; how important forgiveness is in a marriage; and how Christ forgave her when she had done many things worse than this. So she makes the choice to forgive him. They pray together, agree on the way they both should behave at parties in the future, and they go to sleep in each other's arms.

Much More Than an Emotional Episode

This is much more than an emotional episode. By her choice to forgive, Lucinda has made a promise to Mark, just as God made a promise to His people. She has lifted the burden of guilt from him; he doesn't have to get up tomorrow morning shamefaced, trying to stay on her good side. He doesn't carry the burden anymore.

But there's more to the promise than that. God's forgiveness involves never remembering the sin against his people again. Lucinda's promise also includes a three-part commitment, whether stated or not: "I won't bring this up to you again, Mark. I won't bring it up to others either. I won't tell my sister or my best girlfriend, and I won't make a scene with Shirley." And, now comes the hard part, the third part. She also promises, "I won't bring this up to myself again. I will remember it no more!"

Feelings Have Nothing to Do With It

(Note: Lucinda did not feel like making the promise. Not really. She was steamed! How dare he sit and talk to Shirley all evening! But she made the conscious decision to forgive.)

The next morning while she's scrambling eggs, the anger begins slowly building again. Now she has to make the choice to keep her promise whether or not she feels like it. So she asks God to help her show love to Mark, and she greets Mark with a kiss. After breakfast, they have their Bible reading together, and she surprises him by helping him wash the car. (She even vacuums the interior, the part he doesn't like to do.)

When Self-Pity Returns. . . .

By this time, she *feels* warm and loving and they have a wonderful weekend together. All goes well until she's sitting in the dentist's office three days later. Something (she doesn't know what) triggers her memory of that party, and the awful way she felt, and *how could Mark do that to me?!?* Suddenly, she's full of self-pity and in danger, once again, of breaking her promise.

But Lucinda understands how to handle such situations. She does not allow her thoughts to run wild, and she doesn't argue with them. Instead, she looks away from them and occupies her mind in another way. Pulling out her purse organizer, she begins making a menu list for their camping trip in the mountains. The moment passes, and God does His part. In fact, she forgets the emotional pain of the event so completely that when she runs into Shirley at the mall two months later, she can give her an untroubled smile and a friendly greeting. Later, the happening itself fades from her memory, and if remembered at all, she does not relive it. It is like something that occurred long ago and far away. She has forgiven biblically, and God has enabled her to forget.

A Good Pattern Established

Mark learns several lessons, too: (1) that he was a jerk, who needs to give more thought to his wife's feelings, (He confesses his sin to God and asks God to make him more sensitive to her needs.); (2) that his wife is a beautiful person, and not in looks only, (He has more respect and thankfulness for her.); and (3) that the next time she offends him (which does happen occasionally) he'll be quick to forgive her in turn. Lucinda's choice to forgive has established the beginning of a blessed pattern in their marriage.

THE FOUR STEPS OF FORGIVENESS

Here, in review, are the four steps of forgiveness:

1. **Choose, with your free will, to forgive.**
2. **Make the promise to lift the burden of guilt from the person as far as the wrong against you is concerned. Remember the person's sin no more —never naming it again to the person, to others, or to yourself.**
3. **Seal it with your behavior, demonstrating love in suitable ways with tender-hearted kindness, and doing what the Bible shows you to be right in the situation.**
4. **Trust God to allow you to forget and to renew your mind with new attitudes.**

WHEN YOU WON'T FORGIVE

What if you choose not to forgive? What if you prefer to hold on to the resentments, the anger, the hurt? God's Word makes the consequences of this choice plain. So, let's look at the options.

1. If you hold on to your resentments, they will turn to bitterness. As a result, your life will be poisoned, and others' lives, too.

"Be careful that none of you fails to respond to the grace of God, for if he does there can spring up in him a bitter spirit which can poison the lives of many others" (Heb. 12:15 PHILLIPS).

2. By refusing to release the burden of the other person's wrong against you and choosing to carry that burden yourself, you may become crippled in the living of life. God warns us about spiritual lameness,

Make straight paths for your feet, lest that which is lame be turned out of the way; but let it rather be healed. Follow peace with all men, and holiness, without which no man shall see the Lord; looking diligently lest any man fail of the grace of God, lest any root of bitterness springing up trouble you, and by it many be defiled (Heb. 12:13-15).

3. If you are not willing to forgive, there is no way you can expect to walk in personal fellowship with God. A Christian's forgiveness is based on realizing he has been forgiven, as we read in Ephesians 4:32. Choosing to withhold this forgiveness from others will erect a barrier between you and your God.

For if ye forgive men their trespasses, your heavenly Father will also forgive you; But if ye forgive not men their trespasses, neither will your Father forgive your trespasses (Matt. 6:14-15).

David Augsburger in *The Freedom of Forgiveness* challenges his readers to learn the power of love to overcome every bitterness of the heart. But to those who would reject the freedom of forgiveness he warns,

If you intend to claim all your rights in life, to even all scores against you, to demand every penny ever owed to you, then go ahead.

But if you give no inch, expect no second chances; if you show no mercy, do not hope for mercy; if you extend no forgiveness you can expect none. Life, love, mercy and forgiveness are all two-way streets. To receive, you must give. Humbly. Aware that you are constantly in need of the understanding and acceptance of others and the loving mercy of God.[2]

Granted, the scenario we used as an example was not a pivotal moment in life. It was an easy wrong to forgive compared to those we hear about every day from heartbroken and embittered husbands and wives. We trust nothing like that has occurred in your new marriage. But it is good to learn the principles of forgiveness so thoroughly that if the worst should happen, you will be prepared to handle it in God's way. We can assure you that far more suffering results from unforgiveness and its continuing effects than from the original injury.

A CLEAR CHOICE

It's really simple, after all. You either choose love and emotional freedom and fullness of life, or you hold on to old injuries and let them grow inside of you until they take over and you become their prisoner. You are not hurting the one who sinned against you. All the damage you would like to inflict on that one comes back on you instead. It's a principle of life. It's the law of sowing and reaping: "Be not deceived, God is not mocked, for whatever a man soweth, that shall he also reap" (Gal. 6:7).

Love cannot grow in the same heart with negative attitudes and bad feelings—anger, bitterness, resentment, pride, despair, or hostility (veiled or otherwise). So always be careful what you are growing in your marriage.

WHEN IT SEEMS IMPOSSIBLE TO FORGIVE

If you are ever faced with the need to forgive and you feel it's impossible, remember these things:

1. God never asks His children to do anything that He does not provide both the instructions for and the strength to accomplish. You have the instructions in this chapter, and He will give you the strength if you call on Him for it, and then do what is right.

2. You do not have to be controlled by your feelings, and you are not the helpless prisoner of your past. People sometimes picture themselves as enslaved by their own feelings, as prisoners of events that happened in the past. And yet Christians have already been set free. Jesus said,

You will know the truth, and the truth will set you free.... If the Son sets you free, you will be free indeed (John 8:32, 36 NIV).

If you are a Christian, trusting in Jesus Christ alone for your salvation, right now you are *free*. If you believe it and act on it, you will experience the truth of it.

3. Jesus Christ has special deliverance and healing for you if you have been bruised and wounded by the sins of your mate—or anyone else—against you. Recall the words He used to describe His ministry.

The Spirit of the Lord is upon me, because he hath anointed me to . . . set at liberty
them that are bruised (Luke 4:18).

As we explained in *LOVE LIFE,*

There is no bruise, no emotional wound in your marriage that the Lord cannot heal
when you choose to forgive and commit this matter and your subsequent behavior
to Him. No hatred can hold you prisoner when you choose freedom. No negative
attitude can dominate you when you choose to let it go as an act of obedience to
the Lord Jesus Christ. His love simply overpowers old resentments. It is like raising the shade and opening the window in that dark room. The sunshine floods in
and dispels every corner of darkness. The air is fresh and sweet and exhilarating.[3]

DO WE HAVE TO FORGIVE EVERYTHING?

Is there any sin that you can't be expected to forgive? Sometimes people tell
us, "I can forgive everything but *that.*" The answer is that God is not selective
with us. When He forgives us in Christ, He forgives everything. So please
remember that God's grace, (from which comes *churizomui* in Ephes. 4:32)
covers *every category of wrongdoing.*

Dr. Wheat's personal philosophy has always been "Anger against someone
is a big waste of time. It doesn't bother the other person, but it drains your own
energy. You're the loser." He says, "If someone is hostile toward me, it's their
problem, not mine. As for forgiveness, I don't argue with God about it. I just do
it. And I sleep well at night."

As a couple in love, planning a forever relationship, you need to get your
forgiveness skills in good working order: you will have plenty of practice on
the small things. We pray the larger things never put you to the test. But if they
do, you can forgive in the biblical way we have outlined here. Hold to His way
of handling the situation, and God will take care of the "forgetting" part for you.

FORGIVENESS IN YOUR LOVE RELATIONSHIP

Here's how forgiveness can take its place in your love relationship, soothing
the irritations and healing the hurts, which occur even between two people who
love each other very much, and, afterward, restoring your sense of oneness.

1. **Make a habit of forgiving and never keep count.**
2. **Settle your accounts quickly.** It's best to forgive one another before you
go to sleep. Some couples commit themselves to kissing and saying "I love you"

before they go to sleep at night. If they can't do that, they work on the conflict until it is resolved. Then they go to sleep. We encourage you to never, even for one night, withhold your love, mercy, and compassion from your partner.

3. Remember that forgiveness always includes the idea of restoration and a new start. Maintain that sense of newness in your relationship. Whenever you have resolved a problem and given each other the gracious favor of forgiveness, you can enjoy a fresh beginning in your marriage. Then, as the poet says, you "wake at dawn with winged heart and give thanks for another day of loving."

When we forgive habitually, quickly, and expectantly, we can look forward to the continuing inflow of His mercies in our marriage—"new every morning."

5
Communicating:
Your Lifeline in Marriage

COMMUNICATION IS ONE of the extraordinary delights of marriage, when it's working. *Nothing,* not even sexual fulfillment, will bring as much enriching intimacy into your relationship.

But it's more than a luxurious pleasure. Call it the *lifeline* of a love-filled marriage—the means by which indispensable supplies are transported from husband to wife, and from wife to husband.

LIFELINE SUPPLIES

If you have good communication in your marriage, the lifeline will provide these supplies:

- **The knowledge and understanding of one another which you need for intimate closeness**
- **The interchange of information and ideas you need to work together as a husband-wife team**
- **The capability to work out your differences and resolve your conflicts**
- **The continuing "in touch" contact you must have to grow together in the same direction, and to be there to support each other during the changes and difficult times of life.**

Obviously, couples trying to operate without these supplies will encounter major problems. In the troubled marriages we counsel, communication lines are almost always clogged or severed. In fact, researchers believe that 90 percent of all marriage counseling involves the attempt to restore communication, or to teach the couple to communicate effectively for the very first time.

It's easy when you're dating and lulled by soft lights and romance to assume that you communicate well, but under the floodlight of marriage, any flaws or trouble spots in your communication system will quickly show up. Domeena C. Renshaw, M.D., an expert on communication in marriage, explains: "Soon after marriage, as daily routines evolve, there is less talk but many more (frequently inaccurate) assumptions about what the other thinks and wants."[1]

"Less talk and inaccurate assumptions" about one another, if not remedied, will lead eventually to one of these common complaints: "We *don't* communicate;" or "We *can't* communicate," which is most serious because it is perceived as marital failure. In fact, "no communication" has become the catch phrase of the 80s, replacing "mental cruelty" and "incompatibility" as the commonly voiced reason for couples to give up on their marriage.

Why Marriages Fail

In a 1982 survey when four hundred psychiatrists were asked why marriages fail, they gave poor communication as the most common cause.[2] And couples themselves perceive poor communication as the proof that "all is lost." Dr. Renshaw warns,

Once a couple agrees, "we don't communicate," then they may give up, withdraw emotionally, and conjointly decide that nothing can be done.[3]

Researchers report that most husbands express marital dissatisfaction through anger and *withdrawal,* while most wives show their dissatisfaction through depression and *withdrawal.* In all cases, the withdrawal into silence is devastating and should be regarded as a "red alert" for the marriage.

The most urgent indicator of distress in a marriage may not be the uproar of discord, but rather the ominous sound of silence, the lack of any communication.[4]

All Is Not Lost

No couple needs to get to that point, however. Any communication problem can be worked out because communication involves skills that can be learned and practiced. In preparation for your first years of forever, we want you to have some advance knowledge of the communication problems that often spring up in marriages and the skills couples need to develop to overcome them.

This may be a good time for you to pause and evaluate the communication system you're now using. Are you and your partner free to express yourselves spontaneously with each other? Are you able to confide in each other as best friends? Or are there difficulties? Do you hear what she's really saying? Do you understand what he's really feeling? Do you share your ideas, thoughts, and feelings? Or do you just talk about practical necessities? Is your communication on practical matters clear enough for things to go smoothly? When you hit a snag in communicating, do you keep on trying until you have overcome the barriers and the flow of meaning opens up between you again? Or do you give up and not try, get angry, yell, or retreat into silence? When you feel rejected, do you retaliate by rejecting your partner?

Checking Out the System

How can you be sure that your communication system is working as it should? Judson Swihart, who also likens communication in marriage to a lifeline, has given five characteristics of a system in good working order:[5]

1. **A sense of freedom to express yourself**
2. **A sense of being understood**
3. **An absence of win-lose arguments**
4. **A reduction of tension**
5. **A sense of being safe and secure in the relationship**

On the other hand, a system that is shut down and critically impaired will manifest these two characteristics:[6]

1. **One or both partners repeatedly assume negative intent on the part of the other.**
2. **There is increasing distance and silence.**

Most people, however, fall somewhere in between with a partially flawed system, which may reflect some, but not all, of the five positive characteristics listed above. Here's how you can build them all into your relationship.

HOW TO BUILD YOUR LIFELINE SYSTEM

1. **You will feel free to express yourself when both of you accept one another just as you are.**

Acceptance is the key factor in good communication, for acceptance (or rejection) sends one of the most powerful messages known to human beings. We have an enormous need for unconditional acceptance from the person closest to us. Critical comments or attitudes will make us afraid to express ourselves for fear of being judged. A wife wrote us, "How can I communicate with my husband when he makes a value judgment on everything I say? If he decides it's not worthy of his attention, he quits listening, or he tells me, 'That's not important enough to discuss.' What he's really saying is that *I* am not worth his time and attention."

A critical attitude will also make us want to avoid "intimate talks." A husband said, "Intimate talk means I have to explain why I haven't gotten her vacuum cleaner fixed or why I seem to dislike her mother. My wife enjoys getting things out in the open because, once they're there, I usually have to apologize for them."

Replace a judgmental or fault-finding attitude with a positive response and a consistently accepting attitude, and you will have the ideal climate for a loving interchange of thoughts and feelings. This can lead to the deepening of your love relationship. A young husband, who had been admittedly impatient and somewhat critical, told us, "I have become sensitive to Katie's reaction when I criticize or even show impatience. It seems to be a function of the love God has given me for her that now it hurts me so badly when I see her hurt that I have to back off." He's learning the secret: Good communication *begins* with acceptance.

---

2. You will feel understood when both of you learn to listen with your ears and hearts to one another.

Listening is an important, but often flawed, part of the marital communication system. A specialist in interpersonal communication says,

> Even though couples spend over 40% of their communication time listening, it is an underdeveloped skill in most families. Research indicates that we listen at about 25% efficiency, and that much misunderstanding is attributable to poor listening.[7]

Eight Ways to Develop Your Listening Skills

"Half" Is Not Enough

Make it a practice to give each other your *complete* attention when you talk together. If you only half-listen, you will only half-hear and that's not good enough. Try to listen with your heart as well as your ears to hear what the other is really saying and feeling. Remember that "the human heart holds more than speech does."[8]

No Interruptions

Don't interrupt each other! This can be terribly frustrating for someone trying to put his thoughts and feelings into words. Don't jump to conclusions about what the other is saying. Hear your partner out, then respond.

Repeat, Repeat

Prove that you have listened by repeating your partner's thoughts and feelings back to him so that he is sure you have understood him correctly.

Respond with Your Eyes

Real listening involves concentration accompanied by eye contact. When your partner is sharing thoughts and feelings with you, stop what you're doing and respond with your eyes. Stop and make yourself available when you sense your partner may be wanting to talk.

Don't Wait for Commercial Breaks

Give each other focused attention time with the television turned off. Communication squeezed in during halftime activities or the commercial breaks will be unsatisfying and, even worse, is the effort to talk something over while the television continues to blare and one partner tries to keep an eye on a favorite program. So forego television, put away the video movies, turn off the radio, and shut down the stereo. Close the doors, get your children (if any) occupied elsewhere, and take the telephone off the hook. Never listen with split attention. The communication system of your marriage deserves the very best.

A Negative Feedback Unless. . . .

Remember that your silence can be a negative feedback unless you accompany it with a nonverbal signal of approval, such as a smile, or squeeze of the hand, or loving eye contact.

When the Breakthrough Comes

When there is a breakthrough, never overwhelm your partner by demanding more than he or she is ready to give. Just show appreciation and thankfulness for what has been shared with you. And, of course, never repeat what your partner has told you in confidence.

A Love Message

Remember that when you listen to your partner, you are showing love. You are giving your partner the message, "What you have to say to me is important because *you* are important."

---

3. **You will be rid of win-lose arguments in your marriage when you learn what causes them and how to replace them with real communication in resolving disagreements and conflicts.**

Why is it that differences of opinion between husband and wife so often lead to arguments and a breakdown in communication? Usually the differences are not life and death matters. They aren't even right and wrong matters. Just different ways of seeing things or handling a situation. At such times the couple's communication skills are tested. Here are some of the ways the conversation may go wrong.

Six Ways a Discussion Goes Wrong

A War to Be Won

The disagreement becomes a war to be won—a power struggle. But the fact is that no one wins in an argument. Your goal should be to win by reaching an agreement or an understanding, while maintaining your good feelings for one another.

A Personal Rejection

The disagreement is taken as a personal rejection. Unfortunately, people often confuse rejection of their ideas with rejection of themselves. You can benefit in marriage from bringing your varying viewpoints together and discussing them, finding a solution, and gaining a deeper appreciation for one another at the same time.

A Change of Weapons

People change the subject and drag in other issues to use as weapons against their partners, instead of limiting the discussion to the original disagreement. As soon as one feels attacked and reacts with defensiveness, communication and loving intimacy are on the way out the door. If you want to avoid this and resolve the issue, agree ahead of time to discuss only the matter at hand. Let the law of kindness be on your tongue. The Bible says that words can pierce like a sword, but the wise tongue brings health and well-being.

Sweeping Generalizations

People, frustrated by their inability to make their point, resort to sweeping generalizations characterized by the use of these expressions: "You *always. . . .*" and "You *never. . . .*" These are "fighting words" and there is almost no adequate response to them. The temptation is to stoop to the same tactic and argue, "I do not! You always. . . ." or "You never. . . ."

Shouting or Siberia

People sometimes respond to disagreements in even more inappropriate and childish ways. One wife wrote us, "I wish my husband could discuss a matter without shouting. He seems to think that talking loud and fast is the only way to communicate." A husband told us, "My only option is to agree with my wife on every point. Otherwise, she sends me to Siberia for weeks at a time."

Yes, But. . . .

People often pull out this prize communication stopper: "Yes, *but. . . .*" which simply escalates the argument. Once we recognize how thoroughly annoying and disheartening this reaction is, we can choose to learn other ways of responding when we disagree. Here's how: Refuse to use those two words in combination again. Learn to make your point differently, beginning with a favorable response, such as "That's an interesting way of looking at it. I hadn't thought of it that way." Or, "I see what you mean." Move right on smoothly into your point, presented as a question, "Do you think that . . . ?"

In other words, present your original reaction in the framework of a measured and respectful response to the other person's idea by taking it seriously. Then tactfully offer your question in such a way that it is not regarded as an attack or a put-down. The discussion begins without ever using a "but," and your partner will feel more like rethinking the issue because you have recognized the validity of his or her position.

All these childish attempts to "win" the disagreement can be changed, if there is a genuine desire to learn to communicate. Excitable people can learn to talk more slowly and calmly, to take deep breaths while they are talking, and to stop to listen. People who pout, who use the deep freeze to express their displeasure, can learn that open, honest discussion has its rewards. Most importantly, marriage partners can learn to appreciate the peace (the restfulness), which comes when they respect one another's right to hold different views and to express those views in a calm discussion.

When a disagreement occurs, it's important to defuse its explosive potential by reducing what's at stake. When your attitude changes from a win/lose, I'm right/you're wrong position to a "Let's talk this over, but it doesn't affect our love and respect for one another" perspective, you've won the real battle. Here are some principles to follow.

Eight Ways to Replace Arguments with Communication

Response, Not Reaction

Don't interrupt. Listen carefully before you respond. Don't react. Respond. Keep the discussion squarely on the issue at hand. You need to agree, long before disagreements arise, that you will limit any discussion to the present, leaving the past out of it, and limit the discussion to the one issue, refusing to allow side issues to enter in.

Disagreement, Not Disapproval

Acknowledge that you understand what your partner is saying, even though you disagree. Show him or her respect. Don't let your disagreement of this issue sound like *disapproval* of your partner.

The Gift of Empathy

Make it a point to share your feelings, but not in such a way that your partner feels criticized. Encourage your partner to share his feelings and respond to them lovingly. Give him or her the gift of sympathy and empathy. This is one way to teach each other to give what you both are longing for.

Carefully Clarify

Carefully clarify what you are both saying so there can be no misunderstanding. Take turns doing this, with no interruptions.

Truthing in Love

Speak the truth in love. The original expression in the New Testament (Eph. 4:15) is literally *truthing in love*—maintaining truth in love, both with your speech and with your behavior. Honesty and love are needed, so speak the truth but speak it gently.

Say "I Need You"

Be willing to show your vulnerable, needy side to your partner. Don't be afraid to say "I need you." Sometimes we want to conceal our feelings to protect ourselves, but when you begin communicating, you learn the value of being honest, even about your own weaknesses. Real communication means revealing yourself even at the risk of rejection. When both are willing to do this, you are well on your way to building loving intimacy in your relationship.

Surprise and Disarm

Stop being defensive when the issue is a personal one. Surprise and disarm your partner by agreeing there is wrong on your side, since there always is (even if you don't wish to admit it). Be specific. "I was wrong" can stop a fight and demonstrate to your partner how to admit wrong, too.

Apply the B-E-S-T

Apply the B-E-S-T principles in your communication. As you talk with each other, *bless* with your words; *edify* (or build up) your partner by what you say and by your interest in what your partner has to say; *share* openly and honestly; and *touch* affectionately while you talk. *Bless, edify, share,* and *touch*—communicate the BEST to your mate.

> 4. You can reduce tensions by recognizing and correcting the communication practices that cause frustration and by learning to fight the biblical way—a way that deals constructively with anger, resentment, and hurt feelings.

RECOGNIZING THE FRUSTRATIONS

We have already mentioned many of the communication practices that cause frustration. Here are five "deadly sins" in communication, which can blight any relationship.

SHUTTING DOWN: Not listening.

SILENT TREATMENT: Not talking.

STABBING: Using the other's words against him/her.

SCOLDING: Putting guilt, blame on the other.

SHALLOW LIMITS: Surface talk only.

When Silence Is a Sin Against Love

We need to take another look at one of these sins against love, for that is what they all are. The "silent treatment" as a punitive measure may be the most hurtful of all. It makes us feel unloved, even despised, and it taps into old childhood fears of being abandoned and helpless. To be shunned by the person we love severs the links of trust, which are so necessary for an intimate relationship. In short, it is one of the most destructive things a person can do to a marriage.

Silence is often used . . . in a power struggle. . . . The withholder often feels powerful for he can manipulate both the feelings and behavior of the other. This is a favorite ploy in the "something-is-wrong-but-I-will-NEVER-tell-you game. Sometimes a fierce competition takes place and the goal is to see who can hurt whom the most. If the competition is in the form of who can be the coldest and most uncommunicative, breaking the silence becomes a sign of weakness. . . .

Silence can be passive-aggressive behavior, which is indirect, covert, and camouflaged hostility. The hostility is never dealt with openly and, therefore, often feeds on itself and becomes greater. Because the silence prevents hostility from being overtly recognized and dealt with, alienation may result, which is more destructive than fighting.[9]

The Messages We Miss

Alienation leads to more alienation. The more distance you've placed, the more likely you are to miss or distort messages transmitted between you. Considering the delicate and complex nature of the hundreds of messages sent and received in a day's time between husband and wife, with words comprising only seven percent of what is communicated, (the rest coming through tone of voice, body language, and even more subtle factors), is it any wonder that misunderstood messages can seriously damage an already shaky relationship?

The Five-Second Pause

Take this example: The wife asks her husband, "Do you really love me?" The husband waits five seconds and answers, "Of course I do." Every woman knows the important part of that message: the five-second pause. It changes the husband's answer from reassuring to ambiguous and unsatisfying.

The Silence of a Closed Door

There is another sort of painful silence when a partner will not go beyond shallow conversation. It is the silence of a closed door. When this silence refuses the other one's entrance to his heart, their relationship becomes empty, seemingly dead in the water.

To be silent about one's deepest feelings in a marriage often leads to a dead space in which there is nothing to communicate.[10]

This problem will require loving persistence, patience, and prayer, but unconditional love does have power to open doors. The reward for both partners will be a growing and deepening love as they allow themselves to become known without self-imposed barriers.

Other Frustrations

Here are some other frustrating communication practices.

1. Pretending you are communicating, when you're merely attacking your spouse.

2. Not knowing how to express your feelings without putting each other down.

3. Stating your views as though they are the absolute truth. (There's the old proverb, *One who is too insistent on his own views finds few to agree with him.*)

4. Not hearing the message from your partner because you're too busy figuring out what to say next. You can take it as a general rule that you will never be able to send messages successfully unless you are also paying attention to receiving them.

5. Faking attention, but not really listening. This is dangerous business. Faking attention with a glassy-eyed stare while you're thinking of something else will trip you up, and your partner will be understandably insulted. Researchers say that good listening is accompanied by a slight rise in temperature, a faster heartbeat, and a quicker circulation of blood. In other words, listening is not a passive activity! You should establish eye contact, think while listening, and not only concentrate on the words, but observe the nonverbal behavior of the speaker. All of this must be integrated into the meaning of the message.

6. Trying to communicate when you have two different goals for the conversation.

For example, when a wife pours out her problem to her husband, she may not be looking for an instant solution. Her husband, who views himself as a problem solver, gives her a quick way to handle the problem, and then becomes frustrated when she does not appreciate his brilliant solution. She's equally frustrated because she needed just to talk with him about it and to feel his support and understanding. But he says, "Okay, if you don't want my help and don't want to take my advice, then don't talk to me about it." So they are both disappointed. She wants to be listened to and empathized with. He wants to be respected for his ability and smart thinking. Neither is getting what he or she wants!

It's best to know the initial purpose of the conversation. The one who is being approached should be sensitive to the other's needs and goals for the conversation. If necessary, ask in a tactful way. Body language, tone of voice, and facial expressions will tell you a great deal.

Usually, the wife will be more relationally oriented, and the husband more data oriented. He doesn't realize how short he sounds when he asks where the tax file is. He just wants to know to get the job done. She is more concerned about relating to her lover and feels surprised and wounded by the curt, businesslike edge to his voice. The result may be a minor crisis in which fence-mending, for that night at least, becomes more urgent than filing the tax form.

This illustrates one of the most frustrating areas of communication in marriage: the difference between men and women.

7. Husband and wife communicate differently, and this can lead to misunderstandings and mutual exasperation.

At a national seminar session on communication, the speaker suggested that men are outclassed when it comes to verbal facility. Women talk better. They develop the language earlier and are more skillful in its use.

He also said men are more linear in their thinking, moving from a to b to c, while a woman can surround the subject from nine directions. And she is usually more concerned with "people" issues.

The speaker said he had discovered firsthand from his wife that women will repeat the same thing several times to their husbands because to share it you have to say it several times. He added that men do the same thing, but they say it to three different people!

One significant difference to keep in mind is the way men and women use the words *want* and *need.* Women don't mind saying, "I need," and may say it often. Men do not. To express need makes many men uncomfortable. When they say anything, it's usually "I want." Wives need to remember that men have needs, whether or not they are willing to express them.

8. Cultural differences and personality differences also take their toll on patience. In the pressure cooker of marriage, the cool Swede from Rockford, Illinois, may seem too cold for comfort to his Italian wife from south St. Louis. And the girl he loved because she was so vivacious and delightfully unpredictable becomes "noisy and undependable" instead.

Even if you came from similar backgrounds, you will be surprised at the differences, which emerge and the adaptations that are necessary. Strong clashes are inevitable between two people who love each other, but the Bible shows husbands and wives how to deal with their anger, resentments, and hurt feelings constructively.

Learning to Fight the Biblical Way

In Strike the Original Match, Charles R. (Chuck) Swindoll says that Ephesians 4:25–32 "offers seven rules for having a good fight. These rules will allow you to carry on normal, natural, disagreeable times without breaking with Scripture." Here are Chuck Swindoll's *Rules on How to Keep It Clean* from Ephesians 4:25–32.

1. **Keep it honest (v. 25).** Be committed to honesty and mutual respect.
2. **Keep it under control (v. 26).** Make sure your weapons are not deadly.
3. **Keep it timed right (vs. 26-27).** Agree together that the time is right to talk.
4. **Keep it positive (v. 28).** Be ready with a positive solution right after taking a swing.
5. **Keep it tactful (v. 29).** Watch your words and guard your tongue.
6. **Keep it private (v. 31).** Don't swing at your mate in public. When you swing in public, your malice is showing.
7. **Keep it cleaned up (v. 32).** When it's all over, help clean up the mess.[11]

We encourage you to study these "rules" and make them a part of your new life together. They are practical; they are wise; they work! They can guide you through your conflicts in a controlled, constructive way that hurts neither of you and actually causes you to love each other more, after "the fight" is over.

---

5. **You will feel safe and secure in your relationship if you get to know one another through good communication and remain closely in touch for a lifetime.**

Think about this rather melancholy statement spoken by the Duke of Wellington at the end of his life in 1852:

"It's a strange thing that two people can live together for half a lifetime and only understand one another at the very end."

Does it have to be that way? Definitely not. At the conclusion of this chapter we'll share the story of two people who understood each other most of their lives because they communicated all along the way. Their story is a reminder that you can build a lifeline system of loving, unhindered communication that will make it possible for you to become

- Intimate lovers
- Best friends who always enjoy being together
- A team that can accomplish anything because you work together rather than fighting for control
- Two people who understand one another as unique individuals, not as extensions of yourselves, and accept each other just as you are
- A couple who stay in touch during the changes of a lifetime, who "grow up together" and "grow old together" and remain "at home" with each other no matter what else changes

- Compassionate partners who can help one another adjust to the difficult times of life and endure them together

Now that's security!

GUARDING YOUR LIFELINE

Security takes a bit of guarding. In your case, you will know more than anyone else about the sensitive points in your relationship, which need special watchfulness. Here are our suggestions.

Six Warnings for Lovers

Be Alert to Unusual Tension.

Be sensitive to the danger when an uncomfortable tension is felt concerning some topic. Nothing does more harm to a good marriage than the rising of invisible walls because of something that cannot be talked about together. The caring may remain, but the intimacy and trust depart.

Therapists name *loss of effective communication* as the most common cause of distress in a previously stable marriage.[12] When some kind of distress cuts the lines that unite you, you must take quick action to resolve the situation.

Never Betray Your Best Friend.

Be on guard against taking something shared with you in a vulnerable moment and turning it against your mate as a weapon. This is easy to do when you're angry, feeling condemned, and fighting back. But as one husband said, "If you get into a revenge mode of thinking, it's like trying to stop a moving train." NEVER give way to the temptation. Remember, this is the person you want for your best friend.

Beware of the Heat of the Moment.

This is another "heat of the moment" danger. When you have a confrontation (and you will) about something so significant that you both become overwrought, you may say too much—something you'd give anything to take back later. But it's too late then. So have the good sense to stop and cool it when you recognize you're getting to that point. Go in separate rooms for a short time, and write down your feelings just as they are. Then come back together with the intensity of the moment dissipated, remembering that, no matter what, this is your intimate lover whom you don't want to wound, or lose.

It's good to make Psalm 141:3 your prayer and to pray it together before talking: "Set a watch, O Lord, before my mouth; keep the door of my lips."

Never Look at Your Mate Without Compassion.

Never close your heart to your loved one, even in the heat of the moment. To see your *one flesh* partner without feeling compassion is unthinkable. To see your partner in need and not pity him or her is to be without love. The principle—one of the most important you can learn for your marriage—is "We know love by this, that He laid down His life for us; and we ought to lay down our lives for the brethren. But whoever has the world's goods, and beholds his brother in need and closes his heart against him, how does the love of God abide in him? Little children, let us not love with word or with tongue, but in deed and truth" (John 3:16–18 NASV).

First, we are to be willing to lay down our lives for one of our own. To "lay down" means to divest ourselves of something that is part of us, for instance, our selfish desires. We are to love as He loved us. His love is to pour through us and touch others, especially the one closest to us, our own marriage partner. We are to give definite form to the love of Jesus Christ and show it by example. This kind of love reveals itself in details, in acts of behavior, attitude, small words, little smiles, as well as enormous acts of self-giving, done in such a way that there is no hint of martyrdom. If your partner feels you are sacrificing, something is wrong with the way you are showing your love.

Second, we are not to close our heart against a loved one's need. To look at our mate without *splanchna* (pity) is not love. That pity is a deep-seated emotional concern and affectionate sympathy. We must *feel*. Jesus was moved with compassion. He was torn up. He wept, He felt compassion. We need to emerge from our self-centeredness and affirm our solidarity with our partner. We need to open our inner life and feel deeply for and with our mate.

The award-winning movie *Ordinary People* portrayed an outwardly charming woman who is unwilling to open herself inwardly to her husband and son at the time of their deepest needs. They desperately want her compassion, some outward sign of her caring, but she cannot or will not give it. Defeated in his efforts to reach her? her husband says sadly, "I don't know you. I don't know what we've been playing at all this time." He adds, "We could have done all right if there had been no mess in our life." But all lives have "messes." We all need compassion from our partner.

So, thirdly, we must act. Not just love with our words—with our tongue that says pleasant things when we're in the right mood—but in *deed* (action) and truth. That should be our response to the compassion we feel.

Remember the Power of Words.

Remember what power your words have to affect your partner's life. Sometimes we discount their potent influence. Emily Dickinson put it this way,

> A word is dead
> When it is said,
> Some say.
>
> I say it just
> Begins to live
> That day. [13]

Our words have the power to penetrate another person's inner being, and their effects spread outward in a way that seems almost unending. Who can say where a word ends? Here is Derek Kidner's explanation:

1. *Penetration.* What is done to you is of little account beside what is done *in* you. . . . The *feelings,* or morale, may be lacerated by a cruel or clumsy thrust . . . or vitalized by a timely word . . . and the whole body with them. . . . *Beliefs and convictions* are formed by words, and these either destroy a man or are the making of him.

2. *Spread.* Since words implant ideas in other minds, their effects ramify—again, for good or evil.[14]

Our words can wound or heal; weaken or strengthen; depress or inspire; drive to despair or fill with happiness. It's particularly hard to overcome their negative impact. The injurious effects of words once spoken suggests that we sometimes communicate all too clearly. Our partner has no difficulty in receiving the message of our anger, disappointment, and complete dissatisfaction! "Everyone should be quick to listen, slow to speak and slow to become angry" (James 1:19 NIV). Or, "Consider what a great forest is set on fire by a small spark. The tongue also is a fire. . . ." (James 3:5–6b NIV).

If you want to enhance your "word power" and harness it for good, we recommend studying the Book of Proverbs. Make a study together of biblical principles of communication, taking all the verses in Proverbs about this, one at a time, and applying them in your marriage. Here are some to get you started.

Proverbs 12:18 There is one who speaks rashly like the thrusts of a sword, but the tongue of the wise brings healing.

Proverbs 15:1 A gentle answer turns away wrath, but a harsh word stirs up anger.

Proverbs 18:13 He who gives an answer before he hears, it is folly and shame to him.

Watch Out for the Third Partner in Your Marriage.

For at least fifteen years Dr. Wheat urged newlyweds to begin their marriage without a television set in the house. Young people sometimes thought that was asking too much. Now, couples are realizing what a thief television can be, robbing them of their prime time together. A bride told Gloria recently, "We decided not to get a TV, and it's been wonderful. There's nothing else to do but spend time paying attention to each other!"

Even television's voice, *TV Guide,* questions whether TV can cause divorce. Psychiatrist David Hellerstein observes that today

the TV *itself,* that noisy box in the corner of the living room, has become an equal—and essential—partner in many marriages. Even when it's turned off, there's that blank screen waiting to rejoin the conversation or to monopolize one's—or worse, one's spouse's-attentions.

Then Hellerstein asks a pointed question that every newly-married couple, interested in good communication, needs to consider.

Is there any connection between the fact that so many marriages now have three partners (two human, one electronic) and the fact that more than one million American couples now divorce every year? Consider that so much TV viewing occurs in early evening—which, as Miriam Arond points out, "is the time of day that couples are most in need of communication." Does the silent "conversation" with the TV set replace invaluable human communication?

He concludes,

At worst, TV can be an escape from problems that desperately need to be dealt with directly. And an "affair" with TV watching can kill a marriage. The fast pace and slickness of the TV world can, as Miriam Arond says, "promote unrealistic expectations of passionate romance that life should have a pace of passion that your own life doesn't have." One result is "that people are less good at weathering problems than they were in the old days" and the quick fixes suggested by many TV shows can reinforce one's impulse to get out fast.[15]

Whatever conclusions you reach about the part TV should have in your marriage, whether as third partner or infrequent guest, we trust you will see good communication as such a vital part of your love relationship, (so hard won and so easily lost!) that you will guard it to the utmost.

Two people who did this were close friends of ours: John and Richie Wadsworth. For forty eventful years this couple communicated, and when John was diagnosed as having cancer, they were able to support one another through that experience, too. Richie wrote about it afterward, and we asked if we could share it with our readers who are just beginning their journey together.

"I Love You, John"

The seven weeks from the diagnosis of cancer to those last moments when the breath came more and more slowly, and finally not at all, was a vast learning experience and a spiritual growing period for both of us.

Basically we were the same persons who had, for forty years of marriage, been together, laughed, teased, made decisions, argued, agreed, and cried together. We had stubbornly said, "I love you," even when we didn't like each other much. We had said it passionately, contentedly, reassuringly, proudly, and "just because."

Communication was open when cancer invaded our lives, because communication had been kept open during our years of marriage.

Illness didn't change our ability to laugh and kid around. We reminisced lots. We cried unashamedly. Most of all, we communicated every thought we had. Fear was never present because Christ was the center of our lives and He had removed fear on the cross for us. We marveled at that.

Sometimes the medicine gave John fantasies as he slept; usually they were not disturbing ones, but mostly he would be traveling. One day he said, "It is so strange, but I was on this trip and in this house that was mine, and yet not this one; and in this room that was mine, and yet not this one—"

I interrupted, "Well, you're going to be taking a trip and—" Together we said, "In my Father's house are many mansions . . . I go to prepare a place for you."

Communication made our last days together rich. If it hadn't been building through the years it wouldn't have been there for us to enjoy in the last days of our life together.

In the middle of the night, Friday, I came back in the room with fresh water. When John heard the ice tinkle in the glass he turned his head and smiled. I said, "Hey, I love you."

He groped for my hand with his left hand, because by this time the bone in his right arm had disintegrated, pulled my hand to his lips and said, "I love you, too. Oh, my, yes!"

I had prayed so much that John would not lose his ability to speak and God had granted my desire. We had talked about the fact that if we hadn't been open and loving all these years, the last days of our life would have been too late to start.

Saturday and Sunday, the voice I loved became a whisper, but still I communicated, and as I held his hand and his quiet breathing stopped, he stepped over the threshold and I was saying, "I love you, John."

6
The Door Marked Private: Secrets of Sexual Fulfillment

THEREFORE SHALL A man leave his father and his mother, and shall cleave unto his wife; and they shall be one flesh. And they were both naked, the man and his wife, and were not ashamed (Gen. 2:24–25).

"May my beloved come into his garden, and eat its choice fruits!"

"I have come into my garden, my sister, my bride. I have gathered my myrrh along with my balsam. I have eaten my honeycomb and my honey; I have drunk my wine and my milk."

(God to the Couple) Eat, friends; drink and imbibe deeply, O lovers" (Song of Sol. 4:16, 5:1 NASV).

When you feel an overwhelming sexual desire for each another, you can lock out the rest of the world without guilt or shame and express your love physically in total freedom. That's the wonder of marriage!

But there's more. God promises that through sexual union the two of you will become *one flesh*. Real love causes us to long to be as close to the beloved as possible, and God's provision is to meet that longing. The term *one flesh* means the merging of your personalities, the sharing of your entire beings so that you can really know each other. In fact, the biblical word for sexual intercourse is to "know." "Adam knew Eve his wife; and she conceived" (Gen. 4:1). "Then Joseph . . . took unto him his wife: and knew her not until she had brought forth her firstborn son" (Matt. I :24–35).

So, never think of sex as an extra added attraction. It is meant to be at the very heart of your marriage, becoming the most private and priceless expression of your love in the sharing of all that you are with one another.

Here's the way one wife described the relationship. Susan explained,

Sex in our marriage has been a magic thread which sews us together into one person. Even after the lovemaking is over, the thread still holds in this magical way, and we go about our ordinary life smiling at each other with satisfaction, sitting down together to our pasta salad with a special quality of contentment, knowing that we know each other fully and love each other completely. It's a secret delight that we share—or maybe I mean a delightful secret.

Anyway, sharing this secret knowledge with the man I love is an important part of it: the private looks, the private smiles, the private meanings in what we say. It's our time to recapture the feeling of being young and in love. It keeps us in touch with that secret place we discovered ten years ago. Now we have kids to raise, bikes in the driveway, bills to pay, schedules and interruptions, and all kinds of demands on our time and thoughts. But at night when the house is quiet, we can retreat back into our private world and imprint our oneness on our hearts again.

One benefit of what I call the magic thread is that the good effects don't last. It's not a once for all thing; we are drawn back to each other again and again. We just can't do without our reunions. I don't see how any marriage can survive without those times when you can concentrate on each other, and shut the rest of the world out!

It's true from Day One of your marriage into "forever." Some of you are engaged couples preparing for your wedding and honeymoon. Others are newlyweds who have been married long enough to want a different set of questions answered. Some of you may be building a second marriage and bringing the sexual experiences of your first marriage into this one. Or you may have had sex with various people and wonder how this will affect your relationship in marriage. Since we want to speak to all of you and your circumstances, let's begin with biblical counsel about sex—guidelines about how to enjoy sex in marriage from the Inventor of all good pleasures and conclude with the secrets of sexual fulfillment, which every couple needs to know.

BIBLICAL COUNSEL

1. Approach sex with reverence because you know what it means.

If you're clear on this first point, you can avoid the wrong attitudes toward sex that create such deep heartaches in marriages. For example, we have seen many fearful, inhibited people who believe that sex between husbands and wives is something to be ashamed of. Even as Queen Victoria wrote to her daughter, "The animal side of our nature is to me—too dreadful." At the other end of the spectrum, we counsel couples where one of the partners holds a cheap, casual view of sex with self-centered, physical gratification as the only goal, as a "whatever-turns-you-on" encounter. People from both these extremes share a common misunderstanding: They believe that sex is an expression of the animal nature.

If you feel that you are veering toward either extreme in your attitudes toward sex, you can correct your course and safeguard your love relationship with these biblical facts as fixed points in your understanding.

When God originated sexuality, He called it very good.

So God created man in his own image, in the image of God created he him; male and female created he them. And God blessed them, and God said unto them, Be fruitful, and multiply and fill the earth. . . . And God saw every thing that he had made, and, behold, it was very good (Gen. 1:27, 28, 31).

The word "man" (*adam,* not a proper name) denotes two sexual beings made for intimate union with each other. If you read Genesis 1, you'll see that all other parts of creation had been pronounced "good." It was not until man and woman were created as sexual beings endowed with the mysterious qualities and attributes of masculinity and femininity that God called his creation "very good." Also note that God's first word to his new creatures was a command to exercise their sexuality.

God sees sex in marriage as pure and valuable.

Marriage is honorable in all, and the bed undefiled, but fornicators and adulterers God will judge (Heb. 13:4).

The New Testament teaches that sex was not only good at its origin, but when enjoyed in the context of marriage according to the Creator's design, it is highly valuable and beautifully pure. We explained the meaning of Hebrews 13:4 in a secular textbook for college students.

Three words require special attention. The word translated as "honorable" means most precious, costly, of great price. The word translated "bed" is, literally, coitus—a plain reference to sexual intercourse. And the word "undefiled" signifies freedom from contamination—purity. In one cogent sentence, the Bible says that marriage—God's chosen environment for the expression of sexuality—is most precious, of indescribable value, and that sexual intercourse in that setting is so pure that it could take place (and does!) as an act of worship.[1]

This scripture depicts the marriage bed as a sort of "holy of holies" where husband and wife meet privately to celebrate their love for each other. But if sex is holy in that setting, it is no less enjoyable physically. We were created as sensual beings with piercing desires, and our bodies were intricately designed to experience exquisite sexual pleasures. The Bible places high value on the human body for its own sake as "wonderfully made" by the Creator (Ps. 139:14) and inhabited by the incarnate Savior. The same body that enters into the passionate, physical delights of intercourse with one's marriage partner is described as "the temple of the Holy Spirit" (1 Cor. 6:19).[1]

Obviously, we can't uphold this truth and ignore the other side of it. The same verse from Hebrews that assures us of the worth and purity of sexual intercourse in marriage warns us against contaminating God's good gift by engaging in sexual intercourse outside of marriage.

Many of the couples who contact us are having difficulties because of guilt, even when their premarital sex was with one another. If you have violated God's plan for enjoyment of your sexuality please remember that God can forgive, cleanse, heal, and restore. A missionary/teacher offers this good advice.

> You can have a great marriage and future, so don't despair. I've heard women who were once prostitutes say that on their wedding night it felt like the first time. God can do a mighty work in your life! Come to Him and admit that He really knew what He was talking about, and you were wrong to second-guess Him. Repent and then by faith let Him reverse the damage. . . . Let Him direct the river of your sexuality as a river within its banks, and it will become a thing of beauty and fulfillment in your life.[2]

Sex in the environment of permanent commitment in marriage has profound meaning and a spiritual purpose.

> For we are members of his body, of his flesh, and of his bones. For this cause shall a man leave his father and mother, and shall be joined unto his wife, and they two shall be one flesh. This is a great mystery, but I speak concerning Christ and the church (Ephes. 5:30–32).

The Book of Ephesians reveals that the one-flesh union of husband and wife is intended to picture the intimate closeness, total commitment, and permanent love relationship that Jesus Christ has for the church. This puts the sexual relationship of marriage in its true perspective. It is never sinful to love your partner sexually and passionately; it is never meaningless to engage in sexual intercourse with your own mate. Real pleasure begins when you approach your sexual lovemaking with the reverent respect it deserves.

2. Enjoy sex as recreation because God planned it that way.

When you understand the true meaning of sexual intercourse, you're ready to appreciate the delights God has prepared for you in marriage. As we explained in *Intended for Pleasure,*

Sex with your partner is far more than recreation, of course, but it is that as well: the best, the most relaxing, renewing recreation known to man, and God planned that too. No wonder it is often called "love play." It is fun, not duty; high excitement, not boredom; something to anticipate, not a dreary experience to be avoided if you can. It should be and it can be the highlight of any ordinary day, as two people come together to refresh themselves in each other's love, to find forgetfulness from the cares and insults of life, and to experience the total and wonderful relaxation God designed as the culmination of the lovemaking, with both husband and wife reaching release. How ironic that couples search for all manner of recreation elsewhere, never having discovered the fullness of pleasure available to them in their own bedroom.[3]

Read and reread together the Song of Solomon in a modern translation, and apply it to your own love affair. You will find that the sexual relationship of your marriage can provide refreshment, restoration, joy, liberty, and an abundance of delights. And not just now while you are newlyweds! Hear the counsel from the Book of Proverbs, which specializes in down-to-earth wisdom for the situations of life. The theme of Proverbs 5 could be summed up this way: Stay away from people who would lure you into unfaithfulness and always be madly in love with your own wife. Here is a clear description of the sexual pleasures in a lifetime marriage, "Let thy fountain be blessed, and rejoice with the wife of thy youth. Let her be as the loving hind and pleasant roe; let her breasts satisfy thee at all times, and be thou ravished always with her love" (Prov. 5:18–19).

The wife is pictured, both here and in Song of Solomon, as a well, a spring shut up, a fountain sealed for her husband, whose waters will satisfy him to the fullest. To be satisfied, in the Hebrew language, means to have one's thirst slaked, to take one's fill, to be abundantly saturated with that which pleases. And to be ravished with love means to be enraptured . . . intoxicated . . . exhilarated.

The verses from Song of Solomon quoted at the beginning of this chapter describe the consummation of love on the wedding night. S. Craig Glickman calls it "one of the shyest and most delicate of love scenes in world literature." Afterward, the husband describes their love as a beautiful garden he has enjoyed and as a great feast he has celebrated.

Nevertheless, the words of the lovers are not the last words of the night. A mysterious voice is the last to speak. "Eat, O loved ones; drink and be drunk, O lovers." (Song of Sol. 5: IB) Who is speaking to the lovers here? Some have suggested the wedding guests, but of course they are not likely to be around at this moment. And neither is any other person for that matter. Yet the voice must represent someone other than the lovers, for they are the ones addressed here. . . .

In the final analysis this must be the voice of the Creator, the greatest Poet, the most intimate wedding guest of all, the one, indeed, who prepared this lovely couple for the night of his design.

He lifts his voice and gives hearty approval to the entire night. He vigorously endorses and affirms the love of this couple. He takes pleasure in what has taken place. He is glad they have drunk deeply of the fountain of love. Two of his own have experienced love in all the beauty and fervor and purity that he intended for them. In fact, he urges them on to more. . . . Eat together from the feast I have prepared for you. This is his attitude toward the giving of their love to each other.

And by the way, that's also his attitude toward couples today.[4]

3. Recognize your responsibility to your mate.

In 1 Corinthians 7, we are offered four valuable guidelines for the expression of sex in marriage—all of which emphasize responsibility to one another as lovers.

The Principle of Need

But since there is so much immorality, each man should have his own wife, and each woman her own husband. The husband should fulfill his marital duty to his wife, and likewise the wife to her husband (1 Cor. 7:2–3 NIV).

The first principle is simple: The two of you *need* the blessings and protection of sex within your marriage. It's important for you to do everything you can to meet your partner's needs. If both of you take hold of this concept and live it out, the result will be a tender, but very exciting relationship.

The Principle of Belonging

The wife's body does not belong to her alone but also to her husband. In the same way, the husband's body does not belong to him alone but also to his wife (1 Cor. 7:4 NIV).

The second principle is less simple and very sobering. When two people marry, they relinquish ownership of their own bodies and give this right to their mate. Obviously, this requires the utmost trust. People should understand before they marry that when they do, in God's sight, they will belong sexually to each other and will have no right to withhold physical affection. Bluntly speaking, the wife's body now belongs to her husband; the husband's body now belongs to his wife. However, each must love the other's body and care for it as his own. Unreasonable demands are totally excluded.

The Principle of Habit

Do not deprive each other except by mutual consent and for a time, so that you may devote yourselves to prayer. Then come together again so that Satan will not tempt you because of your lack of self-control (I Cor. 7:5 NIV)

The third principle uses a harsh word, "Deprive," *apostereo,* which actually means to rob or defraud one another. In other words, don't cheat your partner by withholding habitual sexual lovemaking except by mutual consent for a brief period of time. If you do, you will open your marriage to satanic temptations. our Creator knows this. That's why He counsels us to participate actively and regularly in sex with our own mates.

The Principle of Equality

This principle comes from the passage we have been quoting and finds its best illustration in the relationship of the lovers in Song of Solomon. Sexual relations are to be equal and reciprocal; each has the right to initiate sex, and neither has the right to use it as a bargaining point.

The husband and wife are *equals.* Their sexual relationship has been designed for two equals—a man and woman permanently committed to marriage—who love, not use, one another. A science fiction novel a few years ago portrayed a futuristic society in which couples are no longer called lovers but *users.* Television reflects a trend toward this chilling future: In one survey of American television, researchers reported that 88 percent of all sex presented on television was sex outside of marriage—people using other people for momentary gratification.

The biblical principles for the enjoyment of sex totally contradict this approach. God's counsel concerning sex advises us to be always loving and concerned for the welfare and happiness of each other. Let's hear again from Susan who told us about the "magic thread." We asked her how she and Don had maintained such a beautiful relationship in their ten-year-old marriage. Her answer shows the biblical guidelines in action.

We follow three simple rules, not laws, but ways of communicating love. First, we keep our sex life separate from our quarrels and disagreements. That's not as hard as it sounds. Our sex life is so good; we don't want any harm to come to it, so we protect that private place, and neither one of us drags other things in. When we fight, we make up; then we make love. We have never in ten years of marriage used sex against one another.

Second, we're almost always available for one another. When one's in the mood the other reciprocates and soon gets in the mood. Of course, we don't make demands when we know our partner is tired or sick or upset. That's just good manners and thoughtfulness.

Third, if one of us just isn't up to it, we ask to postpone it for another time in a way that sounds like loving anticipation, not like rejection. We've always related this way sexually, and a few years ago when we began studying the Bible, we found that by some miracle of love, we had done things right!

4. Remember the privacy factor.

Becoming one flesh in marriage calls for privacy in every sense of the word. Here are some ways to apply this in your relationship.

Don't let another person intrude into your private world for two.

This is one part of your life where close friends, children, and beloved family members do not belong! *Private* means not for common use, secluded, removed from public view.

Beware of the invader—an individual who would like to take your partner's place in your life.

To allow a close friendship marked by affectionate touching and intimate conversation to grow is like leaving the gate open and inviting that person into your heart as a lover.

Avoid family members, friends, or neighbors who encourage you to talk about your partner until you see yourself separately from him or her.

Guard your sense of oneness. It's precious.

Never discuss details of your sexual relationship with anyone except a physician or counselor, if it becomes necessary.

Your sex life should be viewed as sacred. Never permit jokes about your private world or share confidences with others in this sensitive area.

Establish and maintain the privacy of your bedroom.

Keep a lock on your bedroom door and use it. Children should be trained from a very young age to knock on Mother and Daddy's door, never to barge in. Do not allow your children to sleep with you or in the same room with you. When you buy or build a home, try to obtain a master bedroom arrangement that offers as much privacy and quiet as possible. Your bedroom should be a sanctuary of love. Make it beautiful, keep it pleasant, and use it only for sleeping, dressing, and relating as lovers.

BEFORE THE WEDDING NIGHT COUNSEL

It's good that you are preparing now for the physical dimension of your marriage, even though it may be some weeks before your wedding. The sexual relationship involves far more than doing what comes naturally, and no one should feel that he has to be an instant expert. For a new husband to have to pretend that he knows it all can be quite a burden. No one knows it all. Even the therapists in the field are continually researching the subject of sexual response, and new facts are coming to light out of this research. God's physical design for sex between husband and wife is beautiful but intricate, and you need to understand the mechanisms of sexual expression and response to prevent difficulties from arising that could hinder your pleasure and rob you of fulfillment.

Many problems can be avoided if you have the right information ahead of time so that you can begin your marriage with positive experiences in lovemaking, and even enjoy sex on your honeymoon—a time that, frankly, is disappointing for couples who have gone into it unprepared or misinformed. Many of the sex problems treated at the Wheat Clinic can be traced back to a honeymoon which was fearful for the bride and frustrating for the groom. This first experience often leads to an habitual state of disappointment, blundering, and boredom in the bedroom. The wife begins to avoid sex altogether, and the husband's hurt turns to anger.

We want you not only to have a wonderful time together on your wedding night, but to gain the confidence that your sex life will get better and better as you practice communicating physically and discover many special ways to please one another. No one can tell you all you need to know about loving your own partner sexually. Only you can develop this knowledge as you become sensitive to your partner's desires. In fact, it is this sensitivity and desire to give pleasure to your partner that will make you a great lover. You need to begin with mental preparation for your wedding night.

1. Do not expect complete physical harmony right away. Be realistic in your expectations. To avoid disappointment, plan your wedding night together ahead of time, each sharing your secret dreams.

On the wedding night, romance and realism meet at the crossroads. Hopefully, they will become compatible and travel together from then on. Nothing is more realistic and "earthy" than sexual intercourse. But what about the romantic dreams, and the idealism that desires a beautiful experience, and the longing for spiritual union which at least one of you may bring to your wedding night? These are just as valid and just as important as the rapture and passion that the other one may be visualizing.

You do need to communicate your desires. Please do not count on your partner to know what you want without being told. Husband, you will have the opportunity of demonstrating your love for your bride by making this a beautiful night, which she will never forget, as well as fulfilling her romantic dreams and enjoying loving physical intimacy. Probably, the first few weeks of sexual encounters will require maximum self-control on the husband's part to allow his wife maximum comfort.

2. Do not be goal-oriented in your lovemaking.

This is particularly directed to the man, since he would tend to judge himself as a lover solely on the basis of whether he is able to bring his bride to sexual release through orgasm. But don't make this the supreme goal of your honeymoon.

Your goal setting and striving to meet that goal puts pressure on your bride to respond and perform properly, but it can have the opposite effect. She will reach orgasm only in a relaxed atmosphere after emotional as well as physical arousal have occurred, and enough skillful physical stimulation has taken place. When she feels pressured by *your* expectation, *her* fear of failure can hinder the physical response she otherwise would have. It can even sensitize her and inhibit her response in the future.

Your purpose on the wedding night should be to develop emotional intimacy through physical closeness. You have new avenues for demonstrating how much you adore your wife, how beautiful you think she is, and how she is the most desirable of women. If you lack imagination, study the Song of Solomon, which describes a thrilling wedding night for both bride and bridegroom.

Concentrate on pleasing your wife with romantic words and gestures, warmth and tenderness, and caressing her entire body in a leisurely manner, which indicates how much you delight in her. Some hasty mechanical fondling of the breasts or genitals as a means of fast arousal is just not the mark of a real lover. Your lovemaking should be leisurely, but purposeful to be exciting, and the excitement should steadily intensify. Begin slowly, enjoying every sensation and every sign of your partner's pleasure, then build gradually to an emotional as well as physical climax. As we explained in *LOVE LIFE*,

> Husbands who are preoccupied with physical gratification should know that even for their own maximum enjoyment of sexual release, they need to have at least twenty minutes of sexual arousal beforehand. We some times call orgasm a climax and it should be just that: the highest point of interest and excitement in a series of happenings. How do you reach the high point? By climbing to it. Climax is a Greek word meaning "ladder." You move to a climax with a slow, progressive build-up resulting at the highest point in a sudden, thrilling release—something like a rollercoaster ride with its long, slow climb and then its exciting plunge downward from the peak.[5]

This does require self-control on a young husband's part, but his patience will be rewarded with a fulfilling sex life for many years to come.

Don't be disconcerted if you ejaculate before you want on your wedding night. This might be expected because of your intense feelings. It may happen the moment the penis enters the vagina or even while you are still caressing your bride to bring her to arousal. But this is by no means the end of the lovemaking experience. On your honeymoon another ejaculation will probably appear in a few minutes. Continue to bring your wife to sexual release through stimulation of the clitoris. Actually, this may be more pleasing to her because the vaginal muscles will be very tense, and intercourse will bring some discomfort.

This counsel applies to you even if you have been married before or if you have had previous sexual experiences outside marriage. No matter what's in the past, approach your wedding night as though it were the first time for both of you. This is a fresh start by God's grace and should be handled that way. Treat your bride as gently as though she were a virgin and forget that she is not. Besides, sex within the commitment of marriage is profoundly different from a casual coupling outside of marriage. As one person told us, it's like the contrast between a clear, starry night on a mountain peak and the city smog down in the valley. So enjoy!

Here is some important physical preparation you need to make.

3. Plan the right environment for your honeymoon.

The Old Testament law made provision for a newly married couple to enjoy a one-year honeymoon. Deuteronomy 24:5 says, "When a man hath taken a new wife, he shall not go out to war, neither shall he be charged with any business: but he shall be free at home one year, and shall cheer up his wife which he hath taken." The Hebrew word translated to cheer up means *to delight his wife and to understand what is exquisitely pleasing to her in the sexual relationship.* Obviously, God gives this top priority.

If your budget has several thousand dollars allocated for your wedding with a hundred dollars left over for an overnight honeymoon, we encourage you to balance your funds so that you can be free of responsibility for a few weeks while you have time to get to know each other. During that period, you will have clearer communication lines than you may ever have again. If you miss this opportunity, you may find those communication lines becoming progressively blocked as time goes by.

We recommend that you emphasize comfortable privacy during your honeymoon rather than an elaborate trip. Certainly you should be apart from family and friends. Try to stay in a place where room service will bring meals to your room when requested. Come to your wedding night as rested as possible and do not plan a long drive to your hotel or motel for that first night.

Some thought needs to be given to proper lighting in your bedroom. Since men prefer light and women usually prefer darkness, the best compromise is dim, romantic lighting, which will enhance your lovemaking. Some people take candles with them for subdued lighting.

Also a word about sleepwear. The bride will have some beautiful nightwear; in fact, this may be a part of her romantic dreams. It is best, however, if sometime during the first night you are "naked and unashamed" with one another.

4. Come prepared with an artificial lubricant. This is an essential.

Plenty of lubrication is a must for pleasurable intercourse. If you want to enjoy your honeymoon, take some K-Y Jelly along with you. Use it liberally while you are caressing the genital area, particularly the very sensitive clitoral area.

Also, you will want to have a small towel within reach to take care of the discharged material (lubricating fluid mixed with semen) after ejaculation. We do not advise a vaginal douche after intercourse. The semen projected from the penis is primarily protein, similar to egg white, and is not dirty or unsanitary, despite its distinctive odor.

5. Agree in advance on your family-planning measures.

Fear of unwanted pregnancy can be a serious hindrance to sexual pleasure. Determine if you wish to use artificial means of family planning, natural means, or no means, and then make all necessary preparations in advance. You need to discuss this together and agree in advance on what measures, if any, should be taken. The responsibility belongs to both of you, and it should not cause uneasiness or uncertainty on your honeymoon.

You may find these statistics helpful. Studies have shown that 66 percent of pregnancies occur within three months of the initiation of unprotected intercourse. Within six months of continued exposure, 75 percent of the women have become pregnant, and by the end of one year about 80 percent of the women have conceived.

6. Make preparations for a painless first-time sexual experience.

At the time of their first intercourse, 50 percent of all women experience some pain; 20 percent say they have no pain; and 30 percent experience severe pain. The cause of this discomfort is the hymen—a shelf-like membrane that surrounds but does not cover the lower opening to the vagina. In some instances, a baby girl is born without a hymen so that its absence is not necessarily an indication of loss of virginity. In other cases, it is so tough and resistant that at the time of pelvic examination, a physician can predict that intercourse will be extremely uncomfortable for the bride.

The opening in the hymen for a virgin is usually about one inch, but for intercourse a diameter of one and one-half inches is needed. This means that the vaginal opening should be stretched in advance so that a painful tearing will not occur when the husband attempts to insert the penis. The physician can dilate the vagina if the patient requests; or the woman can devote a few moments each day for two to four weeks before the wedding in stretching the vaginal opening herself (the best way, in our opinion); or the bridegroom can be instructed in how to do it on the wedding night.

Here is how to stretch the vaginal opening. Begin by placing one finger, well-lubricated with K-Y Jelly, inside the vagina and push back very forcibly but very slowly. When you are able to insert one finger all the way to the base, then try to place two well-lubricated fingers into the vagina, press downward and backward with quite firm pressure.

If the husband is attempting to stretch the vaginal opening on the wedding night, he may then insert the tips of three fingers, arranged in a wedge shape, well-lubricated with K-Y Jelly. (His fingernails must be filed smooth and short.) Place the fingertips in the vaginal opening, then press down very firmly toward the back, but very slowly. This should take from fifteen to thirty minutes to accomplish, moving the fingers only about one-eighth inch at a time until all three fingers can be inserted to the base.

This procedure will result in the stretching and possibly even the tearing of small areas in the vaginal opening. If a small area of bleeding occurs, do not be afraid. Simply look for the exact spot that is bleeding, take a piece of tissue, put it on the spot and hold it there with a firm pressure. You will be able to stop whatever bleeding occurs in this manner. If another tear and more bleeding occurs when you have intercourse, you can stop it the same way by holding tissue on the exact spot with a firm pressure. The tissue may be left in place about twelve hours and then soaked loose in warm water to avoid new bleeding. Intercourse can begin again the next day.

After this stretching process, the major portion of the remaining hymen lies in a crescent shape across the back of the vaginal opening. You should keep in mind that it is much less in the way when the wife's legs are down flat. If the husband has difficulty in accomplishing initial entrance, try this special position.

The bride lies on her back with two pillows under her hips, with her legs down as flat as possible to move the hymen more out of the way. The husband faces her and approaches from directly above so that the penis is in an almost vertical position at first contact. After applying plenty of K-Y Jelly around the vaginal opening and on the head of the penis, he places the tip of the penis near the front of the vaginal opening and slides it almost straight down, attempting to slip past the elastic hymen. When the penis slips into the vagina, then the wife should slowly and intermittently bring her knees up as far as her discomfort will permit. At this point the husband will no longer force the penis in but allow her to thrust her pelvis upward and forward against the partially inserted penis, which should still be in an almost vertically straight down position.

As a last resort only, if there is a great deal of pain, Nupercainal Ointment may be applied around the vaginal opening, especially toward the back, and left for a period of five minutes. This is a local anesthetic ointment available without a prescription, which you may wish to have on hand if your physician has warned of a vaginal outlet that seems to be unusually tight.

While these precautions may sound unnecessary to many of you, pain on the wedding night does occur in some cases, and it can and often does affect the couple's sexual relationship for years to come. Some patients at the Wheat Clinic come to us after months or even years of avoiding sex because of a painful first experience. By the time they come to us, their marriage is hanging in the balance.

Most pain occurs from entering too quickly, not allowing enough time for the muscles around the vagina to relax. At the time of first intercourse, the husband should not strive to bring his wife to orgasm with his penis in the vagina. This will only increase her soreness and discomfort. After the penis is inserted, the husband should have his orgasm quickly, withdraw the penis, and gently stimulate his wife's clitoral area with his fingers to bring her to orgasm.

If the husband gives his wife tender loving care at this special time in her life, it will establish an attitude of trust within her so that in the weeks to come she can relax totally and enjoy his lovemaking.

Another problem may arise on your honeymoon unless plenty of lubrication is provided for the penis in the vagina. It is a bruising of the urethra, the outlet for urine from the bladder. (This opening is about one-half inch above the vaginal opening and entirely separate from it.) The urethra is a tube that runs beneath the pubic bone and can be easily bruised by the thrusting of the penis unless the penis and vagina are well-lubricated.

This bruising produces a bladder infection commonly called "honeymoon cystitis." It is characterized by pain in the bladder area and by blood in the urine with rather severe burning when the urine passes. The infection and pain will clear up more quickly if the bride increases her intake of fluids and uses medication prescribed by her physician.

Almost all urinary tract infections in women occur within forty-eight hours after sexual intercourse. Voiding within a few minutes after intercourse is important because bladder urine is sterile. Thus, the voiding of urine cleanses the urethral mechanism of bacteria which would cause the infection.

7. Do not be concerned about your lack of experience.

We have never encountered a couple who had problems relating sexually because of their inexperience. In fact, some of the couples who enjoy the most fulfilling relationships came to us for premarriage counsel with no experience because they had chosen to wait until marriage. Their joy in one another was undiluted by past experiences, and they were free to discover what God has prepared in marriage for those who wait for His timing. What one needs for his wedding night is not experience, but correct information.

Now we want to direct our words to all couples, newly married or about to be.

SECRETS OF SEXUAL FULFILLMENT

If you are like most couples today, you are eager to experience every good thing; your expectations are high. If your sexual relationship falls short of total fulfillment, you will consider it a problem and search for the solution. The silent endurance and trial-and-error methods of your parents and grandparents are not for you! We consider this a positive development, for we know that satisfying sexual intimacy has a remarkable power to renew, refresh, and sustain a marriage.

In this section we want to give you seven valuable secrets of sexual fulfillment. Remember that secrets are things either concealed from others or not readily understood by them. Although sex seems to be the Western world's favorite topic with such exhaustive coverage by the media that we wonder if anything *could* still be concealed, the truth is that husbands and wives today are as frustrated as ever because of their inability to please one another sexually. But it doesn't have to be that way! Many troubled people come to the Wheat Clinic with problems in their sexual relationship that could have been avoided if only they had known and applied this counsel at the beginning of their marriage.

1. Forget the past.

"Like a lily among the thorns, so is my darling among the maidens" (Song of Sol. 2:2 NASV).

This is a key point today when so many people are going into a second marriage or may have had previous sexual experience outside of marriage. One mate may be tempted to make comparisons. Or the other mate may be tempted to be jealous and troubled by mental pictures of the lover loving someone else. Either condition may lead to great distress and a breakdown in the sexual relationship.

It is more difficult, at best, to establish the one flesh relationship when you have had sex before with another person or persons. So be forewarned that this is one area of life where experience will hinder rather than help. Here are the best ways to cope with prior sexual experience in a new marriage: Forget it and discipline yourself never to think of it or the person again; never, under any circumstances, discuss it with your partner. If it must be referred to, be careful never to give details—they will be particularly hard for your partner to forget. Do all you can to overcome its negative potential by practicing the art of loving your partner in all ways, not just sexually.

Learn from the bridegroom in the Song of Songs who wisely and lovingly reassured his bride that she was unique, his perfect one; that she was lovely as a lily and all other women were but as thorns in comparison.

Pray that God will enable you to forget your past sexual experience and make all things new for you in your marriage. It is easier to forget what lies behind when we are straining forward to what lies ahead and giving our heart and energies to that. So pour your life into loving your mate and give no emotional energy to things and persons of the past. God will be faithful to do His part: ". . . His compassion never fail. They are new every morning; great is your faithfulness" (Lam. 3:22–23).

2. Gain a lover's expertise.

"Let his left hand be under my head and his right hand embrace me" (Song of Sol. 2:6 NASV).

While it is true that a mastery of technique alone will do little for your love life, there are several things every husband needs to know to bring his wife to a satisfying sexual release.

(1) The clitoris is the trigger of female desire.

Men sometimes expect the greatest sexual sensitivity to be in the vagina, but this is not the case. The clitoris is the most keenly sensitive point for sexual arousal and has, as far as we know, no other function. Sufficient physical stimulation of the clitoral area will produce orgasm in nearly all women, if there has been sufficient foreplay and emotional arousal.

It's important to learn the exact location of the wife's clitoris. The clitoral shaft, which is about an inch long, is closed in by the peak of the inner lips, the labia minora, and extends upward onto the pelvic bone. At the outer end of the clitoris is the glans, a small rounded body about the size of a pea. A fold of skin, called the clitoral hood partly covers the glans.

During the time of sexual arousal when effective physical contact on the clitoris is continued, a firmness and enlargement of the shaft of the clitoris occurs. You can detect this enlarged shaft by placing sensitive, well-lubricated fingertips alongside it. As you move your fingers across the shaft from side to side, it will be like rolling your fingers across a very small telephone cord. Persistent, loving, gentle, sensitive, well-lubricated stimulation alongside this clitoral shaft will bring almost any wife to orgasm in a twenty-minute period. As orgasm is approached, the tempo of the stimulation will need to increase. Beware of too much stimulation on the glans, as it can easily become irritated. It is a supersensitive spot! The wife should lovingly move her husband's hand to show him which area is most responsive to touch and even the degree of stimulation and the tempo she prefers. This is part of learning to communicate physically.

Remember, the clitoris must always be stimulated either directly or indirectly for the wife to achieve orgasm. The physical process of orgasm is the same whether by clitoral stimulation or from sexual intercourse, which also stimulates the clitoris through the movement of the penis as it tugs and pulls at the small lips and the clitoral hood. Also, certain positions will enable the base of the penis to rub against the clitoris during intercourse and bring about orgasm. When the woman experiences sexual release, she will have a generalized sensation of pleasure throughout the pelvis and especially at the vaginal opening. However, the clitoris is always the trigger point of orgasm.

Men should also know that deep penetration of the vagina has no effect on their wife's pleasure. The size of the erect penis has almost nothing to do with how much either partner enjoys intercourse, as only the outer two inches of the vagina contain tissue that is stimulated by pressure on the inside. Most vaginal sexual sensitivity depends on contraction of the PC muscles as they grip the penis, rather than being stretched by a larger object in the vagina. In fact, during the plateau phase of arousal in preparation for intercourse, the lower vagina swells so that the diameter of the outer third of the vagina is reduced as much as 50 percent in readiness to grip the penis.

The Song of Songs describes the ideal position for stimulation. "Let his left hand be under my head and his right hand embrace me," the bride says. The Hebrew word translated embrace usually means to embrace lovingly, to fondle or stimulate with gentle stroking. In this position, the wife lies on her back with her legs comfortably separated, and her husband lies down on her right side, placing his left arm under her neck. In this way he can kiss her lips, neck, and

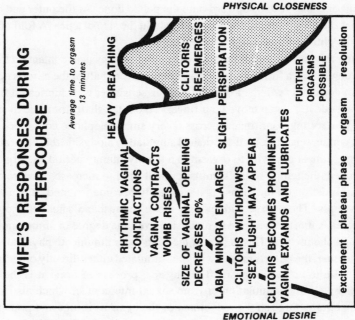

WIFE'S RESPONSES DURING INTERCOURSE

Average time to orgasm 13 minutes

PHYSICAL CLOSENESS

HEAVY BREATHING

CLITORIS, RE-EMERGES

SLIGHT PERSPIRATION

FURTHER ORGASMS POSSIBLE

RHYTHMIC VAGINAL CONTRACTIONS

VAGINA CONTRACTS
WOMB RISES

SIZE OF VAGINAL OPENING DECREASES 50%

LABIA MINORA ENLARGE

CLITORIS WITHDRAWS
"SEX FLUSH" MAY APPEAR

CLITORIS BECOMES PROMINENT
VAGINA EXPANDS AND LUBRICATES

EMOTIONAL DESIRE

excitement   plateau phase   orgasm   resolution

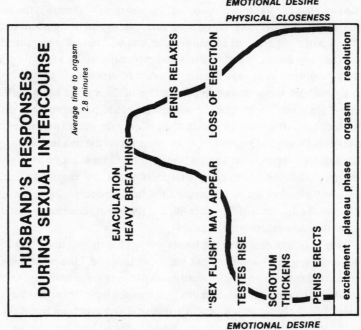

HUSBAND'S RESPONSES DURING SEXUAL INTERCOURSE

Average time to orgasm 2.8 minutes

PHYSICAL CLOSENESS

PENIS RELAXES

LOSS OF ERECTION

EJACULATION
HEAVY BREATHING

"SEX FLUSH" MAY APPEAR

TESTES RISE

SCROTUM THICKENS

PENIS ERECTS

EMOTIONAL DESIRE

excitement   plateau phase   orgasm   resolution

breasts, and at the same time his right hand is free to fondle her genitals and particularly to stimulate the clitoris. In some cases, the wife may experience orgasm before the penis is inserted. In some cases, the two may reach orgasm at the same time. And, if the wife has not reached release before or during the husband's orgasm, he should bring her to release afterward, using his hand to stimulate the clitoris.

(2) After foreplay, the husband can reach orgasm in less than three minutes, the wife requires an average of thirteen minutes. The skillful lover understands and adjusts to this difference.

If you study these response charts, you will see the four phases of the sexual experience, and you can also take note of how much the man and woman vary in their timing of response. The husband must learn to control the timing of his response while the wife learns to let herself go, trusting both her husband and her own body. She needs to concentrate on her physical feelings and communicate her level of excitement to her husband with looks, touches, and sometimes loving words. While his stimulation brings on her orgasm, her caresses of the male genitalia do not speed up his orgasm. Instead, her touch of his genitals is soothing and comforting. The wife's very light, gentle caressing should center around the inner thighs, the scrotum, and the under surface of the penile shaft.

Fondling the head of the penis will increase his excitement and may trigger ejaculation more quickly than desired. By lovingly fondling her husband's genitals, the wife helps him to wait for her own excitement to build.

When is she ready for insertion of the penis? The most observable sign is the swelling of the inner lips on each side of the vaginal opening. These lips may be so engorged that they protrude beyond the outer lips. The wife should signal her husband when she desires the insertion of the penis, and it is best in most cases for the wife to insert it. Never thrust vigorously as soon as the penis is inserted, since this usually decreases arousal in the woman.

Timing is all-important. Take time to arouse each other completely. Take time to ensure her orgasm and his controlled, full response. And after intercourse, take time to express your love and appreciation to each other. The final phase has been called afterglow when the fires of passion and pleasure settle down to a warm, lovely glow. The couple should lie close in each other's arms, enjoy each other's presence, and show tenderness and appreciation with hugs, kisses, love pats, and loving words. This will give a smooth transition to complete relaxation. It may be as long as fifteen minutes before all the physical signs of arousal are gone. A young man's erection may remain as long as half an hour.

Some have wondered why God made men and women so different in length of time required for their sexual arousal. Here is Dr. Wheat's answer:

> If men and women both were satisfied with a short period of arousal, the sex act would become a brief, mechanical experience. If both took a very long time to become aroused, the experience could become boring and monotonous. . . . Because men and women are different, the husband is given the opportunity to learn self-control and encouraged to investigate and employ the imaginative techniques that please a woman. He has the opportunity to develop patience and gentleness in physical communication, while she learns to keep him sexually aroused and intrigued. The differences between men and women provide ground for creative, interesting interaction and enrich the sexual relationship in marriage.[6]

3. Nourish your total relationship.

"Take us the foxes, the little foxes, that spoil the vines; for our vines have tender grapes" (Song of Sol. 2:15).

Sex in marriage serves, in sometimes uncomfortable ways, as a mirror of your total relationship, reflecting the flaws as well as the virtues. You might think of it as a barometer, which fluctuates, depending on how well you are getting along in other areas of your marriage. Negative feelings will often show up first in your sex life.

When people come to us, complaining of difficulties in relating sexually, we usually find that the difficulty began elsewhere and long before. Any unresolved conflict, sooner or later, finds its way into the bedroom where it creates a whole new set of problems. For instance, most of the cases we see of inhibited sexual desire have one root cause: repressed anger and resentment, which produce depression and a chilly indifference toward the mate.

Women are particularly sensitive to factors outside the bedroom. Dr. Helen Kaplan warns that "in general, female sexual desire is more variable than that of males. While women have a greater orgastic potential, their sexuality is also more easily suppressed."[7]

Researchers have found a strong connection between a woman's ability to reach an orgasm and her feelings of trust in her partner. If other problems in the marriage have caused her to question whether she can rely on her husband, it will make a difference in her sexual response. If she is insecure because she does not experience his cherishing, she may not be able to gain sexual release. Since she feels she can't depend on him and has to stand on her own, she finds it almost impossible to trust him in the sexual act and to relax and let herself go to the point of orgasm.

The sex drive of young men is so intense that only strongly negative factors will inhibit their desire. But a man's sexual life is always tied to his sense of manhood and self-esteem. If his wife consistently tears him down and demonstrates her lack of respect for him, over a period of time it will hinder his ability to desire sex or enjoy it. He may even have problems in functioning sexually with his wife.

These are three examples of a principle to remember: The way you treat your partner on a daily basis will determine your partner's responsiveness in the bedroom. On the positive side, this means that good sex at night begins in the morning in the way you snuggle together before getting up for work, the way you talk to each other over breakfast, the way you kiss good-bye with a promise for the time when you can be together again. Any intimacy between you has sexual dimensions whether you're talking together or tossing a frisbee, dressing together for the day or working in the garden side by side, cooking dinner together or sharing a time of prayer. It's all a part of lovemaking.

We encourage you to nurture that relationship with particular attention in these areas:

(1) *Avoid behavior which creates anger and lasting resentment in your partner.* Try to resolve conflicts when they arise and do not let them drag on without getting help from your pastor or a biblical counselor.

(2) *Husband, demonstrate to your wife in every way you can that you won't let her down, that she's safe in the security of your love and permanent commitment.* Be the leader she can lean on and count on. Prove to her that you care about every detail of her welfare. This really can make the difference in her ability to respond to you fully.

(3) *Wife, remember that when your husband's self-esteem is reduced because he feels you do not respect him, your sex life together is sure to suffer.* Respecting your husband and responding to him as the leader in your home will inspire him to be the confident and ardent lover you want him to be.

(4) *Learn to relate as lovers all of the time, not just when having sex.* Feeling mutually loved and admired will keep you turned on sexually. As Dr. Kaplan says, "Love is the best aphrodisiac discovered so far."[8]

(5) *Pray that God will make you sensitive to areas of your relationship that are being neglected.* (Husbands tend to see their sex relationship separately from these areas, while wives never do.)

With proper care given to your total relationship, your sex life can be a joyful affirmation of the love you share twenty-four hours a day.

4. Keep negatives out of your lovemaking.

"You are altogether beautiful, my darling, and there is no blemish in you" (Song of Sol. 4:7 NASV).

Students of human behavior tell us that all human behavior is organized around seeking pleasure and avoiding pain. Apply this to your sexual relationship. You can see how important it is to keep negatives out of the bedroom and to make your lovemaking altogether pleasurable.

You need to look on sex in your marriage as an opportunity for genuine "lovemaking" in the sense of making or building love. This will happen through giving and receiving in ways that are physically and emotionally satisfying for both of you. Remember, the thrills are great, but concentrate on the essentials: physical/emotional closeness and a positive response that will signal pleasure, not the emotional pain of rejection and criticism.

Compare the generous, positive words of the husband in the Song of Songs ("Thou art all fair, my love; there is no spot in thee.") with these examples taken from real life. A husband complains,

"Elizabeth's idea of foreplay is a brief therapy session, which consists mostly of criticism of me. That's supposed to be how we get intimate. Usually, though, it ends in our sleeping reverse spoons."[9]

A wife confides,

"My sex life has become a nightmare because my husband is a dictator in the bedroom. George is always trying to control our lovemaking and wants things his own way without any regard for what I prefer or can do. Now he insists that we reach orgasm simultaneously! I'd like to just forget the whole thing."

A husband says,

I can't believe the way Jill treats me when we're making love. She starts complaining about my technique instead of just showing me what she wants. Or she cracks jokes—jokes that put me down. It hurts.

A wife asks,

"How can I break my husband away from the eleven o'clock news to go to bed? I get up at 5:30 a.m., so by the time Tom is ready to make love, I'm wiped out. His selfishness really hurts me, and it's affecting our entire marriage."

Therapists call negative behavior that hinders a satisfying sexual experience "sexual sabotage." The behavior that creates the deepest resentment of all in wives is the feeling that they are being used, not loved. For instance, a man may feel desire and want sex even when he is angry with his partner. That's the last thing a hostile wife wants. She feels exploited and outraged by his attempts to have sex before their relationship has been put right. The behavior that offends a husband is the critiquing of his performance or, worst of all, a lack of response from his wife, which amounts to rejection.

It's good to follow the biblical principle in your bedroom: "If there be any virtue, and if there be any praise, think on these things" (Phil. 4:8b). The Greek word for think is an accounting term that means reckon these things among your assets. If you are positive in your attitude and your approach, your sexual relationship can mirror a love that values, treasures, and respects.

5. Practice bedroom etiquette.

". . . it is the voice of my beloved that knocketh, saying, Open to me, my sister, my love. . ." (Song of Sol. 5:2).

Here is one of the memorable letters to advice columnist Abigail Van Buren and her even more memorable answer:

Dear Abby: What would you do with a man who refuses to use a deodorant, seldom bathes, and doesn't even own a toothbrush? —Stinky's Wife.

Dear Wife: Absolutely nothing![10]

To approach your partner without being clean and well-groomed is simply bad manners. When married, bathing at night before getting into bed makes sense. Sleeping together, even when not making love, is an intimate contact. When you want to make love, bathing, shaving, and carefully grooming yourself shows respect as well as caring and an anticipation of closeness.

Have you ever thought of applying all you know about good manners and courtesy in your times of relating sexually? The purpose of etiquette is to smooth and improve human relations. Many sexual problems result from ignoring bedroom etiquette, and good manners in the sexual relationship could cure some of the dysfunctions we must treat.

The truly courteous are warm, kind, generous, and flexible in the bedroom. They consider one another's needs and feelings, and approach sex with their partner not as a right, but a privilege. Courtesy is made up of tact and foresight—

looking ahead to see how what you say or do will affect another person. Tact means to touch delicately. As a considerate lover, you will try to relate to your loved one with this "delicacy of touch," and you will avoid being careless or rude in the name of relaxed intimacy.

6. Share the responsibility.

"I am my beloved's, and my beloved is mine . . ." (Song of Sol. 6:3).

Sexual fulfillment requires a sharing of the responsibility for every aspect of the relationship. Both of you are responsible to communicate (lovingly!) your needs and desires—the ways of loving that please you most. You're also responsible to communicate (tactfully!) what you don't care for by suggesting something else in its place.

Sexual communication is important, but so is taking partial responsibility for your own sexual arousal and satisfaction. The wife should realize that her mind is probably the most important part of her sexual anatomy, and that she needs to prepare herself ahead of time for pleasure, fantasizing romantically about her husband and anticipating the experience. She must learn to use her own mental concentration to sustain the emotional mood of lovemaking and then guide her husband in the kind of physical stimulation she desires for orgasm. She also is responsible to initiate sex when she desires it.

The husband can learn to do what will increase the physical intensity and pleasure of his orgasm: (1) waiting at lease twenty-four hours after orgasm to allow the body to store a larger volume of seminal fluid; (2) lengthening the foreplay and excitement periods so that the penis can remain erect about twenty minutes; (3) concentrating on enjoyment of the wife's response; (4) voluntarily contracting the anal sphincter muscles during orgasm; and (5) increasing the force of thrusting while the orgasm is in progress.

If a problem arises in your sexual relationship, you need to take responsibility for it together. It is a couple problem that will require a couple solution, so absolutely refrain from placing blame on one another. Remember that every sexual problem has a solution that can lead to pleasure and emotional satisfaction for both partners. For a full discussion of common sexual problems and what to do about them, we refer you to *Intended for Pleasure,* which will answer your questions.

Remember also that you share the responsibility with God, the Wedding Guest in the Song of Songs, who encouraged the lovers to delight in the sexual relationship He had designed for them. Make your relationship a matter of prayer. When problems arise, it may be necessary to go to a physician or therapist. But the solution also requires patience and purity of love, and a sincere turning toward God. If a couple were to seek the Lord with their whole will, rejoice in Christian fellowship, and spend time both alone and together in heartfelt prayer and study of the Scriptures, they would soon find their love life filled with a rich glow and a mysterious new energy that cannot be discovered through any worldly means. For as the Lord is the author of sex, so He is its interpreter, and it is His therapy that is most to be treasured.[11]

7. Enjoy partner-centered sex.

"The mandrakes give fragrance, and at our gates are all manner of pleasant fruits, new and old, which I have laid up for thee, O my beloved" (Song of Sol. 7:13).

This is the greatest secret of sexual fulfillment we can offer you: to develop a relationship that is not self-centered, not performance-centered, not even sex-centered, but centered in the joy of giving your partner pleasure. In this best kind of sexual relationship, each learns how to please the other; each tries to outdo the other in pleasing; and each gets the greatest thrills from seeing the other's ecstatic response.

When two people enjoy partner-centered sex, their lovemaking is never repetitious, boring, or mechanical. Sex that has become as routine as brushing teeth or as mechanical as mailing a letter signals a dying relationship. It can be revived when both put the focus on their partner's pleasure. The signs of life are spontaneity and sensitivity to one another.

Partner-centered sex depends on your motivation, for it will require careful study of your partner to learn what brings pleasure (and displeasure) to him or her. Becoming sensitive to your partner's needs and desires, implied or stated, means listening with your whole being to that person. It involves reading body language, observing even the slightest word or gesture and discerning what it means. You will lovingly put forth effort to discover your partner's wishes, to find out what "feels good." You will learn your partner's likes, dislikes, what parts of his or her body are most erotic, and the ways of loving that evoke a response at that particular moment.

All of this requires the gift of time to one another and the decision to set your marriage bed apart as an important priority. Knowing that simple exhaustion because of hard work, a demanding schedule, small children, or too much social life will diminish sexual interest, the two of you need to establish a lifestyle that avoids fatigue and saves prime time and energy for one another.

Don't think of partner-centered sex as somehow sacrificial. You don't lose any pleasure by this. To concentrate on pleasuring your partner is a sweet sacrifice that turns out to be no sacrifice at all because the reward is so great! The thrills that come to both of you as you each see your partner responding totally and enjoying your lovemaking cannot be described.

Partner-centered sex will be positive, relaxed, enjoyable, romantic, physically satisfying, and emotionally fulfilling. Partner-centered sex partners will learn to handle their relationship with the care that they would give to anything that can be explosively wonderful, or explosively harmful if mishandled. Yes, there is a risk in being vulnerable. But the same openness that makes you vulnerable to pain is the price of joy. More than that, it is the prerequisite for oneness.

Sexual fulfillment that bonds the two of you in the forever relationship of marriage will include these elements: the assurance of being accepted and desired; the well-being that comes from intimate physical and emotional closeness; the sensuous delights of loving caresses; and the wonderful feeling of belonging to each other in the one-flesh relationship of God's devising.

7

The ABCs of Never:
Warning Signals

∽━━✦━━∽

IN THIS DAY of "instant" everything, when experts are asked to sum up their solution to a pressing world problem "in the fifteen seconds we have left," we offer some almost-instant counsel for your new marriage.

You've read the ABCs of Forever. Here is another set of ABCs, but these form the language of loss, not love: loss of happiness, loss of peace, loss of all good things you hoped to get from your marriage. It's said that most people marry for sex, security, and prevention of loneliness. Turning these ABCs loose in your marriage will destroy your joy in sex and your sense of emotional security; moreover, if allowed to proceed unchecked, they can produce more loneliness in your relationship than you ever felt when you walked this world as a single.

We call these the *ABCs of Never* because they can never bring you happiness. But understanding them, avoiding them, and replacing them with positive attitudes and behavior will go far to guard your love relationship and increase your pleasure in it.

These "ABCs" have their model in the Proverbs of the Old Testament, a book which sets forth a series of momentous rules of life, concentrated into remarkably few words. Although ours offer more words and less genius, they are grounded in biblical truth. They should serve as warning signs and reference points when you feel your relationship is moving in the wrong direction.

Adultery

Sexual intercourse with someone other than your marriage partner.

One of the deadly three destroyers in marriage, it shocks the heart and destroys the lifeline of trust, but does not release you from the vows of marriage.

Only marriage to someone else destroys the marriage bond. Even when a Christian marriage is attacked by unfaithfulness, it can be restored and healed. God says adultery carries severe penalties with it. Read Proverbs 5 and 1 Corinthians 6:9–20.

Anger

Uncontrolled or unresolved feelings of hostility expressed through temper tantrums, hurtful words, pouting, or icy rages during which you refuse to acknowledge the other's presence.

Uncontrolled, unresolved anger destroys love and produces bitterness and depression. It's an ineffectual way of resolving differences. Never go to bed when angry, i.e., never let a quarrel continue on the second day. Stay up and talk, stay up and pray. Resolve it, and go to sleep with your closeness restored. Proverbs 17:14 says a quarrel begins like a small hole in a reservoir, letting out a tiny trickle. But if it is not stopped, the hole is enlarged and a destructive flood pours through. The problem is not the anger itself, but failure to handle it biblically and resolve it with mutual forgiveness. Read Ephesians 4 and 5.

Bitterness

Anger pushed inward until it takes root, producing all manner of trouble and grief including damage to your physical health.

This second deadly destroyer of marriage comes from clinging to an unforgiving spirit. It tortures both you and your partner, ravaging secretly while blocking any attempts to build real intimacy. Because it operates beneath the surface, it may not be recognized until almost too late. Bitterness can be removed only through forgiveness which Jesus Christ makes possible, "To forgive is to set a prisoner free and discover that the prisoner was you." Read Hebrews 12:12–15; Ephesians 4:31; and Colossians 3:19.

Change

What you can't make your partner do, and it would be better never to try.

You can never change another person's behavior, but you can set up the conditions whereby that person motivates himself (or herself) to change—and to seek the Lord's enabling power in changing. Never forget the positive effects of unconditional acceptance. Read Romans 5 and 6. Also the Song of Solomon.

Conflict

An inevitable happening when two are learning to share their life, but when mishandled, conflicts can escalate and lead to disaster for the marriage.

Basically, there are four ways of handling a marital conflict: 1) The *chaos*
principle when husband and wife clash by day and night and fight incessantly,
or quit trying and go their own ways. As a result, anarchy reigns in the home. 2)
The *power play* principle where one eventually "wins" and the other "loses."
In a power play, the entire offense converges at a given point to exert mass pressure on the defense. When this happens in a marriage, both lose. One dominates, the other retaliates with passive-aggressive behavior or deep resentments.
3) The *bargaining table* principle where conflicts are solved by the *quid pro
quo* method (something in return). This is preferable to chaos, but depends on
a selfish assertion of one's rights, although done in a civilized manner. 4) The
grace principle which can be understood and implemented only by Christians.
It is modeled after God's gracious treatment of us in Jesus Christ which gives
freely and does not think in terms of bargains and rights. Grace means to bestow gracious favors unconditionally. Read Ephesians 2:4–9 and Romans 6:14.

Criticism

A bad habit of forming and expressing negative opinions concerning your partners appearance, behavior, personality, and choices in life.

It may seem fairly harmless, even "constructive" under certain circumstances. Yet it has the potential to bring about the slow, painful death of a love
relationship: when criticism drips unchecked, love dies by inches. The third
deadly destroyer of marriage, criticism should be replaced by encouragement
and edifying. Read 1 Peter 4:8; Romans 14:19, 15:2; 1 Thessalonians 5:11; and
1 Corinthians 8:1.

Debt

The habit of spending more than your income, relying on loans and credit cards,
and hoping to make enough in the future to pay for what you are using today.

Two principles can avert the disasters of this approach: Decide you won't
spend what you don't have; and trust God to provide for your needs instead of
trusting loans. Overwhelming financial pressures are a key factor in the majority of divorces today. Obtain personal financial counsel and develop a biblical

approach to money and possessions. When both partners must work, here are some suggested guidelines:

1. Arrange to have your time off at the same time.
2. Live as close to work as possible; eliminate travel time.
3. Try to get jobs in the same area of town.
4. Recognize that the extra money isn't worth it if you're never together.
5. Discuss your work with one another.
6. Respect one another's skills and hard work.
7. Don't make your partner jealous.
8. Plan ahead financially for the time when the wife will want to be home as you begin your family.
9. Avoid consumer debt and multiply your choices.

Read Psalm 112:5; Proverbs 3:5–10, 15:16, 16:8; Matthew 6:19–34; Luke 12:15–21; 2 Corinthians 9:6–15; Philippians 4:19; and I Timothy 6:6–11.

Disloyalty

The harmful practice of criticizing your partner in discussions with friends and relatives, or allowing them to criticize your mate.

The words you speak—or hear—have power to reinforce negative thoughts and influence your attitude against the person with whom you are meant to be *one* in body, mind, heart, and spirit. D. James Kennedy, in his book *Learning to Live with the People You Love*, points out that marriage can be either tremendously constructive or unimaginably destructive to the lives of those involved. What makes the difference? Whether you are building each other up or tearing one another down! Read Mark 10:6–9 and 1 Corinthians 13:7.

Ego Trips

Making yourself look "good" at the expense of your partner's feelings.

This is done by cutting your mate down, humiliating him or her publicly, or indulging in misplaced humor which ridicules your partner. People with low self-images sometimes resort to this unpleasant behavior to build themselves up. Read Ephesians 5:28; Proverbs 31:11, 26; Colossians 3:8; Ephesians 4:29 and 5:4.

Failure to Communicate

Choosing (for whatever reason) to shut the door of your heart and soul, leaving your loved one "on the outside, looking in."

It's most important to seek the help of a biblical counselor to remedy this, for the causes are varied and complex. Read 1 Thessalonians 2:8; John 15:15; and Romans 1:12.

Guilt Trips

Making your partner feel guilty.

Guilt statements, such as "I'm very disappointed in you," quench feelings of love and pleasure in being together. Guilt is a most disagreeable feeling which people prefer to avoid. Remember, the Holy Spirit has the sole responsibility of convicting of sin in a way that brings about healing and redemption. Only the Word of God can effectively reprove, correct, and train us in the way we should go. Read John 16:7–8, 13; and 11 Timothy 3:16–17.

Habits

Habitual practices that are injurious to your health and happiness: anything which alters the thinking part of the mind, distorts the emotions, harms the body, or leads to harmful acts, such as cocaine, marijuana, and all other forms of illegal drugs; misuse of prescription drugs; beverage alcohol ("drinking"); smoking; and eating disorders.

What hurts you hurts your partner too. But God can deliver you! Commit your way to Him and seek help from your pastor, your physician, your biblical counselor or support groups that may be of benefit. Read Proverbs 20:1 23:29–35; Galatians 5:16–25; 6:8; 1 Corinthians 10:13; and Romans 13:13–14.

Impatience

Annoyance at having to tolerate any delay or general irritability expressed in quick, sharp retorts and a "hurry-up" attitude.

This is hard to live with! However, an impatient person can learn to be quiet, steady, and even-tempered, if he or she desires to change. If we allow Him to, the Lord works mighty changes in us. Read Proverbs 17:27; Galatians 5:22; and James 1:2–4 with Psalm 62:5.

Indifference

A lack of response to your partner, sending the message that you really don't care.

This form of unlove can have the most serious consequences, because all the loves of marriage, with the exception of *agape*, require a response to keep them alive. Indifference, rather than hatred, is the opposite of love. Read Song of Solomon and 1 Peter 1:22.

Inequality

An unfair load of responsibility placed on one partner for the necessities of maintaining their shared life.

This includes financial burdens; housekeeping and home maintenance; duties toward parents and children; and the daily tasks and errands which must be done. Neither partner should be allowed to assume all of this, and neither should be expected to carry it. Inequities produce weariness and resentments. Read Proverbs 18:9; Ecclesiastes 4:9, 9:9–10; Matthew 11:28–30; Galatians 6:2; and Colossians 3:23–24.

Insensitivity

Deafness and blindness of the heart toward your partner's feelings and needs.

This is like trampling with clodhopper boots over the other person—not out of malice, but ignorance. Love pays the most careful attention to the beloved. Anyone can learn to be sensitive to another person. Read 1 Peter 3:7–8, Romans 12:15, and Song of Solomon. Also, the Letter of Paul to Philemon as a model of sensitivity to another person in a delicate situation.

Jealousy

An inordinate fear of losing your partner that causes you to behave irrationally.

This is a destroyer which feeds on your own insecurities and suspicions, and makes your partner miserable. But neither should behave in ways to inspire suspicions. Particularly avoid paying undue attention by look, comment, or time spent with another person of the opposite sex. Never give your partner cause to feel ignored, unappreciated, or threatened by your admiration for someone else. Read Song of Solomon 8:6.

"Keeping House" Controversies

Arguments, strong differences of opinion over the way to do things in your shared home.

Disagreements over the toothpaste tube or the best way to rinse dishes may sound like minor difficulties, but this sort of friction in your household affairs can become a source of great frustration. Compromise, tolerance, a sense of humor, and a sense of proportion can carry you through this problem until you have learned to adapt yourselves to one another. Read Romans 12:9–11 with Galatians 5:22.

Lack of Intimacy

A superficial relationship which leaves a dangerous emotional void in your marriage.

Intimacy will cause you to stay in love. Without intimacy one or both may be strongly tempted to seek it elsewhere. Human beings have an insatiable desire for a meaningful one-to-one relationship. Read Song of Solomon 2:3–6; 14.

Messiness

Disorder in the management and arrangement of your possessions which creates havoc in your household.

A comfortable, orderly home which offers a peaceful atmosphere makes for marital happiness. Creative clutter is one thing; messiness which drives your partner (and you, too) "up the wall" needs to be remedied. God, truly, is the God of order, not of confusion. Many fine "help" books are available to take you through this problem. When one determines to keep a *perfect* house, that also can cause discomfort and unhappiness. Your goal should be: a home you both can enjoy and the freedom to invite people into your house without worrying about its "disaster area" appearance. Read 1 Corinthians 14:33; Proverbs 31:27; and Hebrews 13:1–2.

Nagging

Tormenting your partner by complaining constantly to get your own way about something.

With this approach you admit your failure to deal with issues constructively, or to inspire your partner to love you. But nagging never improves the situation, and may be the death blow to love and intimacy. Instead of nagging, apply the potent power of praise. Read Proverbs 12:25, 15:15, 17:1, 25:23–24; Galatians 5:15, 26; Colossians 3:12–17; and Hebrews 10:24.

Out-of-Control Children

The disruptive presence of unruly, undisciplined children.

It is hard to build a meaningful love relationship when your children are out of control. If their misbehavior and unreasonable demands give you no time for intimacy and private enjoyment of one another, it's imperative to deal with the situation. If you're beginning a family, establish the patterns of obedience in their earliest training. Help them to understand that they must respect your privacy and your right to a peaceful, well-ordered home. It will be a blessing both to your children and your marriage. Read 1 Timothy 3:4; Ephesians 6:1–4; and God's principles of disciplining His children: Hebrews 12:5–11 with Proverbs 3:11–12.

Parental Pressures

Interference from your families, in-law strife, family "feuds," or too much closeness to your parents, and dependence on them.

The biblical principle is: Leave your parents and cleave to your marriage partner; establish a new family unit. You are no longer responsible to obey your parents, but you are responsible to honor them and care for them when they need it. Your families, by their influence and example and the respect they show for your new marriage and your mate, can be of great help to you. Unfortunately, some families become a great hindrance. Read Genesis 2:24; Ephesians 6:1–3; 1 Timothy 5:8.

Pride

The thing which keeps you from seeking forgiveness or granting it.

This character trait is most displeasing to God. It's also one of the highest barriers to a loving relationship. In a good give-and-take marriage, both partners recognize their own shortcomings and willingly admit their flaws. When you learn to say things like, "I was wrong . . . I'm sorry. . . . I need you, . . ." you're on your way to overcoming the pride that destroys marriages. Read Proverbs 6:17, 13:10, 21:4; Romans 12:3, 16; and James 5:16.

Procrastination

When your failure to do what should be done when it should be done creates frustrations in your marriage partner and unhappiness for yourself.

Putting off until later what you have time for today becomes a terrible form of indebtedness, and can be a great annoyance to your marriage partner. The Bible calls the classic procrastinator a *sluggard* who will not begin things; or will not finish things, once started; or will not face things that need to be dealt with. Read Proverbs 6:6–11, 10:26, 12:24–27, 13:4, 15:19, 18:9, 19:24, 20:4, 21:25–26; 22:13, 24:30–32 and 26:15–16.

Quick Replies

Sins of the tongue which come from speaking before you think.

Sharp answers and cutting responses fall under the category of verbal abuse. This creates a strong desire to avoid the person who's causing the pain. Be warned that, in time, it can drive your partner away from you. Read Psalm 19: 14, 141:3; Proverbs 12:18, 15:1, 19:11, 29:20; and James 3:5–12.

Rejection, Sexual

Defrauding your partner by refusing sex.

This creates intense grief and loss of self-respect for the rejected partner. When sex becomes a part of the battleground of marriage, or when either devalues sex, both partners have lost something very important. The sexual relationship in marriage is meant to be one of the most mysterious, profound, and enriching of all experiences. God gives clear-cut guidelines in the Scriptures concerning sexual responsibilities in marriage. Read Proverbs 5:18 and 1 Corinthians 7:2–5.

Selfishness

Preoccupation with yourself, putting your well-being before your marriage partner's.

This indicates that you have not yet learned how to love. Love is giving without counting the cost because it is unimportant compared with the joy of serving the beloved. Read John 3:16; Philippians 2:3–8; and 2 Corinthians 12:15; with Mark 14:1–9.

Self-pity

Feeling sorry for yourself and expressing it by whining and complaining.

This is so tiresome for the partner who must listen to it continually. Replace negative feelings with prayer and thanksgiving. Read Philippians 2:14; 4:6–7; and 1 Thessalonians 5:18.

Spiritual Indifference

In essence, a refusal to recognize God as God; a denial of the Lordship of Jesus Christ in your life even though you may consider yourself a Christian, saved by His grace.

The symptoms are a lack of interest in Bible reading, prayer, and church attendance. You are robbing yourself, your mate, and your family of God's blessing. One of the best ways to ensure a lasting marriage is to become active members of a Bible-teaching church. For example: Two economists studied 1,800 families for twelve years. They found that no-fault divorce laws, educational achievements, and the employment of the wives had little effect on whether couples divorced. But one thing did matter: *The risk of divorce was higher for couples who did not attend church regularly!* Read Deuteronomy 5:29, 6:4–7; Joshua 1:8, 24:14–15; Galatians 6:7–10; 1 Timothy 3:15; 11 Timothy 3:14–17; and Hebrews 10:25.

Television

The over-use of television until it becomes harmful to your relationship.

Too much TV-watching produces passive people with neither the motivation nor energy to develop intimate marriages. It can be a serious hindrance to your sex life and communication. Read 1 Corinthians 10:23 with Ecclesiastes 2:10–11.

Ultimatums

The *or else* weapon which people use to try to make their marriage partner change.

This usually involves the threat of divorce; it is unbiblical and *very* unwise. Divorce should not remain in the vocabulary of a couple who want a love-filled, lasting marriage. Keeping divorce as an escape clause indicates a flaw in your commitment to each other which can prove to be fatal. Threats are always non-productive and often backfire. Read Malachi 2:14–16; Mark 10:1–9; and 1 Peter 3:8–9.

Violence

Physical expressions of rage resulting from anger out of control.

This more frequently involves abusing objects rather than people, i.e., throwing things. It is a sign of immaturity which can be overcome by learning effective techniques for dealing with your feelings. The expression of violence toward loved ones is totally unacceptable behavior and has no place in your marriage. If even one instance occurs, seek help from a biblical counselor immediately. Read Genesis 6:11; Proverbs 4:14–17; and 11 Peter 1:3–7.

Withholding Affection

Refusing to give your marriage partner the loving, affectionate, nonsexual physical touching that he or she needs.

A tender touch tells us we are cared for; it can calm our fears, soothe our pain, comfort our hearts, and grant us emotional security. To refuse to touch your partner lovingly sends the opposite message and may send your partner searching for love elsewhere. Read the Song of Solomon and Ecclesiastes 4:11 with the principle of meeting need from 1 John 3:17–18.

Xhaustion

An absence of the vitality you need for your marriage because you are so involved in other areas of life that you have little left to give to your partner and your love relationship.

Work together to resolve this problem. Few things in life are as important as your marriage, and it does take energy to maintain a good relationship. Read Psalm 116:7; 11 Thessalonians 3:16; and Song of Solomon 5:2–8.

Yelling and Other Annoying Habits

Any personal habit which gets on your partner's nerves.

For example, he yells and she "can't stand it." She "pops" her chewing gum, and it sends him out of the room. Marriage puts every problem and even the

smallest annoyance under a magnifying glass because it's so *daily*. We have to
learn to be both tolerant of habits that bother us and sensitive to our partner's
wishes in trying not to offend. (After all, when we love someone, we don't want
to make that person unhappy!) This problem takes time to work through and a
good supply of patience and self-control. Love will work a change if we let it
have its way instead of forcing the issue through nagging, criticizing, and asserting our rights. Read 1 Corinthians 13:7.

Zzz's

Boredom with your partner, your marriage, and your life in general.

Boredom is a tragic waste of the gift of life, and an insult to your partner.
Bored people are boring people. Bored people become depressed people. So
take action to change your attitude, put the spark back in your marriage, and
find joy and excitement in knowing God and discovering how He wants you to
serve Him. Read Psalm 36:7–9; Psalm 118:24; Proverbs 4:18; and Philippians
1:21.

THE MOST DANGEROUS YEARS

We are often asked what are the most stressful years in a marriage. They include these times:

The first two years of adjustment and adaptation

The sixth and seventh years when outside temptations are said to be the
greatest

The period when the "honeymoon" phase is over and each may begin to view
the other separately and critically

Any time when one or both feel bored with their relationship because it is
not vital and growing

The middle years when children leave home and partners must once again
depend on one another for their companionship and love

Any time when people have the financial freedom and the opportunity to be
unfaithful if they choose

The hard times when outside pressures and problems become acute, particularly in the areas of employment and finances or grief and loss

Periods of physical illness and enforced separation, for various reasons

Old age, when people may have less control over their privacy and their circumstances.

At any age or stage, you should be most careful to guard your oneness and never let other people—whether it be children, parents, siblings, co-workers, or friends—intrude into your own private world of love. They have their place in your life, but it is never at the center of your relationship.

8

How to Love Your Wife: The Husband's Handbook

THIS CHAPTER IS for husbands, but we suspect it will be read with great interest by wives. Wives often tell us their husbands do not know how to love them, and men admit that it's a fact. Said one husband to us: "Meet her needs? I didn't even know that she had any special needs when we married. She liked me well enough when we dated, but it was a new game after the wedding, and I obviously didn't know the rules. I've been playing catch-up ever since!"

One observer has suggested that marriages fail because

> all too often, people marry before acquiring the knowledge and skills necessary to take care of their mates: to meet their emotional, mental, and physical needs. One of the ironies in our society is that a person has to have four years of training to receive a plumber's license, but absolutely no training is required for a marriage license. Our educational system doesn't even require communication courses basic to the meaningful development of any relationship. As a result, many men and women enter marriage with virtually no knowledge of how to meet the basic emotional and mental needs of their mates.[1]

Fortunately, God has not left husbands helpless, nor dependent upon our educational system. God holds the answers for those who want, and even long, to love their wives—answers that are spelled out, written with clarity and power, and made as available to us as the nearest Bible. The "love adventure" really begins when we turn to the Scriptures to find out what the Creator recommends for our marriage.

In the next few pages we want to give you, in brief, the biblical counsel that can transform your relationship over a period of years, as you learn to love your wife in the ways her Creator advises. He knows what she needs. You may not, at this point. But He does!

Because He is God, He speaks by commandment and teaches by example. All the knowledge He provides for us on the subject can be compressed into this one imperative which depends upon a luminous example for its force: "Husbands, love your wives, even as Christ also loved the church, and gave himself for it" (Ephes. 5:25).

Your wife needs to be *loved*. But loved how? What will be required of you? To love her responsibly, understandingly, constructively, cherishingly, romantically, realistically, and (as the springboard from which the other loves rebound) sacrificially. When you have learned to do this, you will have loved her according to the commandment: ". . . even as Christ loved the church and gave himself for it."

Now let's take a closer look at each of these ways of meeting your wife's deepest needs.

1. Love Her with a Responsible Love

Love your wife by taking responsibility for her. When couples develop marital problems and seek counseling with Dr. Wheat, he often tells the husband, "It might not be your fault, but that does not matter. It is always your responsibility."

Why do we start with this bare fact? Doesn't it sound rather cold and hard? What does this have to do with the passionate love you *feel* for the woman you have married?

Our answer is *everything*. Passion, romantic adoration, delight, liking, deep friendship—all of this counts for very little in marriage without the husband's acceptance of the basic charge God has given him. Consider this carefully:

Husband, love your wives, even as Christ also loved the church, and gave himself for it; That he might sanctify and cleanse it with the washing of water by the word, That he might present it to himself a glorious church, not having spot, or wrinkle, or any such thing; but that it should be holy and without blemish. So ought men to love their wives as their own bodies. He that loveth his wife loveth himself. For no man ever yet hated his own flesh; but nourisheth and cherisheth it, even as the Lord the church. . . . let everyone of you in particular so love his wife even as himself (Ephes. 5:25–29, 33).

Think back to the beginning of your courting relationship. When did you first realize that you really loved this girl in particular? You will find that at that point you were beginning to take responsibility for her—that you had an active concern about her physical and emotional well-being and, indeed, everything that concerned her. Whether she was preparing for a chemistry final, or coping with a difficult supervisor at work, or striving toward a particular career goal, or even something as small as recuperating from a nagging cough, didn't that involve you too? Didn't you think about her, even worry about her, and try to do all you could to help? If you could do nothing else, did you not try to comfort and encourage her?

As you began to move naturally into this position, you were preparing to take the role God designed for you in marriage. He intends for husbands to look out for their wives in every way, and He gave us the pattern in Jesus Christ's concern and active care over His people, the church. To love your wife responsibly means you communicate to her that she is important, and what is important to her is important to you. By word and by action, you say to her, "I understand. I respect you. I love you. Your concerns are my concerns. I want to take care of you. I want to treat you most tenderly and protect you and shelter you from anything that would hurt you."

In today's world, wives need more protection than ever. In two-thirds of American families, the women work full- or part-time. Nineteen million American mothers work, and it's estimated that within five years three-fourths of the *new mothers* in America will be working outside the home.[2] The husbands of these women have a serious responsibility to meet their wives' special needs.

If your wife works outside the home, always, but especially when you have small children, she needs your tenderest support. If you want to know how God sees her, consider Isaiah 40:11, "He (the Lord God) shall feed his flock like a shepherd; he shall gather the lambs with his arm, and carry them in his bosom, and *gently lead those that are with young*" (italics ours).

You can nurture your working wife by providing nonsexual physical attention—a supportive hug, a back massage, arms around her at night before she goes to sleep—and by guarding her health and her strength. Don't let her overdo. Remind her that she cannot be everything to everyone and help her arrange her schedule so that she has some time for herself.

Give her emotional support. Listen to her without offering quick advice—just listen with understanding and sympathy. Encourage her! Remember that as a woman she is much more apt to blame herself when things go wrong at work. Since she tends to be more subjective and sensitive in her dealings with supervisors and co-workers than you, she will probably suffer more acutely than you when things get out of order in her home—for a woman's house is an extension of herself, whether she has time to give to its care or not.

Do your share of the errands, home responsibilities, and child care—without leaving the impression you are doing it for her *as a favor*. This is not an act of nobility on your part; it's guarding the precious wife God gave to you. And, in simple fairness, if she is contributing to the family income, which is *your* God-given responsibility, then it's up to you to help on the homefront, which is *her* God-given responsibility.

To love your wife responsibly means nothing less than putting her ahead of yourself as you look out for her best interests and highest welfare.

This does not mean "lording it" over her and certainly it does not mean nagging. At a crowded driver's license bureau this week a husband was observed as he accompanied his wife while she obtained a license. Although potentially attractive, the wife appeared nervous and insecure. It was easy to understand why. Her husband watched her pose for her license photo in glum silence. Afterward he observed, "Your collar was all rumpled. It looked terrible. And why didn't you smile?" As they waited for the results, twice he loudly ordered her to "Quit picking at your face," while she wilted in embarrassment.

This husband apparently saw his wife as a second-rate person, not knowing he had set her in that mold by treating her in a second-rate manner. The principle is that the wife in many ways will be a reflection of her husband and his treatment of her. To put it in selfish terms: If you want to be married to a princess, treat your wife like one. To put it in biblical terms: Since the two of you are one in God's eyes, if you love yourself, you ought also to love the one who is a part of you. Do you love her as responsibly as you care for your own body? She needs this, and God counsels you to do it, even though it may go against the grain of your selfish tendencies.

Marriage demands more of us than any other human relationship and demands the most from the husband, who is to follow the example of Christ. He gave His very life for us that we might experience His love and then love Him in return. Just so, your wife needs you to give your love to her so that she can experience it and then love you in return. God designed her to be a *responder* to you; He designed you to be an *initiator*—to love *first and forever*.

2. Love Her with Understanding and Honor

You will also need to love your wife with a three-part knowledge that (1) understands her personally (2) appreciates her inestimable value and (3) recognizes her position in God's sight.

This counsel comes from 1 Peter 3:7: "Husbands, likewise live with your wives in an understanding way, showing respect for the woman as you would a fragile vase, and as joint heirs of the grace of life . . ." (THE NEW TESTAMENT IN EVERYDAY ENGLISH).

Jay Adams comments,

> Husbands are addressed directly, and commanded . . . to be careful and consider-
> ate about how they live with (their wives). They must stop living in ignorance of
> their wives' problems, desires, needs, longings, fears, etc. (as so many men do who
> have never bothered to try to come to an understanding of them), but literally, "ac-
> cording to knowledge"—in an understanding way.

> The old cliche, "You'll never understand a woman," must be squelched. Husbands
> need to be told—as, indeed, Peter tells them—"There is one woman you must un-
> derstand: your woman! God commands it."[2]

How does a man go about understanding his wife? First, by wanting to understand her so much he will give himself over to the adventure of knowing her.
Second, by making a careful and loving study of her. One young husband describes how he spent time noticing everything about his bride—even the rhythm
of her breathing. He discovered that when she was angry she began cleaning
out closets and drawers; that when she was troubled, she stared out of windows.
He knew what it meant when she looked down and did not meet his eyes. He
came to understand what it signified when she turned her face against his shoulder. He observed her blushes, her passing moods, and her changing expressions.
She came to realize that when he asked her, "What are you thinking?" he really
wanted to know, because he longed to know her as deeply as possible. This young
man literally "dwelt with her in knowledge."

Respect for your wife is the second gift of love based on knowledge. This
respect calls for gentleness toward her. Peter explains to husbands that their wives
are not inferior to them, but different. You need to understand that your wife is
physically weaker and emotionally more sensitive and vulnerable, and so, must
be handled with care. Jay Adams observes that many men treat their wives as
they would an old tin garbage can, rather than as a fragile—and valuable—con-
tainer, "a fragile vase, Ming dynasty!"[3]

We have been considering up until now New Testament counsel to husbands,
but to learn how to apply this respect principle, we must turn to the Old Testament where we find the only book in the Bible devoted exclusively to love, sex,
and marriage. The Song of Solomon reveals the pattern of married love as God
designed it, gives a practical model for the love life of husband and wife, and
guides us in living the principles in Ephesians 5 and 1 Peter 3:7. We suggest that
you read this with your wife and make it a part of your own language of love.

In the opening of the Song of Soloman a king brings Shulamith, a chastely-
reared country girl, to his palace as his bride and queen. Observe this bridegroom's gentle treatment of his wife and the great respect he shows her.

His love and approval was not just a private matter. The king showed publicly his adoration and respect for his wife. In the royal banqueting house, his banner over her was love. . . . It became obvious to everyone that Shulamith was the most important person in his kingdom—to be honored, respected, and protected in every way. He treated her like a queen, and that is what she became in truth. At the same time he privately loved her in such a way that she could finally give herself completely to him, withholding nothing of her trust, her thoughts, and her love.

Husband, how do you treat your wife publicly? Do you open doors for her . . . seat her at the table . . . hold her coat for her? These small courtesies give honor to the wife as the more delicate vessel. After all, your wife cannot see your mental attitude toward her. You must show it by simple actions that display your love and your care and protective concern for her well-being. Is your love a banner over her when other people are present? Do you often look at her? Respond to her glances? Listen to her? Make her feel she is the most important person in *your* kingdom?[4]

The word *respect* in 1 Peter 3:7 can also be translated *honor*. *The Expository Dictionary of New Testament Words* explains that this is "primarily a valuing." In this case it becomes a recognition of a wife's value and preciousness. Do you regard your wife as your treasure?

The third knowledge you must have is an understanding of God's spiritual assessment of your wife: She is a join-their with you of the free gift of eternal life. Although you have been given the privilege and responsibility of acting as God's representative in your home, never forget that your wife has an equal status before God and an equal reward to anticipate. Your roles are different, but you are spiritual equals. And if you forget this and dishonor your wife, Peter warns, you cannot expect God to honor your requests in prayer!

Husbands, in the same way be considerate as you live with your wives, and treat them with respect as the weaker partner and as heirs with you of the gracious gift of life, so that nothing will hinder your prayers (1 Peter 3:7 NIV).

3. Love Her Constructively

When, as a new Christian, Dr. Wheat set out to learn how to love his wife, he discovered this compelling truth: *Love is always doing the best for the object of one's love.*

If a husband follows this principle, he will love his wife constructively, just as Ephesians 5:29 counsels. To love a wife constructively means to nourish her—physically, emotionally, and spiritually—enabling her to mature and reach her God-designed potential. Consider these excerpts from four letters, each from a different woman, and each a heart cry from a wife who has not been nourished by her husband:

Wife A: "My husband is the breadwinner. I receive money for the food needs, but no money for my own personal needs or clothing. He seems to resent having to spend money on me. How do I handle this?"

Wife B: "I have to work, and I come home exhausted and feeling as though I need to be ministered to. Instead, I must always attend to my husband's needs and my children's needs. I don't know how to balance my life. Help!"

Wife C: "How should I react when my husband calls and says he will be late for dinner due to work and I don't believe he really needs to stay at work. I try very hard to make our home a pleasant place to be, but I feel he would rather be at work than home with me."

Wife D: "What part should I take when my husband, who's a Christian, does not lead in any of the spiritual areas of the family? The children long for their Daddy to lead them in devotions, and I need his leadership too."

Traditional marriage vows reflect this need for the wife's nourishing. When a husband endows his spouse with all his worldly goods, the provision of all physical necessities is implied. And when he promises to take care of her "in sickness and in health," physical care is indicated. When he pledges to honor and cherish her, this refers to her mental and emotional well-being.

Ephesians 5:26–27 deals with the spiritual care of the wife. In comparing Christ and the church to husbands and their wives, Paul explains that Jesus gave himself to make his bride holy, set apart, cleansed by the Word of God, radiant, without stain or wrinkle or any other blemish. To apply this in your marriage, remember that you are God's representative to bless your wife and nurture her spiritually. You do this, primarily, by taking the lead in bringing the Word of God into every area of your thought and life. Let it speak to both of you and listen to its counsel. Did you know that the word *success* is used only once in the Bible? It appears only in connection with knowing and heeding the Scriptures:

> This book of the law shall not depart out of thy mouth; but thou shalt meditate therein day and night, that thou mayest observe to do according to all that is written therein: for then thou shalt make thy way prosperous and then thou shalt have good success (Josh. 1:8).

We have known couples who began, while dating, to complete their evenings together by reading Scripture and praying. One girl said, "If it were possible, I think I loved him more during those times than any other. He took charge. He was reading the Bible from Genesis to Revelation, so wherever he happened to be in it, he read those chapters aloud to me, his arm around me, sometimes our cheeks touching as he read. Then we would both pray. But he initiated it, and it convinced me even more that this was the husband for me!"

At our LOVE LIFE Marriage Seminars the longing most frequently expressed by wives is that their husbands would become spiritual leaders in their households. Often, they say, "He will read the Bible with me if I ask him to. But I want him to take the lead!"

Their longing is God-implanted, for it is by His design. This way of nourishing will reap the most precious of fruit. Try it and watch your wife become more beautiful, with an inner beauty as well as an outward radiance and serenity.

4. Love Her by Cherishing Her

The Bible tells you in Ephesians 5 that your wife needs to be cherished by you. Cherish surely is one of the most beautiful words in the language of love. It bears several different meanings, each with a message for the husband who wants to know how to love his wife. Look at this list of meanings as a fragrant bouquet of actions, which will bless your wife.

Cherish means to take care of tenderly; to keep warm as birds cover their young with feathers; to protect as a hen shields her chicks from harm. Do you shelter your wife with tender care, warming her with your love? One bride described the way her husband cherishes her. "The most wonderful part of being married," she said, "is going to sleep on my husband's shoulder every night with his arm around me. I feel so safe . . . so loved."

Cherish also means to hold dear, to treat with affection. It comes from the same root word as *caress*. Your wife needs nonsexual caresses, cuddling, kisses, and hugs. She needs to hold hands with you. Concentrate with sensitivity on the wonderful experience of holding her hand. Tuck a kiss into the palm of her hand when you're leaving for the day. Cuddle her on your lap at the end of the day—not as a signal for sex, but just for cherishing.

Finally, cherish means to encourage or support. Let your wife know you value her opinions and enjoy communicating with her. Listen to her! Learn how to build her up. If you have learned to understand your wife, you will know almost immediately in what area she needs support and how to give it to her.

5. Love Her Romantically

Your wife has a deep need to be loved romantically, as we described in chapter one. She needs you to have and to hold a vision of her truest self, to see through her flaws to the image of God in her, to perceive the beautiful person she is becoming, created and redeemed by God through Christ with an eternal identity.

Strangely enough, when lovers become husbands, they sometimes forget how to be romantic—the very thing their wives need and desire. If forgetful lovers could only realize that the sweet thrills of *being in love* provide an expectancy which literally transforms ordinary life. This line from an old book seems to describe what marriage is like when romantic love still flowers: *Our lives were so thronged with small beauties, it was as if we were children of the rainbow, dwelling always in the morning of the world.*

One woman wrote, "I need proof that there is something inherently lovable in me. Through my lover's eyes and words, pursuit or response, I see myself as I need to be seen. Some women writers nowadays scorn romantic love. But the stories of Cinderella, Sleeping Beauty, and Snow White are still locked within our collective memory. They do contain a truth at their heart: each woman needed the Prince's kiss, the Prince's choice, to be brought to fullness of life. God made me that way too."

The best way to learn to love your wife romantically is to study the Song of Solomon and absorb the ways he loved his bride. Note how he talked to her and about her; note his caresses, his love gifts, his occupation with her, his intense desire to know her better, to look into her eyes, to hear her voice.

6. Love Her Realistically

While this may sound like a contradiction, your wife needs to be loved realistically, as well as romantically. If she thinks you have idealized her, she will be afraid of disappointing you. No woman wants to live on a pedestal. Give your wife the security of knowing you see her as she is and that you love her with an unshakable love. When she feels at her very worst in appearance, or in self-image, or in mood or behavior, that's when she needs most to know you love her. So tell her . . . show her by comforting her . . . and don't forget the power of praise.

The husband/lover in the Song of Soloman gives husbands the pattern to follow in meeting this need in their wives. His bride, who was deeply tanned from working in the vineyards, felt inferior to the elegant, pampered, white-skinned women of the court. Her husband, understanding her feelings, skillfully and lovingly built up her self-image by praise. He sensitively praised her in the areas where she felt most insecure. He voiced his appreciation of her physical appearance and of her lovely character in specifics, not in vague generalities. He told her she was "altogether lovely." But he did not say this just when they were courting or on their wedding night. He continued to praise her even as their marriage matured.

Husband, your wife needs to know that you see her as she is, and think that she is beautiful—inside and out. This will actually produce a shining new loveliness to delight you. Wives who believe they are beautiful *are* beautiful.

As one wife told us, "This week I was really down. I'm struggling to lose fifteen pounds, and I hate my new haircut, and I have a cold. I'm tired and my eyes are red, and I feel like I can't do anything right. Do you know what my husband did? He put his arms around me, and looked at me very deeply, very searchingly, and then he said, 'I find you altogether lovely.' The way he said it, I knew he meant it. I honestly believe that moment has changed my whole life. I'll never forget it!"

7. Love Her Sacrificially

It is easy to define this as loving your wife enough to die for her. Some husbands do love their wives this much. But few will have to meet this particular test. Instead, the question is, do you love your wife enough to *live* for her? This, too, requires a sacrificial commitment.

One wife said wistfully, "My husband is so good. I believe he would even give up his life without counting the cost to save me from harm. He would give his all for me. It's just that he won't share his all with me. I mean, he won't share himself and his life with me. I always feel a sense of distance—and it hurts."

Dwight Small reminds us that caring is a sacred trust; we are ultimately accountable to God for the way we care for our mate. He asks several hard questions worth our careful consideration:

Am I willing to order all my values and activities around caring, making it the primary aim of my marriage and all else secondary?

Am I willing to accept the new demands and new disciplines that caring may impose upon me?

Am I willing to pay the ultimate price of caring: to make continual acts of self-relinquishment as caring shall require?[6]

He explains,

Caring has a way of ordering activities and values around itself; . . . Many things previously felt to be important will now fade in significance, and things related to caring will take on a new importance. What is found to be incompatible with caring, you must exclude; what is found to be irrelevant to caring, you must subordinate. In other words, you are to safeguard the conditions that make caring possible.

This is no easy task. It doesn't happen automatically. Rather, it requires conscious and continuous surveillance over all that touches your life. The more precious a relationship, the more it warrants safeguarding. So it is by the safeguards you employ to protect it and the sacrifices you make to sustain it that you show the worth of the relationship in your own value system. Caring partners will realistically count the cost and commit themselves to pay it.[7]

You will love your wife sacrificially when her happiness and well-being are more important to you than your own and when you are ready to give yourself, without counting the cost, for her highest welfare.

To love your wife as God designed becomes the challenge of a lifetime. This is one chapter we hope you will read and reread for the sake of your marriage. Every husband needs to keep these great principles of love in mind. Always remember that the God who commanded them will give you the strength, wisdom, and sensitivity to *live* them with your own beloved wife.

9

How to Love Your Husband: The Wife's Handbook

IF THE HUSBAND'S responsibility can be summarized in one phrase: Love your wife! your calling as a wife can also be summed up in a few words: Respond to your husband!

As we discussed in the previous chapter, the biblical command "love your wife" comes highly charged with meaning. But when we search the Scriptures to find what the wife's response includes, we discover how all-encompassing and significant her part is.

Many girls marry without an understanding of their beautiful opportunity in the marriage partnership. For example, a wife complained recently, "I do love and respect my husband. And I appreciate all the help he gives me with our children and the house. But I get frustrated with him because he doesn't believe I care about him. He just can't seem to understand that I find it very hard to respond physically or even to show my approval verbally!"

Our counsel to her applies to every wife reading this chapter: You must remember there is only one way to convince your husband that you love him, and that is by your loving response—a response that he can see, hear, touch, feel, and enjoy on a daily basis, a response that includes the physical, but also touches every aspect of his life. This is your contribution to a love-filled, lasting marriage. Many wives who have enjoyed lifelong love affairs with their husbands say that this is their secret of success.

A husband simply delights in a responsive wife. And (although this is no excuse) he often looks elsewhere when he does not find it at home. As Gary Smalley warns,

> A man's self-confidence is directly related to the way others respond to him. A man will tie his affection to those who respond to him and remove it from those who don't.[1]

Not only does your husband's self-confidence rest in your hands for safe keeping. The way you respond to him, even now at the beginning of marriage, will be a strong indication of the kind of life you will have together. It's no exaggeration to say that your response (or lack of it) will set the tone in your home, determine the quality of your relationship, and seriously affect—for good or ill—the outcome of your marriage. Because God designed you to be a responder to your husband's sacrificial, protective love, do not lose something infinitely valuable by ignoring this aspect of His plan.

Before we look at the biblical counsel for wives, we want you to consider two things. First, count the special abilities God has given you as a woman to fulfill your part. Unless you were taught unhealthy inhibitions in childhood, you probably enjoy using your natural skills to build loving relationships. You have an instinctive ability to love, to cuddle, to nurture, and an innate desire to give yourself to those you love. You are apt to be intuitive, affectionate, and person-centered. You most likely think in concrete, personal details rather than general ideas, and are more concerned with relevant facts than theoretical discussions. You find it easy to communicate intimately about feelings and perceive happenings below the layer of the obvious. You have, at least, potentially the gift of listening with your heart to the people you love.

Some of these abilities may, as yet, be undeveloped. Some may have been smothered by years of stress in the working world. A career wife once said, "It seems harder to be a woman these days. It's as though I need to be two very different people, all in a twenty-four hour period. I love my job, but I don't want to lose the qualities that make me special to my husband and children!"

In a study of the Type E woman, Harriet Braiker found that although a woman today lives under far greater work and achievement pressures than her forerunners, her defined role as principal nurturer and attender to the emotional needs of others has remained virtually unchanged.[2]

But no matter how demanding or inconvenient, most women do not want to give up this role or exchange their unique abilities for more masculine qualities. Dr. Braiker observes that

> while women want to succeed, need to succeed, few want to give up their cooperative natures in exchange for male competitiveness. While women yearn to be competent and independent, few would forfeit their parallel need to be loved and nurtured by a man; few women would trade their emotionality and need for intimacy for cold rationality and social withdrawal.[3]

She concludes that although women today want to participate in society in meaningful ways beyond their privilege of bearing babies and their responsibility of rearing and nurturing children, "for the most part, American women still want what they have always wanted—a husband and a family, or an enduring love relationship with a man."[4]

As we suggested to husbands in chapter eight, the man who wants to love and nurture his wife will protect her wife's emotional and physical well-being and help her to enjoy her chosen role in the home, even though she works outside the home by necessity or by choice. No woman can expect to be everything to everyone, and the one who tries will soon find herself drained of the ability to respond to those who need her most. We see the dramatic cultural revolution in our country, which has swept more than nineteen million wives and mothers into the labor force, as another opportunity for husbands to learn to love and protect their wives under changing conditions. The Bible speaks to all cultures and all times, and we can never say, "But this truth just doesn't apply anymore." The principle in every culture is that husbands are to love their wives as Christ loved the Church and that wives are to respond to their love.

Now we'd like you to think about ways you can respond to your husband. If you are newly-married you cannot yet know all he really needs and desires. But let's list some things almost every husband wants from his wife.

Your husband needs you to respond to him physically in lovemaking. He needs your emotional response in nurturing him. He needs you to respond in practical ways in helping to establish and maintain your home and family (which may well include financial assistance). Your husband also wants your encouragement in all the activities he is interested in or feels called to do. Perhaps most of all, he needs you to demonstrate consistently your genuine respect and admiration for him as a man who is handling the challenges of life and handling them well.

These are the husband's needs and desires. If it sounds like too much, please remember this: What the husband hungers for almost exactly parallels the Creator's guidelines to the wife.

The Bible communicates these guidelines to us by several different methods. They appear as statement of fact, as example, and as commandment. While four or five earthly authors wrote them down over a period of about 1,500 years, we can see an amazing unity in their message—another proof that they were authored by one mind, the mind of God, for our blessing and happiness in marriage.

Our search of the Scriptures to discover how wives can best love their husbands will take us from the creation account of Genesis to the wisdom of Proverbs; through romantic, scented gardens in the Song of Solomon into the New Testament where the letters to Timothy and Titus offer a wonderfully concrete and concise statement of what the responsive wife *is* and *does*. We will conclude in the epistles of Ephesians and 1 Peter, which reveal two things every wife needs to know: 1) the best gift she can give her husband; and 2) what will make her most beautiful in his eyes.

Here's what to look for on this guided tour. You will find that everything a wife can do for her husband comes under these three ways of loving: A wife loves her husband and meets his needs by (1) helping him; (2) responding to him emotionally and physically; and (3) respecting him.

As you relate to him day by day, you will be meeting (or ignoring) his needs in these areas. In the hectic arena of daily life, nothing falls neatly into categories, of course, so these ways of loving him will all be intermingled, but it will help you to think of them separately, to be reminded of what he needs, and to analyze how well you are doing in the challenge of loving your husband.

IN GENESIS: HIS HELPER

We begin in the Book of Beginnings, which tells us why God created woman. She was made to complement man because he was lonely and incomplete. She perfected him, making him whole and complete. Her first descriptive title was *helper*.

> And the Lord God said, It is not good that the man should be alone; I will make him an help meet for him. And out of the ground the Lord God formed every beast of the field, and every fowl of the air; and brought them unto Adam to see what he would call them: and whatsoever Adam called every living creature, that was the name thereof. And Adam gave names to all the cattle, and to the fowl of the air, and to every beast of the field; but for Adam there was not found an help meet for him. And the Lord God caused a deep sleep to fall upon Adam, and he slept: and he took one of his ribs, and closed up the flesh instead thereof; and the rib, which the Lord God had taken from, made he a woman, and brought her unto the man (Gen. 2:18–22).

Picture Adam in a perfect environment—but alone. He had the fellowship of God and the company of birds and animals, plus a fascinating work of observing, categorizing, and naming all the living creatures. But because he was alone, this was *not good*. So the Creator provided a perfect solution: He made another creature, like the man, and yet wondrously unlike him. She was taken from him; yet she perfected him. God made her totally suitable for him spiritually, intellectually, emotionally, and physically. When Adam first saw her, his response was one of delight and a sense of belonging. He recognized that she was "the help meet for him" (KJV), "The helper suitable for him" (NIV).

Before the Fall we can be sure the woman joyously responded to her husband/lover and helped him gladly. Today women sometimes picture their title "helper" as a subordinate position, one a servant or child might fill. This is far from accurate! In the Bible's original language, the word *helper* refers to a beneficial relationship in which one person aids or supports another as a friend and ally. Exactly the same Hebrew word is used for God Himself in several of the Psalms. For instance, Psalm 46:1 calls God our *helper*—"a very present *help* in trouble." Or Psalm 70:5, "But I am poor and needy: make haste unto me, O God: thou art my *help* and my deliverer. . . ." Or Psalm 115:9, "O Israel, trust thou in the Lord: he is their *help* and their shield."

One wife told us how secure her husband made her feel when he sat close to her, touching her hand or putting his arm lightly around her. When she thanked him for "keeping in touch," he smiled at her. "Don't you know," he said, "that I am drawing strength from you?"

This illustrates a biblical principle you need to remember. While you will do many beneficial things for your husband in the course of a marriage, you can help him most of all by what you *are*. Your character is what really counts in strengthening him and completing him—even in managing your mutual affairs and rearing your children. Character, of course, will express itself in your actions. That's the only way others can see what you are on the inside. Our stopover in the Book of Proverbs will focus on the wife's character in her role as her husband's trusted partner. The next best way to help your husband is to relate to him as his encourager in everything he does (which may involve practical help as well as emotional support.) Your help in consoling him when things do not go well is equally important.

Psychiatrist Paul Tournier explains how a man needs his wife's consolation.

One of the highest functions of a wife is to console her husband for all the blows he receives in life. Yet, in order to console, there is no need to say very much. It is enough to listen, to understand, to love. Look at that mother whose child runs crying to her knees. She utters no word, and yet in a moment the tears have disappeared, the child jumps down, smiles all over his face, and heads out into the world once more where he will receive new blows. In every man, even the most eminent and the apparently strongest, there remains something of the child who needs to be consoled.[5]

If you can keep in mind that a helper is a *friend and ally*, and always check your responses by this standard, you will become the helper God designed you to be. Your husband will perceive your help as a sign that you love him, and his reaction will be to love you even more. Helping means doing even the smallest thing for him in a cheerful, loving manner. It takes only a little effort to do the kind thing at just the right time.

IN PROVERBS: HIS TRUSTED PARTNER

We are going to look now at a passage of Scripture which offers so much to the woman who wants to learn how to love her husband that we are including it here—every word of it. We have added a title: *The Wife's Alphabet of Excellence*, since in the Hebrew language each of the twenty-two verses begins with a consecutive letter of the alphabet. In other words, it has been carefully thought out, and it can yield riches of wisdom to your life, if you will give yourself to it.

Please read it several times. See what these timeless principles have to say to you as a woman approaching the twenty-first century. Do more than read it. Absorb its message through the pores of your being until you can feel what it means to be your husband's trusted partner for a lifetime. Think about how you can become this kind of wife. Consider the long-term rewards.

The Wife's Alphabet of Excellence

A capable, intelligent and virtuous woman, who is he who can find her? She is far more precious than jewels, and her value is far above rubies or pearls.

The heart of her husband trusts in her confidently and relies on and believes in her safely; so that he has no lack of honest gain or need of dishonest spoil.

She will comfort, encourage and do him only good as long as there is life within her.

She seeks out the wool and flax and works with willing hands to develop it.

She is like the merchant ships loaded with foodstuffs, she rings her household's food from a far (country).

She rises while yet it is night and gets spiritual food for her household and assigns her maids their tasks.

She considers a new field before she buys or accepts it—expanding prudently (and not courting neglect of her present duties by assuming others). With her savings (of time and strength) she plants fruitful vines in her vineyard.

She girds herself with strength (spiritual, mental, and physical fitness for her God-given task) and makes her arms strong and firm.

She tastes and sees that her gain from work (with and for God) is good; her lamp goes not out; but it burns on continually through the night (of trouble, privation or sorrow, warning away fear, doubt and distrust).

She lays her hands to the spindle, and her hands hold the distaff.

She opens her hand to the poor; yes, she reaches out her filled hands to the needy (whether in body, mind or spirit).

She fears not the snow for her family, for all her household are doubly clothed in scarlet.

She makes herself coverlets, cushions and rugs of tapestry. Her clothing is of linen, pure white and fine, and of purple (such as that of which the clothing of the priests and the hallowed cloths of the temple are made).

Her husband is known in the city's gates, when he sits among the elders of the land.

She makes fine linen garments and leads others to buy them; she delivers to the merchants girdles (or sashes that free one for service).

Strength and dignity are her clothing and her position is strong and secure. She rejoices over the future—the latter day or time to come (knowing that she and her family are in readiness for it)!

She opens her mouth with skillful and godly Wisdom, and in her tongue is the law of kindness—giving counsel and instruction.

She looks well to how things go in her household, and the bread of idleness (gossip, discontent and self-pity) she will not eat.

Her children rise up and call her blessed (happy, fortunate and to be envied); and her husband boasts of and praises her, saying,

Many daughters have done virtuously, nobly and well (with the strength of character that is steadfast in goodness) but you excel them all.

Charm and grace are deceptive, and beauty is vain (because it is not lasting), but a woman who reverently and worshipfully fears the Lord, she shall be praised!

Give her of the fruit of her hands, and let her own works praise her in the gates of the city! (Proverbs 31:10–31 THE AMPLIFIED BIBLE).

At first reading we may think, "This lady was a doer!" Count the action verbs. At least twenty times we are told what she *does*, and the last verse assures us that her *works* bring her praise in the city. She's obviously a "liberated" woman, a woman of many parts who could fit well into our century. Today's career wife can respect this competent, creative, energetic businesswoman who managed to balance her life so that neither her work, nor her worship, nor her role as a woman was neglected.

What did she do for her husband? Well, she operated as his equal partner in a totally trustworthy manner. The word *willing* summed up her attitude toward her work and way of life. She managed their household well; she benefited the family financially by earning a good income through her creative endeavors; she honored her husband by her good standing in the community; she trained their children with watchfull concern and supervised the servants, taking responsibility for their needs; she helped the poor in the community. She also brought her husband credit by the appearance of the family, the well-kept furnishings of the home, and by her own regal appearance, clothed as she was, not only in fine white linen and purple, but in strength and dignity.

She looked good, and she *was* good! She maintained her honored position with a servant heart that could forget itself to help others. She spoke with wisdom and also with kindness. In the unexpected moment when the pressure was on, the "law of kindness" controlled her tongue. One gets the feeling that this wife met life with enthusiasm because she was ready for anything. She kept herself and her family in a state of preparedness. Today we could say, "she had it all together."

As for her relationship with her husband, we know he was proud of her; he knew how hard it is to find this kind of wife, and he valued her as "far more precious" than jewels. He had a confident trust in her and relied on her. He knew she would comfort him and encourage him and always do him good. He delighted in praising her and was ready to tell the world that she excelled over all other women, even the most virtuous of wives. He respected her. He honored her. And she dwelled in the sunlight of his praise and approval.

This woman could give most wives an inferiority complex! But a deeper look at this passage reveals something more than just positive actions and good deeds on display. This is not just the success story of a biblical superwoman intended to frustrate the ordinary wife who pours over *The Messies Manual*, valiantly trying to keep her husband happy, her children healthy, her home in order, while holding down a job and teaching Sunday School.

No, this Scripture has something powerful to teach about *character*. The message for wives is this: The most important thing a woman can do for the husband she loves is to develop strength of character by fearing and worshiping the Lord. A woman's relationship with the Lord produces the quality of life we read about here, the character and behavior that will honor her husband and bless their entire household.

A noble character . . . strength . . . dignity . . . wisdom . . . kindness. These most valuable characteristics can be yours if you desire them and seek them over the course of your lifetime. God is faithful to produce them in you if you will only cooperate with Him. Remember that the best way to begin is by drinking in the truth of the Scriptures. The wife of Proverbs 31 was able to become a beloved wife, an honored mother, a supervisor at home, a capable businesswoman, a friend to the needy, and a respected member of the community because her focus remained on the Lord and His power. She possessed spiritual beauty and grew more beautiful with the passing of time.

A young husband told us of an experience when he saw these qualities in his wife and how he fell in love with her in a deeper way. "We had had quite a misunderstanding," he said. "I had spoken words to her that wounded her. This was just minutes before people arrived at our home for a couples' Bible study. I knew how hurt she was. But I saw her rise above it and fasten her thoughts on the Word of God. I heard her share some beautiful truths that helped others. I watched her looking after our guests so kindly and graciously. Even when her eyes clouded momentarily and I knew she was remembering the hurt again, she went on. I saw the reality of her faith, and I knew, as never before, how fortunate I was to have a wife like her! I could hardly wait until I had the chance to be alone with her again and make things right—to ask her forgiveness and kiss away the hurt and tell her how precious she is to me."

Dr. Wheat says, "As an older husband, it means everything to me to know that I can count on my wife in all the difficulties of life, as well as the good times and the ordinary days. I can count on her integrity, her commitment, her wisdom, her kindness, her ability to cope, and her determination to do whatever it takes to help me and our household. I think of Proverbs 31 as the description of my own trusted partner, who is always there when needed."

If you want to love your husband and make him grateful every day of his life he married you, then take the wife of Proverbs 31 as your inspiration and model.

IN THE SONG OF SOLOMON: HIS DARLING, HIS LOVE

Is it possible to continue a passionate, romantic love affair with your husband long after the honeymoon? God has given us this beautiful little book on love and marriage, which answers, Yes!

Observe the example of Shulamith, whom we meet first as a girl being courted, then a radiant bride, and finally an experienced wife. Frequently, her husband called her his darling, his love—words that in the Hebrew language were used for physical expressions of romantic love—kisses and caresses. We would like you to see that this wife was adored by her husband because of her physical and emotional responsiveness to him.

If you would learn how to fuel the fires of an ongoing love affair with your husband, study her behavior and responses. Analyze them. You'll find that her husband's lovemaking thrilled her, and she let him know it! She thought about him with longing when he was not present, and she focused her eyes and conversation on him when they were together, complimenting his appearance, expressing appreciation for his skillful lovemaking, and always communicating her high respect for him as a man.

She desired his kisses, responded to his touch, and even danced for his pleasure. Near the close of the book, after they were well beyond the newlywed stage, she promised him still more physical delights and made plans for their romantic times together.

The wife who wants to love her husband *will* respond to him physically and emotionally. For most men that's the *sine qua non* of marriage—the one essential element. Most men would not have married without the expectation of this on a continuing basis. Few women can imagine the pain Dr. Wheat sees when he counsels men who have been rejected physically by their wives. They've been turned down in the bedroom, pushed away in the kitchen when they seek a kiss, and given an indifferent shoulder in the TV room when they offer a caress. It's devastating to them.

A wife's failure to respond sends a clear signal to the husband. He will not feel loved unless you show him you desire physical affection from him. And you should know that your enthusiastic response to his passionate lovemaking is the ultimate pleasure for him. You have it in your power to seal your relationship by your ongoing response to him.

One husband explained, "I think of it as a bonding, almost like the bonding between a mother and a newborn. My wife's 'being there' for me, always responding emotionally to me with a smile and a hug and a sparkle in her eyes when I come home—that draws me to her like a magnet. This becomes a security link between us. It's one of the best things about marriage."

IN 1 TIMOTHY: THE RULER OF HIS HOUSEHOLD

I will therefore that the younger women marry, bear children, rule the house. . . (1 Tim. 5:14).

Here is another way to love your husband: by helping him to rear, control, train, and discipline his children, and to *rule* his household.

Since this comes as a surprise to some couples, let's look at this a bit closer. The word *rule* is a Greek word combining the ideas of house and master (*despotes*) and from which we derive our English word for tyrant: despot, an absolute ruler.

Various versions of the Bible translate this word either as "guide the house," "manage the house," or "run the household." Clearly, the wife owns the privilege and responsibility of managing and directing all household affairs. This does not mean she must do all the work alone or that she alone must make all the major decisions. But she is to plan, direct, and supervise in this area of their shared life. The household is her God-given province. The gracious, tactful, and considerate way in which a wife approaches her responsibility will be an accurate measure of her success. Proverbs warns that "the contentions of a wife are as a continual dropping (of water through a chink in the roof)" (19:13 THE AMPLIFIED BIBLE). "It is better to dwell in a corner of the housetop (on the flat oriental roof, exposed to all kinds of weather) than in a house shared with a nagging, quarrelsome and faultfinding woman" (21:9 THE AMPLIFIED BIBLE).

The Arabs stated this principle aptly in a proverb, which has become an inside joke for one family we know: "Three things make a house intolerable: *tak* (the rain leaking through), *nak* (a wife's nagging), and *bak* (bugs)."

We have already seen in the Book of Proverbs how the wife's management of the household can benefit her husband. Derek Kidner explains,

> The woman is the making or the undoing of her husband . . . his "crown"; or else "rottenness in his bones.". . . On her constructive womanly wisdom chiefly depends the family's stability, and if she happens to possess exceptional gifts she will have ample scope for them.[6]

Love your husband by managing the household. But be careful to do it with tact and grace.

IN TITUS: HIS LOVING WIFE

> The old women . . . should be examples of the good life, so that the younger women may learn to love their husbands and their children, to be sensible and chaste, homelovers, kind-hearted and willing to adapt themselves to their husbands—a good advertisement for the Christian faith (Titus 2:4, 5 PHILIPS).

At the beginning of this biblical tour, we suggested that wives need to love their husbands in three ways: by helping them, by responding to them emotionally/physically, and by respecting them. In these two verses, we find the whole package—a marvel of concise instruction.

First, on the list we find response: The young wife needs to learn to *love* her husband and children with an affectionate, responding love. It cannot be commanded, but it can be learned.

Second, we find help—helping her husband by what she does, which could be summed up in one word: homemaking. And, perhaps even more important, helping her husband by what she is. Three Greek words describe the character traits that are seen as top priority for the wife. Since all three words are words that have been borrowed for women's names—some wives have found this an easy way to keep their character goals in mind. For instance, to be a *Sophronia* is to be sensible and self-controlled, habitually governing yourself from within.

It is a poise maintained with wisdom which keeps you from doing or saying foolish things on impulse, or letting some desire have power over you.

To be an *Agnes* is to share in God's purity, by keeping yourself away from the defilements of the world; to be chaste. It can mean avoiding crude talk, turning off television shows which have the power to pollute the mind, and choosing your friends with care. It does not mean refraining from sexual pleasures with your husband. Remember that Shulamith, a passionate lover, was called "My dove" (my pure and innocent one) by her husband.

To be an *Agatha* is to be kindhearted—a term which implies action. You will be involved in all sorts of kindly activities for those you love.

Finally, the Scripture in Titus counsels wives to demonstrate respect for their husbands. We will look at this more closely on our next stop in Ephesians.

IN EPHESIANS: HIS ADAPTABLE WIFE

The best gift you can give your husband—that's the topic of this discussion. Unfortunately, it's a topic often misunderstood, so let's look at it in its scriptural context from the key passage in Ephesians.

> Be subject to one another out of reverence for Christ, the Messiah, the Anointed One. Wives, be subject—be submissive and adapt yourselves—to your own husbands as [a service] to the Lord. For the husband is head of the wife as Christ is the Head of the church, Himself the Savior of (His) body. As the church is subject to Christ, so let wives also be subject in everything to their husbands. Husband, love your wives, as Christ loved the church and gave Himself up for her. . . . Let each man of you (without exception) love his wife as (being in a sense) his very own self; and let the wife see that she respects and reverences her husband—that she notices him, regards him, honors him, prefers him, venerates and esteems him; and that she defers to him, praises him, and loves and admires him exceedingly (Ephes. 5:21–25, 33 THE AMPLIFIED BIBLE).

As we saw in chapter eight, a wife's rights are awesome. She has the *right* to her husband's complete nurturing, protection, and sacrificial love! God commands a husband to do everything for her highest good, even to die for her if necessary. God asks the wife to do only one thing for him and that is to give him the gift of submission: an attitude compounded of respect and her willing adaptation to him. It also includes, as we read in Ephesians 5:33 (THE AMPLIFIED BIBLE), the admiration, which a husband needs as much as his wife needs romantic attention.

In the context of the Scripture, it seems plain that both partners are to be submissive in their relationship out of reverence for Christ and as a service to the

Lord. The wife's role is to adapt herself to her husband, demonstrating respect and obedience. The husband's role is to show submissiveness by his care and concern for his wife. Both are serving the Lord and building a harmonious partnership.

The wife is to be in submission because the husband is the head of the wife as Christ is the head of the Church. It would be ridiculous to think of the true Church exerting authority over Christ or announcing its independence to do its own thing.

Submission does not mean the wife is inferior. Or that the husband has any right to *demand* obedience from her, or to lord over her. Thus, we can only look at it as a gift, which a loving wife gives to her husband for her protection and their blessing. In doing this she enters into God's perfect design for their relationship.

If a wife does not trust and respect her husband, it is devastating both to him and the marriage. But if she is able to look at her husband with eyes of reverence, he becomes a king among men. They experience a two-way blessing: she gives him the position of respect and as he gives her the place of honor.

Gaye Wheat shared her thoughts on this attitude of submission in *Intended for Pleasure*. She said,

We know we aren't perfect wives. And our husbands know it too. But it is possible to keep them so happy that they think of us as perfect, because in the details which matter most to them, we have learned to please them! Now, I am not talking about devious dealings or cute manipulations designed to befuddle our husbands into adoring us. They are not that easily fooled. And, most importantly, there is a better way to please them—a way that God can honor, because it is rooted in the New Testament principle of servanthood: "Ourselves your servants for Jesus' sake" (2 Cor. 4:5).

Of course, this does not mean that we are to behave like menials around our husbands. To serve one's husband for Jesus' sake does not demand that one be servile and abject. . . . *It begins with the attitude of thinking about him, instead of being preoccupied with myself.* It includes looking for ways, all the time, to help him and please him. In the words of Proverbs 31, this kind of wife will do her husband "good and not evil, all the days of her life." The behavior that pleases him flows out of an inner attitude that I have already chosen for myself—the attitude that my husband is the king of my household and the king of my marriage. Next to the Lord, he is the one I want to please the most. He is my top priority, right after Christ. So it is my joy and privilege to treat my husband as my "lord." And here I am in good company, for Peter in his first epistle instructs the Christian wives to adapt themselves to their husbands . . . and he goes on to point to Sarah as a good example: "Even as Sarah obeyed Abraham, calling him lord . . ." (1 Peter 3:6).[7]

Then Gaye summed up the rewards of this attitude:

The more you please your husband, the more he is going to be eager to please you.
The more he attempts to please you, the more you are going to be happy and satisfied, so even more you are going to try to do the things which make him happy.
This is the glorious cycle of response which we could call a circle, for a circle never
ends. Once we step into that circle of love, we will not want to move out, and although our husbands may still know our limitations only too well, they will feel
that whatever we do is *all right*. We have proved ourselves to be just the right wives
for them.[8]

IN 1 PETER: HIS BEAUTIFUL WIFE

We have toured the Bible in search of the Creator's guidelines for wives who
want to know how to love their husbands according to His design. At this last
stop, we will consider three important questions:

What does a wife do when her husband can't (or won't) love her the way
God commanded in Ephesians 5?

What does a wife do when she feels no respect for her husband?

What makes a wife most beautiful in her husband's eyes?

Now to find God's answers, read these verses from 1 Peter. This passage
follows a section written about the Lord Jesus Christ, who, when He was mistreated, "simply committed his cause to the One who judges fairly" (1 Peter
2:23 PHILIPS).

In the same spirit you married women should adapt yourselves to your husbands,
so that even if they do not obey the Word of God they may be won to God without
any word being spoken, simply by seeing the pure and reverent conduct of you,
their wives. Your beauty should not be dependent on an elaborate coiffure, or on
the wearing of jewelry or fine clothes, but on the inner personality—the unfading
loveliness of a calm and gentle spirit, a thing very precious in the eyes of God.
This was the beauty of the holy women of ancient times who trusted in God and
were submissive to their husbands. Sarah, you will remember, obeyed Abraham
and called him her lord. And you have become her true descendants today as long
as you too live good lives and do not give way to hysterical fears (1 Peter 3:1–6
PHILIPS).

We have stressed the fact that you love your husband by responding to his
love. We have explained that your gift of willing adaptation to him (the attitude
of submission) should be your response to his sacrificial love for you. But what
if your husband can't or won't love you the way Jesus Christ loved the church,
either because he is an unbeliever or because he chooses to reject the way of

love. What if you don't have any love to respond to? Or what if you can't feel any respect for your husband because he's not respectable?

The Bible has one comprehensive answer to these hard questions: In such situations, your husband cannot control your behavior. Live and relate to him in a manner that pleases God, and commit the results to Him—just as the Lord Jesus had to endure hard things, but committed it all to the Father who judges rightly. In other words, go on loving him in all the scriptural ways we have described in this chapter. Respond to the Lord's love by obeying Him in this manner, even if your husband offers little that you can positively respond to. This is a true saying: Living as a Christian does not depend on anyone else!

For example, if your husband is not a respectable man, you may not be able to *feel* respectful toward him, but God requires you to *show* him respect. The Greek word for "adapt," used in the opening of 1 Peter 3, literally means *to be under authority.*

As Jay Adams explains,

Christians must respect the uniform with which God clothed husbands, even if they poorly fit it. The respect is directed toward God and His authority, not fundamentally toward the man in whom it is invested. When a wife speaks disrespectfully toward her husband, she really speaks in a manner that disregards God. That is serious.[9]

At this point in the discussion several questions about submission usually come up. Let us share some principles with you.

1. God does not ask a woman to be submissive to all men in general, only to her husband and as a means of functioning in an orderly way within the home.

2. God never gave a husband the authority to require his wife to sin. Do what your husband asks—as long as it does not involve sinning. He has no right to ask that of you.

3. Since obedience has to do with action, and respect, with attitude, it is possible for a wife to obey her husband, yet not respect him. Likewise, a wife can make a show of respect, but avoid doing what her husband asks. The absence of genuine respect is not submission.

The last question to consider is: What makes a wife beautiful in her husband's eyes? Women will pore over the latest *Vogue*, have their hair done, buy a new outfit, and their husbands will probably enjoy the results. Husbands appreciate every lovely detail of their wife's appearance. When Shulamith's husband praised her, he left out almost nothing!

And yet, God says there's another kind of beauty that counts for more, that never fades, that reaches into a husband's heart, and has the power to melt it. This beauty can't be bought or developed by an application of new cosmetics. It begins on the inside—within the inner life one lives before God—and as it begins to shine forth, something happens on the outside. A man may not notice it at first. Like the dawn that comes so gradually, who can say when it first appeared?

Eventually the husband takes notice. His wife may not be harassing him anymore, nor complaining, nor nagging at him to change. She has become calm and gentle. She treats him with respect and shows a concern for his wishes. She meets his gruffest moments with a quiet spirit. There's a purity about her, a beauty which he may not understand, but he loves it, and he begins to look at her as if he has never seen her before. He watches her to see the source of this change. And the Scripture indicates there is the distinct possibility he may change too; that he may come to Christ because his wife has won him "without a word."

Hopefully, you and your husband are already one in Christ. But even if he already loves you according to God's design, you can delight him and bless his life by developing your inner beauty. Jay Adams, commenting on this passage in 1 Peter, gives you this recipe:

> (Outer) beauty is artificial; it is added to the person. (Inner beauty) is genuine because it is the result of a change in the person herself. Adornment must be inward; the inner person of the heart must become beautiful in order to please God and to be winning. This hidden person, when so transformed, will become visible.
>
> Women who try to hold husbands or win husbands only by making themselves outwardly attractive misunderstand the fact that husbands really want a woman who is *herself* attractive within. Respect and obedience that issue in lasting values . . . such as a gentleness and quietness are *most* alluring and winsome. Wives who carp and criticize, who whine and whinny, who yell and scream, who argue and act stubbornly fail to exhibit this inner beauty. The gentle and quiet spirit (spirit here means *attitude* and *approach*) attracts; other attitudes and approaches repel.[10]

One more way to love your husband: by becoming beautiful on the inside for him!

10
"Forever"

> He has made everything beautiful in its time; He also has planted eternity in men's heart and mind. . . .
>
> Eccles. 3:11a Amplified

WHEN GOD GIVES us something beautiful to enjoy, He gives us the desire to enjoy it forever! He has planted the fact of eternity in our minds, and the longings of our hearts reflect it. When, as lovers, we say "forever," we mean that we choose to be together "for time without end." And yet we realize that time must end for every living thing. What happens then? Does this mean the end of our love and the oneness we have shared? Will we never be together again? Or, if we meet in heaven, will it be only in passing? Will we be separate again, the process working backward: one becoming two?

It's a good idea to confront these questions early in your marriage, because the conclusions you reach will affect the way you live. We encourage you to develop an eternal perspective of love and marriage based on the truth. The Lord Jesus Christ said in His prayer before going to the cross, "Thy word is truth" (John 17:17). Not all of our questions will be answered, but the Scriptures provide all the truth we need on this earth, and the truth never changes. The answers we have to share with you in this chapter are what we believe the Scriptures teach or suggest concerning love and marriage in heaven.

First, we can be sure that there will be no marriages in heaven. The Lord Jesus, answering the Sadducees, said, "Ye do err, not knowing the scriptures, nor the power of God. In the resurrection they neither marry, nor are given in marriage, but are like the angels of God in heaven" (Matt. 22:29–30). Why? Because God has the power to raise the dead in such a manner that marriage is no longer needed.

God designed marriage for our blessing and well-being on this earth, but in heaven it has been replaced by something even better. Notice that we will not become angels, but we will become *like* angels in several respects: We will not marry; we will have immortal bodies; and we will be occupied with the glory of God.

Here are seven reasons why marriage is not needed in heaven

No Death; No Need for Reproduction

1. Our resurrection bodies will be immortal. Mortality will be swallowed up by life (2 Cor. 5:4), and believers will never again be able to die. In the same moment that their bodies become immortal, they also become incorruptible, or immune to change and decay. Since there will be no death in heaven, there will be no need to reproduce and rear children. (See 1 Cor. 15:42–57.)

No Need to Be Healed of Loneliness

2. Marriage will no longer be needed to heal mankind's loneliness, for there will be no loneliness in heaven. The Scripture says, "In thy presence is fullness of joy; at thy right hand there are pleasures as for evermore" (Ps. 16:11).

We Will Find Our Completion in Christ

3. Marriage was designed to bring completion to man and woman, as the two became one, but in heaven we will experience our completeness in Christ, and will be satisfied. The Scripture says, "For in Him dwelleth all the fullness of the Godhead bodily. And ye are complete in Him. . . " (Col. 2:9, 10a).

No Symbols: The Real Thing

4. There will be no need to picture the relationship of Jesus Christ and His church to a lost world through the symbolism of marriage. We will have the real thing at the "wedding of all weddings" when the church, the Bride of Christ, is married to the Lamb. (See Rev. 19:6–9.)

No Need for Protection in a Perfect World

5. Our love needs the protection of marriage (the house of love) on earth, but in heaven we will dwell in an ideal environment. The security of permanent commitment will be unnecessary in "a world perfect at last." (See Rev. 21:3–5.)

All Relationships Will Be Important in Heaven

6. It has been suggested that in heaven everyone will love everyone else with the intensity reserved now for two people who fall in love. The night before Jesus went to the cross, He told his disciples,

> A new commandment I give unto you, that ye love one another; as I have loved you, that ye love one another. By this shall all know that ye are my disciples, if ye have love one to another (John 13:34–35).

From this time forth, love became the signature and insignia of all who believe in the Lord Jesus Christ. What is commanded on earth "comes naturally" in heaven among immortal beings dwelling always in the glory of God—the God who Himself is Love. We can imagine that, as the air we breathe on this earth, so love will be the atmosphere of heaven.

Rodney Clapp suggests that

> At the resurrection, *all* relationships will be taken up to such a high level that the exclusiveness of marriage will not be a factor in heaven as it is on earth. It is not that in heaven marriage will be less. Rather, all relationships . . . will be infinitely more joyful than we can now imagine. . . .

> Imagine being "in love" 24 hours a day, seven days a week, and "in love" not simply with one person, but with everyone you pass on the street. . . . Only resurrected creatures will be strong enough to endure the weight— indeed, to enjoy it and see in each person a unique aspect of God's beauty.[1]

We Will Concentrate on God, Not Each Other

7. In heaven we will be involved with God's glory, even as the angels are. We will no longer be occupied, as we are now, with our marriage partner's needs amid the cares of this world; our lives will center around fellowship with God. (See Rev. 22:1–5.)

But what will happen to our love in heaven? Many couples ask this question after they find there will be no marriage in heaven. True, their union is housed in the public, legal, sacred commitment of marriage, but that's not all of it. In the process of living out their commitment, their relationship has become a living entity of love. They want to know what will happen to this. Although Scripture has told us very little on the subject, we can draw these conclusions.

First, love is the one thing that will last. It's the only thing we can take to heaven with us. Marriage as an institution is superfluous in heaven, but love is not. We can be sure that not one iota of the love, which we have felt and shared and demonstrated will ever be lost. If our love has been centered in God's love, it will grow and abound in the ages to come.

Then, too, we know that God's love is always personal and specific, "not a vague, diffused good-will towards everyone in general and nobody in particular."[2] Because New Testament love involves people and relationships, we can be sure that love will not be a vague and lonely ideal in heaven, anymore than it is on this earth. And if we have individuals to love and to love us there, we can feel confident that our earthly loved ones will be a part of it. If they are in heaven, we look forward to sweet fellowship with them as we adore our Lord God together.

We need to remember that we don't know all the good that God has planned for us. Jesus' answer to the Sadducees concerning marriage in heaven was not a complete discussion of the subject, but a concise response to an insincere question. He did not address the subject so important to us: the eternal relationship of those who are married in this life. We have no way of knowing if a special bond will exist in heaven between those who were husband and wife on earth. Although we cannot have the same relationship which we had on earth, and even though our lives will be too full and complete to miss it, it's difficult to imagine heaven without some closeness with those we have loved best on earth. We believe that we can trust His great loving kindness to arrange all things for our joy in that day.

When we think of our love in heaven, it teaches us valuable lessons for our time together on earth.

Lessons in Loving

1. Gaining an eternal perspective on our love relationship can be very helpful. It reminds us, first of all, that our love affair is not the highest good, the chief end of life. God is greater!

2. We see that our love for one another is everlasting only if its source is God Himself. All that we can offer apart from Him is mere passion, lust, infatuation, or sentimentality. We find that we don't even know how to love one another fully unless we have loved God first.

3. We discover that if we try to keep our love separate from God—jealously guarding our relationship, even from the Lover of our souls—our love will turn into something else. As C. S. Lewis wrote in *The Great Divorce*,

> No natural feelings are high or low, holy or unholy, in themselves. They are all holy when God's hand is on the rein. They all go bad when they set up on their own and make themselves into false gods.[3]

4. We realize that no earthly love, no matter how wonderful and intimate and beautiful, can replace our need for closeness to God. He has created us so that there is a place within which can be satisfied only by intimate fellowship with Him. In the shelter of His love, our love for one another can safely grow and flower until it is transformed by heaven into something even more wonderful.

How To Make Your Marriage Beautiful In Its Time

We have only two more things to share with you, and they relate to your handling of time and eternity. Your love affair began in delight: now, to learn how to value time and prepare for eternity is the apex of wisdom that will bless you forever.

First, the matter of time. "Marriage is the greatest institution ever invented," a woman said, looking back on forty-six years with her husband. *"It means you are the most important person in the world for somebody else!"*[4]

Have you discovered that yet in your marriage? The lady was absolutely right. But for her, it was already over. Like her, we all have a limited amount of time in the classroom of love with our marriage partner. It may be forty-six years or even sixty. It may be much less. Whatever, our time is short, indeed, to love one another with the exclusive, intimate love that belongs only to earthly marriage.

When you come to the reality of this fact, it can well change the way you look at time . . . and love . . . and the miracle of ordinary life with one another.

In the Pulitzer Prize-winning drama, *Our Town*, Emily, a young wife of 26 who has died in childbirth, is allowed to revisit an ordinary day from her past. But she is warned,

> "At least choose an unimportant day. Choose the least important day in your life. It will be important enough."

She begins reliving her twelfth birthday, but soon she cries,

"I can't. I can't go on. It goes so fast. We don't have time to look at one another. . . .
I didn't realize. So all that was going on and we never noticed. . . ."

Another character comments from the grave,

"Yes . . . that's what it was to be alive. To move about in a cloud of ignorance; to
go up and down trampling on the feelings of those about you. To spend and waste
time as though you had a million years. To be always at the mercy of one self-
centered passion, or another. . . ."

But it is Emily's question which echoes in the heart: "Do any human beings
ever realize life while they live it?"

She is told, "No. (*Pause*.) The saints and poets, maybe—they do some."[5]

Yes, the saints—Christians who are the sons and daughters of the God who
inhabits eternity (Isa. 57:15) and created time (Gen. 1)—do possess the spiritual capacity to appreciate the miracle of life on this earth, and to value every
moment of loving as a gift from our Father. But if we have it, we must choose
to learn how to use it. As the old hymn warns, "See how time flies, the time that
for loving and praising was given![6]

James Dobson tells of a trip he and his family made in 1977 to Kansas City,
Missouri, to visit his parents. As they drove to the airport when the visit was
over, he asked his father to pray for their family. He said he would never forget
his father's words, for it was their last prayer together:

And Lord, we want to thank you for the fellowship and love that we feel for each
other today. This has been such a special time for us with Jim and Shirley and their
children. But Heavenly Father, we are keenly aware that the joy that is ours today
is a temporal pleasure. Our lives will not always be this stable and secure. Change
is inevitable and it will come to us, too. We will accept it when it comes, of course,
but we give you praise for the happiness and warmth that has been ours these past
few days. We have had more than our share of the good things, and we thank you
for your love. Amen.[7]

Dr. Dobson says that eleven years later, his dad's final prayer still rings in
his mind:

"Thank you, God, for what we have . . . which we know we cannot keep." I
wish every newlywed couple could capture that incredible concept. If we only
realize how brief is our time on this earth, then most of the irritants and frustrations which drive us apart would seem terribly insignificant and petty. We have
but one short life to live, yet we contaminate it with bickering and insults and
angry words.[8]

Here are seven ways to value time and bless your marriage.

1. Thank God for the daily miracle of time. Arnold Bennett has called it

the inexplicable raw material of everything . . . You wake up in the morning, and lo! your purse is magically filled with 24 hours of the unmanufactured tissue of your life, the most precious of possessions.[9]

2. So live and so love your partner as though it were your last day to enjoy the gift of time together.

3. Ask God what He wants to do with your marriage in the time you have. Share the vision and fulfill it together.

4. Practice, every day, becoming more at home with one another—mutually adapting, mutually accepting.

5. Learn to value the miracle of ordinary days of living together. Ask God to open your eyes, your cars, your mind, your heart, and all your senses to the wonder of it.

6. Beware of wasting your time with self-centered passions, bickering, power plays, unkind words, idle self-pity, petty disputes.

7. Remember what is most important. Henry Drummond says,

We know but little now about the conditions of the life that is to come. But what is certain is that love must last. God, the Eternal God, is love. Covet, therefore, that everlasting gift. . . . You will give yourselves to many things; give yourself first to love. Hold things in their proportion. *Hold things in their proportion.*[10]

How To Prepare Now For Eternity

God has placed eternity in our minds and hearts because we are eternal beings. Our human soul—that part of us which makes each of us a unique and distinctive individual—will live forever. It's a fact. Granted, it's a truth that troubles some people. They would prefer to think that they could do whatever they please during their lifetime and afterward go to sleep, never to awaken again.

But, no. Apart from the unmistakable evidence of Scripture, most people also know in their hearts that while their body will wear out, their soul—their being—will never die. We have no choice in this: we *will* exist forever. But here's the point that some people miss to their eternal grief: We do have a choice concerning *where* we spend eternity and *how.* If we refuse to make a choice and "just let it all happen," that becomes a choice too, and we must live with the results.

Either we will enjoy eternal life in heaven where Jesus Christ went to prepare a place for us, or we will endure everlasting unhappiness and misery, separated from God and love and all that makes life beautiful, not for just a time, but through all eternity.

What is eternity? "Infinite duration without any beginning, end, or limit—an ever-abiding present."[11] What will it mean to spend eternity in heaven? Think of living forever in the vigor of your strength without the uncertainties of childhood, the trials of adolescence, or the frailties of old age. Picture inhabiting a beautiful present without yesterday's regrets or tomorrow's fears. Think of life without death or pain or sorrow. Picture the beauty and freedom and joy that can be yours in heaven. As wonderful as all that sounds, there will be much more which we cannot even imagine now. We are incapable of comprehending it, and we do not possess the language to describe it. We do have this: a sure promise which goes into effect even before we get to heaven, "Eye hath not seen, nor ear heard, neither have entered into the heart of man, the things which God hath prepared for them that love Him" (1 Cor. 2:9).

All these glorious things which God has prepared for us come wrapped in one package labeled *eternal life*. And the best part is that we can begin to enjoy eternal life immediately. It can be a permanent possession, a present experience; we don't have to wait until our earthly body wears out to receive it. Note the present tense of these Scriptures:

He that believeth on the Son hath everlasting life . . . (John 3:36).

He that heareth my Word, and believeth on Him that sent me, hath everlasting life . . . (John 5:24).

He that hath the Son hath life . . . (1 John 5:12).

The other side of this truth is just as true. If eternal life is present tense for some people, so is God's judgment for others. If we do not possess eternal life, we are under God's judgment, already condemned—even before our earthly bodies succumb to physical death. No one is in a neutral state!

God made His choice when He sent His Son to die in our place for our sins. He has provided the way out for us—the way to be saved from the condemnation of sin and the sentence of death which already hangs over us. Now the choice is ours. The Lord Jesus says,

. . . the Son of Man must be lifted up, (on the cross) that everyone who believes in him may have eternal life. For God so loved the world that he gave his one and only Son, that whoever believes in him shall not perish but have eternal life. For

God did not send his Son into the world to condemn the world, but to save the world through him. Whoever believes in him is not condemned, but whoever does not believe stands condemned already because he has not believed (and trusted) in the name of God's one and only Son. This is the verdict: Light has come into the world, but men loved darkness instead of light because their deeds were evil (John 3:14–19 NIV).

And John the Baptist adds his testimony,

The Father loves the Son and has placed everything in his hands. Whoever believes in the Son has eternal life, but whoever rejects the Son will not see life, for God's wrath remains on him (John 3:35–36 NIV).

Again, Jesus speaks,

I tell you the truth, whoever hears my word and believes him who sent me has eternal life and will not be condemned; he has crossed over from death to life (John 5:24 NIV).

The Apostle John explains our condition and our choice:

And this is the testimony: God has given us eternal life, and this life is in his Son. He who has the Son has life; he who does not have the Son of God does not have life (1 John 5:11–12 NIV).

It's plain that the only wise way to prepare for eternity is to obtain *eternal life*. What is it? The life of Christ within you. You do not receive it by joining a church or being baptized or by living a good life. All those things result from possessing eternal life.

You can only receive Jesus Christ by believing on the power of His Name to save you. Here, according to the Scriptures, is what happened on your behalf, and what you need to believe by faith in order to be saved and receive eternal life:

1. The Lord Jesus Christ at a specific moment in history died on the cross for our sins, bearing the sins of the whole world. Through that mighty act, by paying the death penalty, He opened the way for all of our sins to be forgiven. In Jesus our past is pardoned, and our sins are forgotten as though they had been put in the depths of the deepest sea and remembered no more.

2. After dying on the cross, Jesus was buried. On the third day He arose again from the dead, demonstrating to all people for all time that He is God, with all power and authority and resources for the life of the person who believes on Him. It is written, "For as many as received Him, to them gave He the power to become the sons of God, even to them that believe on His name" (John 1:12).

3. Redemption in Christ Jesus does more than pardon our sins. Forgiveness covers the past, but when we believe on the Lord Jesus Christ, receiving Him by faith, God not only forgives our sins and redeems us: We also become sons of God, partakers of divine nature, and possessors of eternal life. We are taken into the family of God, and thereafter God deals with us as children.

J. I. Packer explains,

What is a Christian? The question can be answered in many ways, but the richest answer I know is that a Christian is one who has God for his father.

But cannot this be said of every man, Christian or not? Emphatically no! The idea that all men are children of God is not found in the Bible anywhere. The Old Testament shows God as the Father, not of all men, but of His own people, the seed of Abraham. 'Israel is my son, even my firstborn: and I say unto thee, let my son go . . .' (Exod. 4:22f.) The New Testament has a world vision, but it too shows God as the Father, not of all men, but of those who, knowing themselves to be sinners, put their trust in the Lord Jesus Christ as their divine sin-bearer and master, and so become Abraham's spiritual seed. 'Ye are all sons of God, through faith, in Christ Jesus . . . ye are one man in Christ Jesus. And if ye are Christ's, then are ye Abraham's seed' (Gal. 3:26 ff.). Sonship to God is not, therefore, a universal status upon which everyone enters by natural birth, but a supernatural gift which one receives through receiving Jesus. 'No man cometh unto the Father'—in other words, is acknowledged by God as a son—'but by me' (John 14:6). The gift of sonship to God becomes ours, not through being born, but through being born again. . . .[12]

The human race is made up of two kinds of people—those who are alive unto God, and those who are already dead in their sins. There is no middle ground: Believers possess eternal life; unbelievers are, even now, under the condemnation and wrath of God.

Do you know your own identity as a child of God who can call God your Father? Do you know that you possess the life of Jesus Christ within you because you have already received Him and believed on His name? Are you confident of your destiny when you leave this life?

If your answers to the above questions are "no's" or if you are just not sure, here is a prayer which you may want to follow in expressing your faith in Jesus Christ as your Savior:

Heavenly Father, I know that I am a sinner and cannot do anything to save myself. I do believe that Jesus Christ died on the cross, shedding His blood as full payment for my sins—past, present, and future—and that He rose from the dead, demonstrating that He is God.

As best I know how, I am believing in Him, putting all my trust in Jesus Christ as my personal Savior, as my only hope for salvation and eternal life.

Right now I receive Jesus Christ into my life, I thank You for saving me as You promised, and I ask that you will give me increasing faith and wisdom as I study and believe your Word.

I ask this in the name of the Lord Jesus Christ. Amen.

After this, let all the good things begin! Now you can begin to discover the riches of eternal life, with God as your own Father. To write about those riches would require another book, but to sum it up in a few words: You will live the rest of your life and on through eternity, knowing that God is *for* you. You belong to His family for now and forever, and He will never leave you nor forsake you. *You belong!*

What, then, shall we say in response to this? If God is for us, who can be against us? He who did not spare his own Son, but gave him up for us all—how will he not also, along with him, graciously give us all things? Who will bring any charge against those whom God has chosen? It is God who justifies. Who is he that condemns? Christ Jesus, who died—more than that, who was raised to life—is at the right hand of God and is also interceding for us. Who shall separate us from the love of Christ? Shall trouble or hardship or persecution or famine or nakedness or danger or sword?. . . . No, in all these things we are more than conquerors through him who loved us. For I am convinced that neither death nor life, neither angels nor demons, neither the present nor the future, nor any powers, neither height nor depth, nor anything else in all creation, will be able to separate us from the love of God that is in Christ Jesus our Lord (Rom. 8:31–25, 37–39 NIV).

Here are seven ways to prepare for eternity.

1. Trust in Jesus Christ as your Savior, if you have not already done so, and receive the gift of eternal life.

2. Set yourself on the eternal adventure of experiencing what it means to belong to God's family through Jesus Christ.

3. Become actively involved in a Bible-teaching church. God has designed the local church to be the bulwark and support of His truth in your life; a means of spiritual growth; and a stabilizing factor as you establish your own family unit.

4. Commit yourselves as one to love and serve the Lord Jesus Christ all the days of your life.

5. Continue to grow in His love through Bible study, prayer, and obedience in all He shows you.

6. Bless each other with His love, drawing on His power and resources to be the husband or wife you were meant to be.

7. Look forward to being together. . . "forever"!

Notes

Introduction
[1]Marcia Lasswell, "Illusions Regarding Marital Happiness," *Medical Aspects of Human Sexuality* (February 1985): 154.

[2]Paul Tournier, *To Understand Each Other* (Richmond, Virginia: John Knox Press, 1967), 30.

Chapter 1
[1]Robert Frost, "The Figure a Poem Makes," *Collected Poems*, 1939. Quoted in *A Little Treasury of Modern Poetry* (New York: Charles Scribner's Sons, 1950), 798.

[2]C. S. Lewis, *George MacDonald: An Anthology* (London: Geoffrey Bles, 1946), 123.

[3]C. S. Lewis, *A Grief Observed* (New York: The Seabury Press, 1961), 13.

[4]Maggie Scarf, *Intimate Partners* (New York: Random House, 1987), 79.

[5]Judith Adams Perry, M.D., "Love Related to Marriage," *Medical Aspects of Human Sexuality* (June 1985): 243.

[6]John C. Haughey, S.J., *Should Anyone Ever Say Forever?* (Garden City, New York: Doubleday & Company, Inc., 1975), 62, 64.

Chapter 2
[1]Malachi Martin, *There Is Still Love* (New York: Macmillan Publishing Company, 1984), 207.

[2]Ed Wheat, M.D., and Gloria Okes Perkins, *LOVE LIFE* (Grand Rapids, Michigan: Zondervan Publishing House, 1980), 119.

[3]Jay E. Adams, *Marriage, Divorce & Remarriage in the Bible* (Grand Rapids: Baker Book House, 1980), 4.

Chapter 3
[1]James R. Mannes, "Love the One You're With," *Family Life Today* (March 1985): 41.

[2]David Hegner, *What Will Make My Marriage Work?* (Grand Rapids. Michigan: Radio Bible Class Publications), 8.

Chapter 4

[1]Jay E. Adams, *More Than Redemption* (Phillipsburg, New Jersey: Presbyterian and Reformed Publishing Co., 1979), 228.

[2]David Augsburger, *The Freedom of Forgiveness* (Chicago Moody Press, 1970), 121.

[3]Ed Wheat, M.D., and Gloria Okes Perkins, *LOVE LIFE*, 199.

Chapter 5

[1]Domeena C. Renshaw, M.D. "Communication in Marriage," *Medical Aspects of Human Sexuality* (June 1983): 205.

[2]Martin Goldberg, M.D. "Commentary on Survey: Current Thinking on Why Some Marriages Fail," *Medical Aspects of Human Sexuality* (June 1982): 131.

[3]Renshaw, 205.

[4]Anthony Pietropinto, M.D. "Commentary on Survey: Distress Signals in Marriage" *Medical Aspects of Human Sexuality* (April 1984): 87.

[5]Judson J. Swihart, *Communicating in Marriage* (Downers Grove, Illinois: InterVarsity Press, 1981), 19–20.

[6]Carmen Lynch, MSW and Martin Blinder, M.D., "The Romantic Relationship" *Medical Aspects of Human Sexuality* (May 1983): 155.

[7]Donald G. Ellis, Ph.D., "Listening Creatively to One's Spouse," *Medical Aspects of Human Sexuality* (March 1983): 173.

[8]Czeslaw Milosz, *Selected Poems* (New York: The Ecco Press, 1980), 18.

[9]Barbara E. James, Ph.D., "The 'Silent Treatment' in Marriage," *Medical Aspects of Human Sexuality* (February 1983): 100.

[10]Ibid.

[11]Charles R. Swindoll, *Strike the Original Match* (Portland, Oregon: Multnomah Press, 1980), 102–111.

[12]Pietropinto, 88.

[13]Emily Dickinson, *The Complete Poems of Emily Dickinson*, ed. Thomas H. Johnson (Boston: Little, Brown and Company, 1890), 534–535.

[14]The Rev. Derek Kidner, M.A., *The Proverbs, An Introduction and Commentary* (London: The Tyndale Press, 1964; reprint ed., Downers Grove, Illinois: InterVarsity Press, 1972), 46–47.

[15]David Hellerstein, M.D., "Can TV Cause Divorce?" *TV Guide* (September 26, 1987): 4–7.

Chapter 6

[1]Harold Feldman and Andrea Parrot, eds., *Human Sexuality, Contemporary Controversies* (Beverly Hills, California: Sage Publications, 1984), 130–131.

[2]Dean Sherman, "Singles and Sex, Logical Loving Limits," *The Last Days Magazine* 9, no. 2 (1986): 30.

[3]Ed Wheat, M.D., and Gaye Wheat, *Intended for Pleasure* (Old Tappan, New Jersey: Revell, 1981), 236.

[4]S. Craig Glickman, *A Song for Lovers* (Downers Grove, Illinois: InterVarsity Press, 1976), 25.

[5]Ed Wheat, M.D., and Gloria Okes Perkins, *LOVE LIFE*, 76.

[6]Wheat, *Intended for Pleasure*, 214.

[7]Helen Singer Kaplan, M.D., Ph.D., *Disorders of Sexual Desire* (New York: Simon and Schuster, 1979), 61.

[8]Ibid.

[9]Steve Beauvais, "What Men Hate About the Women They Love," *Glamour* (April 1988): 315.

[10]Abigail Van Buren, *The Best of Dear Abby* (Boston: G. K. Hall & Co., 1982).

[11]Mike Mason, *The Mystery of Marriage* (Portland, Oregon: Multnomah Press, 1985), 127–128.

Chapter 8

[1]Gary Smalley with Steve Scott, *For Better or for Best* (Grand Rapids, Michigan: Zondervan Publishing House, 1982), 14–15.

[2]Harriet B. Braiker, Ph.D., *The Type E Woman* (New York: Dodd, Mead & Company, 1986), 2.

[3]Jay E. Adams, *Trust and Obey, A Practical Commentary on First Peter* (Grand Rapids, Michigan: Baker Book House, 1979), 100.

[4]Ibid., 101.

[5]Ed Wheat, M.D., and Gloria Okes Perkins, *LOVE LIFE*, 158–159.

[6]Dwight H. Small, *How Should I Love You?* (San Francisco: Harper & Row, Publishers, 1979), 191, 193, 194.

[7]Ibid., 191–192.

Chapter 9

[1]Gary Smalley with Steve Scott, *For Better or for Best*, 155–156.

[2]Harriet B. Braiker, Ph.D., *The Type E Woman*, 141.

[3]Ibid., 2.

[4]Ibid., 4.

[5]Paul Tournier, *To Understand Each Other*, 23.

[6]The Rev. Derek Kidner, M.A., *The Proverbs, An Introduction and Commentary* (London: The Tyndale Press, 1964; reprint ed., Downers Grove, Illinois: InterVarsity Press, 1972), 50.

[7]Ed Wheat, M.D., and Gaye Wheat, *Intended for Pleasure*, 143–144.

[8]Ibid.

[9]Jay E. Adams, *Trust and Obey, A Practical Commentary on First Peter*, 96.

[10]Ibid., 96–97.

Chapter 10

[1]Rodney Clapp, "What Hollywood Doesn't Know About Romantic Love," *Christianity Today* (February 3, 1984): 33.

[2]J. I. Packer, *Knowing God* (Downers Grove, Illinois: InterVarsity Press, 1973), 112.

[3]C. S. Lewis, The Great Divorce (New York: The Macmillan Company, Macmillan Paperback, 1946), 93.

[4]Diana Trilling, quoted in *Cosmopolitan*, (March 1987): 229.

[5]Thornton Wilder, *Our Town, A Play in Three Acts* (New York: Harper & Row, Publishers, 1957), from Act III.

[6]Frederick William Faber, "The Remembrance of Mercy" in *The Christian Book of*

Mystical Verse selected by A. W. Tozer (Harrisburg, Pennsylvania: Christian Publications, Inc., 1963), 77.

[7]Dr. James C. Dobson, *Love for a Lifetime* (Portland, Oregon: Multnomah Press 1987), 115.

[8]Ibid., 116.

[9]Arnold Bennett, *How to Live on Twenty-Four Hours a Day*, a condensation in *Getting the Most Out of Life, an Anthology* (Pleasantville, New York: The Reader's Digest Association, Inc., 1948), 166.

[10]Henry Drummond, *The Greatest Thing in the World*, A Revell Inspirational Classic, (Westwood, New Jersey: Fleming H. Revell Company), 55.

[11]William Evans, *The Great Doctrines of the Bible*, Enlarged Edition (Chicago: Moody Press, 1974), 35.

[12]Packer, *Knowing God*, 181.

SECRET CHOICES

*With thanksgiving for my wonderful
dad and mother, Guy and Irene Okes,
who have shown me the reality of their faith
in Jesus Christ, and the generosity of
their love, without end*
Gloria Okes Perkins

Contents

Preface

Secret Choices continues the adventure we began last year with the writing of *The First Years of Forever*, a handbook for newlyweds with high expectations of happiness and the enthusiasm to commit themselves to the process of building a wonderful, lasting marriage.

We made it our prayerful goal to offer, in one volume, the hard-to-obtain, new-marriage counsel that every couple needs at the beginning of their life together. We included the essentials for building a *forever* relationship: understanding and guarding the feelings of love; living by the facts of love; learning the principles of faithfulness and forgiveness; building the lifeline system of good communication; discovering the secrets of sexual fulfillment; and recognizing warning signals. Most importantly, we provided complete handbooks for husbands and wives with specific biblical counsel on *how* to love each other in the ways most needed and desired.

Even so, much remained to be said, which we could not fit into one volume. We knew, also, that couples, still caught up in the wonder of their love, are not ready to take in every principle of marriage at the beginning. With a little experience comes a greater awareness of potential problems and the desire to learn how to deal with the unexpected challenges of marriage.

So we invited our readers to participate in a second book to be used as a companion to *The First Years of Forever*. We asked them to share their experiences with us, their questions and discoveries. *Secret Choices: Personal Decisions That Affect Your Marriage* is the result. We believe you will find, as we have, that these Bible-based concepts, when applied, will change the quality of your marriage and your life.

And the adventure goes on. Let us hear from you at *Secret Choices*, P.O. Box 410, Springdale, Arkansas 72764.

Your friends in Christ,
Ed Wheat, M.D. and Gloria Okes Perkins

Acknowledgements

Our thanks to
George Fooshee, Dow Pursley, and Victoria James, whose wonderful contributions enriched our book,
our friend and pastor, John Glasser, for his timely and well-seasoned comments,
and all our friends and loved ones who prayed.

The choices that determine the success of your marriage are secret ones because they happen on the inside first. Later, the results can be seen by all.

Introduction

All of us know, as a matter of practical experience that there is something within us, behind our emotions, and behind our wishes, an independent self, that, after all, decides everything.

Hannah Whitall Smith

We usually approach major decisions as though they were packages marked: *Handle with care.* But what about the small personal choices we exercise from moment to moment, scarcely realizing we've just made a choice? Do we ever ask ourselves, *What are we really choosing? Where might this take us? Do we want to go in that direction?* We should!

Within the sensitive setting of marriage these small choices have more power to bless or hurt a relationship than we could imagine. For all their seeming unimportance, they carry long-term consequences and ultimately can make the difference between success in building a love-filled marriage or failure.

In this fourth book of marriage counsel, we have a compelling truth to share with you: *Your secret choices have power. You can learn to use them to determine the success of your marriage.* Forget the theory that "if it's meant to work out, it will." Yes, God wants your marriage to succeed, but He has entrusted your relationship into your own care. Please don't hand it over to "fate," "luck," or "wishful thinking." The responsibility—and the benefits—are all yours.

In the next fourteen chapters you will discover how to become aware of your choices and their consequences; how to take charge of them; and how to make the best choices to create the right emotional climate in your marriage and establish an enjoyable partnership that really works. You will also find biblical counsel and spiritual resources to help you explore your potential for growth and positive change.

As you read, watch for the "stepping stones." These enclosed blocks of copy will give you twenty steps to follow in your quest for a marriage that satisfies and delights. Each chapter begins with a question to help you define your present situation and determine where your secret choices have been taking you. The suggestions for action in each chapter will help you apply the material to your life and marriage. Remember, the more deeply you become involved, the more benefits you can enjoy.

Recognize, however, that you won't be able to do it all, or to do it all at once. These chapters are packed with good ideas and valuable principles from Scripture. You'll be delighted with the results if you begin now and simply do what you can—every day. Be consistent, be expectant, and relax in the Lord's readiness to help you. This process offers hope, not more burdens to bear, so enjoy the experience, and remember the Lord's tender word of commendation: "She has done what she could" (Mark 14:8).

If you are pouring yourself into this study of secret choices to win your partner back or to restore a love that shows few signs of life, remember that the awakening and flowering of love cannot be forced. Make the right choices consistently, keep them "watered" with prayer, and wait for the results as patiently as possible. Good choices have a way of producing good fruit.

Part 1
Where are Your
Choices Taking You?

1

Harnessing the Power

Are we aware of our secret choices and their power in our lives?

Choice: The voluntary act of selecting from two or more things that which is preferred.

WHEN THE ALARM went off at six a.m., Mary Lou opened her eyes, then sank back into sleep. Her husband Bill made his breakfast and ate alone. Mary Lou felt rather badly about it, but the choice was simplified several mornings later when she didn't even hear the alarm. Bill began going to the Doughnut Shop for breakfast and companionship where an attractive waitress provided both.

Bill and Mary Lou had established the habit of exchanging kisses and hugs whenever one of them left the house. But Bill, miffed at Mary Lou's failure to get up for breakfast with him, decided one morning to leave without her sleep-fogged kiss. Mary Lou, hurt when she realized what he had done, retaliated by ignoring him that evening. Both were out of sorts at bedtime and turned their backs on one another instead of exchanging good-night hugs.

No major decisions here but a link-up of choices which are affecting this marriage. Life is a series of choices, most of them so small we scarcely realize that we're making them. Or why. Sometimes we call them *reactions* and disclaim any responsibility for them, not recognizing that reactions are choices, too. Not only are we often unaware of our choices, but we seldom give thought to where they are taking us and whether we want to go there. Though our choices are small when counted one at a time, their cumulative effect is more powerful than we can imagine. In reality, these private choices direct our steps, determine our behavior, change the quality of our relationships, and in the end, shape our lives.

To help you focus on your choices in marriage, we have a series of questions for you to consider in the privacy of your own heart. Each section of the book will pose new questions which we believe are crucial to your happiness and the health of your marriage. The first one is this: *Where are your choices taking you?* Or, more specifically, *Are your secret choices moving you in a positive direction toward a successful marriage?*

The point is **They can!** Our goal is to show you how.

> Become aware of your secret choices and discover their power in your life. This is the first step toward harnessing that power to build the marriage of your hopes and dreams.

Start by defining and describing where you want to go with your marriage. If you don't know where you're going, almost any road will do, but to harness the power of your secret choices, you must know precisely where you're headed and how to get there. We encourage you to begin now to develop a strong mental picture of your "destination"—the marriage you consider *successful* because it's the kind of marriage you and your partner desire.

Think about it. What comes to mind when you hear the phrase "a successful marriage"?

For most of us, this depends on whether we're describing someone else's marriage or our own. When it comes to other people, we're likely to measure success by how long they've been married, how well their children and grandchildren have turned out, and if they're still talking to one another after thirty or forty years.

But when it comes to our own marriage, we expect infinitely more, and the passing of time has little to do with our calculations. We want a great marriage *now*—whether "now" is three days after the ceremony, or two years and two children later. Success, we rightly feel, should be enjoyed today, not deferred until our Golden Wedding Anniversary.

And yet, impatience is not the way to a great marriage. It can take us on side roads and rocky detours that we'd rather avoid. Some people today are so impatient for instant success that they throw in the towel if the marriage doesn't feel good and work well from Day One! Unfortunately, these people will never know what happiness they missed out on: they can only wonder.

To create a beautiful marriage that fulfills God's design and meets the deepest needs and desires of our hearts will take time. It is never a fortunate accident, but always an achievement—a work of art. Still, we don't have to wait for success. We can enjoy success all along the way, if we're moving in the right direction. The process of building a good marriage offers moment by moment rewards in love, enjoyment, and satisfaction. If you are going through this book with your partner, make it an experience you'll remember with pleasure for years to come. Take advantage of the opportunities for personal growth while you share the fun of turning your dreams into goals which you can attain by working together. Even if you are reading this book alone, your mate can share in the benefits and blessings as you make positive choices concerning your marriage.

What do people expect from their own marriage? Our conversations with hundreds of couples indicate that most people want to be loved, understood, and cared for by their marriage partner. To put it simply, they want their needs met!

Call this the *happiness factor*, for marital happiness usually reflects the degree to which husbands and wives can relate as intimate friends and lovers. This clearly is the first dimension of a successful marriage. To determine how well our own marriage is working in this dimension, we can ask ourselves: Do we know how to love each other? Do we feel loved? Do we take care of each other, meeting the other's needs freely and without complaint? Are we able to be close without holding anything back? Are we growing in intimacy day by day?

It's worth noting that men and women tend to use different standards in answering these questions, and they judge their relationship in highly subjective ways. However you measure it, the dimension of love and intimacy cannot be regarded as an optional feature. Look into the heart of any happy marriage and you will find exchanges of love and nurturing in an emotional climate where intimacy grows and thrives.

Second, we can measure success in our marriage by evaluating how well we get along as partners. Call this the *contentment factor*, for our ease of mind greatly depends on whether we can function as a good team in the arena of life. Is our partnership reasonably efficient and generally free from bickering, recriminations, and attempts to control one another? Do we agree on most things or adapt and compromise when necessary? Do we complement one another, each contributing to the success of our joint efforts? Can we depend on one another? Are we satisfied with the way our lives are going, (our finances, our social life, our careers, our home setting, our schedules, our in-law relationships, our family planning and rearing of children, and the like)? Do we derive real pleasure from sharing our lives, and working toward long-range goals together? A satisfying partnership is the second dimension of a successful marriage.

The third measure of success reaches far beyond the emotional pleasures of being loved or the practical contentment of sharing life with a good partner.

This dimension connects us on the deepest level and provides us with our *purpose* for living as well as our most valuable *resources* for living. Let's call it *the strength and stability factor.* We all have a built-in need for an active belief system which provides joy, purpose, unity, coherence, and a strong sense of meaning for our lives. Do we share this in our marriage? Are we bonded together by something greater than ourselves? Does our relationship have spiritual dimensions and powerful spiritual resources because we worship and serve God together? A marriage without this shared *reason for being* will, at best, be painfully incomplete.

When couples say "I do," they usually begin with the conviction that marriage will make things easier for them as well as happier because the sorrows as well as the joys of life can be shared. "Double the joy and half the sorrow"—that's the arithmetic of our expectations. The danger is that in such cases we expect our partner to do for us what only God can do. Without spiritual resources, we may disappoint one another badly. Our relationship may become "double the sorrow and half the joy," instead. But when God is at the center of our marriage, He can work in both of us, relieving our burdens of grief and anxiety so that we are free from the weight of them, filling the empty spots, refreshing our spirits, helping us to help each other, and blessing us with an ever-deepening oneness in Him.

To review, here are the dimensions of a successful marriage which can safely be followed in mapping out your own destination. Within the scope of this broad outline, begin to fill in the specific details of the marriage you and your partner desire.

The Three Dimensions of a Successful Marriage
(1) An emotional climate of love and nurturing, with a growing intimacy;
(2) The creation of a smooth-working, satisfying partnership;
(3) A shared faith which provides meaning, direction, and unified purpose for your marriage, and spiritual resources for all your needs.

Always remember how important it is to keep the picture of the marriage you want fresh in your mind. As desirable goals fill your thoughts, you will find yourself making positive choices with more ease, and these choices will steer you steadily in the right direction. Besides that, as your marriage gets better and better, think how much both of you will enjoy the journey.

Establish the picture of the marriage you desire, fill in the details, and keep it fresh in your mind to guide your choices. This is the second step in harnessing your secret choices to build a satisfying marriage.

SUGGESTIONS

1. Set up a large looseleaf notebook labeled *Choices*, which you can use for your own journey as you build the marriage of your hopes and dreams. Put sections in the notebook corresponding to the outline on the Contents page. (Note that Parts II, III, and IV correspond to the three dimensions of the successful marriage.) Make a practice of inserting helpful clippings, notes, and journal entries in the places where they are applicable. Keep your input positive! This will become your private resource book and a source of encouragement.

2. Write a journal entry answering the question in Part 1: *Where Are Your Choices Taking You in Your Marriage?* Base it on your past performance. Then record changes you expect to see as you learn to make choices that lead to success. Again, be patient!

3. If you own our new-marriage handbook, *The First Years of Forever*, or if you can borrow a copy, study the handbooks for husband and wife (chapters 8 and 9). These chapters explain the seven basic ways to love your wife and the seven basic ways to respond to your husband. Make notes on these ways of loving and responding in marriage and enter them in the appropriate sections of your notebook.

2
Who's at the Controls?

Have we learned how to take charge of our choices?

The last of human freedoms is the ability to choose one's attitude.
Viktor Frankl, a concentration camp survivor

EVERY SUCCESSFUL MARRIAGE depends on the ability of both partners to make good choices. Analyze even one enjoyable day spent together as husband and wife, and you'll see that it happened because both of you chose to respond rightly. Was it a pleasant surprise? Or do you consistently choose the best for your marriage? In other words, *have you learned how to take charge of your choices?*

To answer this question, it's necessary to focus on *the real you*, the part of you that weighs thoughts, feelings, and beliefs, and then chooses attitudes and actions.

Granted, this can be perplexing. Human behavior seems to be a hopeless tangle of complexities and contradictions, with an endless line of "experts" on the subject, each putting forth his or her own theories. Which one is right? Who knows? Sometimes we wonder if we will ever understand ourselves!

Fortunately, there is one authoritative book that understands us: the Bible. Recognizing that the Author of this book is the one who created us and knows us thoroughly, we can approach its contents with a thirst to know ourselves and the confidence that what we discover will be the truth and totally dependable.

When we begin in Genesis, we find that God created us with an amazing capacity to make our own choices. Amazing, because *willpower* is power indeed. This independent self called the will sits in the place of personal authority and responsibility, with power to decide and control even the most essential matters of faith and life.

If we were designing a world of new beings, would we allow that? Wouldn't we install built-in safeguards to make sure, at the very least, that our creatures recognized our superior position as Maker.

God, instead, made a world of men and women in His own image with the freedom *to choose* whether or not to love Him. He created us in His image as rational, morally aware, and morally responsible human beings—a fact with great relevance for us personally. It means that we must make our own choices, and live with the consequences.

This is a fact we tend to ignore or overlook. Too often, we forget that every choice has its consequences, or we try to escape those consequences by saying, "Don't blame me. It's not my fault. It's just the way I am." Or, "Someone else is to blame!"

This tendency to try to escape the consequences of our actions had its beginning at the time Adam and Eve made their disastrous choice to reject God's will in favor of their own. In that terrible moment when they had to explain their behavior and face the consequences of what they had done, the man, in effect, complained: "It was the woman's fault. She gave me the fruit to eat. And it was your fault, Lord, because you gave me the woman to be with me, and look what happened." The woman could only blame the serpent: Lord, I was tricked! I was deceived by that serpent."

God responded by telling each of them, beginning with the serpent, the consequences of their actions: "Because you have done this . . . I will. . . ." The aftershocks of their choice go on and on, and we all suffer from the results. Our will has been so adversely affected that we not only find it hard to *do right*, but we find it hard *to choose to do right*, even when it is to our clear advantage.

Because our first ancestors rebelled at God's gracious design for their lives, that same rebellion has now spilled over into our own minds. The control center within us, which was meant to be in charge, is under attack on all fronts. We're besieged by our emotions, threatened by our fears, tricked by our lusts, lied to by the enemy of our souls (who promises that sin will bring us peace and pleasures), and sabotaged by outside influences which can do us no good.

This is why the question, "Who's at the controls?" is such an important one for the person who wants to build a good marriage. Such a marriage won't happen automatically, and it can't, because our control center cannot be depended upon to make good choices without some essential adjustments.

These adjustments become possible only when we are ready to accept responsibility for our choices, large or small, and the consequences which inevitably follow. Yes, God has given us the freedom we crave. Because of the way He created us, we are still free, even in the most oppressive conditions of a concentration camp or a Vietnam POW camp, to choose our beliefs and attitudes. But freedom costs because it makes us responsible.

> Remember that *every choice has its consequences*, and learn to "count the cost" before you act or react. This is the third step in your journey toward the marriage you desire.

Now, let's consider how the process of taking charge of our choices works. On the surface this appears to be a major attempt at self-improvement in which we stop taking the line of least resistance and start managing our life more constructively. Taking charge in this way sounds brisk, decisive, and invigorating, like an October football game. The crunch comes when we find that our self-efforts do not have the clout we expected.

In fact, almost from the moment we try to exert control and make improvements in the ways we think and behave, we find ourselves in a civil war, and the hopes of winning seem slim indeed. On the battlefield of our mind we face a dizzying array of enemies and obstacles. We have already mentioned a few: fears, lusts, and selfish desires, emotions threatening to take control, temptations, deceptions, distractions, doubts, confusions, pressures from outside, and a disturbing inability to operate decisively, no matter how hard we try. Naturally, in most cases, the white flag goes up.

If we can't control our choices, what's the point of writing a book about them? This is a fair question. The Scriptures supply the best of answers: God, who gave us our human will with its power to choose, has not left us helpless before our enemies, whether within or without. The Bible assures us of this in many ways. Here it is put most plainly:

> He Himself has said, "I will never desert you, nor will I ever forsake you" (Heb. 13:5b NASB).

The word "forsake" is a compound of three Greek words meaning, *leave behind in*. He is not going to leave us behind in this battle of our mind and will. As we will see, He has a solution! Another translation of the same verse says,

> I will in no wise desert you or leave you alone on the field of conquest or in a position of suffering. I will in no wise let go, loose hold my sustaining grasp (Westcott).

God has committed Himself to helping us. Because He has the lovingkindness to do this for us and the authority and power to accomplish it, we *can* take charge of our choices through His energizing and by His guidance. "Thanks be to God, who gives us the victory through our Lord Jesus Christ" (1 Cor. 15:57 NASB)!

The New Testament gives the wonderful details of this victory which can exert such a life-changing effect on us. It becomes the absorbing study of a lifetime for those who trust in Him and learn to experience His victory in various areas of their life. In this book we want to concentrate on one area, the choice-making process. Because of God's provision, we can make good choices, stick with them, and live them out in our marriage—not by self-effort, but by linking our will-power (our willingness to behave responsibly) with God's enabling, indwelling power. All the other counsel we have for you depends on this point first.

> Understand this basic principle: *Your willingness to behave responsibly needs to be coupled with God's power.* This is the fourth step in your quest for a fulfilling marriage.

Because all of God's provisions, including His infusion of power and ability, come to us through *salvation*, we must begin there. This is the essential adjustment which makes it possible for us to function as we were originally designed to. If you have not put your trust in Jesus Christ (and this is a very personal matter which only you can determine), please turn at once to chapter 14 for information on how to "choose life," that first and most important decision which will set you free to choose all other good things, including the best possible marriage.

As soon as your personal relationship with the Lord Jesus Christ is established, you can begin to discover the meaning of this important counsel for your life:

Work out your own salvation with fear and trembling. For it is God which worketh in you both to will and to do of *his* good pleasure (Phil. 2:12b, 13 KJV).

We do not work *for* our salvation: that is a free gift. Instead, we "work out" the salvation He has put within us, expressing what God has given us by His Spirit; putting it into practice in our daily living through our actions, words, and attitudes. We are counseled to do this with a sense of awe and responsibility. And as we live responsibly, we have the assurance that God is continually at work within us, giving us both the will to choose and the power to achieve those things which God knows are best for us.

How do we learn what is God's best for us? By consistently referring to the Bible as our guidebook for daily living. As we do this, God is able to direct us and change us by renewing our mind and replacing old, harmful ways of thinking with a fresh, biblical viewpoint which will bless us as individuals and benefit our marriage beyond description.

> Do not conform any longer to the pattern of this world, but be transformed by the renewing of your mind. Then you will be able to test and approve what God's will is—his good, pleasing and perfect will (Rom. 12:2).

In other words, don't allow the world around you to press you into its mold, because God has something much better for you. He wants to transform you! (The Greek verb for transform is the word from which we get our English word *metamorphosis*.)

He's talking about a total change from the inside out, and it is an ongoing process. "Keep on being transformed . . ." the Greek New Testament says.

The key to this change is always our mind, the control center of our thoughts, feelings, actions, attitudes, and beliefs. God, through His indwelling Spirit, can and will make it new again, as we keep the truth of His Word flowing through our mind while maintaining the vital connections of prayer and Christian fellowship. If we allow Him to do so (for we always have the power of choice), He quietly changes our thinking and attitudes, and we discover by experience that His will for us is always good and wonderful—the best thing and the safest thing that could happen to us. As we grow in this confidence, we begin to choose and desire His will above everything else, and in the end we find His promise true:

> Delight thyself also in the LORD; and he shall give thee the desires of thine heart. Commit thy way unto the LORD; trust also in him, and he shall bring *it* to pass (Ps. 37:4–5 KJV).

When we discover that God's will for us is better than our own choices, we also learn to trust Him concerning the caution signs and the red flag warnings He gives us in the Scriptures. His way is to tell us the consequences of certain actions and attitudes—the unpleasant cause and effect of our self-willed choices. We learn to believe Him, for as we grow to know Him, we learn that He is Love, and that His intentions toward us are always *good*.

His concise counsel for us in making and implementing choices can be found in the fourth chapter of Ephesians, verses 22–24:

(1) . . . put off your old self, which is being corrupted by its deceitful desires;
(2) . . . be made new in the attitude of your minds;
(3) . . . put on the new self, created to be like God in true righteousness and holiness.

The choice to do this must be ours; the power, His. "I can do everything through him who gives me strength" (Phil. 4:13). Who's at the controls? Note that the *I* remains, but not the old self-will. You cannot operate the controls effectively by your own power; neither can the Lord do it without your cooperation in choosing to listen to Him and follow His instructions. A teacher of the Word has observed that the secret of power is to discover and to learn from the New Testament *what is possible for us in Christ.* God has never counseled us to do something impossible! Instead, the responsibility we emphasized earlier in this chapter can become what Jay E. Adams has called *respond ability*: the God-given ability to respond as God says man and woman should respond to every situation of life.

The remainder of this book will present you with specific choices that can determine the quality of your marriage, along with other options and their predictable consequences. We have found that the most helpful marriage counseling always emphasizes God's pattern for relating as husband and wife, and we pray that this will become the standard which guides your major decisions and every secret choice.

Keep your mind renewed and filled with the Word of God so that you can learn how to respond in every situation of marriage according to His good counsel. This is the fifth step in building a love-filled, lasting marriage.

SUGGESTIONS

1. In your notebook record some ways you chose to react to your partner this week and note the immediate results of that choice. Then describe a more positive choice you could have made and the probable results. How does this fit in with your picture of a successful marriage?

2. Describe some difficulties you have had in choosing to do right, or following through on your choices. Then write about a special time when you know you experienced God's help and guidance in making a good choice and sticking with it. If you want His power and direction in your marriage, express your longing in the form of a poem, a prayer, or a letter to the Lord.

3. Take the outline in Ephesians 4:22–24, and set some personal goals concerning what you want to "put off," what you want to "put on," and new attitudes you would like God to renew in your mind. See if you can find Bible verses which give guidance related to the subject matter of the goals you have set. Meditate on them "day and night," and see what happens!

4. Read Psalm 1 every day until it becomes a part of you.

3

Consulting the Marriage Map

Are we patterning our marriage after the Creator's original design for our happiness?

Through skillful and godly Wisdom is a house (a life, a home, a family) built, and by understanding it is established (on a sound and good foundation). And by its knowledge shall the chambers (of its every area) be filled with all precious and plesant riches (Prov. 24:3–4 AMPLIFIED).

IN THE FIRST chapter, we encouraged you to develop a strong mental picture of the marriage you desire so that you could harness your secret choices to move in that direction. Now, if you have your "destination" in view, it's time to consult the marriage map—the Bible, which reveals God's perfect design for marriage.

In its pages, from Genesis to Revelation, you can find what you need to build a marriage which will bring lasting happiness because it follows God's original design. This design is conveyed to us in the form of basic principles, specific instructions, clear guidelines, vivid examples, sobering warnings, and wise counsel. Nothing can take the place of God's wisdom in showing you how to build your house—your life, your home, and your family—to last a lifetime, and how to fill every room of your life together with "all precious and pleasant riches."

Although we can't communicate all of this in a single chapter, we can make a survey of God's wisdom on marriage which will show you what God considers most important in your relationship. After all, He created marriage for our blessing, and He knows best how to make it work!

We asked you to define a successful marriage from your perspective. Now, we need to go to the Scriptures to answer the same question from the divine viewpoint. Keep in mind that Paul, in the book of Ephesians, called marriage "a great mystery." *Mystery* in the New Testament usually refers to something we could never solve by ourselves—a secret which God has now revealed to us. Let's explore this mystery together in the light of God's revelations about marriage.

THE MEANING OF MARRIAGE

To look into the meaning of marriage, we need to return to the first wedding (a garden wedding!) where it all began.

> And the LORD God caused a deep sleep to fall upon Adam, and he slept: and he took one of his ribs, and closed up the flesh instead thereof;
>
> And the rib, which the LORD God had taken from man, made he a woman, and brought her unto the man.
>
> And Adam said, This *is* now bone of my bones, and flesh of my flesh: she shall be called Woman, because she was taken out of Man.
>
> Therefore shall a man leave his father and his mother, and shall cleave unto his wife: and they shall be one flesh.
>
> And they were both naked, the man and his wife, and were not ashamed (Gen. 2:21–25 KJV).

This was the first marriage ceremony: *Made he a woman, and brought her unto the man.* God made the woman to complement Adam perfectly, as an artist producing a masterpiece. That is what the original language conveys. Please note that the initiative in marriage, the plan, the design, and the creation of the two human beings for each other—together reflecting the image of God, and yet separately incomplete—began and remains under the watchful care of the Lord God. Marriage is not something devised by a blundering man, full of flaws and bugs needing to be worked out. God's way with a man and a woman in marriage is perfect and beautiful, and His plan is still in effect today.

At this first wedding, the bridegroom provided the special music. His song, *Bone of my bones and flesh of my flesh*, suggests another aspect of the mystery of marriage: the kinship we feel with our mate while still retaining our individuality.

In a sense, we, too, share Adam's experience: we survey the other creatures of the world, finding no one quite right for us, and then God brings us to the one person with whom we feel akin. Even though we may be very unlike one another, yet we know we are closer than blood relatives, as close in heart and being as though we shared bones and flesh. We know within our spirits that *we belong!* God designed this mystery of marriage to heal our loneliness.

At weddings, the music (such as Adam sang) usually provides a lovely prelude to the promises made by the couple, promises so sacred we call them wedding vows. In the perfection of the Garden, where man and woman knew only good, vows were unnecessary. Instead, God taught Adam the terms of the marriage covenant He had established for the human race. The terms have never been revised or replaced, and still provide the most concise and most effective marriage counsel ever given:

Leave all else, giving your primary and wholehearted loyalty and attention to one another;

Cleave to one another until you become inseparable, coming together in spirit so completely that you are one and the seam can no longer be found;

Become one flesh, with your oneness of heart, spirit, and shared life symbolized by and expressed through sexual union.

As we consider this three-part counsel we can see that marriage rests on two pillars which are far more than ornamental. They are *oneness* and *permanence*. God really does expect husband and wife to become *one* and to continue growing in oneness over the course of a lifetime. But the benefits of marriage can bless us only in the context of permanence. Temporary oneness would bring harm, not blessing. If we are to be one with our mate, it must be within a permanent relationship.

We need to *leave* all else, for other pulls must give up their power; we can only know oneness with one person. Even our children, dear though they are to us, must be excluded from the center of this relationship, for we are not one with our offspring; only with our mate. Leaving prepares us for oneness. Cleaving establishes the fact of permanence in our minds and reassures our hearts that we *are* loved and *shall* be loved tomorrow.

After the wedding comes the honeymoon. In the case of Adam and Eve, it was a perfect honeymoon, for in the sunlit and star-bathed delights of marriage in the Garden, both were naked and were not ashamed. No barriers existed between them: there was nothing to hide, nothing to overcome. What liberty of mind, body, and spirit they must have experienced—liberty to love and become one, without the conflicts which tear at us while we painfully learn our lessons in oneness.

Earlier in this book, we referred to the sad aftermath of the Garden wedding. You can read in the third chapter of Genesis how the man and woman failed to obey God in their ideal environment; how they fell from a state of innocence into sin and death; and how God promised redemption and expelled the couple from the Garden of Eden to live a life of moral responsibility under new and difficult conditions. The oneness of the man and woman could no longer be assumed and enjoyed without effort.

Their unity broken, Adam and Eve's relationship became separate and selfish, their love contaminated with hostility and blame. And so, today, we still cope with sin, shame, selfishness, self-centeredness, and separateness. We all have the tendency to withdraw from one another, to concentrate on our own needs and wants, to live for ourselves, and to blame those closest to us when things do not go as we desire.

As an indication of the influence of Genesis 3 on today's society, listen to this wife's words concerning her marital problems.

> "When I married Jeff, I meant it to be forever, but now I'm seriously considering a divorce. A few months ago I began having an affair with a man I met at work. He has invited me to move in with him—and I haven't decided to do that yet, but this affair has made me question whether Jeff and I can ever be happy together."

Her story is ordinary enough by today's standards, yet incredibly off the mark when compared to the Genesis marriage covenant.

Someone may ask, "Does God really expect people in today's world to live out a marriage ordinance that was given in the perfect environment of the Garden? How can His original plan still work in a world alienated by sin? Hasn't He somehow revised His marriage plan to fit prevailing conditions?"

THE QUESTION OF DIVORCE

This may be one of the most important questions you can ever ask, and it's essential to get the right answer firmly implanted in your understanding. The biblical marriage map can guide you only so far without this truth straight from the lips of the Lord Jesus Christ. In Mark 10:2–12 and in the parallel passage in Matthew 19:3–12, Jesus communicates the divine viewpoint of marriage. Listen for truth in a pure form, untarnished by the hardness of people's hearts:

> And the Pharisees came to him, and asked him, Is it lawful for a man to put away his wife? tempting him.
>
> And he answered and said unto them, What did Moses command you?
>
> And they said, Moses suffered to write a bill of divorcement, and to put her away.
>
> And Jesus answered and said unto them, For the hardness of your heart he wrote you this precept.

But from the beginning of the creation God made them male and female.

For this cause shall a man leave his father and mother, and cleave to his wife;

And they twain shall be one flesh: so then they are no more twain, but one flesh.

What therefore God hath joined together, let not man put asunder.

And in the house his disciples asked him again of the same matter.

And he saith unto them, Whosoever shall put away his wife, and marry another, committeth adultery against her.

And if a woman shall put away her husband, and be married to another, she committeth adultery (Mark 10:2–12 KJV).

If we want to know what our own attitude toward marriage and divorce should be today, we can learn from Jesus' response to the Pharisees. He ignored the bickering "religious" authorities of the day and their preoccupation with excuses for divorce; He focused on the Scriptures as the only real authority; and He went back to the original design for marriage in the Genesis account as the only relevant topic of discussion. Matthew records that Jesus first answered the Pharisees this way: "Haven't you even read Genesis 1:27 and 2:24, you people who are always boasting about your knowledge of the Scriptures?" In other words, "Why don't you go to the original teaching on marriage to find your answers?"

Jesus recognized these two Genesis passages as the divine ordinance for marriage which remains very much in effect in a sin-marred world. He made it clear that Moses' concession for the hardness of men's hearts was not the issue for anyone who really wanted to understand God's plan and purpose for marriage. "From the beginning it was not so," He said in Matthew 19:8, directing us back to the beginning where we still find our instructions for marriage and the standards we need to follow.

He did add one new statement to the Genesis ordinance: "*What therefore God hath joined together, let not man put asunder*" (Matt. 19:6; Mark 10:9). When a man and woman marry, God participates in yoking them together, changing what has been two into one. From the divine viewpoint, marriage is a union which all the courts of the land cannot dissolve.

What does this mean to you today? It means that even admitting the possibility of divorce can adversely affect the development of your love relationship. Retaining the idea of divorce in your emotional vocabulary can actually sabotage your attempts to grow in love and oneness, and keeping divorce as an escape clause suggests a flaw in your commitment which may become fatal at some point.

We realize that some of you have remarried after an unhappy first marriage and subsequent divorce.

Please keep this truth in view: God can take us where we are at any given moment and work out His plan for our life. If there are mistakes in your past concerning marriage and divorce, ask God's forgiveness and receive it, knowing that you have been set free from guilt. He always deals with us in the now, and you have every opportunity to go forward in a new way, conforming your new marriage to His original design.

THE BENEFITS OF MARRIAGE

But what are the purposes behind this design? What benefits did God have in mind for us? Let's consider the scriptural evidence. The blessings of marriage seem to fall into three main categories which we have listed below along with Scriptures which can help you understand the way God sees your marriage relationship, and the potential it holds for your happiness. Note that these categories correspond to the three dimensions of marriage which we described in chapter 1: the emotional climate of love, nurturing, and intimacy; the satisfying partnership; and the spiritual dimensions and purposes of marriage.

1. Marriage was designed to provide the security of a "house of love" for the enjoyment of romantic fulfillment, intimate friendship, and sexual delights in the permanent setting of a steadfast covenant relationship.

> My lover spoke and said to me, "Arise, my darling, my beautiful one, and come with me." . . . He has taken me to the banquet hall, and his banner over me was love. . . . Place me like a seal over your heart . . . for love is as strong as death. . . . It burns like blazing fire, like a mighty flame. Many waters cannot quench love; rivers cannot wash it away. . . . (Song 2:10, 4; 8:6, 7).

> May you rejoice in the wife of your youth. A loving doe, a graceful deer—may her breasts satisfy you always, may you ever be captivated by her love. Why be captivated, my son, by an adulteress? Why embrace the bosom of another man's wife? (Prov. 5:18-20).

> You flood the LORD's altar with tears. You weep and wail because she no longer pays attention to your offerings or accepts them with pleasure from your hands. You ask, "Why?" It is because the LORD is acting as the witness between you and the wife of your youth, because you have broken faith with her, though she is your partner, the wife of your marriage covenant. . . . So guard yourself in your spirit, and do not break faith with the wife of your youth. "I hate divorce," says the LORD God of Israel (Mal. 2:13–16).

2. Marriage was designed to heal man and woman's aloneness, to provide a suitable helper, friend, and ally to sustain and support the other in the challenges of daily living, and to encourage one another in following and serving the Lord.

The LORD God said, "It is not good for the man to be alone. I will make a helper suitable for him" (Gen. 2:18).

A wife of noble character who can find? She is worth far more than rubies. Her husband has full confidence in her and lacks nothing of value. She brings him good, not harm, all the days of her life (Prov. 31:10–11).

Two are better than one, because they have a good return for their work: If one falls down, his friend can help him up. But pity the man who falls and has no one to help him up! Also, if two lie down together, they will keep warm. But how can one keep warm alone? Though one may be overpowered, two can defend themselves. A cord of three strands is not quickly broken (Eccl. 4:9–12).

3. Marriage was designed to picture the relationship of Jesus Christ and His church—the oneness, sacrificial love, and submission—and to give an example of heaven on earth to a watching world. It is also the place in which to produce and rear godly families in this setting of love, and to train them to serve the Lord.

So God created man in his own image, in the image of God he created him; male and female he created them. God blessed them and said to them, "Be fruitful and increase in number; fill the earth and subdue it" (Gen. 1:27–28).

"Choose for yourselves this day whom you will serve. . . . But as for me and my household, we will serve the LORD" (Josh. 24:15).

Love the LORD your God with all your heart and with all your soul and with all your strength. These commandments that I give you today are to be upon your hearts. Impress them on your children. Talk about them when you sit at home and when you walk along the road. . . . Write them on the doorframes of your houses and on your gates (Deut. 6:5–7, 9).

Has not the LORD made them one? In flesh and spirit they are his. And why one? Because he was seeking godly offspring. So guard yourself in your spirit, and do not break faith with the wife of your youth (Mal. 2:15).

Submit to one another out of reverence for Christ. Wives, submit to your husbands as to the LORD. For the husband is the head of the wife as Christ is the head of the church, his body, of which he is the Savior. Now as the church submits to Christ, so also wives should submit to their husbands in everything.

Husbands, love your wives, just as Christ loved the church and gave himself up for her to make her holy, cleansing her by the washing with water through the word, and to present her to himself as a radiant church, without stain or wrinkle or any other blemish, but holy and blameless. In this same way, husbands ought to love their wives as their own bodies. He who loves his wife loves himself. After all, no one ever hated his own body, but he feeds and cares for it, just as Christ does the church. . . . "For this reason a man will leave his father and mother and be united to his wife, and the two will become one flesh." This is a profound mystery—but I am talking about Christ and the church. However, each one of you also must love his wife as he loves himself, and the wife must respect her husband.

Children, obey your parents in the LORD, for this is right. "Honor your father and mother"—which is the first commandment with a promise—"that it may go well with you and that you may enjoy long life on the earth."

Fathers, do not exasperate your children; instead, bring them up in the training and instruction of the Lord (Eph. 5:21–33; 6:1–4).

CHECKLIST FOR A GOOD MARRIAGE

Here's a look at the marriage map of the Bible from another perspective. Use these nine scriptural characteristics of a good marriage as a checklist and a basis for making your choices:

1. Both partners have left their parents to establish their own independent family unit. Neither is unduly influenced by their families and neither is emotionally bound to them.

2. Partners are cleaving to one another so that nothing on earth is as important to them as their mate and their marriage.

3. They are growing in physical, emotional, and spiritual oneness which includes Bible reading, prayer, and church participation.

4. They are enjoying the delights of romantic love.

5. They have a strong view of the permanence of marriage and a steadfast faithfulness to one another.

6. They help each other in all the details of living.

7. They meet each other's needs and forgive each other freely so that they no longer feel alone.

8. They relate in mutual love and submission, learning how to love one another by studying the relationship of Jesus Christ and His church.

9. Their marriage becomes a house of love so that it offers the right setting to rear and nurture children; to minister to others in need of love and encouragement; and to portray to the world something of the love which Jesus Christ has for His people to become "a showcase for heaven."

Set against these wonderful benefits of marriage are the misunderstandings and false conceptions of marriage which influence many minds today. Check the chart we have prepared to contrast the two views of marriage, and be alert to these subtle lies which can so easily shape our thinking before we realize what has happened to us.

MARRIAGE: TWO VIEWS

Human Perspective	Divine Perspective
Self-Centered	"Two Become One"
"I" Mentality	"We" Mentality
Temporary	Permanent
Conditional Partnership	Indissoluble Union
"An Experience"	A Lifetime Covenant
"As long as I like it"	Commitment—"No matter what"
" I'll try . . ."	"I Do!"
"Unless I fall in love with someone else"	"Till Death Do Us Part"
No direction or meaning	Purposeful, following God's Design
"Divorce is always an option."	"What God has joined let not man put asunder."
"I have to decide what's best for me."	"Love means doing the best for my partner."
Separateness	Togetherness

One writer has said that marriage, essentially, involves a lifelong commitment to do a good, thorough job of loving one person.

We agree. But this requires work! The mingling of identities, the maintaining of a binding covenant, and the nurturing of a love affair through all the wild clashes of self-assertion which a couple have to survive to find their way into the peaceful place of genuine oneness takes consistent effort, time, and patience. It will help immensely if we hold ever fresh in our minds the picture of marriage as God has designed it, and what that can mean in our life.

Study the Creator's original design for marriage, and live by His design. This is the sixth step in building a good marriage.

SUGGESTIONS

1. Write three ways you need to change your behavior as a husband or wife based on biblical information in this chapter. Be very specific. Exercise your choices as described in chapter 2.

2. Analyze whether there are any differences between the marriage you desire and God's original marriage design. Comment on this in your notebook.

3. Read the Scriptures in this chapter aloud with your marriage partner as though this were a personal letter to you from the Lord. For daily devotions, divide the Scriptures up into a week's portions. Record thoughts shared by your partner and ideas for fulfilling the commands and examples.

Part 2
What Kind of
Emotional Climate
Are You Creating?

4
Distance or Intimacy

Are we moving closer or growing apart?

"This . . . my lover, this my friend" (Song of Songs 5:16).

As YOU BEGIN Part 2, we have another crucial question for you: *What kind of emotional climate are you creating with your secret choices?* Is it an environment of love, nurturing, and intimacy? Or, distance, . . . neglect, . . . indifference?

Your first reaction may be to opt for a gray area somewhere in between. Couples sometimes answer, "Well, we're not doing all that great, but we're not doing so bad either. On a scale of one to ten, give us a five."

The truth is, you are continuing to move in one direction or the other, and at some point, however subtle the change, the scales will clearly shift to show what has been happening all along. Although you may not realize it, you are growing closer or drifting farther apart every day of your marriage. Even the smallest choice—whether to curl up next to your mate on the couch or plump down in a chair across the room—is taking you toward one of two opposing poles: emotional distance or intimacy.

Because of the demands of daily living, we can go for periods of time without realizing what is happening in our relationship. Sometimes we're not even aware of our secret choices because we assume ourselves to be something that we're not. We may pride ourselves on being the kind of marriage partner with a capacity for intimate closeness, but our actions communicate something quite different to our mate. We may describe ourselves as loving, nurturing individuals, but this has little effect on how we behave. Our will—which decides what will happen—has chosen otherwise, and our conduct reflects our true choice.

This is why we emphasize the adjective *secret* when speaking of the choices that determine the success of our marriage. These choices, which take us in one direction or the other, happen on the inside first. Afterward, because of subtle clues communicated through our behavior and attitudes, our husband or wife can sense that change is taking place on the inside, "where the meanings are." Still later, the results (positive or negative) can be seen by all.

When changes are perceived as negative, the question is, Have we changed, or is our partner beginning to know us as we really are? After all, dating affords the opportunity to put on our nicest face, our most agreeable personality, and our best behavior. When we live together twenty-four hours a day in the bonding of marriage, such well-meaning pretense is no longer possible. Under the glare of reality, unrealistic expectations can cause many a problem and forge major obstacles to the enjoyment of intimacy. Because you can only build a rewarding, intimate relationship with a person who is well-known to you and lovingly understood and accepted, it's important to learn to relate to the one you actually married, not to the idealized person you dreamed of marrying.

In real life your "prince" may refuse to hold hands with you at the park. Your "princess" may criticize you and take your boss's side. Your lover may roll over and go to sleep instead of cuddling you in his arms for a good-night chat. Your sweetheart may watch TV until 2:00 A.M. when you want her to go to bed with you at 10:00. It may not be as bad as that, or it might be worse. Any genuine relationship which offers the " magic" of love also contains the seed of disappointments, flaws, and failures.

Few of us are aware of that reality at the beginning of marriage, for our expectations run high. When we meet the person who seems to fill in the lonely spaces in our heart, and the feeling is shared, we say it's too good to be true, but we believe that it is true anyhow! We desperately want to believe we have found the ideal love relationship which will fulfill all of our dreams. After marriage, when discontent slips in, when we discover that our partner is less than "a perfect fit" as a mate, and that our relationship is less than the perfection we counted on, this may disappoint us and disturb us, but it can also mark the beginning of our true love affair. Wisdom tells us that although life will not be a perpetual honeymoon, something much better, much richer, can be ours *if* we're willing to direct our secret choices toward building love-filled intimacy with the *real* person we married.

This means, of course, that we have to be real, too, and unafraid of revealing ourselves in an intimate relationship.

Nothing is more real than intimacy, and to build it in our marriage, we need to begin by converting our false assumptions about ourselves and our unrealistic expectations of our mate and marriage into reality-based thinking.

> See yourself and your partner as you really are, and love, accept, and delight in your partner on the basis of reality. This is the seventh step in establishing the kind of marriage that every couple needs.

Our goal in this chapter is to help you use your secret choices to develop that incomparable closeness of an intimate marriage in which you share the restful assurance that you are fully known and deeply loved. You may have had intimate friends who enriched your life, but this should surpass any other relationship, for intimacy in marriage is as close as two human beings can get. As the quote from the *Song of Songs* at the beginning of this chapter suggests, an intimate marriage involves two roles in combination: lover and best friend. Intimacy enjoyed in the security of marriage offers us the ultimate pleasures of life and, at the same time, heals our innermost loneliness as nothing else can.

To make the best choices for intimacy, it's necessary to grasp the key position of intimacy in a good marriage. This example from the world of architecture offers some interesting parallels. Picture a stone arch representing your love relationship. The stone looks strong enough, but in order to maintain its structure, this arch needs a keystone. Although the keystone is only one of a number of associated parts, (just as intimacy is only one aspect of your relationship), it is the key element that holds the others together. It does this by causing the downward pressure on the arch to be evenly exerted throughout the whole structure.

The same thing happens when two people share everything in their lives through the experience of intimacy. All the pressures of life, bearing down on the marriage and on either or both of the partners, become evenly shared and their impact lessened by the presence of intimacy. Medical doctors have found that an intimate relationship between a husband and wife can determine how well that couple masters the crises of life. A high degree of intimacy can also provide shelter and relief from the ordinary tensions of life. Life becomes richer and more colorful when shared with an intimate partner; it offers love and laughter, pleasure and stability. In fact, we believe the secret of staying in love for any married couple can be summed up in this one potent word: *intimacy*.

Recall the picture of the arch: Its keystone fits into the top of the arch in the central position, strengthening the entire structure; at the same time it provides an ornamental touch. The keystone is seen by all, it's decorative, and it's essential! When thinking of the opportunities to build intimacy in your relationship, remember the lesson of the keystone.

Intimacy in marriage can be defined this way: **The intimate relationship of husband and wife is a deeply satisfying closeness of mind, heart, body, and spirit which is shared and experienced by two equals who relate as lovers and best friends in the permanent context of marriage.**

But keep in mind that marriage never guarantees the delights of intimacy. If you read the current magazines, you know that couples seem to have great difficulty achieving this intimacy. Yet they all expect it, and, without it, marriages often disintegrate. Even in stable marriages, couples sometimes admit to an emptiness at the core of their relationship because one or both do not know how to become intimate lovers or are afraid to try.

You can be the happy exception. Be assured that God desires you to have the best, and in a world of shifting relationships, the two of you *can* experience an ongoing, always growing intimacy which is so different from the norm that a world of lonely people will want to know your secret.

The secret involves understanding the inmost workings of an intimate relationship and then learning to make moment-by-moment choices based on your knowledge, like a good athlete making the right moves without conscious decisions because he or she has thought it all through ahead of time.

One thing is certain: You cannot create intimacy by making an intellectual choice to do it. You can love someone with unconditional love by the choice of your will and continue to do so, whether or not the person responds. But it takes two for intimacy, and response is its "life blood." How then can you use your secret choices to obtain intimacy? By doing those things which will enhance it, promote it, and give it room to grow. By providing an emotional climate which will nurture it in your marriage and *cause* it to grow.

Here are the guidelines we have found helpful in understanding intimacy and "growing it" in marriage.

TEN GUIDELINES FOR INTIMACY IN MARRIAGE

1. Always remember that intimacy depends on the experience of shared feelings.

Intimacy is experiential in nature. It is not perceived in the mind as something that *should* be there: It is felt instinctively and viscerally. You know intuitively—your feelings tell you—whether your intimacy is flourishing or fading. You *know* if something is wrong between you, and you feel relief the moment everything is all right again. In this private, most personal relationship, the two of you become so finely tuned to one another that you can be constantly alert and responsive to one another's fluctuations of feeling and well-being at any given moment.

This means that if you want emotional intimacy in your marriage, you will have to gain a good understanding of your partner's feelings. There is no short-cut for this. You will need to study your partner lovingly and *listen* to your partner with your whole being. Both of you will need to develop your verbal skills and learn how to talk about your inner life with one another. Intimacy can only come out of your free choice to know and be fully known in return—a choice each must make individually, for intimacy is a reciprocal process.

When people marry, each comes into the relationship with different habits formed in childhood concerning closeness and space; togetherness and privacy. It takes time and patient efforts to arrive at a comfort zone which both can accept. A person who has been raised to be "detached" from loved ones will have to learn by experience the delights of intimacy in marriage. Please do not allow this to become a matter of controversy in the meantime. When only one of you desires a more intimate relationship, you will need to set up the conditions whereby your partner also feels motivated to desire it. This, too, develops out of careful, loving study of your partner, and delicate pursuit over a period of time.

2. Learn, by practice, to express your inner feelings to one another.

In shallow relationships, not much exchange of information about inner selves takes place. By contrast, in a meaningful relationship, people reveal how they feel and why, sharing their personal history of sorrows, joys, accomplishments, disappointments, changes, and growth.

A common problem with this sharing is that the husband may find it difficult to talk about his feelings. It's been a long-held notion that women are more emotional than men, but this is only part truth, if truth at all. According to recent research, men and women respond emotionally to events with equal intensity. The real difference is that women are more able to describe their responses and reactions in emotional terms. Women can usually tell you what they're feeling at the moment. A man can talk about what's happening, but may have difficulty expressing how he feels about it.

An understanding wife will make it easier for her husband to talk about his feelings by patiently drawing him out, not by putting him down. If the experience of sharing becomes disagreeable, all is lost. One wife we know got her husband to start sharing his feelings by what she called "Sunday afternoon communication breaks." The two would lie across the bed, sharing thoughts, or go for a leisurely walk together. From sharing thoughts, she would move into sharing feelings, and exhibit such a gentle interest in her husband's feelings that he began to enjoy expressing them.

She says, "I've learned three things about this. First, don't prolong the sharing times. Men seem to get bored easily with this kind of talking, so be sensitive to signs of restlessness. Second, make the experience extremely pleasant for your husband. Third, communicate your genuine interest in knowing him better. Of course, he has to be sure this is all in the strictest confidence and that you'll never use it against him later. I see that it's not easy for men to become vulnerable to their wives. It takes a lot of trust—and practice, too."

The husband who wants his wife to fall in love with him utterly and completely will win her heart by following the example of the lover in the Song of Songs:

O my dove, *that art* in the clefts of the rock, in the secret *places* of the stairs, let me see thy countenance, let me hear thy voice; for sweet is thy voice, and thy countenance *is* comely (Song 2:14 KJV).

What wife wouldn't be thrilled with a husband who wanted to get her alone *to talk with her*, to hear what she had to say to him? A wife is touched when a husband cares enough to ask, "What are you thinking right now?" because he really wants to know what she is thinking and feeling and desiring. This is characteristic of lovers, but husbands and wives sometimes forget that they ever were lovers, that this is how their marriage began! It's important for you to continue to relate as two people in love, sharing your feelings out of your desire for intimacy.

Is there a place for sharing negative feelings in an intimate relationship? Yes, all feelings need to be shared, but you must be careful to share them lovingly and tactfully.

Therapists believe that one of the greatest destructive elements in a relationship is the inability to relate what you're feeling at the moment, and to lapse into brooding silence, instead. Learning to name and share your feelings will not only promote intimacy, but will protect your marriage as well.

We encourage you to study the chapter on communication in our new-marriage handbook, *The First Years of Forever*, while you improve your skills by practice.

3. Display a mutual respect for one another, a mutual hunger to know one another better, and a growing delight in one another.

Intimacy develops between two respected equals who share their inner lives *because they want to*, because they have a vital interest in one another's thoughts and feelings. If one partner is seemingly not interested, the effect may be withdrawal on the other side too.

This wife's comment to us is typical, "I don't feel that my husband is receptive to my emotional needs. I know this is why I have withdrawn from him, and, even when I want to, I can't share with him anymore."

Husbands may not realize what they are communicating to their wives by this apparent indifference. A few years ago a women's magazine carried a short feature on "How to Discourage an Unwanted Relationship." It was, of course, directed to the woman reader, but let's change the focus. Husband, if you want to convince your wife that you are not interested in an intimate relationship with her,

1. don't listen to her.
2. don't look at her.
3. turn down her offers.
4. figure out what she wants and offer the opposite.
5. be in a hurry.
6. be busy.
7. never offer her any encouragement.
8. be supercritical.
9. bring up touchy subjects.
10. say. "I don't have time for you."

The opposite also is true. If you want to convince your partner of your interest and your desire for more intimacy in your marriage,

1. listen.
2. look.
3. respond to offers.
4. figure out what your mate wants and offer it.
5. never be in a hurry when your presence is desired.
6. don't be too busy for your mate.
7. encourage.
8. never criticize.
9. avoid touchy subjects.
10. say, " I always have time for you," and prove it!

Along with interest demonstrated on both sides, there must be a growing *delight* in knowing one another better, for that is the greatest incentive to intimacy. If you enjoy each other's company and the sharing of experiences, you are well on the way to an intimate marriage. In such a setting neither partner minds opening up to the other, because both have the confidence that if they are better known, they will be loved more.

As a husband told us, "Getting to know my wife during the first five years of our marriage has been a fascinating experience. We had gone through the University of Wyoming together, and we considered ourselves best friends when we were engaged. But I found I didn't really know her, after all. She's more beautiful than I imagined she could be . . . and I'm still learning."

4. Remember that sex is no substitute for intimacy.

This is something that women understand, but men sometimes do not. Women have both the need and desire to relate in other ways before they are ready for sex. They tend to be social before they are sexual; in contrast, men have been conditioned to be primarily sexual and to express their needs for intimacy through intercourse.

For instance, when a man comes home to his wife after a week away on business, she wants to hug him and kiss him and talk to him and feel close to him again. He wants to regain closeness by immediately having intercourse with her. She's hurt because "all he wants is my body." He's hurt because she has misunderstood his attempt to be intimate through sexual lovemaking, and he reels rejected.

Men may see no fine shade of difference between sex and intimacy, but their wives will, unless sex takes place after the exchange of mutual tenderness in an environment of emotional closeness. Impersonal sex intensifies loneliness; true sexual intimacy has great power to refresh the entire marriage.

5. Fill your marriage with tender, nonsexual physical touching.

Consider the dictionary definition of *caress*: An act of endearment, a tender or loving embrace. To touch, stroke, pat—tenderly, lovingly, or softly. This is what we are suggesting: touching as a communication of private intimacy, not as a sexual signal. Try hugs, holding hands, and all the gentle gestures which say so much. Even a smile or a wink across the room builds the enjoyment of intimacy. Eye contact provides the spark of understanding that you need. Hold hands when you pray; take time for closeness morning and night; sit so that you are touching in some way instead of choosing chairs across the room; leave each other and greet each other with a special kiss. This kind of touching becomes the tangible base of your intimate relationship.

We will have more to say about touching in the next chapter, for it is also an important part of nurturing.

6. Maintain the we perspective.

When we talk to couples who are having problems with intimacy, invariably their sentences begin with *I*. Seldom, if ever, do they use *we*. People who are only interested in themselves just do not have the capacity to build an intimate relationship, even though they may crave the benefits of intimacy.

To maintain the *we* perspective, you will have to forget what today's culture claims about the importance of self-fulfillment. We've become a nation of individuals operating on the *I must always do what's best for me* principle. This can be disastrous to an intimate relationship, which requires both partners to be open and vulnerable to one another. As one wife said, "Don't talk to me about opening up to my husband. I can't trust myself to him. He only looks out for himself, and I'm on my own." Intimacy in marriage always depends upon the knowledge that each of you will look out for the other, and in that knowledge you can feel secure.

A word of warning: Newlyweds find it easy to use the word "we" at first. But listen to yourself in a year or two. If "I" begins cropping up more and more in the words you speak—as well as in your thoughts—it indicates that a sense of distance and loss of intimacy has already occurred, and you will need to take quick action to restore it.

7. Communicate approval and acceptance of one another.

Everyone fears disapproval, especially from the one we love most. This fear is probably the greatest hindrance to intimacy in an otherwise good marriage. As a husband explained, "It isn't that my wife rejects me. She's really very loving. But she's always pointing out to me—in a nice way, of course—what I did wrong or what I should have done instead. I get so tired of the feeling that she's disapproving of me. I know I don't quite measure up, and I can't enjoy being close to her anymore."

Granted, you will have differences of opinion and even strong clashes as you learn to resolve conflicts in your new life together. But you need to communicate an approval and acceptance of one another that runs far deeper than these surface matters. When you disagree on an issue, do it gently in a respectful way. Always discuss in the context of love for your partner, which is more important than the issue at hand.

Also remember that the major impact of communication comes from body language, facial expressions, and tone of voice. You may be communicating disapproval in those modes even though your words say something else. *Of all the things you wear, your expression is the most important.*

8. Recognize and overcome fear of intimacy by building trust in actions, words, and attitudes.

Although people need and even long for intimacy, they sometimes react to it with fear. Or withdraw if it becomes a possibility. Why? Because intimacy represents a mutual need for closeness, and people are often afraid to *need* someone else. In the past they may have been let down and disappointed by those they depended on (sometimes parents), and they do not want to risk it again. Or they are afraid of revealing their true self to their lover (a necessity in an intimate relationship), afraid that if the lover knew what was "behind the mask" they would be abandoned.

Other related fears include fear of criticism, fear of rejection, and fear of being used. All these fears can be put under one umbrella labeled: *I am afraid of being hurt.*

Without trust, no real emotional intimacy is possible. To build this trust in your relationship, follow these basic principles:

a. Always be very kind to one another.

b. Never reject the other, or shut the door to touching, talking, or sharing your life with your mate.

c. Build trust through *faithfulness*. (See chapter three of our new-marriage handbook, *The First Years of Forever*.)

Here are key characteristics of the kind of intimate relationship which will overcome all future fears:

A Committed Relationship

You know that when you go to your loved one, he or she will always take you in. This is part of the *at homeness* present in an intimate marriage. (Think of Robert Frost's description of home: Home is the place where when you go there, they have to take you in.)

A Relationship Without Exploitation

You demonstrate to one another by deed as well as word: "I don't want to use you. I want to love you."

An Open Relationship

No hiding is necessary because you know you are accepted unconditionally. You can trust each other enough to become vulnerable, knowing you will not be under attack, but accepted and loved just as you are.

A Mutual Support System

You can go to your lover whenever you feel low or lonely or misunderstood. As someone has said, "When you respond to me so that I feel special, it will make up for all those who, during the day, have passed me by without seeing me." You are free to let one another know your emotional needs, and you do it because it is unfair to expect your partner to read your mind.

A Treasured Relationship

You appreciate this as one of the two most valuable treasures of life, the other being a personal relationship with God. You know you possess this intimate closeness by mutual choice and deep desire, and you both do everything possible to preserve it forever.

9. Maintain the spirit of discovery in your relationship.

When you married, each of you left your old world to form a new one together. You have entered into a new reality where two are in the process of becoming one. And the new world you longed for when you fell in love is now yours for the taking. It's up to you to explore the territory, take dominion over it, and make it what you both want it to be. Think of yourselves as pioneers who, because you are entering new territory, must explore it and establish your lives in the new world.

You will need to establish an atmosphere of permanence and safety in which both partners can experience intimacy, a new world in which you can safely express love and grow in love together. You will need your own language of love for this new reality. It's important to gain an awareness of what makes your partner *feel* loved. Both of you should share this information, being as specific as possible. Think back to a time in your past when you felt totally loved. Remember how it felt. Reexperience those feelings and try to find the key ingredient. Then you can tell your partner, (for instance) "The thing that makes me feel most loved is . . . when you touch me gently on the face, and look at me searchingly."

To know specifically what makes your partner feel loved is a major discovery, and one which many spouses never make. It's strange how many people try to love their mate the way they themselves want to be loved, disregarding the fact that their partner has a different language.

Building up this special vocabulary, this collection of private things you say and do which have great meaning for both of you, is part of establishing your new world of intimacy, your new reality. It will include secret names for each other, inside jokes, actions which privately express great tenderness or indicate physical desire, shared memories, and words which send special signals to each other.

Many couples enjoy some of this during courtship but forget it when they settle into their marriage. You not only have to *pioneer* your new world, you have to stay alert and involved to *preserve* your new world.

Here's another reason why you must *maintain* the spirit of discovery. All through life you will be changing—both of you— in your own ways according to the process which has been called "adult unfolding." You must expect this and understand that your marriage is a living, and thus changing relationship. Fundamental, unchanging truths undergird a marriage, but these principles are lived out by human beings who change and grow and encounter problems of one kind or another all along the way. To become one, and to remain one through all the changes and vicissitudes of life is a great challenge.

The surest way of remaining in a state of oneness is to grow in spiritual intimacy, establishing the life-long habit of Bible reading and prayer together in a special private time which is enjoyed daily. If you continue to move in the same direction spiritually, allowing your lives to be shaped and readjusted by biblical principles and the work of the Holy Spirit, you will be able to be flexible in your dealings with one another, and able to change together, instead of separately.

Is your new world a perfect one? Certainly not. If the time of falling in love is a Garden experience, we leave Eden when we marry, and we learn to live in a new environment (at times, a gray world) according to our vision of love. That's why it's so important to share the same vision, and to have it continually reshaped, refreshed, and even refocused by the truth of God's Word—God who is the source of all love.

10. Follow the pattern of Ephesians 4:22–24 in making your choices for intimacy.

Begin by considering what will happen if you ignore the need to create an emotional climate of intimacy in your relationship. The alternative is emotional distance, with its inevitable components of disinterest, or distrust, or even dislike and open hostility. The prefix *dis* generally denotes *separation*, *negation*, or *reversal*. If the two of you want to build a love-filled, lasting marriage, it's safe to assume that you don't want separation from one another, or negatives in your relationship, or reversals of all you have hoped for.

The choice belongs to you. You will have countless opportunities to make choices that draw you together into a wonderful intimacy, and you'll have just as many temptations to make selfish, foolish choices that would certainly pull you apart and set distance between you. This, then, is a good time to revisit Ephesians 4:22–24; it will show you how to defuse the temptations and take advantage of the opportunities.

(1) Put off and discard your old unrenewed self which is being corrupted by its deceitful desires. Note that self-centered desires deceive us and trick us into making mistakes which will harm us. When selfishness runs unchecked in a marriage, it invariably corrupts. The Greek word for *corrupt* has three graphic meanings: shrivel, wither, and spoil. If self-centered desires take control, our love relationship may shrivel up and wither away. But God gives us the ability to discard the behavior which could lead to disaster. As Phillips's translation says, "Fling off the dirty clothes of the old way of living."

(2) Be constantly renewed in the spirit of your mind, having a fresh mental and spiritual attitude. Let God keep your mind refreshed with truth and positive counsel from the Scriptures which can help you think clearly and rightly about the choices of your marriage.

(3) Put on the new nature created in God's image in true righteousness and holiness. As Phillips translates it, " Put on the clean fresh clothes of the new life which was made by God's design." This is the behavior that will bless you and bless your marriage. God says, Put it on. Choose to do it, and God will give you the power to accomplish it.

Intimacy can be yours if you desire it and choose to pursue it. Pursue it patiently, consistently, and delicately, with sensitivity. Nothing is more vulnerable to fluctuations, changes, and influences—positive or negative—than your intimate relationship. It is fueled by shared feelings, and the slightest turning away will be felt by the intimate lover-friend. If the chill of misunderstanding or the heat of annoyance threatens your closeness, forgive freely and be quick to reconcile. Test your choices by these questions: Will this produce a positive response or a negative response? Will it build our relationship or tear it down? As a result of this, will we be closer emotionally or farther apart?

Protect your intimacy as the treasure of your marriage, and enjoy!

Make a once-for-all decision to take the path to intimacy, and test all you do and say by the question, "Will this draw us closer or move us apart?" This is the eighth step in building a great marriage.

SUGGESTIONS

1. Take this "Test for Intimacy," inserting your answers in your notebook. Plan to take it weekly as a means of checking the emotional temperature of your relationship and charting changes. Any no answer should alert you to a possible problem, or to an area which you need to develop. Remember the principle of "delicate pursuit."

Test for Intimacy

(1) Do you and your partner talk about feelings?
(2) Do you usually understand what your partner is feeling? Does your partner understand you?
(3) Do each of you trust the other and feel safe from hurt?
(4) Do you touch lovingly and often?
(5) Do you and your partner usually share a good feeling of closeness that seems to make everything else "worthwhile?"
(6) Have you moved closer this week or drawn apart?

2. Study chapters 3 and 5 on "Faithfulness" and "Communication" in our new-marriage handbook, *The First Years of Forever*. Make notes from these chapters on how to build trust in your marriage and how to communicate your feelings. Record them in the intimacy section of your notebook.

3. Become an expert on the one book of the Bible devoted exclusively to love and marriage. In the Song of Songs, God presents a vivid picture of an intimate marriage which you can use as a model for your own relationship. Read and reread this book in a modern translation, recording ideas and ways to apply what you learn in your notebook.

4. Apply Ephesians 4:22–24 to the phase of your relationship which seems to need attention. These questions can guide you in determining what you want and need to do in God's power.

(1) What do you need, want, and choose to put aside?
(2) What attitudes need to be changed within you?
(3) What new behavior do you need, want, and choose to put on as your own?

5

Neglect or Nurturing

> Are we taking good care of one another or ignoring the other's needs?

"This is now bone of my bones, and flesh of my flesh" (Gen 2:23 NASB).

For no one ever hated his own flesh, but nourishes and cherishes it
> *(Eph. 5:29 NASB).*

IN THIS CHAPTER we leave the delights of intimacy and turn to the area of marital interaction called *nurturing*, which is nothing less than our responsibility to take care of one another and meet each other's needs for a lifetime.

If this sounds like a very large order, it is. Perhaps that's why people seldom write about nurturing: it requires so much from us. Intimacy is an enjoyable sharing of ourselves with one another; nurturing is giving to our partner, even though it costs us. Intimacy requires that we become *we*-centered; nurturing demands that we become *other*-centered—and that's not easy for people who are inherently *self*-centered. Nowhere in marriage does the separation between selfishness and unselfishness show up more distinctly. Nowhere is the opportunity greater to build oneness by meeting the other's needs; by giving. But equally great is the temptation to build a wall of alienation by ignoring the other's needs; by taking all we can get.

As we consider our secret choices in this area of marriage, we need to recognize that on our own we will find it very difficult to make the right choices consistently. And if we fail in this matter, or fail to try, our marriage will bear the scars.

What we cannot do on our own, God will give us the resources to accomplish. We will have good reason to hope if we keep our sights on God's plan for our relationship—His principle of nurturing in marriage; His pattern of love strengthened by loyalty; and His power to enable us to keep our marriage vows with the stubborn, steadfast lovingkindness the Bible calls *hesed*.

THE ARRANGEMENT:
WHO TAKES CARE OF WHOM AND HOW

In every marriage an arrangement evolves which determines "who takes care of whom and how." If both partners are satisfied with the arrangement, their marriage is blessed with harmony and positive reactions to the reassurance and comfort of being loved. When both partners are nurtured in the ways they desire, they feel loved, and when two people *feel* loved, they feel like *loving*. A husband and wife in this frame of mind can give freely to one another, and keep on giving with generosity of heart.

By contrast, where husband and wife fail to care for each other's physical and emotional needs, a cycle of neglect, complaints, resentments, and angry demands gains momentum. Eventually, if no change for the better occurs, chronic disagreements turn into ongoing battles, while lovers turn into enemies, or look elsewhere for the care and attention they desire.

In other words, the stakes are high. Nurturing matters very much in the delicate balance of your relationship. Newlyweds seldom give this a thought when they marry, but it can become an area of conflict rather quickly thereafter.

The fact is that we never outgrow our need for nurturing. It reaches back to our earliest experiences, before language dawned for us, when we learned to trust the person taking care of us. The beneath-the-surface memories of that time have become a part of us and have shaped our needs and expectations today. We still tend to measure how much we are loved by how well our physical and emotional needs are met. And each of us has a unique agenda of needs, charged with meanings, which we expect our marriage partner to give attention to.

For example, one husband expects his wife to remember which foods he likes and dislikes, and gets moody if she serves something on the forbidden list; another wants his clothes kept in top condition and available on demand. One wife needs a luxury gift every few months; another has a strong need for continued verbal assurances of her husband's love. For some people sexual needs take front ranking; for others it's a craving for intimate talks. One wife gets nervous in grocery stores and depends on her husband to do all the marketing; a husband feels inadequate on the telephone and counts on his wife to take care of all the household business calls. Another husband demands pampering in bed when he has the mildest cold, and when his wife has to go to the doctor, she insists on being taken, rather than driving herself. Granted, these may sound (to someone else) like luxuries rather than needs, but that is not the issue. If something represents a serious need to one partner, the other mate, if wise and loving, will be sensitive to it, and will demonstrate a caring, compassionate response.

It's of burning importance to us to feel that our partner cares enough to meet our special needs. If our needs are unmet or, even worse, completely ignored, we may not discuss them directly, but we will express our discontent, anger, and frustration in other ways. The negative words and actions which invade the marriage should be understood for what they are: expressions of protest.

The principle to remember is that everyone desires and needs some kind of nurturing. It's up to each of us to learn what our partner regards as his or her most important needs, and to determine whether we are meeting them or neglecting them. We also should take time to think about other needs our partner has, but will not admit, and how we can help meet those needs. One of the prime secrets of a happy home is finding out what matters to our partner and then *doing it*. When both partners follow this prescription and take care of one another *in way's that count,* the resulting harmony is close to "heaven on earth."

> Create an emotional climate of caring by finding out what nurtures your partner and then doing it, gladly and lovingly. This is the ninth step in building a successful marriage.

As time passes and changes occur, new responsibilities may hinder us from giving our accustomed care and attention to one another. This will place an undeniable strain on our relationship. Even desirable changes, as well as those we'd rather avoid, can produce tensions. Pregnancy, illness, a relative moving into our home, a demanding new job which takes all our attention for awhile, a return to college for advanced education, and the care of aging or ill parents head the list of factors which affect the quality and quantity of nurturing we can give one another. This, in turn, may create strong dissatisfaction with the marriage. Whenever circumstances change, we need to make the necessary adjustments in our relationship with special tact and demonstrations of our continuing love for one another.

No matter what we do to nurture one another, the way we do it is of supreme importance. In fact, if we do it the wrong way, it's not nurturing at all. The value of a willing, glad-to-be-helpful spirit and a gracious attitude in caring for one another generously and without complaint is beyond measure.

Finally, we should remember as we make daily choices that in this area of interaction, little things mean a lot!

NURTURING IN MARRIAGE:
A BIBLICAL PRINCIPLE

Is it possible to go on nurturing our partner when our own needs are being ignored? How about the times when we feel too much is being asked of us, and we're tempted to say, "Take care of yourself. Do it yourself. I'm not your mother (or father)!"

Those words sound a bit like Cain's, don't they? (The selfish displeasure, the fallen countenance, "Am I my brother's keeper?") It's true, we're not a parent (or a sibling); we're much closer than that. We are *one flesh,* and the Bible makes it as clear as sunlight that we *are* responsible for our mate. Pride, self-centeredness, and self-pity will tempt us to react with foolish choices that can harm us and destroy our marriage. In contrast, God's plan is simple and beneficial: we are to give our partner the loving attention we give to our own body. Our ability to make good choices in our marriage, even when we are tempted to do the opposite, depends upon how precise our knowledge is of God's plan for marriage, and how willing we are to trust His wisdom and apply it in our lives.

Here is the biblical principle of nurturing in marriage from Ephesians 5:28–29 in several different translations.

> So ought men to love their wives as their own bodies. He that loveth his wife loveth himself. For no man ever yet hated his own flesh; but nourisheth and cherisheth it, even as the Lord the church (KJV).

> In this same way, husbands ought to love their wives as their own bodies. He who loves his wife loves himself. After all, no one ever hated his own body, but he feeds and cares for it, just as Christ does the church (NIV).

> Men ought to give their wives the love they naturally have for their own bodies. The love a man gives his wife is the extending of his love for himself to enfold her. (Phillips).

We can learn a lot about how to nurture our partner by understanding the two key words in this passage: *nourishing* (feeding and aiding in the other's development by providing what is needed) and *cherishing* (caring for). Let's take a closer look at *cherishing,* for it offers three important guidelines. First, cherishing involves taking care of tenderly, keeping our loved one warm the way birds cover their young with feathers, and protecting our mate as a hen shields her chicks from harm. Second, cherishing involves display of affection. Cherish comes from the same root word as *caress* and speaks of providing the physical affection our partner needs. Finally, to cherish means to encourage or support.

The emotional support and reassurance partners give, and the practical ways they help each other through life are all part of the nurturing process.

The amount of nurturing we provide should be compatible with the love we have for our own self: we are to love and care for our mate as much as we love and care for our own flesh. But note that the commandment to love in this way is directed to the husband; he nurtures, and his wife responds. She has her own responsibilities in the relationship, and they are given to her (1) at the beginning of this passage where she is instructed to willingly adapt herself to her husband—by implication, preparing herself to meet his needs; and (2) at its conclusion where she is directed to hold her husband in a position of respect.

> You wives must learn to adapt yourselves to your husbands, as you submit yourselves to the Lord.... In practice what I have said amounts to this: let every one of you who is a husband love his wife as he loves himself, and let the wife reverence her husband (Eph. 5:22, 33 Phillips).

Why did the Lord arrange it this way? Some have suggested that the Lord knew husbands would have to be commanded to love and nurture their wives, while wives, designed for potential motherhood, would possess the natural ability and the inclination to nurture those they loved. Others have countered that the Lord also knew wives would have to be commanded to demonstrate respect for their husbands and to submit graciously to their leadership. For both husbands and wives, some sacrifice of natural tendencies is involved.

One thing we can be sure of: The Lord has shown us what each partner needs *most*. Women need love; men need respect. Women especially need nourishing and cherishing for their well-being; men especially need a positive response to their leadership to encourage them to carry out the position of responsibility which God has given them. Consider Ephesians 5:33 again, this time in the Amplified translation:

> However, let each man of you (without exception) love his wife as (being in a sense) his very own self; and let the wife see that she respects and reverences her husband—that she notices him, regards him, honors him, prefers him, venerates and esteems him; and that she defers to him, praises him, and loves and admires him exceedingly.

In a good marriage both partners will find pleasure in nurturing their mates physically, emotionally, and spiritually, giving each other all they need to mature and reach their God-designed potential. Because, as we pointed out earlier, this is such a large order, it's well to have a plan to follow in making the right choices consistently. We have one to suggest—a tried and proven prescription for your marriage.

THE B-E-S-T PLAN FOR NURTURING

We originally developed this plan to help couples rekindle their love for one another. Think of it as a formula to remind you of your partner's needs and the biblical way to meet them. The plan is practical—it gives you things to do; uncomplicated—you can remember it easily; and effective—it really works for any couple motivated enough to apply it in their marriage. It doesn't even require both partners to make it work. If only *one* person wants a transformed marriage, this plan for nurturing can be put into motion with positive results. When two live it out, the rewards keep on multiplying.

The B-E-S-T plan is based on three facts:
   (1) Love is the power that produces love.
   (2) Giving is love in action; giving is love made visible.
   (3) You can lovingly nurture your partner and spark an answering love by giving the B-E-S-T:

   ♥ BLESSING
   ♥ EDIFYING
   ♥ SHARING
   ♥ TOUCHING

As we describe the four parts of this plan and give you some suggestions in applying each part, remember that they need to be set into motion simultaneously, not one at a time. When you are blessing, it becomes easier to touch; when you are edifying, it becomes more enjoyable to share. The four patterns of behavior reinforce one another and quadruple the benefits.

Consistency is important too. The B-E-S-T treatment needs to become a habit, not a happy surprise with which to dazzle your partner now and then. Trust comes from steady, unchanging behavior, and one mistake can tear down what you have spent many weeks building.

BLESSING

Blessing is a New Testament word *eulogia*, taken from two Greek words, *eu* which means "well" and *logos* which means "word." This will remind you of the first way to bless your partner: Speak well of him or her and always answer with good words even though you feel you have just been scolded, scorned, ignored, or insulted.

The Lord Jesus, who did not answer in turn when He was reviled, is our pattern of behavior. *In the same way,* the Scripture says, we are to live as husbands and wives. We have no justification for speaking to our partner scornfully, angrily, or manipulatively. Even when our partner behaves badly, we do not have license to retaliate. If we fail to bless, God says that we will miss out on the blessing which He has called us to receive.

Think about it. If you bless your partner by the words you speak, and the times when you choose to hold your peace, you will avoid the damage inflicted on new marriages by two angry people with uncontrolled tongues. Afterwards, when they want to reconcile, there's a lot to forgive and forget. An angry spirit and a raging tongue can never nourish and cherish. The Bible reminds us,

> A SOFT answer turneth away wrath, but grievous words stir up anger (Prov. 15:1 KJV).

> To sum up, let all be harmonious, sympathetic, brotherly, kindhearted, and humble in spirit; not returning evil for evil, or insult for insult, but giving a blessing instead; for you were called for the very purpose that you might inherit a blessing. For "let him who means to love life and see good days refrain his tongue from evil and his lips from speaking guile. And let him turn away from evil and do good; let him seek peace and pursue it. For the eyes of the LORD are upon the righteous, and His ears attend to their prayer but the face of the LORD is against those who do evil" (1 Peter 3:8–12 NASB).

The second way to bless your partner is by doing kind things for him or her—not as a duty but as a gift of blessing. Think about what your partner really likes. His socks put together in a certain way (which seems like a waste of time to you)? Her pleasure in a freshly made cup of coffee before she gets out of bed? It can be something small, but perfectly suited to your partner's private tastes and wishes. You fill in the blanks. You know best how to bless your partner with *kindness in action.*

The third way to bless is by showing thankfulness and appreciation. Whatever you appreciate in your partner, make it known verbally. Thank your partner with the same courtesy you would show to an outsider—plus a lot more warmth!

The fourth way to bless is by calling God's favor down in prayer for your partner's highest good and best welfare. Some people spend time praying for missions and ministries but forget that no one needs or deserves their prayers more than their own marriage partner.

To review, you nurture your partner and enhance your marriage by blessing with (1) good words; (2) kind actions; (3) thankful appreciation; and (4) intercessory prayer. Blessing not only prevents the spread of mutual hostility but opens the door to God's blessing upon both of you and your marriage.

TWELVE WAYS TO NURTURE YOUR PARTNER BY BLESSING

The Key to Love

1. Say something good about your partner to another person.
2. Answer with positive, loving words, no matter what.
3. Do something kind for your mate.
4. Surprise him or her with a gift or thoughtful act.
5. Do the things you know are important to your loved one.
6. Say "thank you" often and mean it. Say "I love you."
7. Be consistently courteous.
8. Thank God for your mate. Be specific.
9. Pray for his or her blessing.
10. Choose to forgive if hurt or offended.
11. Avoid proud behavior and never try to get even.
12. Study more ways to bless your partner.

EDIFYING

D. James Kennedy, in his helpful book, *Learning to Live with the People You Love,* points out that marriage can be either tremendously constructive or unimaginably destructive to the lives of those involved. What makes the difference? In essence, **building up** or **tearing down** one's partner.

He reminds us how, when we fell in love, we knew we had met the most wonderful person in the world, and we had no patience with family or friends who tried to point out a flaw in our loved one. Our way of seeing one another had positive results, because we began to become the person our beloved thought that we could be.

But what if, instead of continuing this constructive and encouraging pattern, we discovered that our mate did indeed have faults? If we concentrated on the negatives, our view of the good points would become blurred, and all that made us discontented with our partner would move into sharp focus.

If we began to communicate our changed viewpoint and our new opinion to our partner, our partner would slowly become what we believed him or her to be. *What you say is usually what you get!*

To prevent this destructive cycle of behavior, learn to nurture each other with the gift of *edifying.* This biblical term, often used in the New Testament, refers to the building up of individuals. When you edify your partner, you build her up in every aspect of her personality. You cheer him on in every area of life and increase his sense of self-worth so that his capacity to love and give will be increased too. To edify is to personally encourage. Because edifying builds up and never tears down, you give your partner freedom to grow and develop as a person without fear of failure or hurtful criticism.

Edifying begins in the life of the mind, where Philippians 4:8 is applied: "If there is any excellence and if anything worthy of praise, let your mind dwell on these things" (NASB). Practice thinking about things you find attractive in your mate—every positive quality your partner possesses. Ask yourself this before you speak: Will these words build up or tear down? And ask yourself: What can I say to my partner right now that will edify and build up, encourage, strengthen, and bring peace?

Did you know that praise is actually a source of fresh energy which can be measured in the laboratory? Dr. Henry H. Goddard pioneered these studies, using an instrument devised to measure fatigue. When an assistant would say to the tired child at the instrument, "You're doing fine, John," the boy's energy-curve would actually soar. Discouragement and fault-finding were found to have an opposite effect which could also be measured! Imagine the miracles you could achieve by nurturing your partner with genuine appreciation and encouragement.

When you nurture, you provide a place of emotional safety. The husband and wife who are afraid of hurt, rebuff, criticism, and misunderstanding from the other will find it difficult to touch and share freely. So it's important to learn how to establish trust. Let this be your guide:

(1) Love covers over a multitude of sins (1 Peter 4:8).
(2) Love builds up (1 Cor. 8:1).

Edifying not only offers a place of safety, but will quickly spark an interested response in a partner who has been showing indifference. All people love to be edified and will be drawn to the one who builds them up.

TWELVE WAYS TO NURTURE
YOUR PARTNER BY EDIFYING

The Key to Well-Being

1. Decide not to criticize your partner again. Back up your decision by action until it becomes a habit.
2. Discern where your partner can use extra encouragement and think of ways to build him or her up.
3. Spend some time thinking about every positive quality you admire in your mate.
4. Edify your partner with words of praise and appreciation. Be genuine, specific, generous.
5. Recognize his or her talents, abilities, and accomplishments.
6. Communicate your respect for the work he or she does.
7. Keep your attention focused on your partner rather than expressing admiration for others of the opposite sex.
8. Seek your partner's opinions and show that you value his or her judgment.
9. Demonstrate your confidence in him or her.
10. Respond to your mate with eye contact, smiles, and body language (turning toward him or her).
11. Treat your partner as a VIP in your home and in the presence of others.
12. Provide a peaceful, relaxed atmosphere of acceptance and unconditional love.

SHARING

The more ways you can find to be in relationship with each other, the less lonely you are, and the stronger your love will become. People are drawn into loving closeness because of what they share. In fact, *sharing* has been called the central secret of enduring love.

Sharing should touch all areas of life—your time, activities, pleasures, interests and concerns, ideas and innermost thoughts, family objectives and goals, and, most important, your spiritual values and the way you express them.

This might be a good time for you to think creatively about how to give one another the gift of sharing. Consider your life in these five areas, incorporating your ideas and conclusions into your Master Plan:

♥ Common Ground. Think of the things you share right now. How can you enjoy it more?

♥ Separate Ground. Areas of work and responsibility may be separate, but how can you bridge the gaps to share your different worlds?

♥ New Ground for One. What interests can you learn to enjoy because your partner enjoys them? How can you develop new enthusiasms to match your partner's?

♥ New Ground for Both. Can you think of some absorbing new interests to develop together?

♥ Higher Ground. Are you sharing your spiritual life through prayer, Bible reading, church participation, and special ministries? Is it satisfying to both?

At no time is your sharing more meaningful than when the values supremely important to you are held in common, supported, and expressed together. The most beautiful song of marriage is not a duet (pleasant though that is), but a three-part harmony which husband, wife, and the Lord God produce as a sweet agreement—an inner togetherness. And when you have a common faith, *prayer together* is the key to sharing the joy of it.

Billy Graham, married for more than forty years, believes also that a successful marriage is made up of three people: husband, wife, and God, and he says that he and his wife have never faced a problem which could not be solved with love, forgiveness, and prayer.

Unfortunately, it's estimated that only about one percent of husbands and wives in America have meaningful prayer together. This has been called a tragic statistic, because prayer can cement a marriage together. Many couples find that the problems in their relationship—anger, pride, hurt, misunderstandings, or resentments—seem to melt away in the presence of a holy and loving God as they pray together.

One husband told us, "When we pray for each other, about eighty percent of it is thanksgiving. It energizes us and keeps us in harmony, and open to one another, when otherwise we might choose to keep our distance (and hurt our relationship in the process). I wonder how married couples manage without a prayer life together!"

When couples spend a lifetime nurturing one another through sharing, the result is the *oneness* God designed to alleviate man and woman's loneliness. A husband described it this way, "It is difficult to know where 'she' begins and 'I' leave off."

TWELVE WAYS TO NURTURE
YOUR PARTNER BY SHARING

The Key to Oneness

1. Enjoy some quality time together every day.
2. Do a special project together.
3. Develop some new interest in common.
4. Learn more about one another's work. Share the challenges and the rewards.
5. Enjoy a special date together once a week. Plan for it.
6. Listen to him or her attentively without interrupting.
7. Be understanding. Share your feelings. Say "I care, I love you."
8. Make plans, set goals together.
9. Do housework or yard work together and make it fun.
10. Study communication skills together and practice them.
11. Treat your partner the way you would treat your best friend. (Your partner *should* be your best friend.)
12. Pray together, grow in faith, share a ministry together.

TOUCHING

The fourth element in the B-E-S-T plan for nurturing is the easiest to implement and, in some ways, the most important. Touching, of course, represents the physical care and attention we must give to one another, but it means much more than that. Touching kindles a flame which every marriage needs. In fact, physical contact, apart from sex, is absolutely essential in keeping the fires of romantic love lit between husband and wife. The people who come into Dr. Wheat's office saying, "I love my partner but I'm just not *in love* with him (or her)" are the ones who have very little affectionate touching in their marriage—no hugs or love pats or holding hands, no kisses "just because," and no snuggling close to each other at night.

It's ironic that young couples who have built an intense love relationship by holding hands, kissing, hugging, and cuddling while they were dating often quit touching after marriage. Why give it up when it's so enjoyable? Because touch has become only a sexual signal in their relationship, and something irreplaceable has been lost.

Touching is important to us all of the time! Scientists believe that the inescapable need for skin contact is more crucial than hunger for food. Researchers have found that human infants and baby monkeys have trouble surviving without skin touch in their early months. Touch deprivation causes withdrawal, failure to thrive, infant depression, and even death.

Adults can also suffer from touch deprivation, and *touch hunger* is a common marital problem. Your partner's need, as well as your own need to be held nonsexually for comfort and to be touched tenderly and gently in nurturing ways, should be recognized and met in the security of marriage.

Anyone can learn to touch by doing it. People may claim that they don't enjoy it (usually because their family never learned to touch), but we have found in our work with couples that when people actually try it, they like it! People who had never learned to say freely, "I love you," find that they can do so and want to do so after a little experience with touching and being touched in loving, nonsexual ways. Authorities on touch say that one of the measures of our development as healthy human beings is the extent to which we are freely able to embrace and enjoy the nonsexual embraces of others.

In marriage touching is the least threatening way to bridge the distance created by other problems. In times of strong emotion, people respond best to physical contact rather than talking. Remember how a hug from Mom made everything feel better, how a little child goes to Mom or Dad to get the hurt kissed away? We need to go back to the beautiful simplicity of this in our marriage. Couples who have learned how to give and receive affectionate touching—a pat on the shoulder, a squeeze of the hand, a caress of the cheek, a strength-imparting hug, physical closeness, whether watching TV or listening to a sermon—say that this brings them feelings of comfort, optimism, support, and togetherness that are truly wonderful.

Stop and appreciate the way God designed touch as a blessing for your marriage. It is the most personally experienced of all sensations available to human beings. Our skin has been created to register this good experience. Experts say that the skin's sensitivity is so great and its ability to transmit signals so extraordinary, that for versatility it must be ranked second only to the brain.

So, explore the pleasures of touch, apart from sex. Learn to give each other gentle, nurturing massages, using a pleasing lotion or scented oil. This produces relaxation, a lowered heart rate, lowered blood pressure, and lets you experience the thrills of being in love. That's a lot of benefit for an hour's enjoyable activity. Have times of pleasure-oriented caressing without sex as your goal. Avoid the genital area and discover other sensitive areas of your body. Learn to please and to anticipate one another's desires. Teach one another what you like best by responding positively to the touch sensations you enjoy. Most people learn the language of loving through touch rather quickly, once they focus their attention on it.

Then become sensitive to the ways you can keep in touch in daily life. (Dr. Wheat prefers love seats in his house!) Hold hands when you walk, never separate without a good-bye kiss, and find times to hug when there is no reason except the good feeling it gives to both of you.

Use our list of suggestions as a take-off point to spark the individual creativity you can put into your own marriage through the avenue of touching.

TWELVE WAYS TO NURTURE YOUR PARTNER BY TOUCHING

The Key to Romance

1. Hug often for no particular reason.
2. Always greet or leave with a kiss. Kiss when there's no occasion.
3. Sit close to each other, whether in church or at home watching TV.
4. Go to bed at the same time and cuddle before you go to sleep. Allow a few minutes in the morning to hold each other before you get up.
5. Show as much concern for your partner's body as you do for your own.
6. Practice expressing your love through the medium of tender touch. Find out what feels good to your partner.
7. Give each other back rubs, massages. Use a pleasing lotion or scented oil. Enjoy!
8. Take your shower or bath together. Be lighthearted and sensuous.
9. Develop positive feelings toward your own body (See Ps. 139:13, 14).
10. Stay in physical contact while going to sleep.
11. Hold hands when you take a walk. Enjoy the thrill of holding hands anytime.
12. Think of ways to say *I love you* by tender touch.

If you want to know how the B-E-S-T plan can transform a marriage, read the book *Rekindled* (Revell, 1985), which tells how a husband set out to nurture his wife and restore intimacy to their marriage by applying the B-E-S-T principles as he found them in our book, *LOVE LIFE for Every Married Couple.* *Rekindled* describes, in vivid detail, what happens when even one partner cares enough to put this plan into practice. But please remember that the B-E-S-T plan is not just an emergency measure for crisis situations. It's one of the best things you can do for your marriage right now.

> Put the B-E-S-T plan for nurturing your partner into effect and follow it consistently. This is the tenth step in creating a marriage filled with all good pleasures.

When Nurturing Becomes a Necessity

Nurturing one another in marriage can be pleasant and delightful, but at some point it may become a hard necessity. As adults, we prefer to think we will always be capable of looking after ourselves. Yet we realize the time might come when we will need help. After a serious accident or an emotional collapse, during the course of a terminal illness, or if other infirmities of mind or body should overtake us, will our marriage partner be there to do for us what we cannot do for ourselves?

Almost all wedding vows include promises to cherish one another in the worst as well as the best conditions. Did your vows follow this pattern? *In hardships and in triumphs . . . in want and in plenty . . . in sorrow and in joy . . . in sickness and in health . . . forsaking all others . . . for as long as we both shall live.*

One of the comforts of a good marriage is experiencing the peace of knowing that, no matter what happens, we can count on our mate. So it's vital, from the day we marry, that we build our sense of confidence in one another.

The Scriptures say that "Confidence in an unfaithful (person) in time of trouble is like a broken tooth or a foot out of joint" (Prov. 25:19 AMPLIFIED). Two sad examples of this in marriage come to mind. We recall a young wife named Sarah, who was left stranded in a state-operated facility in a northern city without family, friends, or financial help. Sarah was paralyzed in an automobile accident caused by her husband, who deserted her when the extent of her injuries was known. We also remember a wife of retirement age in a western state whose husband suffered a stroke which took away his ability to speak. His illness so upset her that she visited him only once in the nursing home and eventually moved to another state to be with relatives, leaving him behind.

In contrast to these stories, we have seen many more faithful wives and husbands caring for their mates in the hospital and at home with great devotion, and, if a nursing home was required, spending a part of every day there with them.

The answer to whether we will be able to count on one another in the future lies in how well and how graciously we are caring for one another now on a daily basis. We store up trust for the darkest times of life by the way we live in the light, and by the way we handle the minor crises. A warm hug, a reassuring word, a helping hand, a willingness to do whatever is needed without complaint—these prove what kind of marriage partners we are. For a successful marriage, we need the assurance that as long as both of us live, we will *be there*, looking after one another to the best of our ability.

It's been said that the simplest definition of trust is the feeling that another person is *for you*. Add the element of loyalty—the person is *for you* and *won't change*—and you have the trust that is essential for a happy marriage.

Do you want to be this kind of husband or wife—loyal, steadfast, unchanging in your love and your commitment to do the best for your partner? We have talked to people who said, in effect, "But I can't be like this. I really want to be, but I'm weak, I'm changeable, and I can't be expected to handle problems. When it's too much for me, I'll have to walk away."

This too is a choice, and the people who say, "I *can't*" have just made one. When you say, "I *will*, and I *can* because God will show me how," you are choosing to stay in the mainstream of God's plan for you, and He will provide exactly what you need.

Both the pattern for this steadfast, loyal love, and the power to live it, come from God, who nurtures His people with the faithful lovingkindness the Bible calls *hesed*. To help you make the best choices in your marriage, you need to acquaint yourself with this word and the special quality of love it describes.

STUBBORN, STEADFAST HESED LOVE

It's amazing that in one beautiful, comprehensive word, God has fully described the attitude which partners in a marriage covenant can and should demonstrate toward one another. Found in the Old Testament 245 times, *hesed* (sometimes spelled *hesedh* or *chesed*) possesses such extraordinary richness and depth of meaning that no equivalent word in the English language exists. Bible translators have used a wide range of words to try to convey its multifaceted message. Often the word love appears with a variety of adjectives: steadfast love, true love, unfailing love, constant love, strong love, wonderful love, and the like. Other families of words are used to denote mercy, goodness, favor, promise, devotion, kindness, and loyalty. Certainly it is one of the most important of God's words for love, and it offers sure guidance for our marriage. By consulting the studies of *hesed* by biblical scholars, we can draw out these facts to apply in our own relationship.

1. *Hesed* always indicates some kind of relationship; it is used to express the feeling between people who are in a close relationship, such as couples in a marriage covenant. This is a concept we can take for our own as husband and wife.

2. The central meaning of *hesed* is love expressed in two significant ways: first, through kindness; and second, through loyalty. These two qualities can be considered as the main building blocks in a stable, love-filled relationship.

3. The kindness of *hesed* blesses the relationship with a continuing attitude of goodwill which proves itself in action—good, kind actions which demonstrate favor out of deep affection for the beloved. Our marriage should be characterized by kindness—seen, experienced, and felt. Here is a scriptural example of *hesed* which we could take as a model for our own love relationship:

> The LORD appeared of old to me (Israel), saying, Yes, I have loved you with an everlasting love; therefore with lovingkindness have I drawn you and have continued My faithfulness to you (Jer. 31:3 AMPLIFIED).

4. The unshakable loyalty of *hesed* is dictated by duty as well as desire, so that if feelings fluctuate, our loyalty does not. This loyalty is directed in two ways: (1) to the persons involved and (2) to the promises made in the relationship. Here is a scriptural example of *hesed* which we could adopt as the love song of our marriage:

> "Though the mountains be shaken and the hills be removed, yet my unfailing love for you will not be shaken nor my covenant of peace be removed," says the LORD, who has compassion on you (Isaiah 54:10).

5. *Hesed* is faithfulness in action; fixed, determined, almost stubborn steadfastness which, in God's case, lasts forever, and "is better than life" (Ps. 63:3). Psalm 136 with its continuing refrain: *His steadfast love endures forever* presents *hesed* as an essential and unchanging part of His nature. "To thee, O Lord, belongs steadfast love," the psalmist says in Psalm 62:12. The fullness of meaning in *hesed* can only be found in God, but because the Holy Spirit now indwells believers, we also possess the potential to love in this way. The choice is ours! We can operate on the basis of our own selfish interests, always putting ourselves first, or we can allow the greatness of His love to enlarge the narrow capacities of our own hearts.

Recognize that God is the true source of faithfulness for your marriage, and choose to demonstrate His faithful *hesed* love to your partner. This is the eleventh step in forging a marriage that endures.

SUGGESTIONS

Form the B-E-S-T habit of nurturing by following these steps:

1. In your notebook make your own list of ways to apply each part of the prescription to your relationship. Transfer them to 3x5 cards you can keep with you as reminders. As you make new discoveries about what your partner desires, add them to your list.

2. Launch your new plan with strong initiative. Give your new beginning such momentum that the temptation to break down will not occur as soon as it otherwise might. Each day you continue on, you are strengthening your resolve and building for the future.

3. Never allow an exception to occur until the B-E-S-T habit is securely rooted in your life. William James says that each lapse is like dropping a ball of string which one is carefully winding up; a single slip undoes more than a great many turns will wind up again. By continuity and consistency, you will train yourself to respond rightly with less effort.

4. Take the first possible opportunity to act on each specific B-E-S-T goal you set. Concrete actions will establish your behavior as habit. When a resolve or a fine glow of feeling is allowed to evaporate without bearing practical fruit, it actually works to discourage us from making future decisions.

5. Practice every day. Do a little more than you ordinarily would to establish the habit so that when you are tempted to let up, you'll be nerved and ready to stand the test.

6. Don't let the discouragement of a "failure" cause you to quit. Instead, go back to the B E-S-T principles and see how you can remedy the situation, and go on from that point. The idea is not to become a perfect person, but to nurture your partner in the ways that he or she needs and desires most.

7. Commit your way unto the Lord and your plans will be established.

6
Indifference or Loving

> Are we taking our relationship for granted, or are we learning more about loving each other as time goes by?

Love never fails (1 Cor. 13:8).

ONE OF THE momentous choices you will make in marriage is whether to allow indifference to set the emotional tone of your relationship, or to learn and practice the very personal art of loving your partner.

But where does indifference come from, and how can it take over a relationship? As counselors, we see that nothing is started with such high hopes and shining expectations, yet fails as often as the love which propels newlyweds into marriage. God's Word says that "love never fails." So the problem lies not with love, but with "lovers" whose choices too often are based on misconceptions, rather than the truth about love.

God Himself is Love. He communicates this truth through the Bible so that we can be free to love, but we have an enemy who attempts to destroy love by disseminating lies about it. Satan's lies, some of them quite subtle, are successfully spread like viruses throughout the world, and as a result we're likely to be infected, even while growing up. Almost all of us, without realizing it, accumulate a mixed bag of myths and misconceptions about love. Unless we learn better, we take them into marriage with us.

A wife told us, "I can see that I've been emotionally illiterate for most of my married life. And, oh, I've paid the price of ignorance!" Her husband, of course, had to pay a price in unhappiness, as well, for the false ideas about love which had dominated her behavior.

You see, what you believe about love—true or false—will always influence your behavior toward your mate. This will certainly affect your marriage and will help determine your future happiness and well-being. What you believe is that important.

For example, people who believe the world's lies about love tend to take their relationship for granted because they think love is a feeling that should happen automatically and get even better without effort on their part. Or, if the feelings stop happening, they believe nothing can be done about it anyway.

Be warned that if you don't choose to actively practice the art of loving, an emotional climate of indifference will develop almost by default. A love relationship left to itself will not improve with time; the original momentum will not continue. In fact, the principle of deterioration sets in as soon as apparent indifference opens the door. It may be only laziness, or ignorance, but the same harmful effects result. People have to work at their relationship to keep it working, and loving one's mate always requires knowledgeable effort.

In the next few pages we want to give you some truths which will help you make the best choices in your love life. These truths can revolutionize any love relationship. If you absorb them and live by them, there will be no room for Satan's deceptions, and no way they can control you. Here, in visual form, are the topics we'll be covering, beginning at the foundation and moving upward—from basic principles of love to a clear vision of the love which will keep you on a steady course throughout your married life.

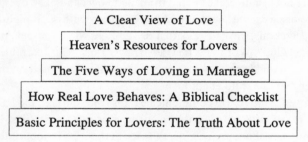

A Clear View of Love

Heaven's Resources for Lovers

The Five Ways of Loving in Marriage

How Real Love Behaves: A Biblical Checklist

Basic Principles for Lovers: The Truth About Love

BASIC PRINCIPLES FOR LOVERS: THE TRUTH ABOUT LOVE

We begin with four basic principles every lover needs to know. Each principle answers and corrects a false belief commonly held about love which hinders us from learning and practicing the art of loving our partner. It's vital to make these truths a part of your belief system if they are not already.

1. I can learn what love is from the Word of God. It is rational, not irrational. I can understand love and grow in the understanding of it throughout my lifetime.

Contrast this truth with Satan's most subtle lie about love: that it is a misty, uncertain, irrational thing which we can never "get a handle on." (Rather like a big, beautiful soap bubble!) This lie tries to diminish our vision of love and dilute its influence upon our life by suggesting that, since love is irrational, we can never understand it. If we can't be sure and clear about it in our minds, love is reduced to something as weak as wishful thinking.

The fact is that love is the one thing in life about which we can have a blazing certainty. There is nothing more realistic and powerful in the history of the world than that moment at the crossroads of time when God's Son, Jesus Christ, died for us, so that we might live forever in the eternal circle of His love. There is nothing more sure than His love for us, and we too can love realistically and powerfully "because He first loved us" (1 John 4:19).

> Let us go on loving one another, for love comes from God. Every man who truly loves is God's son and has some knowledge of him. But the man who does not love cannot know him at all, for God is love.

> To us, the greatest demonstration of God's love for us has been his sending his only Son into the world to give us life through him. We see real love, not in the fact that we loved God, but that he loved us and sent his Son to make personal atonement for our sins. If God loved us as much as that, surely we, in our turn, should love each other!

> If we love each other God does actually live within us, and his love grows in us towards perfection (1 John 4:7–12 Phillips).

In other words, if we want to learn what real love is, we can go to the Scriptures—our only accurate source of information about love—to discover how God loves. Basically, we will find that love is always drawing the beloved with lovingkindness, always *doing* the very best for the beloved. Why? Because love recognizes the unique value of the beloved and chooses to affirm it always. The Lord's words to His frequently unlovely people offer the best example of this: *"Because you are precious in My sight, and honored, and I love you, I give"* (Isa. 43:4 AMPLIFIED). Love is a steadfast choice consistently backed up by action—a rational choice made with the full power of the will.

We know that real love is always rational, consistent, purposeful, and creative because God, who *is* Love, is also the One whose wisdom created and maintains the world. Think of it! All the incredibly diverse life forms of our world and all the heavenly bodies in the galaxies of space with their majestic, mathematical order have been conceived and kept in motion by the God of love. Love makes sense. The principles of love can be understood and lived by, just as seafaring men can find their way across trackless oceans by the fixed positions of the stars.

2. Love is neither easy nor simple. It is an art that I must want to learn and pour my life into.

Although real love can be understood, it does not come easily or automatically. This fact answers the common misconception among young people that love is the simplest thing in the world, that it's easy to love, requiring neither thought nor effort. No one has to learn about love or even think about it—it's just a matter of doing what comes naturally! With this lie, Satan tries to cheapen love.

The fact is that if you do what comes naturally, you'll be wrong almost every time. By nature we human beings are selfish, not generous. True love demands a generosity of spirit and life which gives gladly and freely for the benefit of the beloved—and keeps on giving. Real love costs! It will require much from you even when the giving is pure joy.

You can't become a skilled lover by treating love as a pleasure you dabble in when you're in the mood. The art of loving must be learned as a discipline just like the art of music, or medicine, or any other work which requires the most skilled craftsmanship and mastery of technique. You must want to learn this art so much that you are willing to pour your time and strength into the process. You can become an expert lover if you will put forth the effort to learn what you need to know about the art of loving, and practice it on a daily basis. We're recommending action, not just theoretical knowledge. As the language experts point out, Science *knows*; art *does*.

3. Love is an active power that I control by my own will. I am not the helpless slave of love. I can choose to love.

Most of the man-meets-woman, man-loses-woman plots of films and television come from the premise that love is a feeling that just happens. Or else it doesn't happen. Or it happens and then stops happening so that nothing can be done to recapture that feeling, once it goes.

The truth is that love is an active power which you were meant to control by your own will. You are not "just a prisoner of love" as the song claims. If you are a Christian with the love of God in your heart, you can choose to love your marriage partner moment by moment, no matter what the circumstances are, or how you are feeling. (Remember that you are *more* than your emotions.)

4. Love is the power that will produce love as I learn to give it rather than strain to attract it.

Most people today worry about finding someone to love them and keep on loving them. Advertising plays on those worries by sending the message that people have to learn how to be desirable in order to be loved and to hold on to their lover. This means choosing the right toothpaste, perfume, shaving cream, shampoo, deodorant—the list of products almost guaranteed to bring love into your life is endless.

But not everything can be blamed on television commercials. Our media-oriented society unashamedly measures desirability by three flimsy yardsticks: popularity, sex appeal, and great looks. (It also helps to have a rising career and the income for an exciting life-style.) But although people may be paying more attention to their appearance, taking more exotic vacations, earning more money, and becoming more knowledgeable about sex than ever before—their longing for someone to love them, really love them, has not abated in the least. With the rising divorce rate, people are even more lonely, and more desperate for a love relationship based on reality.

The Bible holds the secret. It can show you how to be so lovable and desirable that your marriage partner will adore you and never let you go. The secret involves learning to give love rather than straining and striving to attract it—a powerful secret which only a few people know. One word of caution: Many mistakes are made in the name of love. You must learn how to love in ways that correspond to your partner's own measurement of love. What will make your mate *feel* loved by you? When you become skilled at the art of loving, you will know the answer.

HOW REAL LOVE BEHAVES: A BIBLICAL CHECKLIST

Here is another dimension of learning to love (and thus becoming the most desirable of marriage partners). We need to learn the characteristics of true love and let those become our pattern of behavior to follow. One passage of Scripture holds a mirror before our eyes so that we can compare how we love with the way real love thinks, speaks, and behaves, especially when tested. And tested we will be!

So toss out your unrealistic expectations and accept the fact that you will be tested all too frequently while you are learning to adapt to one another in marriage. As the process goes on, don't be surprised if marriage magnifies every flaw in your disposition while self-centeredness is being replaced by real love.

The truth of 1 Corinthians 13, given here in chart form, can help. Study it, pray over it, live with it until its influence transforms your behavior, especially toward your mate.

WHAT LOVE IS AND IS NOT:
THE DEFINITIVE STATEMENT
As found in 1 Corinthians 13

Love Is. . .	Love Is Not. . .
1. patient, long-tempered	impatient, short with others
2. kind, gracious, good	unkind, indifferent
3. glad when good things happen to others	envious, jealous
4. modest, undemanding	a show-off, a bragger
5. humble, seeing itself realistically	haughty, conceited, proud
6. polite, courteous	rude, apt to behave badly
7. more concerned with the well-being of others than its own welfare	selfish, self-centered, always insisting on its own way
8. even-tempered under pressure	touchy, irritable, easily annoyed

Love does. . .	Love does not. . .
1. overlook grievances	keep score of wrongs, nurture grudges
2. rejoice with the truth, become happy when truth is honored	rejoice at unrighteousness, feel good when things go badly for others
3. bear up under anything and everything	give up on others and drag the worst out into the open for others to gloat over
4. believe all things, give others the benefit of the doubt	believe the worst about others
5. hope all things under all circumstances	accept failure as the last word
6. endure all things without weakening	give up, admit defeat

THERE IS NOTHING GREATER THAN LOVE!

THE FIVE WAYS OF LOVING IN MARRIAGE

Loving one another requires "know-how" as well as consistent effort. But our English word *love* is an overworked and inadequate term for someone who wants to know *how* to love. The word has been used in so many meaningless ways that authors feel the need to qualify it when they want to say something important. For instance, the poet Edgar Allan Poe wrote, "We loved with a love that was more than love." And in a currently acclaimed television fantasy, the Beauty and the Beast describe their profound caring for one another as "a bond stronger than love."

When we developed the *love life* principles for thousands of couples who wanted to rekindle love in their marriage, we went back to the precise language of the Greek New Testament along with some vibrant Hebrew terms of the Old Testament to distinguish and describe the various aspects of love and to explain how they could enrich a marriage. We will give you these five ways of loving now, not as a language exercise, but as a practical explanation of what your marriage can be when love finds its full expression in your relationship. (Refer back to chapter 5 for the sixth way of loving, the steadfast lovingkindness called *hesed*.)

Please understand that we're not suggesting window shopping. You can't major on one kind of loving and discard another. Each builds on the other. Each has its own special place, as you will find when you put them into practice, and yet all are interrelated.

We'll briefly describe each facet of love, then give you guidelines on experiencing its delights in your relationship. Pay special attention to the key words!

1. Epithumia—Sexual Desire

Thy **desire** shall be toward thy husband (Gen. 3:16, KJV).

I am my beloved's and his **desire** is for me (Song 7:10).

This facet of love—a strong craving and physiological desire—is suggested by a Greek word which the Bible never calls love. However, it describes a crucial aspect of the love affair between husband and wife. *Epithumia* is a strong desire of any kind—sometimes good, sometimes bad. It means to set the heart on, to long for, rightly or wrongly. When used in the Bible in a negative way, it is translated lust. When used in a positive way, it is translated *desire*, and this is the meaning we refer to. In marriage, husband and wife should have a strong physical desire for each other that expresses itself in pleasurable sexual love-making.

HOW TO LOVE YOUR PARTNER SEXUALLY

a. You need complete, accurate medical information.
b. You need to understand sex from the biblical perspective.
c. You need to develop the right approach in your marriage:

  ♥ by eliminating the negatives, avoiding all criticism.
  ♥ by building a series of enjoyable physical experiences together based on physical touching and emotional closeness.

The Key Words: INTIMACY and RESPONSE

2. Eros—Romantic Love

Let him kiss me with the kisses of his mouth: For thy **love** *is* better than wine (Song 1:2, KJV).

This way of loving—literally, to boil—never appears in the New Testament, but its Hebrew counterpart is used in the Old Testament. *Eros*, more than any other kind of love, carries with it the idea of romance. *Eros* is not always sensual, but it includes the idea of yearning to unite with and the desire to possess the beloved. Romantic, passionate, and sentimental—this love often provides the starting point for marriage. It has been called rapture; exquisite pleasure; a strong, sweet, and sometimes terrifying emotion because it is so all-absorbing. At its best, romantic love is pure and beautiful and ennobling, and will add all manner of delights to your marriage.

It's important to remember that eros is always "the love of the worthy." When a young man or a young woman falls in love, it is always because the beloved is perceived as attractive. How you *see* each other will determine the quality of *eros* in your marriage in the months and years ahead.

HOW TO BUILD ROMANTIC LOVE

A. Eros love is a pleasurable learned response to:

  ♥ the way your partner looks and feels,
  ♥ the things your partner says and does,
  ♥ the emotional experiences you share.

B. Think about all these ways your mate pleases you.

♥ Use your God-given gift of imagination to build this love in your mind.

♥ Never allow criticism or ridicule of your mate to enter the picture.

C. Remember—you are teaching your mate to respond to you all the time, either positively or negatively. So send out pleasant and pleasurable signals.

♥ Provide the right emotional climate for your mate to experience romantic feelings.

♥ Provide the physical stimulus of closeness, touching, eye contact.

♥ Set up the conditions in which your partner will find it easy to love you.

The Key Words: PLEASURE and ROMANCE

3. Storge—Natural Affection

Be **kindly affectioned** one to another with brotherly love, in honor preferring one another (Rom. 12:10, KJV).

This term represents the natural affection of marriage, a warm, devoted loyalty which you feel and show to one another because you *belong*. It's such an unspectacular, down-to-earth love, its importance may be underestimated. But listen to this report (quoted in our book *Love Life*) from a couple who developed *storge* love early in their marriage. They've been together more than thirty years now, but here's what *storge* meant to their relationship during what they look back on as the "rocky years."

"On the way to our June wedding, we thought we had everything going for us. Our friendship was warm, our romantic feelings even warmer, and, as for the fires of passion, they were just waiting for the match! After we settled into married life, the companionship and sexual desire and romantic thrills were still there. But it was all a little less perfect than we had expected because we were such imperfect people. The pink glow of romance hadn't prepared us for that! We weren't Christians then, so we didn't know that *agape* love could glue us together.

"Fortunately, something else brought us through those first rocky years when wedded bliss almost got buried under the unbliss. You might call what developed between us a sense of belonging. We had decided right from the start that it was us against the world—two people forming a majority of one. So whatever happened, or however much we clashed in private, we stuck by each other. We were like a brother and sister on the playground. We might scrap with each other, but let an outsider try to horn in and he had to take us both on! If one of us hurt, the other wiped away the tears. We made a habit of believing in each other while our careers got off the ground.

"We showed each other all the kindness that two impatient young people could be expected to show—and then some more. It really wasn't long until we discovered something stupendous about our relationship: We found out we belonged. We came first with each other, and always would. Because we belonged to each other, no one could spoil our love and togetherness from the outside. Only we could do that, and we weren't about to! It was too good to lose. A lot of people seem to spend their whole life looking for a feeling of belonging. Maybe they don't know that marriage is the best place to find it."

This facet of love we call *belonging* is essential to your happiness in marriage. We all need an atmosphere at home which is secure, where we feel completely comfortable with one another, knowing that we belong there, and that our happiness and well-being are supremely important to our partner. Here's how to turn your marriage into a place of *homecoming* for both of you.

HOW TO GIVE THE GIFT OF BELONGING

A. Establish the viewpoint of oneness in your marriage.

- ♥ Do not see yourselves separately.
- ♥ Refuse to let pressures divide you.
- ♥ Be loyal to each other under all circumstances.

B. Reinforce your sense of family solidarity.

- ♥ Spend comfortable time together.
- ♥ Always be supportive and kind.
- ♥ Show your partner you can be counted on.

The Key Words: RELIABILITY and KINDNESS

4. Phileo—Friendship Love

That they may teach the young women to . . . **love** (phileo) their husbands (Titus 2:4, KJV).

Phileo is the love one feels for a cherished friend of either sex. Jesus had this love for a disciple: "One of His disciples whom Jesus loved—whom He esteemed and delighted in . . ." (John 13:23 AMPLIFIED). Peter expressed his *phileo* love for Jesus: "Lord . . . You know that I love You—that I have a deep, instinctive, personal affection for You, as for a close friend . . ." (John 21:17 AMPLIFIED). And Jonathan and David provide an Old Testament example: "The soul of Jonathan was knit with the soul of David, and Jonathan loved him as his own soul" (1 Sam. 18:1, KJV).

This same *phileo* is the cherishing love of marriage. It takes on added intensity and enjoyment as part of the love bond of husband and wife. When two people in marriage share themselves—their lives and all that they are—they develop this love of mutual affection, rapport, and comradeship. They become best friends, delighting in one another's company, and caring for each other tenderly. None of the loves of marriage offers more consistent pleasure than *phileo*. The camaraderie of best friends who are also lovers seems twice as exciting and doubly precious. As you put your energies to building and maintaining this love in your marriage, remember two important things. First, sharing is the key that unlocks the emotions of friendship. Second, the conditions you set up in your marriage must be conducive to friendship. Through personal experience you already know how to make and keep friends. Now it's a matter of applying what you know to build this most important friendship of your life.

HOW TO BECOME BEST FRIENDS

A. By genuine togetherness.

- ♥ Spend quality time together.
- ♥ Focus your attention on each other.
- ♥ Share your activities and interests.

B. By developing real communication.

- ♥ Share your thoughts, goals, ideals.
- ♥ Develop a safe atmosphere in which you can share inmost feelings, and totally be yourself.

The Key Words: COMRADESHIP, RAPPORT, and REVELATION

5. Agape—Unconditional Love

God commendeth his **love** toward us in that, while we were yet sinners, Christ died for us (Rom. 5:8, KJV).

Agape is the love so often spoken of in the New Testament because it is God's love. *Agape* is that showering of grace and favor which transforms our life; of unshakable commitment and unselfish giving; of great kindness and concern for our highest welfare; of unconditional acceptance as though arms were open always to receive us, no matter what. Everyone wants and desperately needs this unconditional love. But it cannot be purchased; it cannot even be earned by good behavior. God is the *source*, and until we understand this we will be unable to love each other in marriage with the love that brings every good thing into our lives.

As you learn to give this priceless gift to one another you will find that there is no substitute for the emotional well-being that comes from feeling loved and accepted, completely, unconditionally, and permanently.

HOW TO LOVE THE AGAPE WAY

A. Choose with your will to love unconditionally and permanently.
B. Ask God to enable you to love with His love.
C. Develop the biblical and personal knowledge of your partner's needs and how to meet them. If the loving actions of *agape* are not guided by precise knowledge of your partner, they will miss the mark.
D. Apply everything you know in communicating this love. Agape love is an action word: always doing the best for the object of your love.
E. Give your partner what he or she needs most: the assurance of being

♥ totally accepted.
♥ permanently loved.

The Key Word: GIVING (based on knowledge)

HEAVEN'S RESOURCES FOR LOVERS

This conversation was reported to us recently. Young granddaughter: "Grandma, I don't think I'm going to get married when I grow up." Grandma: "Why is that, Kristy?" Child: "Because I don't want to be divorced."

Children have a way of going to the heart of the matter. For this little girl and thousands like her, divorce does seem to be a natural consequence of marriage— the second part of the story, the unhappy ending.

But here are some facts to count on, facts which more than balance today's dark statistics. These truths give solid reassurance of God's readiness to help you build the kind of marriage that happily lasts a lifetime.

1. It is God's will in every marriage that the couple love each other with an absorbing spiritual, emotional, and physical attraction that continues to grow throughout their lifetime together.

2. God is the one who made you, who thought up the idea of marriage and ordained it for your blessing, and who gives you the capacity to love. He is the One who knows best how to build love into your particular relationship. You can trust Him to be intimately involved in your efforts to develop a love-filled marriage.

3. It is possible for any Christian couple to develop this love relationship in their marriage because it is in harmony with God's express will.

If the time should come when you feel the temporary urge to "give up," refresh yourself with these truths. Remember that heaven's resources are at your disposal. Any couple who wants and chooses to build a love-filled marriage *can* do so.

A CLEAR VIEW OF LOVE

No matter how long we study *love*, we find that our vision is still too small!

In the beautiful little book, *Hinds' Feet on High Places*, which tells of the climb to the High Places of Love, the heroine and her friends reach "the beginners" slopes and realize how much more lies beyond. They see that there are ranges upon ranges which they had not even dreamt of while they were still down in the valleys with their limited views.

The thirteenth chapter of 1 Corinthians, which we considered earlier, gives us a hint of these "ranges upon ranges" of which we know nothing yet. But we do know this much: Love is the most important thing in the world. There is nothing that matters more than love. Love is stronger than death itself. There is nothing more powerful than love. Love is the only thing that lasts, the only thing that will endure forever. There is nothing as permanent as love.

We trust that these truths will be a launching pad for your own discoveries.

> Decide to pour your life into learning the art of loving your mate, and avoid any hint of indifference. This is the twelfth step in establishing a happy marriage.

SUGGESTIONS

This chapter contains the core information you need to learn the art of loving and practice it. What will you do with it?

1. Think about your marriage at this point. Would you describe the emotional atmosphere as loving or indifferent? How have you contributed to this climate? Do you feel a change is needed? If you continue moving in the direction you're now going, will you be pleased with the outcome?

2. Consider making a definite decision to commit yourself to the art of loving your mate, for out of this decision will flow all the small secret choices which characterize your life together. A decision is a signal that you have made up your mind. The word *decision* literally means "a cutting short." It indicates a cutting short of uncertainty and sets the stage for action. Record what you decide in your notebook.

3. Use the five ways of loving as a checklist to determine where your marriage needs extra attention. Based on the information in this section, plan some specific ways to enhance your relationship.

Part 3
How Well is Your Partnership Working?

7

In Conflict: Choices That Make You a Winning Team

> How well do we handle the conflicts which inevitably arise when two human beings try to build one life together?

"Live together in harmony, live together in love, as though you had only one mind and one spirit between you. Never act from motives of rivalry or personal vanity, but in humility think more of one another than you do of yourselves" *(Phil. 2:2–3 Phillips).*

IT'S BEEN SAID that marriage presents one of the most difficult personal problems in life, because the most emotional and romantic of all human dreams has to be consolidated into an ordinary working relationship.

Many of us would agree. And yet the statment is not precisely true, for marriage is no ordinary relationship. God designed it to be the ideal *partnership* in which each partner supports and complements the other; a partnership which is continually renewed and refreshed by the presence and power of love.

Still, marriage, (though far from ordinary) is very much a *working* relationship. Reverse the comfortable myth that says "If two people love each other, everything will work out," and it becomes truth: *If two people want to keep on loving each other, they will need to work out everything!* An enormous difference of approach lies between these two ideas. By inspecting your secret choices in marriage, you can see which statement you actually believe and which approach you have been taking.

Every married couple faces the same challenge: how to create a good partnership. The success of your marriage may well turn on this point. Since marriage is not an endless romantic encounter, but a sharing of life as it really is— the problems as well as the joys; the routine responsibilities as well as the rewards—nothing can take the place of your ability to function happily and effectively as a team. And this never happens without a great deal of understanding and effort.

The roadblock which most couples encounter almost immediately could be labeled, simply, *conflict*. Some couples try to pretend it's not there, and thus make no progress at all. Some attempt to detour the long way around, only to find that they can't avoid it. And others keep smashing into it and retreating, dazed and wounded, to make another run! There's only one adequate way to deal with this barricade: It must be removed (stone by stone, if necessary), and that takes teamwork. It's a hard fact of marriage that your partnership will never work well unless the two of you learn to work together in resolving the hundreds of conflicts that arise whenever two human beings try to build one life. How you approach conflict and how well you learn to manage it will be key factors in determining the course of your marriage. Here are some suggestions which can help.

HOW TO APPROACH THE CONFLICTS
IN YOUR MARRIAGE

1. Approach conflicts with acceptance.

Accept conflicts, especially in the early years, as a normal and potentially useful part of marriage. Granted, they may come as an unpleasant surprise on the honeymoon or soon after. Dating, no matter how frequent, is never the same as living together constantly. We think we know our loved one at the time we say "I do," but human beings are so complex that it takes years for us to begin to understand one another well.

Conflicts, though painful, nudge us into adjusting our expectations and needs to harmonize with those of our marriage partner. Because of the fall of man and our inheritance of a sinful nature, the process of two learning to become one frequently includes conflict. How much, and how painful, will depend on whether we respond in biblical ways and follow biblical counsel in building our marriages. When the red light of conflict clicks on, we can be thankful for the warning signal which shows us an area of our relationship that needs attention. If we allow them to, conflicts can motivate us to build a stronger marriage, and if we are sensitive to the issues, we will learn more precisely how to please one another—always a prerequisite to a happier marriage.

Just as we must accept the reality of conflict in our marriage, we also need to accept our marriage partner, even while the disagreement is raging. Marriage seems to act as a magnifying glass, emphasizing our every imperfection, and nowhere is the view in the glass quite as grim as during a quarrel when anger momentarily distorts our vision. This is our great opportunity to choose to grant our lover the gift of unconditional love; to see him or her without the flaws.

Acceptance also neutralizes the possibility of harmful aftereffects when the clash is over and the matter has been resolved.

2. Approach conflicts with a perspective of oneness.

Approach conflicts in your marriage with a viewpoint that eliminates much of the sting and keeps the positive juices flowing, even while the flak is flying. In short, keep sight of yourselves as the insiders, and this conflict as an intruder with no right to control your relationship. It's a matter of perspective. If you begin to see yourselves as two adversaries, engaged in open warfare or sniper attacks, you have reason to be dismayed, because you are, in reality, *one flesh.* If you turn on each other to retaliate, it is like trying to retaliate against yourself. Always remember that you and your mate are not enemies. The quarrels pose the threat, for they can bring deadly harm to your marriage if not controlled. How much better to approach conflicts as two people who belong together—an indivisible unit—and who refuse to let anything come between them.

The Scriptures counsel us to live together as though we shared one mind and one spirit. Not possible, you say? As believers, indwelt by the Holy Spirit and guided by the Scriptures, it is wholly possible to develop this oneness of approach and remain united even while confronting and resolving our differences.

And so we need to view ourselves as one, to seek oneness of mind and spirit, and to act as one against that conflict which threatens to divide us. If we maintain our sense of unity, neither helplessness ("What can I do?") nor hopelessness ("What's the use?") can ever defeat us.

3. Approach conflict with established guidelines.

We have already suggested the need for biblical counsel in times of conflict. But how about preparing for it ahead of time by establishing in your mind some guidelines to direct your choices? The biblical guidelines suggested in Philippians 2 are harmony and love: "live together in harmony; live together in love. . . ." The hope of harmony will not settle every difference of opinion in marriage, but the standard of harmony can modify your behavior while you are dealing with the problem at hand. The yardstick of love, as found in 1 Corinthians 13 (see chapter 6), provides the perfect model of behavior and attitude. Let this shape your choices, and you will have nothing to fear from the times of adjustment in your marriage.

4. Approach conflict with commitment to teamwork.

Up to this point we have used the illustration of warfare, because our disagreements in marriage often seem more like battles than anything else. But the unique partnership of marriage requires strong teamwork, and that image can also add to our understanding of how to approach conflicts.

If your differences in marriage were a game to be won or lost, how would it usually go in your relationship? Think about it. When you have a conflict about something—anything, large or small—what often happens? Does one of you "win" most of the time while the other usually backs down or gives in?

What does winning really consist of? Having the last word? Convincing the other to change? Talking the loudest or pouting the longest? Is it a reluctant submission by one of you in order to keep your relationship intact? Would one or both of you rather be *right* at the other's expense, than be in harmony? Do you get your own way by applying some sort of pressure? Is winning your way more important than your partner's happiness or the well-being of your marriage?

Winning, as we've already suggested, can mean something else entirely. It doesn't have to be a contest with the two of you pitted against one another, one winning, one losing. It can be a *win-win* approach where you join together as a team in resolving the problem rather than "playing against" one another. If you handle the conflict in such a way that your love and commitment are actually strengthened by the solution you find together, you both come out the clear winners.

It's important to see yourselves, not as competitors against one another, but as co-laborers in the field of marriage. The Bible cautions against "motives of rivalry or personal vanity." We know that when members of a team begin competing with one another, the team's "win" statistics usually take a plunge. In marriage, such rivalry chips away at the peace of the home. The effects of personal vanity are even worse, for a narcissistic person, once offended, can easily switch from "love" to hatred and a thirst for revenge.

Pride, that ferocious refusal to bend an inch, is the most common obstacle to the resolution of quarrels and the healing that forgiveness can bring. It's also the thing that God hates most, according to the Bible. "God opposes the proud, but gives grace to the humble," warns the proverb, quoted twice in the New Testament (James 4:6 and 1 Peter 5:5).

In contrast, humility can bless your marriage by applying the sweet oil of harmony to every point of friction in your relationship. As the saying goes, "The cure for conflict is a humble spirit." How does humility behave? Unassumingly. Unconcerned with status because it does not have to compensate for insecurity. Not self-occupied. It accepts what God has done and what He has given, and does not go to extremes by putting itself up or down. Humility, by biblical definition, considers others better than itself, and looks after the interests of others as well as its own concerns. (See Phil. 2:3–11.) Humility may sound like a foreign term to a generation raised on the benefits of self-fulfillment and assertiveness training, but remember that it is our Creator's prescription for harmony and peace in human relationships. He has given us the living example of strength with humility in the person of the Lord Jesus Christ.

5. Approach conflict as a crucial test.

How you handle your conflicts will be a crucial test of your partnership. Much hangs in the balance. The survival of your marriage may even be at risk, for the manner in which couples handle their disagreements has a strong impact on both the *quality* and the *stability* of their marriage.

In the olden days when divorce was rarely granted, Queen Elizabeth I of England complained to the churches: "How few matrimonies there be without chidings, brawlings, tauntings, bitter cursings, and fightings." People suffered but remained married.

Today, in a society brought up with the idea of "instant relief," only those strongly committed to marriage are willing to put up with the "chidings, brawlings, tauntings" and so on. Even a temporarily strained relationship is apt to be written off the way an interviewer summed up the broken marriage of a famous television personality and her husband. "They had great times," the writer blithely said, "and then the great times were over and it was time to take separate paths."

Married couples today tend to give themselves too little time to adjust to one another and to make the changes which may be necessary in order to build a good marriage. Patience has never been in shorter supply. That's why it is essential for couples to learn and practice the skills which can enable them to understand their conflicts and work them through satisfactorily.

6. Approach conflict with confidence that it can benefit your marriage.

If we learn to handle conflict so that we encourage and build one another up rather than tearing each other down, we can find the experience beneficial. Think of it as a means of increasing your closeness, for if you manage your differences effectively, the result will be a deeper intimacy to bless your marriage.

In our marital partnership we have the privilege of creating many things—conceiving and rearing children; forming a life together, building a home, shaping a loving environment for others to enjoy; pouring our energies into work or a ministry which we can share; creating and sharing experiences of beauty; and providing a role model to help others who are looking for examples of steadfast love between husband and wife. Doing away with the barriers of conflict by moving the stumbling blocks out of the way, one by one as they appear, is another constructive work which we can give ourselves to with joy.

We can never take happiness in marriage for granted, as something owed to us. The Arabian Nights fantasy, *The Thief of Bagdad*, a spectacular silent film of 1924, which was restored and revived on PBS, ends with a subtitle on the screen lest anyone miss the point: "Happiness must be earned." Even the magic of the Arabian Nights was not enough to ensure happiness for the lovers. Happiness—then and now—must be earned by our behavior and attitudes: by our sacrifice, courage, endurance, and patience; and by our secret choices.

HOW TO MANAGE THE CONFLICTS IN YOUR MARRIAGE

We've discussed the best ways to approach conflict when it appears. Now we want to suggest three ways to manage it constructively and resolve it satisfactorily.

1. Analyze the situation.

This requires some objectivity, but it's an essential part of the problem-solving process. Your purpose is to discover what each of you are doing to set off the quarrels, and how you contribute to their escalation. Recognize that you have a strong influence on one another, and share the responsibility for what's happening. Note what triggers the disagreement and how each of you responds. Be very specific.

For instance, one couple made a valuable discovery when the wife realized that issues were not the problem. It was her husband's practice of raising his voice (she called it "yelling") which made her feel attacked. In response, she became defensive and resentful, and soon they were off in a spate of ill feelings that had little to do with the subject they were discussing. The husband discovered that raising his voice at certain times was nothing more than a bad habit learned from his father many years before, and that it had small significance—except to trigger a hundred unnecessary confrontations.

Another wife found that although she had always perceived herself as the "victim," in reality her complaints, voiced in a weak, self-pitying manner, were setting off explosions of frustration in her husband. When she recognized her own power of choice and took equal responsibility for the problems in their life, they were able to establish new, productive ways of interacting.

It's especially important to note clashing patterns of behavior which the two of you have unconsciously picked up from your families. One of your primary

tasks in the critical first year of marriage is to work your way out of these behavior patterns and to develop a new style which represents the way you want
to live together. It takes time to unlearn behaviors, but the process will speed
up when you decide on positive ways to replace the undesirable behavior patterns, and put them into practice.

When couples can freely discuss their family homes and analyze the behaviors and customs they admire and want to retain, and also agree on the destructive behaviors and practices they want to abolish, they eliminate many of the
controversies of marriage. This detachment from families of origin and the
couple's choice to see themselves as a new decision-making unit is a key factor
in building a marriage that lasts.

Your analysis should include the topics you fight about. Is there one issue
that comes up frequently and is never resolved? Money? Personal habits? Sex?
Child rearing? In-law problems? Or do you quarrel constantly about anything
and everything? If so, the chances are good that you are substituting irrelevant
issues for a problem or problems you have not yet confronted. Is there hurt so
deep within that it has never been exposed to healing? Is there a topic on which
you are unable to communicate? Is there a sense of anger or outrage which you
can scarcely explain yourself?

In some cases, your problems may go deeper than the ordinary conflicts of
marriage which we are considering here. After reading the next chapter, "Power
Struggles: The Secret War," if you still feel confused about what is happening
in your relationship, we encourage you to consult a biblical counselor who can
help you to understand your conflicts and resolve them.

Finally, analyze how you are handling your conflicts. By pretending they
aren't there? By trying to avoid them through elaborate means which only make
you angrier inside? Or by living on the treadmill of love/anger cycles where
you are first alienated, then reconciled, only to go through the process again
and again, never dealing with the underlying causes of the quarrel? Peace at the
expense of truth will never last, because the disruptive factor has not been removed, and it will return to strike again.

It's been estimated that only one couple in five knows how to move in the
direction of lasting peace and harmony. Most, if not all, of these couples are the
fortunate ones who know how to apply biblical principles in resolving and healing conflicts.

2. Apply biblical principles.

The Bible addresses these principles to believers. It is not that they will not
work for all people, but that people will find them difficult to live out over a

period of time without the power of the indwelling Holy Spirit. The fourth chapter of Ephesians explains that believers can apply these truths because they have been made new in their mental attitudes. They are no longer empty in their thinking, darkened in their understanding, and ignorant of the true state of affairs. Here are seven principles from Ephesians 4 which will prove invaluable in managing the conflicts of married life.

1. In your anger do not sin (v. 26).

Anger is only a human emotion—raw material—which can be directed in good ways or bad. God does not command feelings, but He instructs us how to behave, no matter what our feelings are. It is possible to be legitimately angry without sinning, but it will require the greatest care and attention to following the rest of the counsel in this passage.

2. Do not let the sun go down while you are still angry, and do not give the devil a foothold (vv. 26, 27).

The enemy of our souls looks for a place to stand nearby, to find even the smallest piece of territory he can claim in our lives. He would like to use our momentary anger to lead us into sin where our anger will seize control of us. But he cannot succeed in this if we "keep short accounts." This means, in marriage, that we do not "call it a day" until we have resolved our conflict and reconciled. We may not be able to work out every detail of the right way to handle the issue in the future, but our anger should be dispelled, our hearts forgiving and forgiven, and our spirits reconciled before we go to bed, preferably lying close to one another as we fall asleep.

The wisdom of this counsel is obvious to therapists who deal continually with embittered people, choked by old resentments which were never dealt with. To become angry is part of the human condition. To nurture the anger in your heart— to allow it to take up permanent residence—is sin.

3. Do not let any unwholesome talk come out of your mouths, but only what is helpful for building others up according to their needs, that it may benefit those who listen (v. 29).

It is also sin to express your exasperation, fury, or indignation in foul words or cruel speech which tears down the listener. When conflict arises, restrain your tongue, and do not speak until you can say healing, helpful, upbuilding, and beneficial things to your mate.

Good counsel can be found in Proverbs, where we are reminded that "A fool's wrath is quickly and openly known; but a prudent man ignores an insult" (Prov.

12:16 AMPLIFIED). "Good sense makes a man restrain his anger, and it is his glory to overlook a transgression or an offense" (Prov. 19:11 AMPLIFIED). "He who foams up quickly and flies into a passion will deal foolishly" (Prov. 14:17 AMPLIFIED), but "A gentle tongue (with its healing power) is a tree of life" (Prov. 15:4 AMPLIFIED). It's a wise practice to pray the prayer of the psalmist when you feel anger coming on: "Set a guard over my mouth, O LORD; keep watch over the door of my lips" (Ps. 141:3).

4. And do not grieve the Holly Spirit of God, with whom you were sealed for the day of redemption (v. 30).

How do we know what will offend or sadden the Holy Spirit who indwells us? We need to become intimately acquainted with the Word of God which tells us and shows us in a myriad of ways what will please and displease the Lord. This should become our standard of behavior, particularly when we are tested by the heat of anger. We should allow the Spirit of Christ to be the umpire in our hearts whenever differences and conflicts arise between us.

5. Get rid of all bitterness, rage and anger, brawling and slander, along with every form of malice (v. 31).

In these seventeen words six dangerous and disagreeable manifestations of anger and conflict are catalogued: bitterness—that ugly build-up of old anger turned inward; rage—anger expressed in outbursts; settled feelings of anger—animosity; brawling—shouting, clamor, or contention; slander—abusive evil-speaking; and malice—an active ill-will which demonstrates its spite in various kinds of wickedness and injury. We are told: Get rid of them! Remember, the choice is ours, and God will work within us, if we allow Him, both to will the right choices, and to give us the power to carry them out.

6. Be kind and compassionate to one another, forgiving each other, just as in Christ God forgave you (v. 32).

This is the positive behavior designed to replace the vices of anger listed above. First we are to be kind, even in the midst of conflict. The word means, literally, "what is suitable or fitting to a need." Be and do what is suitable and what your loved one needs. It is more than attitude; it is action. Second, we are to be compassionate, looking on our mate with a deep-seated emotional concern and affectionate sympathy. The word involves strong feelings and an empathy with our mate in what he or she is going through. Third, we are to be forgiving. This word means to give freely and graciously as a favor. What we give is a promise to lift the burden of our partner's guilt and to remember it no more. Individuals who use their spouse's past wrongdoings like a cattle prod to keep the erring one in line evidently have not yet experienced the free and gracious forgiveness available to them in Christ Jesus.

When you are attempting to communicate and negotiate differences with your mate, begin with mutual confession of wrongs and forgiveness, freely given. If you do not do this, your discussion will never get beyond replays of old offenses. Clear the air and begin afresh with the grace of forgiveness.

7. *Be imitators of God, therefore, as dearly loved children and live a life of love, just as Christ loved us and gave himself up for us as a fragrant offering and sacrifice to God* (Eph. 5:1–2).

The counsel is simple and all-encompassing: Follow God's example through the life of His Son, just as children who are loved imitate their father gladly. Live a life of love with your marriage partner, giving yourselves freely to one another, and differences can be resolved as quietly as they arise.

3. Adapt to one another.

Listen to the experience of a couple who have been married twenty years. According to the husband, "We negotiated—but not without hassle, a lot of conflict, and accommodation. Looking back, we concluded that it was our ability to meet conflict head on, and not to avoid it, to utilize it as a means of becoming closer instead of permitting it to drive us apart, that enriched our relationship."

What this couple accomplished is the challenge of every married couple—to learn to adapt when differences arise (after all, no two people are going to have the same needs, desires, moods, preferences, hang-ups, or beliefs all of the time); to adjust to changing conditions; and to grow together while resolving the conflicts of their shared life.

To accomplish these tasks, a couple has to learn to negotiate, accommodate, communicate, and tolerate. Moreover, they must learn to investigate problems in their marriage and create solutions, and, always, to demonstrate certain positive ways of relating to one another.

To negotiate is, very simply, *to talk over and arrange terms*. It also means *to solve a problem or surmount a difficulty so as to be able to proceed toward something*. This is precisely what we must do in marriage, with the goal of overcoming our conflicts and differences and proceeding together toward a harmonious, smooth-working, enjoyable partnership.

Negotiation can accomplish little without accommodation at its side. To accommodate is *to make suitable, to bring to harmony or agreement, to become adjusted and adapted, to settle differences.* We can only arrange the terms of negotiation by being willing to fit ourselves to one another's needs and wishes in marriage. Always, the goal as we negotiate is to find that proper fit together, so that we can become suitable for one another in the details and choices of our common life.

We negotiate and accommodate just as the couple married twenty years did— by refusing to allow conflicts to take control of our marriage. Instead, we confront them and utilize them to become closer and to forge deeper understanding and a stronger partnership.

But to negotiate effectively and accommodate ourselves to one another, we must learn to communicate. Although this is not a chapter on communication (see chapter 5, "Communicating: Your Lifeline in Marriage" in our book *The First Years of Forever*), here are some suggestions.

First, avoid sweeping statements and broad generalizations as though they were poison to your relationship. They are! Instead, be positive and be specific. Pinpoint changes which you would like to see, item by item, rather than heaping clouds of general disapproval on your partner. At the same time communicate your respect and appreciation for your partner in every discussion. Remember that negative statements will leave conflicts unresolved and even intensify them. Many couples do not know how to express their needs in a nonblaming way, but like any other skill, this can be learned. Speak carefully, clearly, and always in a nonattacking way. Listen as carefully as you speak, and make sure you have the message. Take turns and don't interrupt.

It's important to discuss these matters in a calm, private environment. Approach the negotiations as problem-solving sessions in which you investigate the problems and then come up with creative solutions *together*. Removing the emotional weight from your discussion is the first step. Agree to love one another, no matter what, and discuss within the context of belonging, not as adversaries. After you have removed the emotional threat, add the element of togetherness: you will solve your couple problem together. Expect to put mutual effort into the solutions you come up with, and look at it as an opportunity for deeper intimacy.

The basic principles of problem-solving should be followed in your discussions. First, define the problem clearly, taking input from both and coming up with a description of the problem in which both can concur. List possible solutions in a "brainstorming" session where you bring forth ideas and refrain from shooting them down. Be creative; be flexible. Later, you can analyze the suggestions and agree on the alternative which seems best. If both spouses have different suggestions, strike a compromise solution. When you have come to an agreement, write down your solution—the result of your negotiations—as specifically as possible, including the behaviors which will be required of each partner.

You will also need to tolerate the situation while you work to bring about the desired improvements in your relationship. It is a matter of accepting short-term dissatisfaction to attain long-term goals and rewards. One thing can help immeasurably: to demonstrate consideration, tact, and good manners.

A survey of four hundred counselors has reported *lack of consideration* as the chief cause of marital incompatibility. We also find that bad manners are often a primary source of marriage problems. In marked contrast, treating one another tactfully with careful thought given to the other's feelings will go far to carry you through periods of conflict.

Tact has been defined as the way in which we verbally handle and touch others so that they feel a sense of worth and security. It is, after all, a kind of mind-reading," Sarah Orne Jewett says. But we lose the ability to do this when we are preoccupied with other things. When personal wishes, distractions, or exhaustion take over, we lose touch with our partner's feelings. Thus, it is better to save discussions for special times when neither is tired and both are free to concentrate on one another. In the meantime, even in the heat of stress, remember that tact plus thoughtfulness equals the consideration your marriage needs.

Understanding and resolving your conflicts will always require consistent, patient effort and a great commitment of emotional energy. This is the work of marriage which catches couples by surprise. As one wife said, "Who would think we could find that many things to argue about in the course of the first year? We had to work through every detail of our life, from when to go to bed at night to which family to spend Fourth of July with. We even had our disputes about how to rinse dishes and which personal possessions we were willing to share. But we've learned how to adjust to each other—to negotiate and accommodate, and to change when change is needed. Now we're a couple, not just individualists trying to live together. We've made it! At least, we're ready for the next test."

Commit yourselves to resolving conflicts in ways that bring you closer and forge a stronger partnership. This is the thirteenth step in building a marriage that can survive any difficulties.

SUGGESTIONS

1. Open a new section in your notebook entitled "Conflicts." Record major conflicts in your marriage and how you have resolved them. Go through the steps you took, and compare them with the suggestions in this chapter.

2. Observe your secret choices as you relate to your partner during periods of conflict. Do they help or do they spark fresh turmoil? Make some written commitments concerning more constructive behavior which you intend to put into practice.

3. Study the communication techniques in chapter 5 of our book *The First Years of Forever*.

4. How would you rate your tact/consideration/good manners quotient? Note three times recently when you have been less than tactful or thoughtful with your mate. See what you can learn from the timing and circumstance of these happenings to avoid this behavior in the future.

8

Power Struggles:
The Secret War

> Have we learned to respect, adapt, and compromise, or are we locked in a power struggle, both trying to take control?

What causes fights and quarrels among you? Don't they come from your desires that battle within you? You want something but don't get it . . . (James 4:1–2).

HAVE YOU CONSIDERED the possibility that when you're fighting about money, sex, personal habits, child rearing, or in-laws, that's not what you are fighting about? The real issue may be *control*, with the answers to these questions at stake: Who's in control in this marriage? Which one of us has the power to tell the other what to do and when? Which one of us gets his or her own way? Whose rights take precedence? Of course, these questions are seldom verbalized, but they remain the issue.

For instance, counselors and researchers agree that in today's culture, money causes more marital difficulties than almost anything else. They also say that money is not the real problem. It is only a symbol, the sign of power and self-worth. Because the myth that money power buys happiness has been widely accepted, the use of it triggers explosive disagreements. After all, most people today feel entitled to happiness, and those who believe the myth are threatened if money is not available to attain it. The battle over personal habits, also a leading cause of marital discord, boils down to the individual's right to be him or herself and behave accordingly—or the partner's right to demand change. Again, a contest for power. Power struggles are the most common conflict of marriage. They are also the least understood. Think of them as a secret, mostly silent war fought with diversionary tactics, amid confusion as to who the enemy really is. They agitate quarrel after quarrel over matters that are beside the point, and, ultimately, they can destroy your partnership.

Consider these examples of control and the struggle for it, as taken from life in a one-week period.

Couple A fight over who controls the money. He demands that she prove her commitment to their marriage by getting a full-time job. He will handle her paycheck and give her a weekly allowance.

Couple B fight over his right to free time. Although he works two jobs, she tries to control how he spends the rest of his waking hours. "You can't go fishing tonight; remember, it's your turn to clean the bathrooms."

Couple C fight over his enjoyment of wine with his dinner. A new Christian, she tells him, "I will not tolerate social drinking in my house."

Couple D fight over the way he dresses. She: "That shirt and tie look terrible together. And why are you wearing *that* suit?" He: "I don't tell you how to dress. So don't tell me. You're always trying to change me."

Couple E fight over *everything*—sex, dealings with their children, decisions concerning the upkeep of their house, where and when to vacation, the kind of car to buy—the list of controversies in their home is endless. (The first hour of cleaning the garage together can result in World War III.) Neither is in control, neither trusts the other, and both are miserable.

Couple F never fight. She fulfills his expectations to be all things to him when she gets home from a demanding job—to cook the meals he likes, to listen to him, and to be absorbed in him, even though she longs to have time to herself after the pressures of the day. She also runs his errands on her lunch hour, does all the tasks he finds disagreeable, and somehow keeps life moving smoothly for him. She is desperately tired and unhappy.

The secret war depicted in these examples defeats all parties involved, but may give a false sense of victory to one. The tactics employed during power struggles range from nagging, withholding sexual favors, pouting, or totally withdrawing, to threats, yelling, even hitting, and other disagreeable behavior, such as trying to gain control by exposing the partner's weaknesses in front of others. Battering one another with cruel, abusive words is a method frequently used. Bickering becomes the daily diet of many a couple who have not resolved the basic issue of control.

Because each ongoing power struggle is as unique as the two individuals engaged in it, it is difficult to make predictions as to the outcome. There are several possibilities. The war may continue, bitterly unresolved. One partner may gain the upper hand with the other partner unable to resist. Both may react in passive-aggressive ways with no one at the helm. The couple may fall into the miserable habit of feuding as a way of life. "Partners" may become disgruntled individuals residing in one house but going their separate ways, their marriage existing on paper only. Divorce may be their "final solution." Civil war, dictatorship, anarchy, perpetual unrest, or the annihilation of the marriage are disagreeable choices, indeed.

Ready for the good news? It doesn't have to be like that. Remember the God-given power of your will, not bestowed so that you can trample your mate and obtain your own way, but so that you can make positive choices which will ensure the blessings of marriage for yourself and your partner. By understanding the cause of power struggles and applying biblical solutions, you can eradicate them from your relationship. Only the ordinary differences will remain, to be worked out with courtesy, compassion, and grace. Is that promising too much? It will depend on your response to biblical counsel.

To understand the cause of power struggles we need to return to the Garden where the first man and woman began their marriage under ideal conditions. God intended husband and wife to be a spiritual, functional unity, centered in Him, and living and loving without sin. The marriage ordinance given in Genesis 2:21–25 made no provisions for headship, for the first couple began their marriage in joyous unity with perfect order in their relationship. But when sin entered into the world through Eve's deception and Adam's deliberate disobedience, it changed everything.

The couple became *self*-centered and ill at ease, not only with God, but with one another. Their symptoms of mistrust and alienation took root and sprang up like giant weeds in the fertile soil of humankind's newly-acquired sinful nature, with the capacity to choke out love and mar or destroy marriages from that time forth.

Since then we have seen, historically and personally, that the working of sin produces disorder, disintegration, and chaos. And yet we find a greater power at work: God, desiring to restore order and blessing to our lives, if we choose to follow His plan in faith and obedience.

Threaded throughout the Bible is the motif of blessings and cursings. We find this motif imprinted upon marriage, as well as other aspects of life. The verb "to bless" (the great benediction word of the Bible) basically means "to enrich." God is always the source of our enrichment and blessing. "To curse" means "to impose a ban or a barrier, a paralysis on movement or other capabilities." Thus, marriage was designed to enrich our lives, but when sin takes charge, it literally paralyzes the love relationship. The marriage can go nowhere, and the power struggles between husband and wife form what appears to be an insurmount-able barrier to blessing.

We know that sin lies at the root of these struggles, but the specific problem is selfishness in its many forms. James explains,

> For wherever there is jealousy (envy) and contention (rivalry and selfish ambition) there will also be confusion (unrest, disharmony, rebellion) and all sorts of evil . . . practices (James 3:16 AMPLIFIED).

Selfishness has three children—ugly offspring named Lust, Pride, and Fear. These are the three forces which produce the power struggles of marriage, and, indeed, all power struggles. In every case, the problem can be traced back to one of the Gruesome Threesome running amok in human affairs. These three prefer to go by other names which suggest that right is on their side. My Rights, My Needs, What's Best for Me, My Position, I Deserve, and I Am Important are just a few of their aliases, but the New Testament writers dispose of all their pretensions.

John says,

> For all that *is* in the world, the lust of the flesh, and the lust of the eyes, and the pride of life, is not of the Father, but is of the world (1 John 2:16 KJV).

James concurs,

> What causes fights and quarrels among you? Don't they come from your desires that battle within you? You want something but don't get it (James 4:1–2).

It is our lust for *what we want*—for pleasures, for possessions, and for our own way about things—which motivates us to quarrel. In a marital partnership, colliding lusts will inevitably produce power struggles. So will a situation where one partner thwarts the other's efforts to obtain what he or she wants.

Pride also produces power struggles. Philosopher Ralph Waldo Emerson asserts that "Life is a search after power." The desire to dominate, to prove one's own power and authority, and to authenticate one's sense of self-righteousness, by some form of force if necessary, is as old as Cain.

Finally, there is fear which manifests itself in many forms. We may fear being controlled—losing our self-hood under the domination of a partner. We fear our own weakness and suspect that, unless we fight, we'll be cheated out of our rights. We sometimes fear change and thus fight it all the way, thinking that if we can keep control, we can stop change from happening. Most often, we fear not being in control of our situation; the more fearful we are, the more control we want to exert. In fact, control literally means a counter-roll against the roll or list of a ship. When we fear the ship of our life is rolling too far in one direction, we try to exert control over our partner to correct the situation. Our partner may over-react to compensate for the imbalance in the other direction, and so on. Power struggles!

A key fact to remember about fear is that it is incompatible with love. When fear takes over, there is no place for love. The two cannot stay in the same room (or heart) for long. Which will you choose? John explains,

> There is no fear in love; but perfect love casteth out fear: because fear hath torment. He that feareth is not made perfect in love (1 John 4:18 KJV).

Lust. Pride. Fear. Under this broad outline each of us can fill in the details of our own struggles. Remember that it always takes two for a power conflict. Neither mate is exempt from responsibility.

If we choose, we can look in the Bible as in a mirror to see ourselves the way we really are. As the saying goes, it's not a pretty sight! But always the Bible moves quickly to solutions which can heal, restore, and transform the human condition. In the remainder of the chapter, we want to concentrate on the biblical cure for power struggles, focusing on the epistle of James, which points us to the kind of behavior and perspective which can end the secret war.

Does James understand the conflicts of marriage? You bet! We have only to read his description of the tongue at work:

> We all make mistakes in all kinds of ways, but the man who can claim that he never says the wrong thing can consider himself perfect, for if he can control his tongue he can control every other part of his personality! The human tongue is physically small, but what tremendous effects it can boast of! A whole forest can be set ablaze by a tiny spark of fire, and the tongue is as dangerous as any fire, with vast potentialities for evil. It can poison the whole body; it can make the whole of life ablazing.
>
> No one can tame the human tongue. It is an evil always liable to break out, and the poison it spreads is deadly. We use the tongue to bless our Father, God, and we use the same tongue to curse our fellowmen, who are all created in God's likeness. Blessing and curses come out of the same mouth—surely, my brothers, this is the sort of thing that never ought to happen! (James 3:2, 5–6, 8–10 Phillips).

What's the solution? Wisdom, James says. *True wisdom.* Wisdom *from above* in contrast to the wisdom produced by this world and our own lower nature guided by the Devil. True wisdom from above gives us the kind of behavior and perspective which can end the war. How do we know it when we see it? Its first characteristic is humility.

> Are there some wise and understanding men among you? Then your lives will be an example of the humility that is born of true wisdom. But if your heart is full of rivalry and jealousy, then do not boast of your wisdom—and don't deny the truth . . . you may acquire a certain wisdom, but it does not come from God—it comes from this world, from your own lower nature, even from the devil. For wherever you find jealousy and rivalry you also find disharmony and all other kinds of evil. The wisdom that comes from God is first utterly pure, then peace-loving, gentle, approachable, full of tolerant thoughts and kindly actions, with no breath of favoritism or hint of hypocrisy. And the wise are peacemakers who go on quietly sowing for a harvest of righteousness (James 3:13–18 Phillips).

Let's take a closer look at this wisdom "from above" (called "skillful and godly wisdom" in Proverbs 24:3 AMPLIFIED) to determine what it is and how one obtains it. At the core of the New Testament we discover that Jesus Christ, the Son of God and Lord of Life, "has become for us wisdom from God" (1 Cor. 1:30). Through Him we gain an understanding of the true nature of things, and this becomes the basis for the way we live and think. As we recognize who God is, and as we enter into a vital relationship with Jesus Christ, we develop a clarity of insight which makes it possible to understand more and more from the divine perspective. And that is godly wisdom: "the ability to see things from God's viewpoint."

Is this some mystical knowledge which comes in mysterious ways? Not at all. We have been given the Bible in order to learn God's will on almost every issue of life. While not all our questions are answered, we have all of the principles we need to conduct our lives wisely. "Skillful" wisdom comes to us as we spend time reading and studying the Bible on a consistent basis, and putting what we learn into practice. This is how to develop the practical wisdom and mental good sense needed to live life in all areas—including the important area of choices.

The epistle of James reminds us that wisdom also comes from God in response to our asking,

> If any of you lacks wisdom, he should ask God, who gives generously to all without finding fault, and it will be given to him (James 1:5).

No one should think, however, that God offers instant wisdom on demand, like a heavenly Coke machine. When James speaks of the wisdom that is from above, he uses a present tense participle: "Wisdom *is coming* from above." In other words, we don't get a chunk from the commissary to last us a lifetime, and we don't purchase it on the installment plan. Wisdom comes to us in a steady flow from the mind of God and keeps on coming to meet the demands of our lives, from hour to hour. The supply never runs out, and it is always available to us as we walk with Him in the light of His Word.

Not only does God's wisdom enable us to see rightly and truly from the divine perspective, it also makes it possible for us to behave in wonderfully constructive ways. James describes seven expressions of wisdom in the lives of those who receive it from the Lord moment by moment. This wisdom is:

1. undefiled by our lower nature.
2. peace-loving, rather than combative and contentious.
3. considerate, courteous and gentle.
4. submissive, respectful, willing to yield to reason.
5. full of compassion and good actions.
6. wholehearted, free from doubts and waverings.
7. straightforward, sincere, and not manipulative.

What would happen in your marriage if one or both of you began living out these seven expressions of wisdom? First and foremost, the heat of controversy and bad feelings would be dispelled. Obviously, you can gain much more cooperation from your spouse with this kind of behavior than with threats and acts of war. Therapists warn couples to provide positive reinforcement to one another. Can you think of anything more positive than these expressions of wisdom lived out in your marriage?

Note that wisdom does not close the door to discussions of issues which will inevitably arise in a marital partnership. It does direct those discussions in channels of straightforward, nonmanipulative courtesy and sweet reason. You see, wisdom also knows how to communicate. In a few words James shows us the essence of good communication in marriage: "Everyone should be quick to listen, slow to speak and slow to become angry" (James 1:19). The couples who begin listening to one another, controlling their tongues and refusing to take offense are well on the way to moving from war into a state of negotiated peace.

When the heat is off and the bad feelings dispelled, what remains are ordinary conflicts to be resolved by the techniques given in chapter 7. And now, once the issue of power struggles and control has been cooled, you are set free to see all things differently. Wisdom includes both a godly perspective and godly behavior.

For example, in the case of Couple D, the issue of what clothes he wears may no longer be symbolic of the issue of control. She will learn to express herself tactfully, and he will feel free to accept her advice. In fact, he may be pleased that she loves him enough to advise him on his appearance. Now that the war has ceased, he can appreciate her good taste and her valuable assistance.

Similarly, when a husband asks his wife to keep her hair long, she may resent it as an attempt at control. When wisdom sweetens their relationship, she may be flattered by the delight he has in her long hair, and glad to please him by wearing it that way. It's all in the perspective, and the perspective can be changed by wise behavior.

We need to remember that because we have a sinful nature, pride, fear, and the lust to have our own way will always be controlling factors when the Lord is not in control of our lives and our choices.

James shows us how to turn the control over to the Lord in three important steps.

1. Submit yourselves, then, to God (James 4:7).

He reminds us of a basic principle: God opposes the proud but gives grace to the humble. The word for "opposes" is a military term: He *battles* against the proud. As long as we arrogantly fight against Him, we are conducting a losing battle. But if we humble ourselves before the Lord, "He will lift us up" (James 4:10). Anyone who has been lifted up by the Lord knows what a wonderful, life-transforming experience that is. The price we must pay for it is agreement with God about our own foolishness and sinful behavior, and the desire to exchange our lack of wisdom for His grace and love to be poured through our lives.

Lest we forget, He warns us again about arrogant, self-assertive behavior:

> Now listen, you who say, "Today or tomorrow we will go to this or that city, spend a year there, carry on business and make money." Why, you do not even know what will happen tomorrow. What is your life? You are a mist that appears for a little while and then vanishes. Instead, you ought to say, "If it is the Lord's will, we will live and do this or that." As it is, you boast and brag. All such boasting is evil (James 4:13-16).

Since our lives are no more than a puff of smoke, we have no grounds for our arrogant assertiveness in marriage. These are the biblical facts:

1. We don't even know what is going to happen tomorrow.
2. His will, not ours, will be accomplished.
3. Our life is no more than a mist which vanishes away.

When we come to see that our plans are not our own, our time is not our own, and our lives do not even belong to us, we will develop a true perspective of life in which there is no room for self-assertion, but a dependency on God's will. This dependence can bring peace to our hearts and to our marriage.

James also directs us to the principle of taking our needs to God in prayer, rather than trusting power plays and negative approaches to gain our own way with our partner. But the motive of our hearts must be good:

> When you ask, you do not receive, because you ask with wrong motives, that you may spend what you get on your pleasures (James 4:3).

The Greek word for "spend" actually meant *squander*: God knows that when we get what we think we want, we're apt to throw it away, like the Prodigal Son who went to a far country and squandered his inheritance before returning to his father. God wants us to pray for every need in our marriage—to pray together, with no ill feeling between us hindering our prayers. He always delights to meet our genuine needs.

Submitting to God also involves submitting to one another. One of the attributes of wisdom, as described by James, is a submissive, respectful, willing-to-yield-to-reason attitude. We are instructed to "be subject to one another out of reverence for Christ" (Eph. 5:21 AMPLIFIED), and the next verses in Ephesians 5 and 6 deal with the order and stability of the home—wives being subject to their husband's loving and protective leadership, and children obeying their parents. In a good marriage, unmarred by power struggles, clearly defined boundaries exist. Everyone knows what is expected of husband and wife; of parents and children.

Such balance does not signify a rigid establishment—a pecking order—but a stable arrangement for relationships and interaction in the home which allows room for variations as needed and mutually agreed upon. The husband and wife are equal partners before God with different roles and responsibilities, and they must be free to work together and interact for constructive change. (In marriages where one is afraid to talk to the other, nothing can change.) Think of compromise as a promise to work things out, a flexible and reasonable approach to the issues to be decided. When our compromise is based on a realistic attitude and a godly perspective it will work!

Within God's order are varied ways of setting up the details of the marriage partnership, sharing responsibility and control according to biblical guidelines and the gifts and preferences of each partner. Marriage partners must achieve a fine balance between dependence and support, with a fair division of the household/family responsibilities, for if both partners are present and in reasonably good health, one partner should not have to bear the burden of the other person or of the family and home all of the time. Partners are to be *helpers*, aiding and supporting one another as friends and allies. (See Gen. 2:18–22.)

When we submit to God, we gain the capacity to submit graciously to one another. When we go to God, freely confessing our sins, we receive the ability and desire to go to our mate, confessing where there has been offense; forgiving, and being forgiven. At this point, real healing begins.

2. Resist the devil, and he will flee from you (James 4:7).

God wants us to recognize the real enemy: the Devil himself. Our mate is not our enemy. We have only one real adversary, and he is the enemy of our souls, the enemy of our marriage, the one who is anti-love, who works to bring about divisions, disintegration, and chaos in human affairs.

After we recognize the enemy, we need to know this powerful fact: If we resist him, he will have to flee from us. But if we accept his subtle promptings without resistance, we will slip into evil-doing as naturally as a fish sliding into a stream. According to James, we must exert ourselves to:

(1) submit ourselves to God's control and authority.
(2) learn from the Bible what good we ought to do.
(3) do it! (See James 4:17.)

3. Come near to God and he will come near to you (James 4:8).

Responding to this gracious invitation is the third step in turning the control of our lives and our marriages over to a loving God. When we do this, control problems seem to melt away. We still have problems, challenges, decisions, and the difficulties of life before us. We still will have to learn to adjust, adapt, and compromise in the details of our partnership. But the fierce war for control because of our out-of-control fears, pride, and lusts is settled. We can be moved out of this place of established peace *only by our own choice*.

> Turn the control of your life and the power struggles of your marriage over to God to settle the war once and for all. This is the fourteenth step in forming a marriage filled with peace.

SUGGESTIONS

1. In the "conflict" section of your notebook, add your observations on power struggles in your marriage. Do they exist? To what extent? Think of issues which

produce fights and quarrels because they represent *control* in your marriage. What area do you most want to control? Why?

2. Which one of these phrases best describes your marriage at this time: civil war, dictatorship, anarchy, feuding, armed truce, state of negotiations, or established peace? Work on your desired goal and come back to the question to answer it again, one month from now.

3. How can you implement the biblical plan outlined in this chapter? If you are already in the process of doing so, at what point are you?

4. Read the seven expressions of wisdom at least once a day and ask God to display them in your life. Keep a daily record of how He answers this prayer.

5. Take one small issue which has bothered you from time to time and attempt to resolve it by a combination of compromise, respect, and adaptation.

9
Confusion or Order:
A Master Plan

Do we manage our life together in an orderly way according to a master plan, or do we live in confusion, without plan, purpose, or vision of what is most important to us?

For He . . . is not a God of confusion and disorder but of peace and order (1 Cor. 14:33 AMPLIFIED).

MARRIAGE HAS BEEN described as a continuing exercise in problem solving. Here's another way to look at it: Marriage is an unending parade of decisions demanding your attention—decisions complicated by the fact that two people are sharing one life.

Many of these decisions are major ones which should never be dealt with piecemeal: What sort of life-style do we really want? How should we spend our time and energy? How should we handle our money and what do we want to accomplish with it? How many children should we have and how should we raise them? What about our career goals and plans for further education? How can we nurture our relationship? What kind of environment do we need? What church will we attend? Who will we choose for friends? How do we balance the demands of our respective families on the holidays? How should we allocate responsibility for housework, yard work, paper work, phone calls, grocery shopping, and errands—all necessary in operating our new household? And so on, moving into the less crucial, but necessary decisions connected with establishing your working relationship as lifetime partners.

At the bottom line is a compelling question which must be answered before you can make clear, constructive, and consistent decisions on the other issues. The question: *What is **most** important in our life?*

Have you asked yourselves that question? Do you know the answer? (There may be two answers; it takes some time to become *one*.) When you have agreed on your priorities, (whatever soul-searching and debating it takes to come to that point), many of the pressing questions listed above will be resolved, with only the details to be filled in as the need arises.

In other words, your marriage needs a Master Plan, based on your priorities and reflecting what is most important to you, which can guide you in making the decisions which will shape your new life together.

This Master Plan will need to be kept up to date. Some couples schedule an annual or semi-annual "retreat" away from home in a relaxed, secluded setting to re-evaluate their Master Plan, determine how well it's working out in daily life, and set goals for the next year. This also serves as an important "touching base" time for deeper communication concerning their relationship and their individual needs. All sorts of issues can be addressed in a loving, non judgmental atmosphere with the attitude that this is the time set aside to discover better ways to relate to one another, because it's so important to both of you. It can also be a good time to plan improved ways of running your home or organizing your financial papers. Many useful books are being written on the subject of organizing one's home, possessions, finances, and life in general. You may want to study some of these ahead of time to get new ideas for your planning retreat.

Having a Master Plan and setting aside private times for updating it will eliminate the danger of following two sets of individual dreams which inevitably collide. The Master Plan has room for your dreams as well as goals, but they should be shared, understood, and turned into prayers by both partners. You can, at least, agree to pray, "Lord, if this dream is not in Your plan for our life, please take it out of (his, her, or our) heart. And if the desire is from You, show us how to delight ourselves in You so that You can fulfill the desires of our heart."

The alternative to having a plan is to have none. Couples who muddle through life without a plan face a maze of decisions, large and small, which must be anguished over, one at a time. Then they have to live with the problems which result from indecisiveness or from decisions made haphazardly. Ongoing conflicts and confusion can be expected as the two yoked together pull in different directions.

Your Master Plan should reflect (1) your priorities, (2) your specific goals, and (3) the strategies you want to incorporate to achieve those goals. But, ideally, it begins with *vision*.

What is vision? It's mental sight: the capacity to see what has not yet come to pass, but has potential fulfillment. It is unusual foresight which looks beyond the ordinary and unifies our thinking and planning and expectations. Vision should not be confused with ordinary daydreams. A daydream is a wish made with no real hope of fulfillment, unsubstantial as a cloud. By contrast, vision is forward-thrusting and strong, with power to shape your goals, integrate your marriage, and bring order into your home and your life.

Vision in the Scriptures describes a prophet's revelation from God, but in Proverbs 29:18 it also signifies the entire truth of God's revealed Word: *Where there is no vision, the people perish*. The meaning is plain: Without God's Word, people abandon themselves to their own sinful ways and suffer the consequences. On the other hand, the person who follows God's Word will be "blessed, happy, fortunate, and to be enviable" (Proverbs 29:18 AMPLIFIED).

We often apply this warning to our nation, but how about our marriage? Our home? Our family unit? If we have no vision, no consistent standards or guidance from the Bible, God's revealed truth, what will happen to us? The answer can be found in the word *perish*. The people perish without vision. The picture of perishing that comes to mind is dying in a storm at sea. But the Hebrew word for perish means "run wild, casting off all restraints. Letting your hair down literally or figuratively and becoming disheveled." Related to it are the ideas of becoming loosened, exposed, broken loose and out of control.

As counselors we see families in this kind of upheaval and marriages torn apart by the effects of "perishing" because they had no vision of truth to shape and direct their lives. Without this vision to bind everything together and to give purpose, meaning, and order to the way we conduct our affairs, sooner or later the loose ends of our tangled lives will begin to fray. Unless order takes over, they are apt to unravel completely.

In the New Testament, when God's Word addresses our tendency to anxiety, something like this unraveling is pictured. If you know any Bible verses by memory, you probably have learned this one: "Casting all your cares upon Him, for He careth for you" (1 Peter 5:7). The word for "cares" or "anxiety" is a Greek word which has the idea of *drawing in different directions*. The Scripture says that we need not be pulled this way and that by distracting anxieties because He cares for us *with forethought and interest*. Think of what it will mean to you to make this truth a part of the vision which integrates your life and keeps it together. The vision we're talking about is not only the truth as revealed by God in the Scriptures, but your personal application of that truth to your lives—in other words, the way you live it out.

Your vision for your marriage will not be exactly like any other couple's, but it can be according to God's exciting and specific plan for you, based on scriptural truth. We urge you to share your vision. Put it down on paper in a purpose statement to which you can both agree. After you have clarified your purpose, keep referring back to it; remind each other of it, or it may dissipate. You have a shared life. So wait on God together to discover the unique things He wants you to do with your shared life. Then do what He shows you, and keep the vision fresh.

If your vision is shaped by your commitment to God's truth, it will not only provide the groundwork for a Master Plan; it can lead to finding *the Master's Plan* for you.

> Share your vision and work out a Master Plan for your partnership. This is the fifteenth step in building a marriage that succeeds.

OUR SHARED VISION

What Is Most Important in Our Life

_____

_____

_____

_____

_____

_____

Our Purpose Statement for Our Shared Life

_____

_____

_____

_____

_____

_____

Signed _____ and _____

Date _____ Place_____

Bible Promise or Instruction _____

_____

_____

_____

Our Priorities

1. _____

2. _____

3. _____

4. _____

5. _____

6. _____

7. _____

Dreams to Pray About

_____

_____

_____

_____

Long Range Goals

1. _____

2. _____

3. _____

4. _____

5. _____

Specific Goals This Year

1. _____

2. _____

3. _____

4. _____

5. _____

Strategies for Accomplishing Our Goals

1. _____

   _____

   _____

2. _____

   _____

   _____

3. _____

   _____

   _____

4. _____

   _____

   _____

5. _____

_____

_____

Insights on Long Term Goals and Dreams

_____

_____

_____

_____

Master Plan Retreat

To be held where: _____

To be held when: _____

Evaluation and Update of Master Plan

Priority Changes? _____

_____

_____

_____

Long Term Goal Changes? _____

_____

_____

_____

How Well Did We Do in Achieving Short Term Goals?

_____

_____

_____

Strategy Improvements _____

_____

_____

_____

_____

New Short Term Goals? _____

_____

_____

Bible Verses—Promises, Instructions, Insight _____

_____

_____

Signed _____

10

Strategies for Your Master Plan

Have we developed any strategies for achieving our goals in marriage?

Authors' Note: Dr. Dow Pursley, a counselor at the Wheat Clinic, spends much of his time working with married couples who are taking positive steps to grow in their relationship. We have invited him to share some of his good ideas.

by Dow Pursley, Ed.D.

GOOD SEX, GOOD communication, good jobs, good school performance, and good marriages all have one thing in common: good preparation and planning. The sad truth is that although most people plan their education and jobs, they do the minimal planning for the relationship that they should be involved in for the rest of their lives: marriage.

Desiring a good marriage is noble, but unless a couple sets goals and develops a good plan to reach those goals, their marriage is only a potential waiting to be actualized! The following strategies are designed to help you plan for and achieve the goals you've set for your marriage.

STRATEGIES FOR MARRIED COUPLES

Spiritual Life Planning

Developing a spiritual plan together is essential. My wife, Joanne, and I went to Dr. Tim LaHaye for premarital counseling. He gave us many things to think about, but he strongly suggested three things which I've never forgotten:

1. Pray for each other in the presence of the other every day, calling down God's blessing and favor on each other.

2. Move one thousand miles away from each set of parents for at least the first year of marriage.

3. Telephone Dr. LaHaye, wherever he might be, before taking the step of separating under duress, even for one night.

The idea of praying for each other daily is a good practice for several reasons. Praying with our mate shows that we both are depending upon God for the outcome of our life together. Dr. Wheat says, "It's a time of shared vulnerability before God." Praying and reading the Scriptures together strengthen the marriage bond and makes it less vulnerable to the assaults of the world, the flesh, and the Devil.

Successful devotions involve both the husband and the wife and, later, the whole family. Many wives feel that if they initiate devotions, they usurp spiritual authority from their husbands. While it is true that the man is the spiritual leader in the home, I am sure the Lord didn't mean that the wife could never initiate any spiritual activities. Just as the wife often needs help with feeding and dressing the children and other so-called "domestic duties," so the husband can use some help with the spiritual oversight of the home. Only the most insecure man would object to his wife's reminders and offers to help.

Our spiritual plan should also include praying with our children as they come along. This transition from couple praying to family prayer time is much easier if the couple have started out their life together in prayer. I also strongly suggest keeping a family prayer journal, recording the date the prayer was requested, what was prayed for, and finally, the date the prayer was answered. Then highlight the answered prayer in some fluorescent color which will serve later as a reminder to your family of God's faithfulness and goodness.

Sometimes devotions are a problem for couples and families. The start-stop approach is not unusual. If the husband feels pressure that he must always give the devotional, doing all the reading and teaching, he may feel resentful, and the rest of the family may feel bored. However, it can be a source of spiritual growth for parents to watch their children enjoy learning God's principles together, as they take their turn at reading and leading.

In one family I know, family members take turns reading a passage in the Scriptures, and then, starting with the youngest, each asks the child ahead of him or her in age a question about the passage read. This brings out some friendly competition, and the husband tells me that the only problem is that he is the last to answer! Their method is a sure way to keep the college student listening to devotions because the high schooler is bound to ask an obscure and esoteric question.

Many good books are available to help you initiate devotions. I recommend Charles Swindoll's book *Growing Strong in the Seasons of Life*—his book reflects that practical application of biblical truth so needed among our "knowledge-overloaded" Christian generation. Another good tool for elementary school children is *Keys for Kids*. (Children's Bible Hour, P.O. Box 1, Grand Rapids, Ml 49501). It can be read by the youngest reading child, and is sure to be a big hit with them. (My children have the habit of reading it from cover to cover the day it arrives and still enjoy reading it as a family.)

Take Five (Radio Bible Class, Lincoln, Nebraska) is a short devotional for teenagers which can be read at devotion time. Daily, or at least every other day, the Scriptures should be read along with this.

I think every family should read at least two missionary stories per year—stories about people like George Muller, Hudson Taylor, Elisabeth Elliott, and Amy Carmichael. These will acquaint your children with missions and the stuff great men and women of God are made of. Some other books I suggest your family read are *The Chronicles of Narnia* by C. S. Lewis, *Pilgrim's Progress* by John Bunyan, and *John Foxe's Book of Martyrs*.

It helps to begin small with your devotions, ten to fifteen minutes, and then gradually add new ideas as you think of ways to enhance this time of meditation together. It doesn't have to be done on a daily basis to be effective, but it should be done consistently.

Another area of spiritual life planning has to do with the church. It is important to settle on one church where both husband and wife feel free to worship God. Situations where this simple rule has been ignored can prove troublesome to a new relationship. For example, a couple came in for counseling because they had been married six months and neither wanted to go to the other's church! They finally settled on going to his church Sunday morning and hers Sunday night, reversing the order each week. This lasted several months, and then they tried several churches that neither had attended before. Eventually they found one they both liked and could serve in.

Once you've found a church to attend together, you'll need to plan how many services you will attend each week. Some churches equate faithfulness with church attendance, and people are made to feel guilty if they miss even a midweek service. Remember that church is not there as an opportunity to impress your pastor or friends, but to facilitate your family's worship of God. Sometimes staying home from a service at night or mid-week provides valuable time for fathers and mothers to spend, both physically and spiritually, with their family.

Communication Strategies

Communication does not come naturally, but talking does! Most of us are good talkers, but few are good at the skill of listening. Genuine communication involves three qualities: "listening, taking the person seriously, and trying to understand."

When any of these qualities are absent, problems in communication result. Beware of failure to listen, lack of eye contact, physical contact, or nonverbal acceptance. Make sure ideas, thoughts, motives, and intentions are clarified. Failure to take the other person seriously (discounting his or her sincerity, feelings, statements, or beliefs) and failure to understand the person's background, emotional state, needs, goals, and desires will close the door to good communication.

Responding is a choice; reacting is a disaster! If we listen, take the person seriously, and try to understand, we can choose to respond in a way that will build the relationship rather than react in a way that will tear it down in a way that will help the other person rather than hurt that person emotionally.

Most hostility results from reacting to the way a person is feeling at any given moment, i.e., angry, upset, or irritated. Remember that ninety percent of communication is *how* something is said (tone, pitch, infections) and only ten percent involves the content of what is said.

The principle to remember is this: "A soft answer turneth away wrath, but grievous words stir up anger" (Prov. 15:1 KJV). We can, by using this principle, learn to defuse the other's anger by being calm and reassuring him or her of our intentions.

Learning to be a good communicator is important. In marriage, being able to approach each other about what we want, need, and feel is essential, but we need to do it in a Christ-like way which communicates our intentions and helps clarify our motives, thoughts, and actions for our partner.

Beware of communicating the exact opposite of what you truly want. People often do this because they believe they can get the other to change through manipulation. The word *divorce* in marriage is the ultimate manipulator. It invokes fear, anger, depression, rejection, uncertainty, and unreliability. Many people, when confronted with that word, will apologize, try to change, or even make gallant attempts to be different. But manipulation produces no long term changes, and usually comes back to slap the manipulator in the face.

In the case of one couple, for twelve years the husband regularly threatened his wife with divorce if she didn't change whatever current situation he was complaining about. After years of anxiety, she went to the lawyer and had divorce papers drawn, put them in her top drawer and waited. Sure enough, six months later, he used the magic word again, to which she replied, "Well, I took the liberty of having the papers drawn up the last time you threatened to divorce me, and they are in the top drawer. If you will be kind enough to sign them, this marriage will be history." He was angry, so he signed the papers and their divorce took place.

They saw me later for premarriage counsel before they remarried. Neither had really wanted a divorce. I am convinced that many people who get a divorce never intended to do it; instead, they are attempting to get their mate to change. When it backfires, their pride won't let the process stop.

The only way to see lasting changes develop in anyone is through unconditional love, not manipulation. Unconditional love will evoke lasting change in almost anyone over a period of time.

Financial Planning Strategies

Ninety percent of successful people have written plans and evaluate their plans yearly. The other ten percent are just so smart they don't need to write the plans down!

A spending plan must be agreed upon, and our mates should know the source of our income so they understand where we are financially at all times. The spending plan should include a one year budget and a seven year plan. How we give our money, how we save our money, and our accounting of our money all require understanding, compromise, planning, and good verbal communication about long range goals.

Financial problems are listed in eighty percent of divorces; therefore, having a good plan is not optional, but critical. Most people who come in for counseling have problems in the area of finances, and the most common problem is debt. I always recommend "plastic surgery" on credit cards, and even volunteer my scissors.

More helps for financial planning strategies are found in the following chapter of this book.

Educational Planning

Life is an ongoing educational project for most of us. Teachers need to stay certified, builders need the latest information on their trades, and real estate agents need to upgrade their selling techniques and people skills. As Christians we should plan to be the very best we can be in the calling God has given us. This is part of the creation mandate to subdue the earth.

As a couple, this means we should always encourage our mate to stretch toward excellence. Many couples are so insecure that they see any new challenge taken on by their mates as a threat to their relationship. For example, many women feel a desire to return to college after their children are in school. Sometimes an insecure husband will feel threatened when his wife expresses this desire. One husband told his wife when she said she wanted to attend college, "You are too old." She was twenty-five!

Some insecure wives panic every time their husbands must take a business trip or attend an out-of-town seminar. One woman told me that she gets so depressed when her husband leaves town that she doesn't get out of bed the whole time he is gone. This is a sign of over-dependence and creates great anxiety for the husband.

When a relationship is not growing and healthy, anything becomes a threat to it. But planning for some of these possibilities at the beginning can certainly reduce the anxiety when changes come. We should always encourage our mates to take, or subscribe to courses, workshops, journals or trade magazines which will help them be more effective in their respective callings.

Self-Esteem Strategies

How we look affects the way we feel about ourselves and how our mates feel about us. I have counseled women with drab clothing, no make-up, their hair arranged in a bun, who were surprised when their husband ran off with a woman who looked just the opposite. There is nothing biblical or spiritual about looking bad. Each person should look his or her best.

Our self-esteem plan should include, when necessary, a diet plan, an exercise program, and attention to our physical appearance, including what we wear and the appearance of our home.

Strategies for Families and In-Laws

Most of us have been taught to honor our father and mother. When they come under verbal attack, we are quick to defend them. If our mate says something unkind about them, it puts us in the unnatural position of choosing between our partner and our parents. Even if our parents have shortcomings (all parents do), we also know their strengths and feel we should point them out to the one doing the criticizing.

I recommend that couples never say anything negative about each other's parents. Always point out the positive. Even if our mate is focusing on negative characteristics in his or her own parents, we must stay positive, or anger toward parents may quickly shift our way.

It is important to decide how often we should visit in-laws and on what basis, including holidays and vacations. It is also important to know what is appropriate to share with our family. As a general rule, we should share as little about our marital difficulties as possible.

Strategies for Relating

Every couple needs a plan which includes dating every week. Here is the dating exercise I recommend.

THE DATING EXERCISE

There are three rules to follow:

1. Alternate choosing the place you think your mate would like to go. It doesn't have to be expensive.
2. Go alone. Do not spend time with friends or relatives.
3. No arguments, not about past issues, current "hot" issues, or potential issues.

Some general guidelines include the following:

1. Treat your mate as you would a first date whom you were trying to impress, and dress for the occasion.
2. The date should include eye contact, physical closeness, and upbuilding conversation.
3. Keep your date out a little longer than you think her parents would appreciate!

THE MARRIAGE CALENDAR

Doing things as a couple or family unites the couple and solidifies their relationship. A marriage calendar enables you to plan weekend activities together or as a family.

I encourage six-month planning with some flexibility. This will allow you to sit down twice a year and plan the weekend activities for the next six-month period. Such planning builds toward the future, solidifies commitment and gives short-range events to look forward to and talk about. Because most couples with children are extremely busy, do not be discouraged if some of the activities are already "planned," but be innovative and build your future together.

The Common Project Exercise

This exercise is designed to help couples re-establish communication over a joint project, perhaps a household task like refinishing furniture, painting a room, planting a garden, or landscaping the yard. Working on a project together builds memories and keeps a couple future-oriented.

The Jar Exercise

Learning our mate's needs is vital. Many couples married for years continue to do things for each other with the intention of giving them pleasure only to find that their mate would have preferred something different, didn't like it at all, or felt that the mate was doing it for himself or herself. This exercise is a good way to learn what your mate really needs.

Find two jars and place them on your respective dressers. On Sunday night place five slips of paper into your mate's jar with one of your needs written on each slip. The needs should be of a personal nature, for example:

1. I need you to hold me fifteen minutes before you leave for work this morning.
2. I would like to have thirty minutes to relax after I get home tonight before I am asked to do anything.

Each day, Monday through Friday, one need is pulled out in the morning and fulfilled before bedtime, so make sure the need can be met in one day. And remember, keep it personal.

Only about five percent of couples who remain together actually grow in their relationship, and this is through their careful planning and conscious effort. Growing a marriage has been likened to growing a garden. Neither happens by accident!

> Develop strategies to achieve your goals and carry out your Master Plan. This is the sixteenth step in building an exciting marriage.

11

The Way to Financial Freedom

> Are we free from financial pressures because we manage our money, or are we
> trapped by our habit of overspending?

**Authors' Note: Because mishandling of money has become one of the
major problems of marriage today, we offer you the financial counsel from
an expert who will show you how to free yourselves from the debt trap and
avoid the stress of financial worries.**

by George Fooshee,
author of *You Can Beat the Money Squeeze*

A FEW YEARS AGO, the Holiday Inn's advertising slogan was "The
best surprise is no surprise." After all the excitement and glitter of the wedding
is over and real living begins, the best surprise for any young couple is no financial surprise.

Just prior to celebrating their fifth wedding anniversary recently, a couple
revealed to me some startling facts about their financial mess. They still owed
for their wedding flowers! And the doctor and hospital bill for their first baby
was not yet paid.

It has been said that "A panicky present is the result of a planless past." With
more than $10,000 in past debts, there is no doubt that the previously mentioned
couple has lived in financial panic for their five years of marriage.

FINANCIAL SUMMARY

To eliminate any surprises with money, the couple should fill out a Financial
Summary, listing what they own and what they owe. The honest detailing of all
resources and obligations will bring about real openness. Completion of this
form is an essential first step in facing reality about personal finances, regard-

less of how long you have been married. You will find that genuine communication about your financial situation will be a tremendous start toward communication in your total marriage relationship. The book of Proverbs confirms the necessity of communication in marriage. "Reliable communication permits progress" (Prov. 13:17 LB).

FINANCIAL SUMMARY

WHERE WE ARE NOW   DATE _____

What we own	Total
Money in the bank, savings	_____
Stocks, Bonds, Investments	_____
Real Estate	
Home (price house would readily sell for on today's market)	_____
Other real estate	_____
Automobiles (current price car would sell for readily)	_____
Special Property (cameras, guns, hobbies, motorcycles, silver, camping equipment, stereo equipment, jewelry, etc.)	_____
Interest in retirement or pension plan	_____

What We Own Totals	
Cash & Other Savings	_____
Real Estate	_____
Other Property	_____

GRAND TOTAL OF WHAT WE OWN   _____

	Amount Due	Monthly Payment	Total
To the mortgager of our home	_____	_____	_____
Banks, Loan Companies, Credit Unions, Credit Cards	_____	_____	_____
School Loans	_____	_____	_____
Medical	_____	_____	_____
Other—Family Loans	_____	_____	_____
GRAND TOTAL OF WHAT WE OWE	_____	_____	_____

RECAP

What We **Own** Grand Total   _____
Less What We **Owe** Grand Total   _____
What We Have Accumulated (Net Worth)   _____

Analyze the resources. Do you have surplus items? Are you car rich (two relatively new costly cars) and cash poor (too little cash savings)? Do you have surplus items that could be sold or traded for other items you need? The financial summary will enable you to face the facts about your existing marital finances.

Warning! If what you owe exceeds what you own, face these facts. You are in hock! You are a debtor! Your financial past has revealed desires beyond your means. These figures should be shared with a wise Christian counselor. If you are an engaged couple, some questions to discuss are: Should our present financial condition change the kind of wedding we have planned? Can we afford the honeymoon we want?

The Bible says, "The wise man looks ahead. The fool attempts to fool himself and won't face facts" (Prov. 14:8 LB).

THE BUDGET

Don't panic and try to avoid doing a budget because you aren't an accountant or figures aren't your thing. Two simple definitions of a budget should put you at ease.

First, a budget is simply *planned spending*. Having a plan for spending will help build marital harmony and reach family goals.

A second definition of a budget is *telling your money where you want it to go rather than wondering where it went*.

Weekly I talk to couples in all stages of life who have made a mess of money management, and I see the trauma, the tears, and the tension resulting from mismanagement. Of the hundreds in trouble, I've asked the same question: "Do you have a budget? Do you have a plan for your spending?" None of these couples in financial distress has ever answered this question with a "yes."

As a first step to establishing a budget, you should estimate your living expenses on this Financial Goals form. The categories include the most common expenses.

OUR FINANCIAL GOALS

		Monthly	Annually
1.	Tithes & Offerings	_____	_____
2.	Federal Income Tax	_____	_____
3.	State Income Tax	_____	_____
4.	Social Security Tax	_____	_____
5.	Other Taxes	_____	_____
6.	Shelter	_____	_____
7.	Food	_____	_____
8.	Clothing	_____	_____
9.	Health	_____	_____
10.	Education	_____	_____
11.	Life Insurance	_____	_____
12.	Gifts	_____	_____
13.	Transportation	_____	_____
14.	Personal Allowances	_____	_____
15.	Vacations	_____	_____
16.	Savings	_____	_____
17.	Household Purchases	_____	_____
18.	Debt Reduction	_____	_____
19.	_____	_____	_____
20.	_____	_____	_____
21.	_____	_____	_____
	TOTALS	_____	_____
	Total Estimated Income	_____	_____
	Difference Between Income and Expense	_____	_____

NOTES FOR OUR FINANCIAL GOALS

These explanations of each category will guide you in arriving at the amount for each spending category. Start with the first category and work through them in order. If you have a monthly estimate, multiply it by twelve for the annual figure. If you have an annual figure, divide it by twelve for the monthly figure. Refer to your checkbook to obtain previous expenditures. Don't quit because you can't come up with a figure. Make a guess. The budget process will let you find out how close your guess is.

1. Tithes and offerings: all charitable giving.

2. Federal Income Tax: all amounts withheld, plus estimates paid, plus any amounts due with tax return.

3. State Income Tax: same as above.

4. Social Security Tax: Determine current percent withheld.

5. Other Taxes: any additional tax on your wages.

6. Shelter: a. If renting, include rent, utilities, household supplies, appliance repairs, telephone, other home related expenses. b. If you own a home, include house payments, insurance, real estate taxes, repairs and maintenance, other items listed under renting.

7. Food: grocery store items, paper goods, cleaning supplies, pet foods, all eating out, carry-out items, and school lunches. May also include entertainment.

8. Clothing: purchases, cleaning, repairs. May be divided with separate budget for each family member.

9. Health: health insurance, medical, dental, hospital expenses, prescriptions, cosmetics.

10. Education: school supplies, lessons, college expenses, uniforms, equipment.

11. Life Insurance: all premiums whether paid monthly, annually, or quarterly.

12. Gifts: birthdays, anniversaries, special occasions, Christmas, weddings, funerals, office collections, dues for organizations.

13. Transportation: gas, oil, repairs, licenses, personal property tax, auto insurance, car payments or an amount set aside to purchase your next car.

14. Personal allowance: for each family member to spend personally, such as hair care, recreation, baby sitting, hobbies, children's allowances.

15. Vacations: Trips, camps, weekend outings, trips for weddings, funerals, family visits.

16. Savings: Amounts set aside now for future needs.

17. Household Purchases: For major appliances, furniture, carpeting, and major home maintenance such as roofing and painting.

18. Debt Reduction: Includes all payments on debt not included in other categories, such as school loans, amount owed to relatives, banks, or on credit cards.

After you've discussed and added the figures, and discussed and added some more, realistically face the total. Can you live within your income? Did you grow tense while talking about money? Angry? Non-communicative? The Bible asks: "Can two walk together unless they be agreed?" (Amos 3:3). Can you be cheerful givers? (If you don't start giving early as a married couple, you will tend to be always stingy toward God.) God loves a cheerful giver.

Are you now saving, "The wise man saves for the future, the foolish man spends whatever he gets" (Prov. 21:20 LB)? Putting off saving while you are young is a real trap. It will never be any easier to save, especially if you procrastinate now. To manage money well, savings must become a habit on paydays, just as giving must be a holy habit.

Warning! If your budget won't work on paper, it won't work period. You may find that your budget won't balance.

Most of us want more than we can afford. So-called "easy payments" and readily available credit cards seem to make it possible for us to spend more than we make . . . for a time.

The average American family has to pay out twenty-three percent of net monthly income just for those "easy payments." For a young couple to achieve this heavy debt position requires only two debt areas—two student loans and one new car payment.

With student loans of $16,000 and a car loan of $8,000, monthly payments can easily be $400 (figuring eight percent for ten years on the $16,000 and fourteen percent for four years on the $8,000).

Most couples will discover that they can't balance their budget with any debt payments at all, let alone $412 a month. What's the solution? GET OUT OF DEBT! Great idea! But how?

By *emergency action!* Sell your new car. Buy an old car for a few hundred dollars that will most likely get you every place you need to go. Move close to work. Use public transportation. Ride a bicycle or moped. Share a car with another couple.

Move into free or very inexpensive housing. Share a home with another couple. Pray for an older couple who will allow you to live in their upstairs, basement, or extra bedrooms in return for lawn mowing, car washing, house-cleaning, and other services. The couples I know who have escaped debt in a short time have made temporary short term sacrifices, usually in the areas of housing and cars—their two largest expenses. By eliminating a $200 to $400 car payment and at least $500 a month for rent and utilities, from $700 to $800 per month is available to pay on the student loan payments. The debt can be paid off in 18 months rather than 120 months!

You may think such action isn't possible. Yet, by prayer and standing on God's promises of provision, thousands of couples annualy leave homes and jobs and follow God's leading to attend seminary or graduate schools. Adopting the same kinds of living action that I term "emergency action," they experience His provision.

KEEPING THE BUDGET

Not only do you need to balance your budget, but you also have to keep your budget. Each of your financial goals represents a spending category such as shelter, food, and clothing.

A budget page is similar to a checkbook register, but each page includes only one spending category. For example, visualize a checkbook register that contains only your income and spending for the Shelter Category of your budget.

CATEGORY SHEET

Category **Shelter**   Budget Amount **$560.00**

Date	Description	Income	Out-Go	Balance
1-1	Deposit from pay	$560.00		$560.00
1-3	Rent		$400.00	160.00
1-5	K-L Electric Co.		52.00	108.00
1-9	Clear Water Co.		12.00	96.00
1-10	Clean Trash Co.		8.00	88.00
1-12	Bell Telephone Co.		12.00	76.00
1-14	Daily News Subscr.		36.00	40.00
2-1	Deposit from pay	$560.00		600.00

This shelter category sheet shows where and how much was spent for housing and gives you a means of monitoring your progress. A total budget is done by having similar pages for each spending category. My wife Marjean and I have kept records for more than thirty-four years of marriage. In addition, we made it a rule never to borrow money to buy anything other than our home.

If only we could sit with you and share how God will bless your decision to live debt-free, even if you have to pay off debt now with *emergency action*. The discipline of your personal finances will encourage discipline in other areas. You will learn to say *no!* to this, in order to say *yes!* to that. The result may well be the abundant life that Jesus promised.

You can experience God's peace and blessing as you learn to plan your giving, saving, and spending. Christ came to set us free. You can achieve freedom from debt depression by carefully and realistically budgeting your wedding and living expenses. Budgeting will ensure that you grow as wise stewards of what God provides.

Learn how to manage your money to accomplish your goals and to avoid the unhappy consequences of over-spending. This is the seventeenth step in establishing a strong marriage.

12
In-laws and Other Challenges

> Are our relationships with our in-laws moving toward loving harmony, growing tensions, or open warfare?

Authors' Note: In-law clashes, stepparenting, age differences, and unexpected career changes will trouble many a marriage in the 1990s. We have asked one wife to share her learning experiences in these areas. We believe that her hard-won victories coming out of seeming defeat testify to God's grace and the importance of one's secret choices more powerfully than anything we could say to you about in-laws and other challenges.

by Victoria James

THE TITLE OF this chapter implies that in-laws are a challenge—something to be conquered or overcome. I'd rather think of the in-law relationship as an adventure, one not unlike that of building a bridge. Sometimes you feel as if you are trying to cross the Grand Canyon and other times it seems to be just a few stepping stones across a brook. It is an adventure that does, admittedly, present some challenges.

The term *in-law* can immediately conjure up every bad mother-in-law joke you have ever heard and bring visions of your mate's family dissecting you, just hoping to find something wrong. Every insecurity you ever felt suddenly rears its ghastly head because you know that *they* are going to see only the worst in you. Naturally, up goes the defensive wall!

Unfortunately, every segment of the entertainment industry has for years used the in-law relationship, especially the mother- in-law, as negative comic relief. Waiting in grocery store checkout lines, we can leaf through periodicals with headlines like the one emblazoned on the *National Enquier:* **HOW TO KEEP YOUR IN-LAWS FROM DESTROYING YOUR MARRIAGE.** No wonder we dread, even fear, these terrible people who are going to make our lives miserable. We have been "trained" to see our in-laws as the cross we must bear in order to be married to the one we love. But I, personally, see the in-law relationship as a vital and positive force in marriage. At least, it has been that for me.

Right now you may be thinking, *This gal's in-laws probably adored her from the moment they met, and the worst argument they ever had was over who was going to bring what to the family reunion.* Wrong! My in-law relationship has not been a merry little jaunt down Happiness Lane. It has been more like a roller coaster ride, running the gamut from loving acceptance to painful rejection. I was, of course, the victim of *in-law persecution*—completely blameless and totally baffled by the disagreements that seemed to keep popping up out of nowhere. (If any of you believe that, I know of a bridge in Brooklyn I'd like to speak to you about.)

Before you decide that I have just confirmed your worst suspicions about in-laws, let's take a look at a different picture. I hope that sharing my own experience with the in-law relationship will give you some insights that can help you build your bridge to a positive, loving, and rewarding relationship with your partner's family. The main components, for me at least, have been understanding, patience, and communication (none of which were my strong points). Although understanding, patience, and communication may seem obvious, there are times, in the stress of the moment, when the obvious becomes obscure and simplicity becomes a complicated jigsaw puzzle.

My first visit to my future in-laws' home was to celebrate my fiancé David's birthday. David didn't think to warn me that his family celebrates birthdays (and all traditional occasions) more formally than I was used to. My first thought when I saw the dining room was, *This is a three-fork family, and I'm a one-fork woman.* At least I hadn't worn my blue jeans and tee shirt!

The next surprise came when we all gathered around the table, held hands, and said grace. At this point, David and I had been dating for three months, but he had never told me that he came from a Christian family. In retrospect, I realize that his Christian character, which made him stand out from the other men I knew, should have been at least a clue. Don't misunderstand. I had trusted Christ as a child when my Grandma took me to Sunday school. But I was not reared in a church-going, grace-saying, Christ-centered home, and, sadly, I had for some time been wandering off course in my walk with the Lord. To be honest, if I'd wandered much further, the Lord would have had to send out a search and rescue team. (On second thought, maybe He did when He brought David and his family into my life.)

At this birthday dinner, I got my first glimpse of one of the most important things that needs to be understood and dealt with in the in-law relationship: diversity of background. In other words, this *ain't* your family, and they may do things differently than you're used to. For me, those differences encompassed broad territory: differences in religious upbringing; different traditions and different ways of celebrating them; the closeness of the extended family unit; and differences in the way problems, especially anger, were handled. This was one of those Grand Canyon times; David's family background seemed about as far removed from mine as you could get.

This is where *had I known then what I know now* comes in. Had I acknowledged and voiced my concerns to David and his family from the beginning, it would have saved us all a lot of heartache and confusion. I failed to begin building that bridge and, instead, started piling up "junk"—resentments, false assumptions, and insecurities—that began creating a wall between my in-laws and me. Ironically, they weren't even my in-laws yet!

They were unaware of the problem because of my failure to communicate. I had even managed to fall into the role of a child with my mother-in-law: she is a very motherly person. It was refreshing to be mothered at the tender age of thirty-one after so many years of being totally responsible for myself and my daughter. It was a nice change of pace to have someone making a fuss over me, and I basked in the glow of attention. It's a shame I didn't have enough sense just to enjoy it.

But my independent nature became contrary when the time came to plan the wedding. Since I had been married before, I wanted a simple, informal, outdoor wedding—very low-profile. My family had long since decided that I could make my own decisions (they weren't going to be able to attend anyway), so I expected to do things the way I wanted. David, however, was the first child in his family to get married, and his family wanted a more traditional, formal affair. Knowing that we were both short of money, they generously offered to pay for flowers, a reception, and even offered their home for the ceremony. Here was another prime opportunity to work on that bridge. A little patience, understanding, and communication would have gone a long way, but, instead, I just kept piling up that "junk."

I grudgingly agreed to suits, ties, dresses, and all the other traditional trappings, but I insisted on an outdoor ceremony. As is usually the case, stubbornness had its price, for our wedding day was windy and chilly. Because it was early spring, my hay fever went crazy and I was miserable. I'd really shown them! Anyway, I reassured myself, I was marrying David, not his family. We could go on from there and build our own little world. We would, of course, include our families in our life, but we would *not* let them dictate to us.

Unfortunately, I was ignoring a few basic facts: (1) Both of you bring your family history, good and bad, into your marriage. (2) You will always have to deal with some sort of in-law relationship. Remember, "in-law" does not stop at mother and father; it extends to brothers, sisters, grandparents, aunts, uncles, and cousins. And (3) "old habits die hard." I had had a tumultuous history in relating to my own parents, and even more difficulty in coping with my former in-laws, so I was prickly about anything that even hinted of parental interference. This led to unnecessary tension with my in-laws, most of which came out of a lack of understanding on both sides.

You see, my lack of communication and failure to be open about my past family relationships gave my in-laws no opportunity to get to know the real me—the person behind that defensive wall I'd built. My self-protective caution prevented me from getting to know my in-laws. As a result, I made a lot of assumptions that just weren't true. Assumptions can be a negative force. I have found since that when I made assumptions about someone else's thoughts or feelings, I was taking the easy way out, for I was afraid to openly confront the problems. It was easier to assume the worst. Today I am very thankful that my in-laws had more patience than I did, or we would probably still be "on the outs."

Our relationship has, at times, been very strained. I was like a keg of dynamite with a short fuse. When I got mad, I was mad all over and very vocal. I lashed out at whoever made me angry and anyone else who happened to be in the line of fire at the time. My in-laws tend to be more analytical and reasonable when dealing with anger. That's not to say they don't speak plainly, but they also listen to the other side. Not me! When I'm mad, there is only one side to be heard—mine.

David's family handled anger so differently! The problem was that they were *nice*—totally new territory to me. I didn't know how to deal with *nice*. I had grown up learning by example that anger was the way to deal with almost any unpleasant thing. I had been trained to deal with pain, hurt feelings, grief, and other negative emotions with either the "brave little buckaroo" attitude or anger. Anger was the method chosen most often in my family; thus, I found anger the most comfortable approach to handling anything other than "jump in the air" happiness. It was not a good approach, believe me! No one knew how to take my anger, including my husband, and it got pretty lonely over there in my mad corner!

My in-laws must have seen me as some kind of wild woman and wondered how their poor son would ever survive living with such a shrew. But don't give up on me yet. (My husband didn't!) I have come to see that the old patterns in my life were very destructive and have worked heart and soul to develop new patterns. I've learned to confront my true feelings and deal with them appropriately. My husband and my in-laws are aware of the true problem now, and we all work together to deal with the actual emotion (hurt feelings, or in some cases, anger) involved in the disagreements that do inevitably arise in human relationships. This wise saying from Alexander Pope's *Essay on Criticism* has come to mean a lot to me:

Good nature and good sense must ever join; To err is human, to forgive divine.

Anger was not the only thing our families handled differently. In my family, personal grief is just that: *personal*. In David's family, it is something to be shared; they have a strong support system and rally around each other to offer comfort and help. I believe that is a healthy, loving attitude, and I feel comfortable with it if the other person needs help. But when I need help, I tend to withdraw into myself, not wanting to "impose" my pain and hurt on others. It took a very painful loss for me to see the error in my thinking and to realize yet another difference in our backgrounds.

I suffered a miscarriage shortly after we had announced that the first grandchild for David's family was on its way. David and I desperately wanted this child. Even though David was an excellent stepparent and loved my daughter, he wanted a child of his own blood. His family was, of course, ecstatic. But when we lost our baby, I wanted to be left alone to suffer our grief and loss. (I didn't know then the old Jewish proverb, *A friend is not a friend until you have cried together.*)

My parents have several grandchildren, and, though they welcome each new addition enthusiastically, they held the attitude, "Something must have been wrong and it is probably for the best. We are glad you are okay. Just go on with your lives and try to forget about it."

In contrast, David's mother and grandmother came to be with me in the hospital and brought me flowers. I would not even see them. I was totally insensitive to David's family and refused to share my grief with them, even though they had suffered the loss of their much-anticipated grandchild. My bridge was getting no attention whatsoever. Not only was I failing to build a bridge to my in-laws; I was destroying the framework that was already there!

As you might have guessed, it all got worse before it got better. My in-law relationship did, in fact, completely deteriorate. It reached a point where, because of a monumental misunderstanding based on false information about a very serious matter, I was disowned by David's family and told I would never be welcome in their home again. The details of this strange episode are not important, but the principle is. It never could have happened if we had kept the lines of communication open. But God used this situation, terrible as it was. Believe it or not, things started turning around.

It was very painful for me to accept the fact that I was never going to be a part of David's family. I didn't realize how much I would miss them and how precious they were to me. If only I had done more bridge building when I could!

I had made so many mistakes. I had expected my in-laws to be the "perfect family" I had always dreamed of. I had put my mother-in-law on a pedestal (a mistake we should never make in any human relationship, for pedestals will inevitably crack and crumble), and then felt betrayed when she fell off. I wanted understanding and total acceptance, but didn't give any. I needed patience and had none; worse yet, I did nothing to develop any. And I had managed to create a rift between my husband and his family. Talk about feeling lower than a snake's belly—I had to look up to see the snake!

But I didn't give up. God graciously helped me to see a flicker of light at the end of the tunnel. I needed to work through that tunnel to climb back to the surface and start building the all-important bridge. I took the first step by calling my father-in-law at his office. (I knew my mother-in-law was too outraged to talk to me just then.) I tried to open the door to some sort of communication, and he advised me to let things be for awhile until everyone had calmed down. Much to my surprise, my mother-in-law called me that very afternoon.

I think we both felt at the time that there was nothing to lose, so we had a frank, open, and painfully honest discussion. It took a heart-wrenching effort on both sides, but we did manage to reach some agreements on developing a better relationship. One of the most important steps for me was removing the titles and beginning to think of my in-laws as people with whom I wanted to build a friendship. To me, certain titles, especially that of *in-law*, carry negtive connotations, which I can't yet put aside. This is a personal hang-up and I hope it's not true for you. I surely do get along better with my *friends* than I did my *in-laws*, and we have managed to traverse the Grand Canyon. The little creeks we occasionally encounter are definitely crossable.

In-law problems, like problems in any other relationship, are never one-sided. But the truth is that I *was* stubborn, prideful, and ornery. None of these traits are conducive to good communication, and without continuing, open, and honest communication no relationship will have a solid base.

I don't want to project a completely bleak picture of the last six years. It wasn't all bad. We had happy, fun-filled experiences. We went on a family camping trip, had many joyful family celebrations, and, at my request, my mother-in-law and I had a daily one-on-one Bible study hour during my first year in David's family. Our times of good fellowship around God's Word and her gentle guidance led me back to what I had truly wanted all along—a closer walk with the Lord. I believe God laid the foundation then which made it possible for us to reconcile later at a time when the division between us stretched miles-far and chasm-deep.

My in-law relationships are an important part of my life today, and I know that my husband is much happier when those he loves are in harmony. Thus, the building of the bridge that closed the gap between David's family and me has strengthened our marriage and enriched my life.

One of the most important things I have learned is that you can never have too much love or too many friends. My in-law relationship has been a wonderful source of both. I pray that your adventure in building a happy in-law relationship will be an exciting, positive experience which brings more love and new friendships into your life.

SOME OTHER CHALLENGES

Stepchildren

This is definitely a big league challenge! May I quote some research results which suggest a less than bright future for the marriage where stepchildren are present.

Two sociology professors from the University of Nebraska, Lynn White and Alan Booth, interviewed more than 1,600 families in 1980 and again in 1983, and found that the most difficult marriages to hold together were second marriages to which both partners brought children from a previous union. White said, "Our evidence indicates that if these couples divorced, *it was because they wanted to get rid of the stepchildren, not the spouse.*" White went on to mention *the striking early divorce pattern* due to the special stress involved in stepparenting. And having a child together to unite the families more strongly didn't help the marriages last either, according to the researchers. (Findings published in *The American Sociological Review*, Vol. 50, No. 5, and reported by *Psychology Today*, June 1986.)

When David and I made our lifetime commitment, I did not know just how difficult it can be to marry a second time with an adolescent child to incorporate into the new family. Ann, my daughter, turned twelve the day after our wedding, and we wanted so much to become a family unit that David and I postponed our honeymoon to celebrate her birthday with her.

Ann and David had related well as long as we were merely dating, and even during our engagement period, but the day we married she suddenly turned hostile, defiant, and just plain difficult. It shocked me, but David took it all in stride and acted as if nothing had changed. He was still kind and loving, even when she was sullen and ornery, but it tore me apart—to be pulled between the two people I loved most in the world. We did our best to reassure Ann that we had no intention of trying to cut her off from her father, and David made it clear that he was not trying to replace her father. We did want to create a solid family base for Ann, something she had never experienced.

David and I had joyfully entered into our marriage with a fairy tale dream of becoming "the perfect family." It was a nice dream, but Ann had her own fairy tale in mind—something along the line of Cinderella without the happy ending. David and his family did everything possible to make Ann feel accepted and loved. She was treated like a princess, and acted like a hag. She resisted all efforts to draw her into her new stepfamily, and I was more than a little upset with my daughter's pigheadedness. My fervent desire for a happy family unit blinded me to the emotional conflict and pain that Ann was going through.

Ann felt, as many stepchildren do, that if she liked David and accepted his family, she would be showing disloyalty to her father and his family. I found it hard to understand the blind loyalty she suddenly developed toward her father. He could do *no* wrong, even when he remarried without telling her and just showed up one weekend with a new wife (and another stepparent for her).

Although David was hurt, he remained steadfast and consistent in his relationship with Ann. Together we have tried to maintain a united parental front, sharing in the decision-making process, but I have not always been as consistent as David. As the natural parent, it was hard for me to let go of my overly-protective single-parent attitude and learn to share my parental role with someone who had never been a parent. (The truth was that David could deal with Ann better than I because he could remain objective.) Although I never voiced the "that's my child, not yours" routine, David could sense it in some of my reactions.

David was not the only one sensing my protective attitude. Ann seemed to have a radar system even the Navy would envy! She could always hone in on the slightest discord and try to plant seeds of discontent and doubt to separate David and me.

Parenting a testy, obstinate adolescent is difficult at best, and beginning a new marriage with a teenager in the house is like trying to mix water and oil. Things like privacy, quiet time together, and little romantic candlelight dinners at home become treasured luxuries.

Ann did everything she could to make her presence felt. Some of her tactics were less than subtle. If David and I were seated on the couch together, she would find a way to wriggle in between us; if we were trying to talk to each other, Ann suddenly needed my immediate help with some problem. In fact, she had a wide assortment of tricks to keep my attention focused on her.

She had reveled in my attention for so many years. Actually, we were too close. I had lost some of my parental authority, and she had become very possessive of me. It was understandable, but frustrating, that she resented having to share me with another person, especially someone she was expected to accept in an authority role. I began to feel like a circus juggler as I tried to divide my time and attention evenly between David and Ann. It was an impossible task: a woman's roles can never be equally divided. I kept hoping Ann would see that David was not taking anything away from her. But in trying to keep everything equally balanced between David and Ann, I was forgetting God's clear plan for marriage: that husband and wife leave all else and cleave together and become one. A child, no matter how deeply loved, can never be a part of that oneness and should not be allowed to compete with it.

I made the mistake of trying to make my husband and child equal priorities when my marriage should have been my first priority. If I had kept my "house" in proper order, we all would have been happier. Ann could not have found those tiny little cracks where she was able to drive a wedge, and David would not have had to suffer the insecurities which those wedges created.

In our case, Ann's natural father actively worked to prevent Ann from getting close to David. He did all that he could to foster her resentment. Nevertheless, for the past six years David has faithfully assumed the responsibilities her natural father cared little about. He has attended school functions, parent/teacher conferences, and every extracurricular activity where she needed support. He has helped her with her schoolwork, acted as a buffer during mother/daughter clashes, and this year he even taught her to drive!

I asked David what he thinks it takes to be a stepparent, and he gave six suggestions which I pass on to those of you who may be in similar situations:

1. Don't try to replace the natural parent.
2. Be consistent and steadfast.
3. Let the child know you are there as a friend.
4. Maintain the authority role, however.
5. Don't try to "win the child over" or buy love.
6. Don't expect thanks or recognition for your efforts.

I realize now that unless a child is very young, the child will probably not be receptive to a stepparent, and it is better to approach the marriage with a realistic acceptance of that fact. After talking to friends and acquaintances who have been either in the stepchild or the stepparent role, I find a general consensus that stepparents are not outwardly accepted or appreciated until the child has been away from home for awhile. But then, do any of us truly appreciate our parents, step or natural, until we are out on our own and using the skills they've taught us?

Yes, stepchildren will be a challenge in almost any marriage, but when two become one in a biblically-based marriage, the challenge becomes less intimidating. Actually, there's more love to go around for the children, and they have the benefits of stability and order and security in their home setting. This can only do them good, not harm. They may demand more unconditional love than you ever thought you could give, but God will provide that too.

What a comfort to know that the Lord does guide us through this most prickly area of a second marriage.

Age Differences

When David and I married, he was twenty-three and I was thirty-two, but neither of us considered the fact that I was nine years older a challenge. Unfortunately, some of our friends seemed to think it was a critical area of concern and felt compelled to remind us of it—constantly!

As I look back on it, I wonder if these people were truly concerned about our future together, or if they thought we were just too dumb to do simple arithmetic. The fact was that David knew how old I was all along, and I assumed he was older than he was. He has one of those ageless faces—neither young nor old—and by his own choice he had been working since the age of fourteen and living on his own since the age of eighteen. David was more mature and responsible than any man I had ever dated, and by the time I found out about the age difference, my heart had already made a private but eternal commitment to him.

True love knows no age limits, and I am glad that David and I were unconventional enough not to worry about what other people thought, and to follow our own best judgment on the matter. We did not let our emotions blindly lead us into marriage, for we were both committed to the permanence of marriage and we wanted no mistakes. We spent a lot of time getting to know each other on an intellectual basis; we knew early on that we had connected at the emotional level! We found many common interests and just enough differences to make life interesting. Our age difference did show up in our taste in popular music, but we found a compromise between the Beatles and Three Dog Night—we listened to Alabama instead.

Have there been any "age" problems? I have felt a bit insecure occasionally—after all, he is gorgeous and women are always attracted to him. But he has never wavered in his love, devotion, and total loyalty to me. Our marriage has not always been in perfect harmony (that might be boring), but our discord has rarely been because of the difference in our ages.

I have seen people walk away from what could have been happy relationships because "society's" opinion frightened them. One of my best friends suffered two years of loneliness because she was older than the man she loved. After seeing how happy David and I were together, she finally accepted the younger man in her life when he proposed for the umpteenth time, and they are now happily married.

Today, the trend is changing. More marriages between younger men and older women are taking place—a satisfactory arrangement for both, according to all I have read on the subject. In our case, age played no part in our attraction to one another—we just belonged together and knew it! From our experience, the anticipation of problems connected with age differences can be much worse than any actual problems that may emerge.

When people ask my opinion, I say, "Don't look at the birth certificate; look at the person, his (or her) mind, heart, and soul. You're not going to be cuddling up to a birthdate, but to a person."

Adapting to Career Changes

As a career woman with a secure job in the social work field at the time I married, I valued my independence. Since then I have learned some hard lessons in the process of adapting to my husband's plans.

First, David took a new job which required us to move to another town, and I accepted a position as a bookkeeper. That move wasn't so bad, for, in that city, our Christian foundations were strengthened. (How much I would need that a little later on!)

Two years later, David made the decision to go to college in another state, and so we were off and moving again. As it turned out, Ann hated her new school, I couldn't find a position in my field, and David decided school could wait for awhile. We missed our friends, and as far as I could see, the only good thing that happened there was David finding a job in his profession at higher wages. During this time I nursed an elderly relative through a seven-month illness which proved to be terminal—a traumatic experience—and I myself had to be hospitalized with stress-related symptoms and exhaustion. After a few months of much-needed rest, I found a secretarial position with a salary of less than half of what I had been making before we moved. By now I was convinced that this independent career woman had lost control of her life. I also suspected that God was punishing me for something, but I was soon to know the truth about that.

Just as I was beginning to settle into this new life-style, something truly shocking occurred. My husband came home and told me he had decided to join the Army to receive the education he needed to enter a new profession in the mental health field. As if in a bad dream, the wheels of the United States Army began to roll over the secure life I had tried to construct with my husband. David was stationed a thousand miles from home, and after basic training, he was shipped to another base, more than a thousand miles away in the other direction, for Advanced Individual Training. For seven months David and I were separated—we who could never bear to be separated, even for a night.

David's income went from $600 a week to little more than $600 a month, and I took on two extra part-time jobs to keep a roof over our heads while he was away. To say that I was angry, that I felt deserted, would be an understatement.

David's timing could not have been worse, as far as I was concerned. The longer he was away, the more desolate I became. As I grew more tired and more lonely, my coping ability bottomed out. One night I collapsed in bed and began praying from the very depths of my soul. I poured my heart out to the Lord and confessed my weaknesses, and my sins of hardheartedness, judgmental behavior, and many other sins of the heart. I asked forgiveness and pleaded with God for the strength, patience, and guidance I felt I had lost. I told the Lord that I couldn't make it on my own resources any longer—I needed Him to take control of my life and lead me in His will.

And then I discovered that the Lord had not been punishing me at all, but "child-training" me. He saw me falling back into my old patterns of willful independence and proud self-reliance, and He used this surprising turn in my life to bring me to Him with a heart hungry for His guidance and comfort.

David had already followed the Lord's guidance, and although he was lonely and homesick, he was doing his best to follow that guidance in an honorable way. I am so proud of his strength of character, of the honors he has received, and of the rewarding work he is doing now. I also see how the Lord used my husband's decision (the decision I so bitterly resented) to draw me to Himself. This week David and I will celebrate our sixth wedding anniversary—together again and closer than ever after the pain of our time apart from one another.

What have I learned that could be of help to blended-family couples? That God can—and *will*—use anything in our situations to help us grow up into Christ. This includes the challenges of marriage—whether it be in-laws, or stepchildren, or personality clashes, or changes and adaptations which we rebel against. The point is that He never gives up on His children.

I have found that the Lord will let me butt my head against the stone wall of challenge until I realize that the wall isn't going to budge. With a bruised and battered spirit, I fall on my knees before Him and ask for a bandage and a ladder. He is the only One who can either break down that wall or boost me over it.

My Grandma, who led me to the Lord when I was very young and knew about my secret childhood dream of becoming a professional writer, told me, "Honey, always write the truth, and don't make God mad!"

The truth I believe God wants me to pass on to you is that every challenge you will face in your marriage is designed not for your hurt, but to strengthen you, your marriage, and, most important, your faith.

"As *for* God, his way *is* perfect: the word of the LORD is tried: he is a buckler to all those who trust in him. For who *is* God save the LORD? or who *is* a rock save our God? *It is* God that girdeth me with strength, and maketh my way perfect" (Ps. 18:30–32 KJV).

Establish a harmonious relationship with your in-laws. This is the eighteenth step in building a marriage that works.

SUGGESTIONS

1. Write your own "in-law" story, touching the high points of your relationship with your mate's family. Has it gone in the direction toward war or peace? Why?

2. Think of something you could do this week to improve the situation, if it has moved toward war. (The principles in chapters 7 and 8 can help.) If you already have a good relationship, plan to write a note of appreciation to your in-laws, or telephone just to say, "Thanks for being you. I love you!"

Part 4

What Resources Are You Depending On

13

If You'd Like to Change

Have we discovered how to change for our own well-being and for the good of our marriage?

The Lord my God illumines my darkness. . . . And by my God I can leap over a wall (Ps. 18:28, 29 NASB).

WE HAVE ASKED you to consider three key questions which can make an enormous difference in the quality of your life:

1. Are your choices moving you in a positive direction toward a successful marriage?
2. What kind of emotional climate are you creating together?
3. How well is your partnership working?

In answering these questions honestly, almost everyone will uncover the need for constructive change—somewhere, somehow! Letters often arrive from couples who are at this perilous point. *Perilous* because everything good depends on how they proceed. Will they give up in discouragement? Will they blame each other and demand unilateral change? Or will they take a positive approach, with each partner willing to accept his or her responsibility? And, no less important, will they learn to draw upon spiritual resources for the change that is needed?

If you are at this point, you have plenty of company. When we begin to think seriously about our desires and goals for a happy marriage, we usually find that changes are required both "without and within." Not only do we need to make changes in the ways we relate to one another, but we find that we both need to change on the inside where behavior originates, and that's not a comfortable prospect. It's human nature (the old sin nature, actually) to begin by focusing on the improvements our partner needs to make. The greater our problems, the more loudly we tend to demand change—in the other person. In fact, most people who come for marriage counseling have a hidden agenda which (put in the form of a question) goes something like this: *How can I make my partner change so that I can be happy?* Few of us would voice it so bluntly, but there the belief is, lodged deep within us: If only the other person would change, everything would be all right!

The truth is blunter still. No marriage can work well unless *both* partners are willing to change and keep on changing throughout the long process of establishing their life together.

When your relationship comes right up against this implacable need for change on both sides, it can feel like running into a brick wall. Along with the surprise, hurt, and disappointment come disturbing questions: Will we be able to change enough to make it work? What can I do if my partner won't try to change? And what am I going to do about myself and the ways I need to change? At such times it can look like a wall too high to climb.

If you long to bring about constructive changes in your life, take heart and look at the possibilities. Are you aware of the assets and resources for change which are already available to you—like money in the bank? No matter how you feel at any given moment, the truth is that you are "well-fixed" with assets (valuable possessions and qualities) and resources (sources of aid and support) for transforming yourself, your marriage, and your life. We want to help you learn how to use your assets and how to draw upon the spiritual provisions which can turn the possibilities of your life into shining realities. But please note that these depend upon your eternal connection to the Lord Jesus Christ. If you are not sure of this connection in your life you will need to turn first to chapter 14, to consider the Alpha and Omega choice.

ASSETS AND RESOURCES FOR CHANGE

1. Your Decision-Making Power

We described this asset in chapter 2. You may want to review that chapter after reading this section. Remember that God gave you the gift of freedom of choice by providing you with a will which possesses the power to make decisions based on your best judgment as well as your "want-to" mechanism. And your will was designed to do even more. It has the power to mobilize every part of your being to follow through and carry out your decisions with appropriate actions. Whether you realize it or not, you have the capability of turning your dreams into goals and pursuing those goals to a successful conclusion, even when the way is extremely difficult.

Here is an example of will power which dramatically illustrates what can be accomplished when we choose to use this valuable asset. The example focuses on mountain climbing, an apt comparison for those of us who have found that straightening out our lives can seem like climbing Mount Everest! In an article entitled "Cold Courage" (*Sports Illustrated*, January 16, 1989), Ed Webster describes the goal he and three other men set: to climb the east face of Mount Everest without Sherpas to carry supplies, and without radios, eliminating the possibility of rescue. They would chart a new and challenging route and make the ascent to 29,000 feet without bottled oxygen. This exercise in courage and will power kept them moving for days in what climbers call the Death Zone— any elevation above 26,200 feet—where they had to rest after every second step and suffered hallucinations and periods of passing out on the knife-sharp ridges. Their route took them to the South Summit where one man attained the highest peak and Webster obtained incredible photographs; then, eventually, in a prolonged, nightmarish ordeal brought them back down to their base camp past gaping crevasses, their fingers and toes partly frozen, but their lives preserved and their expedition a success.

The steps they took to transform their dreams into attainable goals demonstrate for us what we need to do to achieve the changes we desire: They made their decision; they operated on a belief system, and continually affirmed their beliefs. They prepared themselves through study, training, and practice; they carefully planned their strategy for success; they made sure they had the necessary equipment and supplies; they followed their plan, but adopted new strategies when necessary. They reassessed their goals and acted according to wisdom; they kept their objectives clearly in mind; and they rejected self-pity and kept moving!

Not many of us are looking for adventure of this magnitude. However, bringing about changes in ourselves, our relationship, and the way we live our lives can offer adventure of another sort, equally bracing, sometimes more taxing, and surely more rewarding over the course of a lifetime.

What kind of motivation can impel us to the decision point? What needs and desires can prepare us for this personal "mountaineering" in which all of our being comes together in a positive effort to attain our goals? It often begins with powerful negatives. We are unhappy with ourselves, discontented with our lives, or perhaps, disturbed at what we see happening in our relationship with our marriage partner. We may be painfully aware of our wasted opportunities and discarded dreams, or concerned by our spiritual emptiness, and thirsting for something more.

Just to recognize the negatives will not be enough. Think about it. What do you hear yourself saying at this moment? If you are saying, "I *should* change," you probably won't. The statement implies, "I wish I could, but I can't and I don't choose to try." If you are saying, "I would try to change if only. . .," that's not a good indication either. People who wait for circumstances to change first seldom ever take the positive step. As Thoreau said, "Things don't change. People do." A wishy-washy, indecisive, non-affirmative approach will never pack the power to take you where you want to be.

Instead, begin with a decision. Not the sort of choice one easily, privately, slips into, hut a clear-cut, open decision which you will back up with action. The word *decision* literally means "to cut away" so that nothing is ever quite the same again. Once doubts, waverings, worries, and various options which you have considered and discarded are "cut away," your will has the all-clear signal to gear up for action.

Decisions should be stated where others can hear; not kept secret. Sometimes we "think" a decision which seems clear-cut enough, but it can slip away from us when we become distracted by other things. Verbalizing our decision in the hearing of others will help hold us to it, and we need to take advantage of every benefit. It's important to launch our decision with a strong initiative which provides the momentum to establish our choices and turn them into the changes we desire. Thus, action to carry out our decision should be taken or scheduled immediately, for delay can weaken our resolve.

All this adds up to *commitment*—a promise you make to yourself, which others know about. But be careful to state your promise to yourself clearly and affirmatively. When strong negatives motivate you to change, restate them as positive goals. If you're climbing the snowy slopes just to get away from your old self, it will never work. Instead, consider what you are adventuring toward. Merely "to be different" is not enough. What is your goal, your desired destination?

For instance, instead of saying, "I don't want to be fat anymore," set a positive goal: "I choose to find the right balance of eating and exercise to maintain my normal weight—for the rest of my life." Other goals follow, such as these: "I will sign up for the *Eat Slim* class at the local hospital, and go with it all the way until I've reached my desired weight loss," "I will commit one-half hour a day to exercise," "I will establish the habit of eating air-popped corn whenever I get a craving for potato chips, or low-fat yogurt in place of ice cream." Note the positive statements. A positive vocalized confession is most important. What you say and what you hear yourself or others say will actually affect the way you think and the way you behave.

Not only be positive about your goal when you speak, but be as precise as possible. Pinpoint it. Only then can you map out a systematic plan to reach a very specific goal. As we have already illustrated, your plan will involve the setting of small goals to be reached one by one as you move toward your main objective.

As you make your plans, remember this: Although feelings will help motivate you to change, do not base your decision or your plans on feelings. That would be like trying to ride on a cumulus cloud. Your feelings can never provide a solid base for progress because they are continually changing—fluctuating day by day and hour by hour. For example, after successfully following a weight loss program for two weeks, something so upsetting may occur that you *feel* like giving up and going back to your old ways. Fortunately, your will and not your feelings are in charge, so this is the very time to renew the commitment you have made publicly and the private promises you have made to yourself, and to go right on with your adventure.

Ironically, many of us have created our own problems or intensified them by our unremitting efforts to make ourselves *feel* better. The way we humans choose to comfort ourselves can be as unproductive as eating three giant cinnamon rolls because our feelings have been hurt, or arguing with our mate because we've just been chewed out by our boss. We know of even more destructive ways—cigarettes, alcohol, abuse of prescription drugs, and you name it.

Not only do we want to make ourselves feel better. We also want to do whatever we can to avoid taking responsibility for our less than satisfactory situation. That's human nature. Remember how Eve blamed the serpent and Adam blamed Eve, along with God, for giving him the woman? We hate to admit that we alone are responsible for the choices we have made.

But unless we are ready to take full responsibility for our situation, or our reaction to a situation of someone else's making, it will be very difficult for us to achieve constructive changes in ourselves or our marriage. The decision that brings forth a genuine turn-around begins with the recognition that what we have been doing is not working.

When we come to this point, we are ready to search for spiritual resources. And so we look to the next asset which God can give to those who belong to Him, who call Him Lord. That asset is Hope.

2. A Dependable Hope

When believers begin reading the Bible as a personal letter written to them, they find a word scattered like stars throughout the Scriptures, and each time they read the affirmations and promises connected with that word, the sense of encouragement, expectation, and energizing occupies a larger place in their lives. The word is *hope*. It is what we must have to stay on the path of change and make progress.

Here are a few of the verses concerning hope to carry in your mind and heart as life-sustaining equipment. Study them, memorize them, keep them on 3 × 5 cards in your pocket or purse, or stick them on the refrigerator as a continuing reminder. Mountain climbers say that knowing what to take with them on the climb can mean the difference between success or failure. These Scriptures which keep hope burning in our hearts as a steady flame provide us with one of our most powerful spiritual resources in the quest for change.

> Why are you in despair, O my soul? And why are you disturbed within me? Hope in God, for I shall again praise Him, the help of my countenance, and my God (Ps. 43:5 NASB).

> The hope of the righteous is gladness. . . (Prov. 10:28 NASB).

> "For I know the plans that I have for you," declares the LORD, "plans for welfare and not for calamity to give you a future and a hope" (Jer. 29:11 NASB).

> Now may the God of hope fill you with all joy and peace in believing, that you may abound in hope by the power of the Holy Spirit (Rom. 15:13 NASB).

> Blessed be the God and Father of our Lord Jesus Christ, who according to His great mercy has caused us to be born again to a living hope through the resurrection of Jesus Christ from the dead (1 Peter 1:3 NASB).

How does hope benefit us? Hope builds and strengthens two valuable aspects of our character which actually determine the way we approach life. The first, *expectation*, makes it possible for us to live with vigorous optimism, and the second, *endurance*, helps us to function with steadfast perseverance. Expectation provides the confidence and enthusiasm to fuel our efforts, and endurance provides the inner steel that keeps us moving forward even when we're tempted to quit. Anyone who has embarked on a program of positive change only to slip back into destructive old patterns of behavior knows that the last state can be worse than the first. Expectancy and persistence founded on biblical hope prevent that kind of devastating backward slide. Expectation keeps us glad, and endurance keeps us going. Both are critical to our success and survival whether we're climbing a mountain or building a love-filled marriage.

Can "hope" really do all that? Yes, if it's biblical hope. The hope God gives us is not an "I hope so." It has nothing to do with wishful thinking. Instead, it means something sure and certain which we anticipate with confidence. Biblical hope has two dimensions. It looks to the future when we can fully enjoy our inheritance in Christ, but it also encircles the present and points to the abundant new life we can enjoy here and now because of Him.

What do you base your hope on? Let's be very practical, for blind hopefulness based on nothing in particular will melt away just when we need it most. Your hope should rest squarely on the fact of the living God and His participation in your life. Every detail of your situation matters to Him. If you are pressed hard by problems right now, if you are longing for changes in yourself, your marriage, and your life, you can count on this: God is in control of everything; God is involved in your problems; God has the answers and provisions you need; and God has promised to provide them for you if you are willing to receive them.

In the beloved classic *Hind's Feet on High Places* by Hannah Hurnard, the heroine collects a bag of small "stones of remembrance," each representing a lesson learned about the Shepherd and His involvement in her life. When she reaches the high places, she discovers that the stones she had gathered—common, ugly stones—have been turned into precious jewels, and the Shepherd reminds her of His promise,

> O thou afflicted, tossed with tempest, *and* not comforted, behold, I will lay thy stones with fair colours, and lay thy foundations with sapphires . . . and all thy borders of pleasant stones (Isa. 54:11– 12 KJV).

If you were keeping a collection of remembrances, what would the contents of your tote bag represent? There should be at least four kinds of precious stones there, each representing hope for you at this very moment.

First are the promises from God's Word, the Bible. These promises do not fail, for God cannot lie, and there are literally thousands of them in the Scriptures relating to the believer on this earth—plus the heavenly promises relating to the future. Build your hope on God's promises.

The second category consists of the commandments in God's Word. Every command in the Scriptures inspires hope, for God never tells His children to do something that He will not supply the power and direction to achieve. These commandments give added reassurance of His provisions for our daily life. Biblical counselors use this equation:

$$\text{Command} + \text{Provision} = \text{Potential for Change}$$

In the third category is God's counsel for us through the Scriptures. Because He Himself is our Counselor, we can have hope, knowing that His loving wisdom is committed to guiding and directing us into the paths that will bless us beyond anything we have yet experienced. Sometimes we struggle just to get back to the status quo. But He is able to give us much more than this, and He desires to do it. He wants to be our counselor, to provide us with wisdom for living, and He waits for us to consult Him!

In the fourth category, we find all the ways He participates in our efforts to bring about constructive change. He is the one who actually does the transforming when we cooperate with Him. As we discussed in chapter 2, when God speaks of the changes He will perform in our lives, the Scripture says, "Be transformed," (Rom. 12:2). Note the passive tense of the verb. The work is done in us by none other than the Holy Spirit.

All these reasons for hope are summarized by the apostle Peter who recognizes that God has given us everything we need. Everything.

His divine power has given us everything we need for life and godliness through our knowledge of him who called us by his own glory and goodness. Through these he has given us his very great and precious promises, so that through them you may participate in the divine nature and escape the corruption in the world caused by evil desires (2 Peter 1:3–4).

What about the times when difficulties come at us like driving snow in a blizzard? It does seem that it often happens just when we're trying our hardest and tasting some success. God's Word shows us how the cycle of hope goes right on at such times. The apostle Paul explains,

Therefore, since we have been justified through faith, we have peace with God through our Lord Jesus Christ, through whom we have gained access by faith into this grace in which we now stand. And we rejoice in the hope of the glory of God. Not only so, but we also rejoice in our sufferings, because we know that suffering produces perseverance; perseverance, character; and character, hope. And hope does not disappoint us, because God has poured out his love into our hearts by the Holy Spirit, whom he has given us (Rom. 5:1–5).

The word translated *suffering* in this passage includes the idea of distresses and pressures. Most of you know about those kinds of afflictions. The letters some of you have written to us describe the pressures and distresses that have invaded your marriage and your life, but they often lift our hearts with a message of the peace and victory that we have experienced as a result of all that has happened. This Bible passage explains the positive chain reaction that takes place when we face challenges and difficulties with an attitude of expectation.

First, we expect (*know* by intuition or perception) that some very good things are going to take place as a result of the way we meet the difficulty. It's only by going through the pressures and trials that we are able to develop steadfastness, the ability to stand firm under heavy difficulties. This, in turn, develops a proven character in us that reassures us of our ability to live with strength and grace in the future, no matter what comes. And that assurance results in even more hope, a confident hope that God will always see us through. We don't have to be afraid anymore. When our hope is centered in God and His promises, it will never disappoint us (or, as the King James Version says, "put us to shame"). God's love, which reached out to us when we were unbelievers, helpless in our sins, continues to pour into our hearts. The reality of His love in our hearts guarantees that our hope is not misplaced and will never fail. And so the cycle begins with expectation and ends with a guarantee.

If you have times of inner distress and feelings of panic, God has a special provision of hope for you. We've been discussing hope as a settled state of mind and heart, and so it is. The Epistle of Hebrews calls it "an anchor for the soul, firm and secure" (Heb. 6:19). But it is also a refuge in times of sudden fear. At such times we need to know that biblical hope is there for us, to protect us and stabilize us. The same passage in Hebrews 6 explains this: "that . . . we who have fled to Him for refuge might have mighty indwelling strength and strong encouragement to grasp and hold fast the hope appointed for us and set before us (Heb. 6:18 AMPLIFIED).

Undoubtedly, the writer to the Hebrews was familiar with Psalm 25 which reinforces the message for us. The Psalm begins, "To Thee, O LORD, I lift up my soul. O my God, in Thee I trust. Do not let me be ashamed" (vv. 1–2). To trust in this way means to be confident; to be sure and expectant; to have biblical hope. In God we place our security: this is a settled state of being.

But even though we *trust*, there still are times when we will fear and flee to God for immediate refuge. The King James Version translates that as *trust*, too. At the conclusion of Psalm 25, we read, "Let me not be ashamed; for I put my trust in thee" (v. 20 KJV). That Hebrew word for trust means "run to for protection": "Do not let me be ashamed, for I take refuge in Thee" (v. 20 NASB). It means that while we live in a settled state of hope, we always have the prerogative of running to God for protection, and this is biblical hope, as well. Whatever your need and condition, God understands and has made provision for it.

Hope is a spiritual resource we cannot do without.

3. The Power of the Written Word

We described the first asset for change (which you already possess) as "decision-making power." Now we want to discuss another kind of power which can operate in your life. This is the remarkable power of the Bible to produce change in people.

Of course, it's neither remarkable nor surprising when we recognize the source of this book. We know from Genesis 1 that God brought the worlds into existence by speaking. His spoken word has power; when He speaks, it is so. We know from John 1 and 1 John 1 that the Lord Jesus Christ Himself is called the Word, who took on human flesh and lived among us; who had only to speak and the waves were calmed or the sick were healed. And from Psalm 119, Hebrews 4:12, 1 Peter 1:23, and many other portions, we know that the Bible is called God's Word, literally, *God-breathed* and written down for us, with the same authority and power to bring order out of personal chaos; peace in the midst of the storms that beset us; meaning to fill our emptiness; and wholeness to heal our hurting, disrupted lives.

The Bible, in short, is a unique book which matter-of-factly claims to have unique power in the lives of those who read it. Even unbelievers respect its wisdom and benefit from it, but only those who come to the Bible with a willing heart can be sure of discovering its dynamic ability to work changes in their lives and transformations deep within their beings.

The Bible works its wonders within us in two phases. First, the Bible has the power to bring us to faith in Jesus Christ; only then can it mold us into new people by working changes in our character, personality, and manner of living which will please Him and bless us. This ongoing change may be dramatic, or as steady and imperceptible as the warming of winter into spring, but whether it occurs quickly or slowly, the effects will be far-reaching.

C. S. Lewis illustrates the surprising extent of the transformation by borrowing a parable from George MacDonald. He suggests that we imagine ourselves to be a living house. When we put our faith in Christ, God comes in to rebuild the house. We know a few repairs are needed, and we expect Him to rebuild us into a decent little cottage. Instead, we discover that He is building a palace. He intends to come and live in it Himself!

Look at 2 Timothy 3:15–17 to find how these changes are accomplished. First,

"the sacred writings . . . are able to give you the wisdom that leads to salvation through faith which is in Christ Jesus" (v. 15 NASB).

Once saved, the adventure of transformation begins. The next verse of 2 Timothy 3 reveals the four ways in which the Bible produces beneficial change in us:

Every Scripture is God-breathed—given by His inspiration—and profitable for instruction, for reproof and conviction of sin, for correction of error and discipline in obedience, and for training in righteousness [that is, in holy living, in conformity to God's will in thought, purpose and action] (2 Timothy 3:16 AMPLIFIED).

The Scriptures (1) instruct us, (2) reprove us, (3) correct us, and (4) train us. At first glance, these four processes may seem to overlap, but in reality they fulfill four distinct functions, each essential for permanent change.

First, they *teach* us. The Scriptures teach the truth about the way God designed human beings to live and love. As we read the Bible we are instructed by word and example so that we can understand what God's standard is for our life and faith, our character and conduct. New norms are set; we have something to model after, a standard for measuring ourselves, and goals to reach for.

Second, they *reprove and convict* us. The process is not comfortable, but it is beneficial. The word used for "reproof" is a legal term meaning more than to accuse; it includes the meaning of trying a case to its end *successfully*. This is one case we will never win. The Scriptures show us how we have failed to live by God's requirements, and as they hold up a mirror in which we see our own sin, the sight flattens us to the dust. The beneficial result? Repentance! It is only when we recognize how far removed we are from God's design for His creation and how far away we are from the standards set for His redeemed people, that we can begin to change.

Third, the Scriptures *correct* us. They have halted the negative drift of our life. Now they can reset our direction by putting us on our feet and pointing us in the right way. The word for "correction" means literally "to stand up straight again." The Bible has knocked us down; now it lifts us up and gets us moving toward God and all good things. It has wounded us; now it heals us. It has plowed us up like fallow ground; now it plants us and promises a beautiful harvest. The Holy Spirit, through the Scriptures, not only helps us put off sin like a falling of withered leaves from the tree, but enables us to put on righteousness like a new green growth pushing off the dead remnants of our old life.

The concept of "standing up straight again" speaks to many of us. In a time of self-searching, one woman sadly concluded that she was like a sack that was all fallen together. Another woman responded, "I felt like that too. But the Scriptures are helping me to stand strong and straight!"

Finally, the Scriptures *train us in righteousness*. They literally "child-train" us in a new way of living in which we walk in God's ways until they become our own. If we did not have this final phase of training, we would soon revert to old, destructive habits. But the Holy Spirit, by means of the Scriptures, lovingly disciplines and works with us until our new character reaches maturity.

And what is God's purpose in this four-phase program? It is briefly stated, but all encompassing:

That the man of God may be adequate, [well-fitted and thoroughly] equipped for every good work (2 Tim. 3:17 NASB).

God wants to make us *adequate*—a wonderful word! It is translated "perfect" in the King James Version, but most of us do not expect perfection: We would be glad to be completely adequate in the living of life. Actually, the Greek word *artios*, which is used only here in the New Testament, means "complete" as an instrument with all its strings, or a machine with all its parts, or a body with all its limbs, joints, muscles, and sinews in good working order. If we give ourselves to the Scriptures, they not only make us complete and thus adequate, but they also equip us for what we will be called to do. The picture is that of a ship being properly fitted out for the voyage. We can be properly equipped for our personal journey through life, if we choose to allow the Scriptures to do their work within us. Remember, the choice is always ours.

4. Your Ability to Form Habits

This is a natural resource everyone can use, but we tend to take it for granted. Think, for a moment, how many of your daily activities are guided by habit. Because God has given us the ability to form habits by repetition, we are able to move smoothly and automatically through most ordinary tasks, with freedom to think about more important matters while we brush our teeth, make the morning coffee, stop at red lights, or, for example, perform our work at the computer on the job.

Originally we learned how to do those tasks and performed them self-consciously until they became an extension of ourselves. It took longer to learn to drive or use the word processor than to fill up the coffee maker. But we gained these skills by means of consistent practice. If we should move to England, we would have to establish a new habit of driving on the other side of the road. It would not be comfortable at first, but we could soon learn. If we begin using a new program on the computer, it requires careful thought and repetition until we master it. We find the process tiring or challenging at first, but soon it has become second nature and we're back on "auto pilot" again.

This capacity to learn to respond unconsciously, automatically, and comfortably is a tremendous asset when we want to change ourselves or the way we live. Knowing how to "put off and put on," thought patterns and behaviors is really the key to change, according to the New Testament. But the process can be misused, for our habit-forming capability makes it easy to establish harmful patterns of thought and conduct without realizing what we're doing. William James observed that if we realized the extent to which we are mere walking bundles of habits, we would give more attention to what we are forming. Now our challenge is to replace destructive patterns of living with positive, beneficial ones. When we choose to do this in conjunction with the transforming work of the Holy Spirit and the guidance of the Scriptures, our potential for success is great.

Sometimes people have the despairing belief that their personality cannot be changed. Personality is simply the sum total of what we are at any given moment. The Bible views it as a changeable factor which depends, first, upon what we believe, what we affirm, and the way we think. "As [a man] thinketh in his heart, so is he," the Scripture says (Prov. 23:7 KJV). If we habitually fill our minds with faith and biblical principles and set positive goals before ourselves, our behavior will inevitably change to reflect our thinking. As we establish new constructive patterns of behavior, our feelings will invariably correspond. Eventually, (sooner than we might expect) others will notice "a personality change."

Biblical counselor Jay Adams writes of a man who had formed the habit of saying sarcastically, "Oh great!" whenever something failed to go his way. Recognizing that his personality was reflecting a complaining spirit, the man chose to *put off* that behavior and *put on* a positive spirit of praise, no matter how he felt. He began substituting the expression, "O great . . . is Thy faithfulness!" (Lam. 3:23 KJV). After a time of consistent practice his new response became habitual (a part of him), and his attitudes and feelings changed. Now his personality could be described by others as "upbeat"—even radiant.

The question is, how can you take the spiritual resources and natural assets which we have described and use them to produce desired changes within yourself or your marriage?

First, you must diagnose the problem. What do you want to change? (Remember that you are seeking to change yourself, not reform your marriage partner.) What behaviors, responses, and attitudes are not working in your life? What do the Scriptures say about them? Get help on this if necessary.

Second, when you have diagnosed the problem and understood the counsels of Scripture in this area, then target the habitual practice or pattern of response that must be unlearned—*put off*. The only way to do this effectively is to replace the old habit with a new one—*put on*. Decide on the biblical alternative and make that your goal which you will promptly put into action, practicing the positive new behavior until it becomes automatic and habitual. If you need to develop a new attitude, you must find the corresponding action which expresses the new attitude and act it out immediately and consistently. Never let a rosy glow of feeling and high resolve dissipate without acting upon it. You will have lost momentum that will be difficult to regain.

Third, structure your situation for the changes you desire. To know how to do this you will have to give some thought to what seems to trigger your undesirable thoughts and behaviors. You may want to keep a record of the times during the day when they occur. What stimuli do you respond to? If you analyze the behaviors you want to change, you will notice that they develop in a series of steps, or links in a chain. You must break a link in the process to prevent the undesirable behavior. That means developing a new response to the same old situations. The circumstances of your life may not change, but your response to them *can*, and that will make all the difference.

Fourth, to build a new response and break the old chain of habit, you will need to develop your own helpful techniques and search out scriptural affirmations which apply to your situation. All depends on your beliefs, so check them out. Are they rational or irrational? Do they line up with biblical principles? If not, change your beliefs.

One man says he pictures a tool box full of beliefs and affirmations. He says he needs a lot of them to cover the needs of his life—a 1,000-piece set as opposed to a 100-piece set. "Could I repair the Queen Elizabeth II with one rusty screwdriver?" he asks. "Not only do I expand my 'tool box' of truth, but I throw out the rusty, unworkable ideas that I collected along the way—ideas that really make no sense. I want my attitudes and actions to be controlled by beliefs that I know are trustworthy and true."

If, then, you want to change yourself, your relationship with your mate, or any other part of your life, you will need to set systematic goals and have a specific plan to form specific desirable habits which will replace undesirable patterns of thought and behavior. What you *believe* will lie at the heart of any positive change. But while you are taking constructive steps toward change, you may have periods of discouragement and sudden strong temptations to simply quit and slide back into old habits, old ways, old sins. This is the time to draw upon the spiritual resource the Bible calls "help in time of need."

5. Spiritual Help

It's always important to have the assurance that the Lord offers you the resources you need, and it is even more critical at a time when you are taking action to bring your life into line with God's design for you. Do you know the Lord as your great high priest who once lived on this earth as a man and has now gone into Heaven where He is "seated at the right hand of God" (Col. 3:1 NASB) to intercede on your behalf?

Please consider the following scriptural passage very carefully. It can make a great difference in your life.

> Therefore, since we have a great high priest who has gone through the heavens, Jesus the Son of God, let us hold firmly to the faith we profess. For we do not have a high priest who is unable to sympathize with our weaknesses, but we have one who has been tempted in every way, just as we are—yet was without sin. Let us then approach the throne of grace with confidence, so that we may receive mercy and find grace to help us in our time of need (Heb. 4:14–16).

As you have quietly read these verses today, what do they tell you that can make such a difference? First, *you are not alone.* The Lord speaks on your behalf, acts on your behalf, and represents you before the throne of God.

Not only that. He *understands you.* Because He lived on this earth as One who was not only God but fully man, He knows what this life is like. He is able to sympathize with you, to feel with you in times of weakness and pain, and to feel the reality of the temptations you face. In fact, His capacity for compassion is greater than anyone else's, for He is the only man to have ever fully resisted temptation and to have felt the full extent of its force.

Third, He *has the power to help you.* He is sovereign God who sits on a throne of power.

Fourth, He *has invited you to come to Him.* His throne of power is the *throne of grace,* and He gives you freedom to come to Him confidently to pour out your needs and your heart before Him.

Fifth, because He is God and thus Spirit, *you have access to Him at all times.* You can draw near to Him at any moment in prayer, in thought, in the depths of your inmost being, and know that He hears you.

Sixth, *you can be sure of finding mercy at His throne of grace.* This mercy is the indescribable experience of God's pardon, acceptance, and love.

Finally, *you obtain special grace which is precisely suited to your need of the moment.* The Greek word literally means "well-timed help." He will strengthen your inner life at the moment of temptation. He will answer your cry for help. When the way of change seems long and hard, He will give you the patience and perseverance to take that next step and the next and so on. When you are hurt because your marriage partner does not recognize the efforts you have made, and it seems your efforts are in vain, then He understands and strengthens you with the kind of strength that no human being can give.

You can count on this special grace and well-timed help to meet you at the point of your need because your faithful and compassionate High Priest makes this commitment:

God is faithful (to His Word and to His compassionate nature), and He (can be trusted) not to let you be tempted and tried and assayed beyond your ability and strength of resistance and power to endure, but with the temptation He will (always) also provide the way out—the means of escape to a landing place—that you may be capable and strong and powerful patiently to bear up under it (1 Cor. 10:13 AMPLIFIED).

THE WAY OF SPIRITUAL GROWTH

As we try to produce change in ourselves while drawing on spiritual resources, we encounter a principle of life that seems to contradict itself. Nevertheless, it is true, and so we call it a paradox of the Christian life.

The paradox consists of these contradictory facts:

1. To change demands my concentrated effort.
2. God does it for me.

To understand how this can be, think of the psalmist's affirmation, quoted at the beginning of this chapter: *By my God I can leap over a wall* (Ps. 18:28 NASB). To leap over a wall demands tremendous effort on our part: Our feet and our legs and the rest of our body (and mind!) do the work. But God puts the spring in our feet and the lift in our legs. Because of Him, we can clear the barrier, no matter how impossible it may seem when we first consider it.

The Christian life requires all the consistent, concentrated effort we can pour into it, and yet God does it for us and in us and through us. While we "work on ourselves" from the outside, He works on the inside, deep within. We call this spiritual growth, and through this process we are transformed.

The Greeks had a word for this change of condition and character which we still use: *metamorphosis*. This describes the happening when *the outward appearance becomes comparable to the inner reality*. How can the earthbound caterpillar become an exquisite flying creature? The metamorphosis occurs because on the inside he already *is* a butterfly even when he looks like a woolly worm.

What are we on the inside and what are we becoming? If we have trusted Jesus Christ as our Savior and Lord, we already carry a new life within us which is sure to produce new growth in its season. God progressively changes us into His likeness so that our outward expression of character and personality correspond more and more with the inner reality of our life in Christ.

We cooperate in this adventure through the exercise of our choices. C. S. Lewis has said that every time we make a choice, we are turning the central part of ourselves into something a little different from what it was before. Adding up all the choices, we are becoming either a heavenly creature in harmony with God and self and all creation—or a hellish creature that is at war with everything including itself. When we make choices, we are deciding more than the quality of marriage we shall have; we're choosing quality of life for time and eternity.

Spiritual growth means positive change! The New Testament resonates with the possibilities of growth and progressive change into something more glorious. We are assured that

> we all, with unveiled face beholding as in a mirror the glory of the Lord, are being transformed into the same image from glory to glory, just as from the Lord, the Spirit (2 Cor. 3:18 NASB).

If you continue to look at Him with the gaze of faith, you will become like Him. Thus, change in yourself, your relationships with others, and the way you live, will require faith as well as obedience. As the old hymn wisely says, "Trust and obey, for there's no other way. . . ." Real faith in the Lord always expresses itself in obedience to His Word. Your side of the change process involves both obedience in choosing the behavior and attitudes that will produce the best conditions for spiritual growth, and faith that trusts the Lord to accomplish in you what He has promised.

His side of the change process? We hope you will experience it for yourself in the days and weeks ahead!

Are there desires of your heart which have been awakened or strengthened while you have been reading *Secret Choices?* We want you to know that we are praying with you concerning this. God will fulfill the desires for good which He has placed in your heart.

Our prayers for you are very specific, and we know that these requests are according to His will because we are following the biblical pattern of Paul's prayers for his friends at Philippi.

Paul began by expressing his confidence that the Lord who had begun a good work in them would never give up half-way through, but would continue the positive change process until "the day of Christ Jesus." We are equally confident that the good things the Lord has begun in you will be carried through to a successful completion. We believe He will do even more for you than you ask or think at this moment.

Here is what we are asking for you at the Throne of Grace: first, that God's wonderful agape love will increase in your heart until it fills and overflows your life to bless your marriage partner and many other lives.

Second, we pray that you will grow in the personal knowledge of the Lord Jesus Christ, gaining a clear vision of His beauty and character, and receiving insight into all His ways. We especially ask that you will apply what you read in the Bible and practice it in your own life on a daily basis.

As you translate the Bible into your personal experience, we pray that you will develop discernment, the ability to distinguish between good and evil; between things that are helpful and things that are not; between what is of benefit and what is subtly wrong and potentially harmful.

Third, we pray that you will develop the capability of understanding *what matters*—the literal wording of Paul's prayer. We ask that you will learn how to choose well between better and best, in order to make the best choices in your life; that you will always put your seal of approval on the very best because it has met the standard of the Word of God. We pray that you will look beyond what is merely good to find what the Lord's will is for your life.

We also ask that you will develop the joy of living which comes from sincerity that is unafraid of the bright sunlight shining on all its actions. We are requesting that the Lord will enable you to build pure, unmixed relationships, and that He will protect you from being a stumbling block to others, especially your own mate.

And, finally, we pray that as you grow spiritually, you will be filled with all the fruits of righteousness which are from Jesus Christ, particularly the fruit of the Spirit. We ask that the love, joy, peace, patience, gentleness, goodness, faith, humility, and self-control which characterized our Lord will be seen in your own personality; that you will be strengthened to live out His love and grace through all the days of your life; and that you will see His glory.

These are very personal requests, for the process of change under the Lord's guiding is an intimate one-on-one experience with Him. Neither of you can do it for the other one. But we know this: If even one of you puts yourself in the Lord's hands, He will use that to bless your marriage.

Commit yourself to the process of change where change is needed, and draw on spiritual resources to bring it about. This is the nineteenth step in forming a marriage that gets better and better.

SUGGESTIONS

1. Decide what changes would most improve your marriage. List three, remembering that change must begin with you alone, unless your partner is equally motivated. What behavior patterns are involved? What do the Scriptures coun-

sel in these circumstances? (Use *Secret Choices* along with our other books, *Intended for Pleasure, Love Life,* and *The First Years of Forever* as reference sources.)

2. Make your own list of "put-offs" and "put-ons" from the Bible, beginning with the New Testament epistles. In your notebook, fill in three columns headed

Put Off   **Put On**   **Scriptural References**

Use your habit-forming ability to make these changes a part of you. Remember that even desirable changes make us feel uncomfortable at first, like a fish out of water, until we have formed the new habit and expanded our self-image to correspond with our new behavior.

3. Write out your own plan for personal change, following the general pattern set by the Mount Everest climbers. Make each phase a matter of prayer, keeping a record of requests, answers, temporary setbacks, and victories.

4. Mark Philippians 1:9–11 in your own Bible and read it daily for a month. This is our prayer for you. Assess your life one month from today and thank God for what He has already done today, and thank God for the progress you already see.

And this is my prayer: that your love may abound more and more in knowledge and depth of insight, so that you may be able to discern what is best and may be pure and blameless until the day of Christ, filled with the fruit of righteousness that comes through Jesus Christ—to the glory and praise of God (Phil. 1:9–11 (AMPLIFIED)

14

The Alpha and Omega Choice

Have we met the eternal One, the all powerful One? Have we heard His invitation? Are we able to draw on the resources of the living God for every need of our life?

I am Alpha and Omega, the beginning and the ending, saith the Lord, which is, and which was, and which is to come, the Almighty. . . . And whosoever will, let him take the water of life freely (Rev. 1:8; 22:17 KJV).

WE HAVE BEEN discussing personal choices that can take you in the direction you want to go—choices which will make it possible for you to build a marriage that lasts and that wholly satisfies both of you for a lifetime.

In the first chapter we described the three dimensions of a successful, satisfying marriage, and in later chapters we outlined the choices involved in creating an emotional climate of love, nurturing, and intimacy, and in forming a smoothly working, enjoyable partnership. The third dimension is a faith you can share—a vital faith in God's son, Jesus Christ—and your choice in this area is the most important one you will ever make.

More than any other choice in life, it is a solitary one. It involves your willingness to make connections, first, with the living God, and then with your marriage partner on the deepest level possible, but only you can arrive at this decision, and you must come to it alone. Others can give you helpful information, but you must decide, in the privacy of your own heart, what to do with the truth when you read it or hear it spoken. Doing nothing is also a choice with eternal consequences.

It's possible that many of you have already acted on the truth and responded to God's gracious invitation through His Son Jesus Christ. If so, you know the benefits of your shared faith, and the fulfillment you find together in His love. We know, from personal experience and from the testimonies of hundreds of married couples, that it is this shared faith which gives marriage its meaning, stability, and settled joy over "the long haul" of a lifetime. It also provides the spiritual resources we need in the course of our years on this earth and assurance for our future.

We would like to give you information that can assist you in making a choice, if you have not already done so. Others provided this information for us, and we are passing it on. In Dr. Wheat's busy world as a family physician, a concerned patient told him about the Lord Jesus Christ, and his life dramatically changed course. In Gloria's case, her family directed her to the Bible where, as a young wife, she met Jesus Christ along with the woman who came to touch the hem of His garment. And so she made the choice which has shaped her life and work.

Come with us to the last book of the Bible which opens with these words: *The revelation of Jesus Christ.* He is the subject of this book which presents Him as He truly is: the King of Kings and Lord of Lords.

A revelation means an unveiling or a disclosure. Let's consider the disclosures made here concerning Jesus Christ, a man whom the world respects, but does not understand.

1. He is the eternal One who is the beginning and ending of all things.

I am Alpha and Omega, the beginning and the ending, saith the Lord, which is, and which was, and which is to come, the Almighty (Rev. 1:8 KJV).

The man whom the world considers a good, humble man and a wise teacher is much more: He is God Himself, the eternal, self-existent One. Alpha and Omega are the first and last letters of the Greek alphabet, indicating the fact that Christ is before all creation and will continue to exist after the present creation is destroyed. Other Scriptures tell us that all things were created by Him and for Him. (Read Rev. 21:5–6 and 22:13.)

For by him were all things created, that are in heaven, and that are in earth, visible and invisible, whether they be thrones, or dominions, or principalities, or powers: all things were created by him, and for him: And he is before all things, and by him all things consist [hold together] (Col. 1:16–17 KJV).

In the beginning was the Word, and the Word was with God, and the Word was God. The same was in the beginning with God. All things were made by him; and without him was not any thing made that was made. In him was life; and the life was the light of men (John 1:1–4 KJV).

2. He is the Almighty, the all-powerful One.

I am Alpha and Omega,. . . the Almighty (Rev. 1:8 KJV).

The man whom the world saw meekly dying a criminal's death on a Roman cross—and forgiving those who participated in His death—is none other than the "Lord God Almighty," the *pantokrator* who controls all things and possesses all power and authority in heaven and earth. (Read Rev. 4:8; 11:17; 15:3; 16:7, 14; and 2 Cor. 6:18.)

His name is called The Word of God. . . . He treadeth the winepress of the fierceness and wrath of Almighty God. And he hath on his venture and on his thigh a name written, KING OF KINGS, AND LORD OF LORDS (Rev. 19:13, 15, 16 KJV).

That at the name of Jesus every knee should bow, of things in heaven, and things in earth, and things under the earth; and that every tongue could confess that Jesus Christ is Lord, to the glory of God the Father (Phil. 2:10–11 KJV).

3. He is both the eternal One and the resurrected One.

Fear not; I am the first and the last: I am he that liveth, and was dead; and, behold, I am alive forevermore, Amen; and have the keys of hell and of death (Rev. 1:17–18 KJV).

After dying on the cross and spending three days in a tomb guarded by Roman soldiers, Jesus demonstrated to all people for all time that He is God by rising from the dead—one of the most legally authenticated facts of history. He spent more than a month on this earth in His resurrection body, seen by hundreds of people including the disciples who became vibrant witnesses of the Resurrection, willing to give their lives for the truth. He then ascended to heaven as many witnesses watched, with all power and authority in His possession, including authority over death and the place of the dead. The Christian's death and resurrection are both in His hands.

For I delivered to you as of first importance what I also received, that Christ died for our sins according to the Scriptures, and that He was buried, and that He was raised on the third day according to the Scriptures, and that He appeared to Cephas, then to the twelve. After that He appeared to more than five hundred brethren at one time, most of whom remain until now, but some have fallen asleep; then He appeared to James, then to all the apostles; and last of all, as it were to one untimely born, He appeared to me also (1 Cor. 15:3–8 NASB).

But we see Jesus, who was made a little lower than the angels for the suffering of death, crowned with glory and honour; that he by the grace of God should taste death for every man. . . . Forasmuch then as the children are partakers of flesh and blood, he also himself likewise took part of the same; that through death he might destroy him that had the power of death, that is, the devil; and deliver them who through fear of death were all their lifetime subject to bondage (Heb. 2:9, 14–15 KJV).

4. He loves us! The eternal and almighty God loves us.

To Him who loves us. . . (Rev. 1:5).

For this reason, Jesus Christ came to earth to live as man and to taste death for us so that we might have everlasting life. If we believe this, and enter into an eternal relationship with Him, nothing can separate us from the love of Jesus Christ.

For God so loved the world, that he gave his only begotten Son, that whosoever believeth in him should not perish, but have everlasting life. For God sent not his Son into the world to condemn the world; but that the world through him might be saved. He that believeth on him is not condemned: but he that believeth not is condemned already, because he hath not believed in the name of the only begotten Son of God (John 3:16–18 KJV).

Who shall separate us from the love of Christ?. . . In all these things we are more than conquerors through him that loved us. For I am persuaded [completely convinced], that neither death, nor life, nor angels, nor principalities, nor powers, nor things present, nor things to come, nor height, nor depth, nor any other creature, shall be able to separate us from the love of God, which is in Christ Jesus our Lord (Rom. 8:35, 37–39 KJV).

5. When He died for us on the cross, He set us free from our sins by shedding His own blood.

To Him who loves us and has freed us from our sins by his blood . . . (Rev. 1:5).

At a specific moment in history, Jesus Christ, the only man who ever lived without sin, chose to die by crucifixion in order to bear the sins of the whole world and pay the death penalty for them. Through that mighty act, planned in eternity past, He opened the way for all our sins to be forgiven. In Jesus our sins are forgotten as though they were put in the depths of the deepest ocean and remembered no more. And we need never be under the dominion of sin and at its mercy again. He is called the Savior for He has saved us from our sins. On our side, it is required that we believe on Him and what He has done, and receive Him as our Savior and our Lord.

The Father . . . hath delivered us from the power of darkness, and hath translated us into the kingdom of his dear Son: In whom we have redemption through his blood, even the forgiveness of sins (Col. 1:13–14 KJV).

But as many as received him, to them gave he power to become the sons of God, even to them that believe on his name (John 1:12 KJV).

6. He has given those who believe on Him a new identity and a new purpose which is life-transforming.

From Jesus Christ the faithful and trustworthy Witness, the First-born of the dead (that is, first to be brought back to life) and the Prince (Ruler) of the kings of the earth. To Him Who ever loves us and has once (for all) loosed and freed us from our sins by His own blood, And formed us into a kingdom (a royal race), priests to His God and Father, to Him be the glory and the power and the majesty and the dominion throughout the ages and forever and ever. Amen, so be it (Rev. 1:5–6 AMPLIFIED).

We are a special people—special because God has chosen and preserved us for Himself. His purpose. That we will live in His wonderful light as witnesses to His glory and grace.

But you are a chosen race, a royal priesthood, a dedicated nation, (God's) own purchased, special people, that you may set forth the wonderful deeds and display the virtues and perfections of Him Who called you out of darkness into His marvelous light (1 Peter 2:9 AMPLIFIED).

7. He makes all things new for the believer.

And he that sat upon the throne said, Behold, I make all things new. And he said unto me, Write: for these words are true and faithful (Rev. 21:5 KJV).

Salvation and new life come through believing in Jesus Christ, the Son of God, as our Savior and receiving Him by faith. When we put our trust in Jesus Christ and our lives link up with His, we become new people. Our problems may seem the same, but our ability to cope with them is all new. We have a source of love beyond ourselves. We have a sufficiency of grace for every situation. We have a new kind of strength from the power of the Lord Jesus Christ that manifests itself through our own weakness. We now have the ability to behave in the ways that will bring an abundance of blessing and order into our lives. We discover new wells of creativity and a new zest for adventure with God.

Therfore if any man be in Christ, he is a new creature: old things are passed away; behold, all things are become new. And all things are of God, who hath reconciled us to himself by Jesus Christ. . . . (2 Cor. 5:17–18 KJV).

8. He offers the water of eternal life to anyone who is thirsty.

It is done. I am Alpha and Omega, the beginning and the end. I will give unto him that is athirst of the fountain of the water of life freely (Rev. 21:6 KJV).

We have called this the Alpha and Omega choice, because the eternal and all-powerful God who is at the beginning and ending of our life, and who encompasses all that is in between, gives us a gracious invitation: "If you are thirsty, come and drink freely of the waters of eternal life. Come to Me and drink and be satisfied."

If you are thirsty, come and drink.

Is it really that simple? A Bible teacher once said, "The questions that matter in life are remarkably few, and they are all resolved by coming to Him."

But how do we come? How do we receive Him by faith? The Scripture explains,

The word is near you; it is in your mouth and in your heart, that is, the word of faith we are proclaiming: That if you confess with your mouth, "Jesus is Lord," and believe in your heart that God raised him from the dead, you will be saved. For it is with your heart that you believe and are justified, and it is with your mouth that you confess and are saved. As the Scripture says, "Anyone who trusts in him will never be put to shame." For there is no difference between Jew and Gentile—the same Lord is Lord of all and richly blesses all who call on him, for, "Everyone who calls on the name of the Lord will be saved" (Rom. 10:8–13).

Where does our faith come from? Scripture explains,

Faith comes from hearing the message, and the message is heard through the word of Christ (Rom. 10:17).

And so we have given you the message straight from the Scriptures. The Word of Christ is clear and plain. God, who is "the root and fountain of all being" loves us with a personal, everlasting love that has made provision for us to belong to Him. This is possible because of the sacrifice of Jesus Christ which paid the penalty for our sins, past, present, and future. The Lord Jesus Christ is not only the eternal One and the all-powerful One: **He is the all-sufficient One who waits to meet every need of our life for now and through all eternity.**

We find that because He is the eternal One, life has continuity; life makes sense. We find purpose and meaning and vitality in living. It is not just that we have entered into Life; Life has entered into us. God is doing something in us and through us, and it will go on forever.

We find that because He is the almighty One, He is in control. Our life is never again out of control. He is at the helm, and works all things for our eternal good. He holds us together even when we feel as though we are falling apart, for He is our center point.

We find that because He makes all things new, we have a wonderful sense of freshness and newness and hope. We find that His mercies never come to an end: They are new every morning.

We find that because He is our all-sufficient Savior, we are never alone. We are delivered even from the burden of ourselves. He Himself is our environment, and we can trust Him for everything we will ever need on earth or in heaven.

Here is a prayer you may want to follow in expressing your faith in Jesus Christ as your Savior:

Heavenly Father, I realize I am a sinner and cannot do one thing to save myself. Right now I believe Jesus Christ died on the cross, shedding His blood as full payment for my sins—past, present, and future—and by rising from the dead He demonstrated that He is God. As best I know how, I am believing in Him, putting all my trust in Jesus Christ as my personal Savior, as my only hope for salvation and eternal life. Right now I am receiving Christ into my life. I thank you for saving me as You promised, and I ask that You will give me increasing faith and wisdom and joy as I study and believe Your Word. For I ask this in Jesus' name. Amen.

If you have made your choice and acted upon it, a wonderful new life is before you with the Lord. You will want to seek out other believers and find your own place of worship and service in a local church which clearly teaches the Bible. We hope you will write and tell us, so that we can pray for you by name. We welcome you into the family of God!

The last chapter of the Book of Revelation contains one final invitation. This time the Holy Spirit joins with "the bride" which is the church in extending the invitation to all who will hear. Those who hear are encouraged to respond and to pass the invitation on to others. Will you hear the Lord Christ and receive His gift of eternal life by faith in Him? The choice is yours.

And the Spirit and the bride say, Come. And let him that heareth say, Come. And let him that is athirst come. And whosoever will, let him take the water of life freely (Rev. 22:17 KJV).

Share your growing life of faith in the Lord Jesus Christ. This is the twentieth—and most important—step in building a love-filled marriage and a wonderful life.

How to Use the Power of
Your Secret Choices:
Twenty Steps Toward a
Wonderful Marriage

1. Become aware of your secret choices and discover their power in your life.
2. Establish the picture of the marriage you desire, fill in the details, and keep it fresh in your mind to guide your choices.
3. Remember that *every choice has its consequences* and learn to "count the cost" before you act or react.
4. Understand this basic principle: *your willingness to behave responsibly needs to be coupled with God's power.*
5. Keep your mind renewed and filled with the Word of God so that you can learn how to respond in every situation of marriage according to His good counsel.
6. Study the Creator's original design for marriage, and live by His design.
7. See yourself and your partner as you really are, and love, accept, and delight in your partner on the basis of reality.
8. Make a once-for-all decision to take the path to intimacy and test all you do and say by the question, "Will this draw us closer or move us apart?"
9. Create an emotional climate of caring by finding out what nurtures your partner and then doing it, gladly and lovingly.
10. Put the B-E-S-T plan for nurturing your partner into effect and follow it consistently.
11. Recognize that God is the true source of faithfulness for your marriage, and choose to demonstrate His faithful *hesed* love to your partner.
12. Decide to pour your life into learning the art of loving your mate, and avoid any hint of indifference.
13. Commit yourselves to resolving conflicts in ways that will bring you closer and forge a stronger partnership.

14. Turn the control of your life and the power struggles of your marriage over to God to settle the war once and for all.
15. Share your vision and work out a Master Plan for your partnership.
16. Develop strategies to achieve your goals and carry out your Master Plan.
17. Learn how to manage your money to accomplish your goals and to avoid the unhappy consequences of overspending.
18. Establish a harmonious relationship with your in-laws.
19. Commit yourself to the process of change where change is needed, and draw on spiritual resources to bring it about.
20. Share your growing life of faith in the Lord Jesus Christ.